The Comparative Political Economy of Development

This book illustrates the enduring relevance and vitality of the comparative political economy of development approach promoted among others by a group of social scientists in Oxford in the 1980s and 1990s. Contributors demonstrate the viability of this approach as researchers and academics become more convinced of the inadequacies of orthodox approaches to the understanding of development.

Detailed case material obtained from comparative field research in Africa and South Asia informs analyses of exploitation in agriculture; the dynamics of rural poverty; seasonality; the non farm economy; class formation; labour and unfreedom; the gendering of the labour force; small scale production and contract farming; social networks in industrial clusters; stigma and discrimination in the rural and urban economy and its politics. Reasoned policy suggestions are made and an analysis of the comparative political economy of development approach is applied to the situation of Africa and South Asia.

Aptly presenting the relation between theory and empirical material in a dynamic and interactive way, the book offers meaningful and powerful explanations of what is happening in the continent of Africa and the sub-continent of South Asia today. It will be of interest to researchers in the fields of development studies, rural sociology, political economy, policy and practice of development and Indian and African studies.

Barbara Harriss-White is Director of Oxford University's new Contemporary South Asian Studies programme, and was formerly Director of the Department of International Development at Queen Elizabeth House. She has been studying India ever since driving there in 1969, focussing on the political economy of long term rural development.

Judith Heyer was formerly a Tutorial Fellow of Somerville College, and Lecturer in the Department of Economics, at Oxford University, before which she held posts at Nairobi University's Institute for Development Studies, and Economics Department. She is now an Emeritus Fellow of Somerville College. A specialist in rural development and in micro-economics, she has written and edited a number of books on rural and agricultural development in Kenya and Africa.

Routledge Studies in Development Economics

The Comparative Political Economy of Development

Africa and South Asia

Edited by
**Barbara Harriss-White
and Judith Heyer**

Routledge
Taylor & Francis Group

LONDON AND NEW YORK

First published 2010
by Routledge
2 Park Square, Milton Park, Abingdon, Oxon OX14 4RN

Simultaneously published in the USA and Canada
by Routledge
270 Madison Ave, New York, NY 10016

*Routledge is an imprint of the Taylor & Francis Group,
an informa business*

© 2010 Selection and editorial matter, Barbara Harriss-White and
Judith Heyer; individual chapters, the contributors

Typeset in Times New Roman by
Florence Production Ltd, Stoodleigh, Devon
Printed and bound in Great Britain by
Antony Rowe, Chippenham, Wiltshire

British Library Cataloguing in Publication Data
A catalogue record for this book is available
from the British Library

Library of Congress Cataloging in Publication Data
The comparative political economy of development Africa and South
Asia/edited by Barbara Harriss-White and Judith Heyer.
　　　　p. cm. – (Routledge studies in development economics; v. 77)
　　　Includes bibliographical references and index.
　　1. Africa – Economic policy.　2. Africa – Social conditions.
　　3. Asia, South – Economic policy.　4. Asia, South – Social
　　conditions.　I. Harriss-White, Barbara, 1946–　II. Heyer, Judith.
　　HC800.C6533 2010
　　338.954—dc22　　　　　　　　　　　　　　　　　　　2009028292

ISBN10: 0–415–55288–5 (hbk)
ISBN10: 0–203–86133–7 (ebk)

ISBN13: 978–0–415–55288–2 (hbk)
ISBN13: 978–0–203–86133–2 (ebk)

Physical Processing   Order Type: NTAS   Sel ID/Seq No:

Cust/Add: 240950003/02   TGHR-T   UNIVERSITY OF GUELPH   2331191
Cust PO No.   new   Cust Ord Date: 19-Mar-2010
BBS Order No: C1246635   Ln: 26   Del: 1   BBS Ord Date: 19-Mar-2010   /3
0415552885-4165982   Sales Qty: 1   #Vols: 001
(9780415552882)

The comparative political economy of development

Subtitle: Africa and South Asia   Stmt of Resp: edited by Barbara Harriss-White and J

HARDBACK   Pub Year: 2010   Vol No.:   Edition:

Heyer, Judith   Ser. Title:

Routledge

Acc Mat:

Profiled   Barcode Label Applicati Affix Security Device US Spine Label Protector U:
Tech   Base Charge Processing   Security Device US   TechPro Cataloging US
Services: Circulation (Author/Titl Affix Spine Label US
            Property Stamp US   Spine Label BBS US

Fund: BLKW-1604   Location: BLKW-1604
Stock Category: Department: BLKW-1604
Class #:   Cutter: Collection:

Order Line Notes:

Notes to Vendor:

Blackwell Book Services

371107

From Barbara Harriss-White and all the other contributors to Judith Heyer for her decades of inspired teaching and discussion grounded in the open approach to political economy which rests on the fine-grained field research that is her trademark; for her comparativist scholarship, her own dedication and her friendship

Contents

Figures

Maps

Tables

xvi *Tables*

Contributors

Lucia da Corta: independent researcher currently working for the Chronic Poverty Research Centre in London, taking a lead intellectual role in the CPRC Comparative Life History Project. Author of numerous publications on unfreedom in Indian agricultural labour markets, focusing on both the feminisation of agricultural labour in South India and the heavy use of unfree child labour, and of a book, *Peasant Household Mobility, Class Differentiation and Gender Transformations: A Study of Agrarian Change in South Indian Villages*, to be published by Frank Cass.

Stephen Devereux: Fellow, Institute of Development Studies, University of Sussex. Author of many publications on famine, vulnerability and social security in Africa. Known for his book *Theories of Famine* (1993) and for several edited and co-edited books, including *The New Famines: Why Famines Persist in an Era of Globalization*, published by Routledge in 2007.

Frank Ellis: Professor, School of Development Studies, University of East Anglia. Author of many publications on African agricultural development. Known for his books *Peasant Economics, Farm Households and Agrarian Development* (1988) and *Rural Livelihoods and Diversity* (2000). Joint editor of *Rural Livelihoods and Poverty Reduction Policies*, published by Routledge in 2005.

Elizabeth Francis: until recently, Senior Lecturer, Development Studies Institute, London School of Economics. Author of many journal articles and book chapters, focusing first on rural development in Kenya, and subsequently on rural development in South Africa. She has published a book with Routledge, *Making a Living: Changing Livelihoods in Rural Africa* (2000).

Hugo Gorringe: Lecturer in Sociology, University of Edinburgh. Author of many articles in refereed journals on untouchability and caste. Has also published a book based on his doctoral thesis, *Untouchable Citizens* (Sage 2005).

Barbara Harriss-White: Professor of Development Studies, Director of Oxford University's Contemporary South Asian Studies Programme and Fellow of Wolfson College. Committed to a political economy practised through field research, she has published widely. Recent books include: *India Working*

(2003); (with S. Janakarajan and others) *Rural India Facing the 21st Century* (2004); *India's Market Society* (2005); (edited with A. Sinha) *Trade Liberalisation and India's Informal Economy* (2007); (edited with Frances Stewart and Ruhi Saith) *Defining Poverty in Developing Countries* (2007), and *Rural Commercial Capital and the Left Front* (2008), which won the 2009 Edgar Graham Prize for original scholarship in development.

Judith Heyer: for three decades from 1975 Lecturer in Economics, Oxford University, before which she held posts in Nairobi University's Institute for Development Studies, and Economics Department. Now also an Emeritus Fellow of Somerville College, Oxford. A specialist in rural development and in micro-economics, she has written and/or edited the following books: (with D. Ireri and J. Moris) *Rural Development in Kenya* (1971); (edited with J.K. Maitha and W.M. Senga) *Agricultural Development in Kenya: An Economic Assessment* (1976); (edited with P. Roberts and G. Williams) *Rural Development in Tropical Africa* (1981); *Kenya: Monitoring Living Conditions and Consumption Patterns* (1991); and (with F. Stewart and R. Thorp) *2001 Groups, Institutions and Development* (2001).

Karin Kapadia: independent researcher and currently an Associate of Queen Elizabeth House, Oxford. Her publications include her monograph: *Siva and Her Sisters: Gender, Caste and Class in Rural South India* (1995) and three edited books: *The Violence of Development: The Politics of Identity, Gender and Social Inequalities in India* (2002); (edited with T.J. Byres and J. Lerche) *Rural Labour Relations in India* (1999); and (edited with Jonathan Parry and Jan Breman) *The Worlds of Indian Industrial Labour* (1999). She has also published numerous articles in edited books and refereed journals.

Jens Lerche: Senior Lecturer, Department of Development Studies, School of Oriental and African Studies, University of London. Editor in Chief, *Journal of Agrarian Change* since January 2008. Many publications in edited books and refereed journals on rural labour in India, and on Dalits, and joint editor of two major collections: *Rural Labour in Contemporary India* (1999) and *Social and Political Change in Uttar Pradesh* (2003).

Kate Meagher: British Academy Post-Doctoral Fellow, African Studies Centre, Oxford University, now Lecturer, Development Studies Institute, London School of Economics. Author of a number of articles in refereed journals, and of the book based on her doctoral thesis, *Identity Economics: Social Networks and the Informal Economy in Africa* (forthcoming). She published an earlier book in 2001, *The Bargain Sector: Structural Adjustment and Non-Farm Incomes in the Nigerian Savanna*.

Cosmas Ochieng: formerly at IFPRI (from March 2005 to September 2007) and currently Lecturer, Sustainable Agriculture, Land and Water, Lancaster Environment Centre, Lancaster University. Since getting his doctorate in 2005 he has published several articles in refereed journals on the political economy of agricultural institutions in Africa. He is currently working on contested landscapes and livelihoods in East Africa, particularly the conflicts involving agriculture, forestry and water eco-systems.

Adam Pain: has combined a career working in the theory and practice of rural development. He is currently a Visiting Professor in Rural Development at SLU (the Swedish University of Agricultural Sciences), Uppsala, and co-principal investigator of an ESRC-funded research programme on livelihood trajectories in Afghanistan. He has been writing on Afghanistan since 2001, before which he wrote on natural resource management and rural development, in countries as diverse as Bhutan, Botswana, Nepal and India. He is currently preparing an edited book on rural change in Vietnam.

Aseem Prakash: Fellow of the Institute for Human Development, New Delhi, and a Visiting Fellow, Queen Elizabeth House, Oxford University in 2007–8. He is the joint editor (with Jan Breman and Isabelle Guerin) of *Bonded Labour in India* (2009), and the editor of *State, Market, Civil Society and Dalits in India*, which is currently with a publisher under review. He has published a number of articles in refereed journals.

Kaushal Vidyarthee: in 2008–9 Vice-President (International) of Oxford University Students' Union having completed his MPhil in Development Studies. A graduate of the Indian national School of Planning and Architecture and expert in GIS mapping, he has collaborated with Barbara Harriss-White on the forthcoming *Atlas of Dalit and Adivasi Discrimination* (Three Essays Press). He now reading for a D.Phil. under her supervision.

Gavin Williams: Fellow of St Peter's College, and a Lecturer in the Department of Politics, Oxford University. He has published extensively on rural development in Africa, with a particular emphasis on Nigeria and South Africa. Influential publications include *Rural Development in Tropical Africa* (co-edited with Judith Heyer and Pepe Roberts), *The Sociology of Developing Societies: Sub-Saharan Africa* (co-edited with Chris Allen) and a seminal article, 'Taking the part of the peasants: rural development in Nigeria and Tanzania'. He continues to write on sociological theory, on democracy, and on the wine industry in South Africa.

Preface

In September 2007 an international workshop, 'Rural development retrospect and prospect', was held for Judith Heyer to celebrate her formal retirement. It drew twenty participants from seven nationalities ranging from Frances Stewart, who has known and worked with Judith Heyer for nearly five decades, all the way to a group of current doctoral students.

Of her work, Judith Heyer has written as follows:

> My African work focused on the importance of taking smallholders seriously, of seeing them as 'rational' economic actors similar to anyone else rather than irrational and not amenable to economic analysis as was still often argued at the time; and fighting all the biases in favour of the large-scale farming sector and agri-business interests that were still dominant in the Kenya economy. My work focused on understanding smallholders, understanding the smallholder economy, and the large-scale farming biases undermining it. This ran through my lectures, my teaching, my work on government committees, and my research and writing while I was in Kenya (1963–75). In the latter part of my time in Kenya I began to think about differentiation among smallholders too – and the fact that there was too little recognition of this.
>
> The initial link between my work in Kenya and my work in India was the fact that the government of India appeared to recognise differentiation among smallholders, through its targeting of the poorer among them in programmes such as the SFDA (Small Farmer Development Agency) and the MFDA (Marginal Farmer Development Agency). I was also attracted by the fact that there was much more awareness of class issues in the literature on Indian agriculture than there was in the literature on African agriculture. I started my work in India by looking at the SFDA and the MFDA in 1978–80. I was struck both by the extent to which the programmes were subverted by the local elite, and by the vulnerability of the local elite as well. I felt that I was getting a very misleading view of the economy by looking at short-term cross-sectional data, so I moved into looking at long-term data instead (what my economist colleagues thought of as history, not economics). My concern was still with the poor in agrarian society. In India,

unlike in Kenya, this meant agricultural labourers as much as anything else. I started out intending to concentrate on class and not caste. I thought that the role of caste was over-rated. I gradually changed my mind. I now think that caste is an extremely important aspect of the (village) society I have been studying – an instrument of control over labour, an instrument that is used to differentiate between different categories of labour, subordinating Scheduled Caste labour to other types of labour, putting them in a position that is grossly inferior (and unfair).

I have always been interested in rural urban interactions. These were less central in the villages I was studying in South India in the late 1970s and early 1980s, but very central when I picked the study up again in the mid 1990s and thereafter. What I am now looking at is villages at the centre of an industrialisation and urbanisation process in which Scheduled Caste groups have got left behind.

I have become much more sensitive to gender issues than I was before. But I have not focused on gender. My data are particularly weak where gender is concerned. My current stance is to recognise this, and to try to factor gender into my understanding of the other issues on which I am concentrating, so far as it is possible for me to do so, but not to change my focus.

The workshop was successful in exploring rich comparative themes from Africa and South Asia – linking them with Judith's work on rural development in general and on Dalit labour in South India in particular, including gender. It was immediately clear that its proceedings could be made into a useful book. Rather than produce a Festschrift, however, we have done something unusual but entirely appropriate to the spirit of the workshop and the comparative political economy seminar that, along with Gavin Williams and Megan Vaughan, Judith and I convened.

With her long personal and intellectual engagement with all the participants and in the light of her interest and engagement with their workshop papers, Judith agreed to commission further papers and collaborate in the process of creating and editing this book.

Our book is being sent to press when the entire world is reeling from the impacts of a series of burst bubbles caused by a financial system permitted to speculate on future assets and collateralised, poor-quality debts, which collapsed when it was finally realised that the latter's value was unknowable. As yet there is little reliable information about the impact of this crisis.

While most of the developing countries in the Africa and South Asia regions we cover have current account convertability, their capital accounts remain in various stages of protection for the reason that, were this not the case, it would be possible to speculate in local currencies and to further attack the already fragile balances between the fiscal deficit, interest rates and exchange rates.

Nevertheless, the two major regions we cover are expected to suffer from the seizure in international lending, from outflows from local stock markets and from shrunken flows of remittances. There is no theory of the likely impact on the unprotected informal economies which are the focus of this book and where reductions in growth rates will be translated into losses of millions of livelihoods. Drops in demand for exports and lack of export credit will certainly hit the relatively labour-intensive sectors, exposed by structural adjustment and liberalisation to the instabilities of international markets. Already political and current affairs reporting, as well as the first state-commissioned reports, testify to job losses across a range of manufacturing and service sectors either linked to exports or to high income domestic demand.

Official responses in developing countries can be of two types: the first involves a coordinated counter-cyclical expansion in state investment and expenditure to sustain the effective demand of victims of the crisis in the real economy, while the second is a fiscal expansion confined to underwriting finance capital. All evidence to date suggests that states are drifting towards the latter rather than the former. Yet, large fractions of these economies consist of citizens whose enterprises or households have never been near a bank, who are 'financially excluded' and for whom such palliative measures will be irrelevant.

Changes in the economy are bound to have far-reaching effects on social and political relations outside it. Reduced returns and incomes will put stresses on household budgets and gendered relations of social reproduction. Women's work is certain to increase, as labour and production for use is substituted for purchased goods. The extent to which this substitution is possible depends on the availability of common property rights to resources to gather and glean. This may be easier in rural sites than urban.

The retreat of the state tracked in this book has also triggered the substitution of private expenditure for former public goods and services, such as education and healthcare. The state will struggle to maintain subsistence guarantees, the costs of which will rise as revenues may shrink. Households will be left with reduced incomes and greater expenditure needs; the impact greatest on the most vulnerable.

The essays in this book trace the dynamics of capital/business under duress of various kinds, and the fortunes of socially differentiated and segmented labour forces. They analyse the pauperising seasonal rhythms of the economy, rural–urban relations, the attempts by states to underwrite and regulate these processes and sustain their victims. They will be highly relevant to the development of a framework through which the impact of the crisis can be understood.

Barbara Harriss-White

Acknowledgements

Specific gratitude streams through the acknowledgements at the foot of many chapters. Here we wish to thank the participants' home institutions for their help towards the travel costs of the workshop. We are grateful to Wolfson College and Somerville College, Oxford and to the Research Support Fund of Oxford University's Department of International Development (Queen Elizabeth House) for resources making the workshop so productive and successful, to Denise Watt and Rachel Crawford for help in organising it, and to Paul Kadetz for very competent assistance in the final phases of preparation of the book. We wish to thank Dorothea Shaefter, Suzanne Richardson and others at Routledge for their interest and support, and Sue Leaper of Florence Production Ltd. BH-W would also like to thank the Institut d'études du développement économique et social (IEDES) of the Université Paris 1 (Panthéon-Sorbonne) for a fellowship which enabled the book to be completed.

Barbara Harriss-White and Judith Heyer

Abbreviations

ACCIMA	Aba Chamber of Commerce
ADB	Asian Development Bank
ADMARC	Agricultural Development and Marketing Corporation
AIADMK	All-India Dravida Munnetra Kazhagam (major Tamil nationalist political party)
AISE	adverse incorporation and social exclusion
AL	agricultural labourer
ANC	African National Congress
APM	Ambedkar People's Movement
BC	Backward Class Caste (lower class caste group)
BIG	basic income grant
BJP	Bharathiya Janata Party
BPO	Business Process Outsourcing
BSP	Bahujan Samaj Party (low-caste North Indian party)
CBO	community-based organisations
CDC	Commonwealth Development Corporation
CEPREMAP	Centre pour les recherches économiques et ses applications (Centre for Research in Economics and Applied Economics – in Paris)
CGIAR	Consultative Group on International Agricultural Research
CM	chief minister
CPGTA	Central Province African Grown Tea Association
CPIAL	Consumer Price Index for Agricultural Labour
CPI(M)/CPM	Marxist Communist Party of India
CPRC	Chronic Poverty Research Centre
CSED	Centre for Social and Economic Development
CTGPA	Coffee and Tea Growers Parliamentary Association
CTO	chief technical officer
DARE	Deagrarianization and Rural Employment
DFID	UK Department for International Development
DLA	Department of Land Affairs
DMK	Dravida Munnetra Kazhagam (major Tamil nationalist political party)
DSF	Dalit Student Federation
DTC	District Tea Committee
DTDC	Desk to Desk Courier (India's domestic delivery network company)
DYFI	Democratic Youth Federation of India
FDI	foreign direct investment
FELDA	Federal Land Development Authority
FRA FRA	region and people in north-west Ghana

GDP	gross domestic product
GEAR	Growth, Employment and Redistribution
GFDC	Ghana Food Distribution Corporation
HIV/AIDS	Human Immunodeficiency Virus/Acquired Immune Deficiency Syndrome
ICT	Information and Communication Technology
IDC	International Development Committee
IDS	Institute of Development Studies
IFAD	International Fund for Agricultural Development
IGC	intergenerational contract
IGNOU	Indira Gandhi National Open University (a distance-learning enterprise)
IGT/I	intergenerational transmission of poverty
IHD	Institute of Human Development
ILO	International Labour Office
IMF	International Monetary Fund
ISI	Import Substitution Industrialisation
ISRDS	Integrated Sustainable Rural Development Strategy
IWPR	Institute for War and Peace Reporting
KTDA	Kenya Tea Development Authority or Kenya Tea Development Agency
KUSSTO	Kenya Union of Small-Scale Tea Owners
KWV	Ko-operatieve Wijnbouwers Vereeniging van Zuid-Afrika
LADDER	livelihoods research project (conducted in Uganda, Kenya, Tanzania and Malawi)
LDC	Less developed country
LP	Liberation Panther
LRAD	Land Redistribution for Agricultural Development
MAN	Manufacturers' Association of Nigeria
MASAF	Malawi Social Action Fund
MBC	Most Backward Caste (official classification)
MFDA	Marginal Farmers Development Agency
MFF	National Fish Forum (the fish workers' union)
MI	methodologically individualist
MLA	Members of the Legislative Assembly
MNC	Multinational corporation
MP	Member of Parliament
MSFC	Maharashtra State Financial Corporation
MVAC	Malawi Vulnerability Assessment Committee
NAMPO	National Maize Growers' Association
NASSI	Nigerian Association of Small and Medium-Scale Industrialists
NASVI	National Alliance of Street Vendors
NCEUS	National Commission for Enterprises in the Unorganised Sector
NCL	National Centre for Labour
NDE	New Development Economics
NGO	non-governmental organisation
NIE	New Institutional Economics
NREGA	The government of India's 2005 National Rural Employment Guarantee Act
NREGS	National Rural Employment Guarantee Scheme
NRU	Nutrition Rehabilitation Unit
NSSO	Indian National Sample Survey Organisation
NTUI	New Trade Union Initiative

OAE	own account enterprise
OBC	Other Backward Class Caste
OC	Other Castes
OXFAM	Oxford Committee for Famine Relief – major British NGO
PASDEP	Plan for Accelerated and Sustained Development to End Poverty
PCP	petty commodity producer
PEACH	political economy of agrarian change
PERP	Public Enterprises Reform Program
PI	Participation Indices
PO	producers' organisations
PRSP	Poverty Reduction Strategy Plan
PSNP	Productive Safety Net Programme
PTB	Provincial Tea Board
QEH	Queen Elizabeth House, Department of International Development, University of Oxford
RDP	Reconstruction and Development Programme
RNF	rural non-farm
SAB	South African Breweries
SAP	Structural Adjustment Programme
SATA	South African Temperance Alliance
SC	Scheduled Caste
SCDA	Special Crops Development Authority
SCE	Scheduled Caste Enterprise
SCP	Scheduled Caste Population
SDPRP	Sustainable Development and Poverty Reduction Programme
SEWA	Self-Employed Women's Association
SFDA	Small Farmer Development Agency
SFW	Stellenbosch Farmers Winery
SGR	Strategic Grain Reserve
SL	sustainable livelihoods
SOAS	School of Oriental and African Studies, University of London
SSA	sub-Saharan Africa
SSLC	Secondary School Leaving Certificate
ST	Scheduled Tribe
STO	Senior Tea Officer
TAHDCO	Tamil Nadu Adi Dravidar Housing and Development Corporation
TBK	Tea Board of Kenya
THDR	Tamil Nadu Human Development Report
UEA	University of East Anglia
UNDP	United Nations Development Program
UNODC	United Nations Office on Drugs and Crime
VAO	Village Agricultural Officer
VCACS	Village Cooperative Agricultural Credit Society
VCK	Viduthalai Ciruthaigal Katchi
VIKALP	Adivasi Forest Workers Association
VLS	village-level studies
VP	vegetative propagation
WB	World Bank
WIEGO	Women in the Informal Economy Globalizing and Organizing
WPM	Working Peasant's Movement

1 Introduction

Barbara Harriss-White and
Judith Heyer

The project

The chapters in this book celebrate the enduring vitality of a comparative political economy approach that is empirically grounded and based on an undogmatic and critical engagement with Marxist theory in which agency, non-class institutions and structures and struggles expressed through them play roles in capitalist transformation alongside class formation and class structure. The approach is historical, comparative and interdisciplinary. It is also one that assumes that the macro context is important for understanding the micro level and vice versa. Most of the chapters in this collection are based on these ideas, or some variant of them, though not all use the language of capital and class.

Most of the chapters also trace their origins to the Oxford University Comparative Political Economy seminar run by Judith Heyer, Gavin Williams, Megan Vaughan and Barbara Harriss-White from the 1980s until the mid 1990s. It was the crucible for Oxford's MPhil in Development Studies, which started in 1996. The seminar was also a crucial starting point for many masters, doctoral and postdoctoral projects, and generated a body of work the continuation of which is in evidence today. This work was strongly influenced by, and closely linked to, work in political economy being published in the *Journal of Peasant Studies* (and now the *Journal of Agrarian Change*) and in the *Economic and Political Weekly*.

The focus of the researchers associated with the Oxford Comparative Political Economy seminar was rural. Judith Heyer's retirement was an opportune moment to reflect on the vibrancy of this research – rural and non-rural – and the contemporary implications of its findings. The original group's comparative political economy was centred on comparisons within and between Africa and South Asia. That is also the focus of this book.

Central to our approach is the notion of class conflict. Class formation and class conflict are understood to be the prime movers behind processes of social change and the expansion and deepening of capitalist relations of production and social reproduction. Class relations are defined through the ownership of land and assets, through conflicts of interest and class struggle. In turn, the study of social structure, social relations and their transformation is indispensable to our understanding of the attempts to manage this process in the name of development.

Some of the criticisms levelled in the 1980s at this Marxian political economy as applied to rural change were that it is homogenising and reductionist; that it places too much emphasis on structure, and has little room for agency; that it underplays the role of politics, culture and ideology; that it ignores aspects of identity such as gender, sexuality, caste, race, ethnicity and religion; and that although ostensibly empirically based it uses empirical material to confirm rather than question its preconceived view of the world. As da Corta shows here (Chapter 2), this was the result of a selective reading at the time. It has certainly not been true subsequently.

The comparative political economy exemplified by the chapters in this book is the result of a continuing critical engagement with theory, grounded in empirical evidence, with analytical space for social agency. It incorporates open, context-dependent and pluralist accounts, within which Marxist theory is often an important ingredient but not a totalising referent (see, for example, Rogaly, Harriss-White and Bose 1999), on agrarian structure in West Bengal). It also draws on Karl Polanyi's concept of embeddedness, with many studies not only of the rural economy but also of state and policy which reveal the inability of secular states or apparently neutral markets to wrench themselves free of social and political relations of class, ethnicity, religion and patriarchy. Indeed, rather than conceiving of non-class relations and institutions as 'epiphemonena', 'impurities' or 'residuals' expected to be dissolved or destroyed by 'modernity', it sees them as enduring and constitutive of modernity. Our comparative political economy draws on the concept of social structures of accumulation adapted and developed in *India Working*, Harriss-White's 2003 book on India's informal economy – see also Meagher, Chapter 8 in this volume.

Some of the followers of this approach to political economy also drew on the sub-discipline of socio-economics, but while the latter attempts to incorporate social structures into economic analysis, it neither mentions class nor considers seriously politics and power (Heyer, Stewart and Thorp 2001).

Political economy approaches have regularly neglected agency on the part of poor and exploited classes. A key feature of much of the work published in this book is that it examines the idea that the poor have strong capacities for political and economic agency. Their mobilisation, however, may be constrained by structures and settings in which the room for manoeuvre and agency is restricted. In this book, for instance, Francis explicitly examines constraints on the agency of poor people in rural South Africa (Chapter 5); Devereux looks at coping strate-gies due to seasonality and extreme food shortage (Chapter 6); Ochieng (Chapter 7) analyses the role played by political patronage in the agency of smallholder tea growers; and while Meagher shows the networked agency of self-employed manufacturers faced with the pressures of liberalisation, mass unemployment and informalisation in Nigeria (Chapter 8), Prakash shows the resourcefulnesss of Dalit entrepreneurs faced with an array of institutional and political obstacles in India (Chapter 15). Several other chapters in this book address the political agency of Dalits around class and identity. Centuries of contemptuous and oppressive treatment have placed huge obstacles in the way of Dalits' development. Subject to positive discrimination and dedicated development projects, euphemised as 'backward' and 'weaker sections', generally confined to casual agricultural labour, low- status artisan crafts, construction, carcass and sanitary work, they remain disproportionately excluded and/or adversely included in India's capitalist transformation. This book puts them centre stage. The role of gender relations is another important theme, given attention particularly in Chapters 5 by Francis and 13 by Kapadia. Kapadia shows that it is low-paid women at the bottom of the hierarchy that support the low-wage economy of India, and that subordination within the household reinforces women's subordination within the wage economy. The questions best answered by feminist political economists about the sites and relations of authority, subordination, exploitation and oppression in the cycles of production and reproduction (see Pujo 1996) can also be asked of other economic manifestations of identity such as caste and ethnicity.

Ochieng and Meagher (here, as well as in her forthcoming book on 'identity economics') show the importance of regional and ethnic identities in shaping and unravelling economic opportunities and development.

While followers of political economy have always been interdisciplinary, history has been as integral to the comparative political economy of development as has been geography. Later followers also had considerable analytical room for political ideologies and practice. Some looked at contested agrarian relations in response to changes in national and global political economy (Harriss-White and Janakarajan 2004; Basile, forthcoming). Other research explored rural-urban political economy through agro-commodity chains, rural-urban clusters and agro-industrial districts (Pujo 1996; Jayaraj and Nagaraj 2006; Roman 2008; Ruthven 2008; Basile, forthcoming). Yet others looked at elite accumulation strategies as well as the politics of the marginalised (Williams 1975; Moore and Vaughan 1994; Fernandez 2008; Sarkar 2009). Yet other work explored how the dialectics of negotiation, bargaining and struggle helped to explain why specific forms of social relations either persist or change (Olsen 1996; Rogaly 1997; Majid 1998; Razavi 2003; Kim 2008). Another way comparative political economy developed was through the interrogation of theories of institutional change in the light of evidence for institutional innovation, destruction, persistence and reworked roles (Basile, forthcoming; Ochieng 2005). The relation between agency and deviance, and responses to both in resistance to institutional change and in institutional reworking, are also being explored. Tools were also developed for the processes and relations that dominate when formal regulative institutions including the state do not operate (Basile, forthcoming; Meagher, in this volume; Harriss-White 2003, 2008).

Practical method

The comparative political economy approach was strongly linked to South Asian and African village studies, in what da Corta (Chapter 2) describes as a 'collision of Marxist methods . . . with concrete village economic, social and cultural reality' (see Harriss-White and Harriss 2007; Harriss-White 1999).

Its empirical grounding is a key feature of the work represented in this book. Empirical work – what the anthropologist Polly Hill called 'field economics' but extended to political economy – is necessary to understand what is going on on the ground, to give specific answers to questions about social change and thereby to engage with theory. Fine detail matters here.

Empirical work in comparative political economy involves an iterative process consisting of several stages. (i) Theory gives rise to questions as well as to presumptions about what data need to be collected to answer these questions. The method is deductive at this stage. (ii) Data collection, involving fieldwork and/or archival work, based on an initial reading of theory, but also open-ended and interdisciplinary, looks out for – and follows up on – whatever may be relevant in order to be able to answer the questions chosen as the focus of the research. It is important at this stage to allow evidence that challenges initial positions to emerge, making it possible to discover the unexpected, to discover additional dimensions that might not have been anticipated. The most valuable fieldwork/data collection is the fieldwork/data collection that produces surprises, data that do not conform to preconceptions, to what we think we know. This is surely the way that agency came back into (if it had ever left) what was essentially Marxist research. In collecting data, one may find that one has misunderstood – in which case (if one has gone through the literature well) it is likely that many have misunderstood – the problem, the explanation and often the theory as well (see Olsen 1996 for a good example of the development of theory on the basis of what was found in the field). (iii) Data processing and analysis – not foreswearing socio- or econometric analysis where appropriate (see Meagher, Chapter 8 and Harriss-White and Vidyarthee, Chapter 15 in this volume) – leads to what are often a revised set of research questions, and a set of explanations that go beyond the range of those originally anticipated as possibilities. Data collection and processing should allow one to reflect on theory, modify theory and develop theory, inductively.

This method takes empirical material seriously, deductively and inductively, and engages with theory from the perspective of local peoples' experience, mediated by first-hand research. Many of the chapters in the book are based on research that has used this methodology or one similar to it.

Non-policy research and its relation to policy

Much of the research does not feed directly into policy. It is important to recognise the value of such research. Non-policy-oriented research has produced a corpus of work that is highly relevant to the policy process – because it helps us understand the processes that may be managed through policy, as well as understanding the policy process itself. Non-policy-oriented research is just as necessary to the development of good policy as is good policy-oriented research. Without a fundamental understanding, research that feeds into policy is most unlikely to have the impact intended. Examples of important non-policy research in this book include Heyer showing the marginalisation of Dalits in a development process that looks in many ways 'successful' (Chapter 11); Williams showing how state support made what was an essentially unviable sector viable (Chapter 9); Kapadia showing the way in which women at the bottom of the socio-economic hierarchy make possible a low-wage economy that persists at their expense (Chapter 13); and Francis showing the implications of development policies that are unsustainable in the medium or the longer term (Chapter 5). None of this research was directly policy-oriented. All of it is essential to our understanding of development dynamics.

It would be difficult to get such research funded in contemporary circumstances. This is because the relation between policy-driven research (where enquiry is contained and room for analytical manoeuvre limited) and non-policy-driven research is currently unbalanced towards a restricted vision of policy. This problem results from the way that research is funded, especially research on development ... Funding is increasingly restricted to research that feeds into an aid-defined policy agenda, and much less readily available for fundamental research, let alone research which is justified for teaching and learning. This means that there is far too little research that is not governed by what funders identify as policy relevance or themes which the policy agenda of funding institutions puts up for investigation. This is what makes independent research, such as much of that offered in this book, increasingly rare, and increasingly important, today.

The contributions to this book adopt different approaches to development policy. For Africa, Ellis, a long-time champion of rural livelihood creation, presents a policy menu for an urban response to agrarian poverty and crisis. The relations between agriculture and the non-farm economy need synergising by active support to very small businesses. Francis signals the importance of a 'basic income' and of labour market reform to address the barriers to economic and social mobility and to create livelihoods. Devereux shows the importance of seasonality in perpetuating and reinforcing poverty and inequality and examines the limited role that social protection policy can play in addressing this. Policy and its effects in Afghanistan are an integral part of the political economy approach of Pain too.

Many of the contributions to this book are concerned with the effects on social transformation of there *not* being policy, or of unintended consequences of policy, or of paradoxes stemming from the nexus of oppressive and exploitative interests of class, state or status groups which sabotage redistributivist development policy through neglect or plunder. Heyer, Gorringe and Ochieng illustrate two further aspects of a political economy approach to policy. (i) The general importance of politics (party/movement/local/informal) for economic opportunities. If politics is seen to be about power and if the state cannot enforce development policy that it may accept on paper, then the politics of markets, the politics of social status, of social movements, of identity and social accountability call for reinterpretation as development policy. This is an ambitious agenda which is only starting to be explored. (ii) The fact that even if phrased in technical universalistic discourse and representations, policy is always political. Policy is also always affected by the law of unintended outcomes. It is far from being an epiphenomenon. It is always revealed as filtered through political contexts and social structures with a range of specific outcomes and practices alongside its more systematic and purposive effects (Fernandez 2008).

The way our non-policy-oriented political economy might engage with policy debates can be illustrated with reference to the World Bank's 2008 World Development Report on agriculture (World Bank 2008; henceforth referred to as WDR 2008). After a gap of a quarter-century in which the Bank has played its own semi-acknowledged role (among other aid/development agencies) in the egregious neglect of agriculture and the depression of rural development under liberalisation, this clearly structured report re-justifies an 'agriculture first' policy.

While we cannot launch here into a full-blooded critique of the report (see www.sol.slu.se/rural/ for a set of political economy critiques; and see Devereux, Scoones and Thompson 2009 for a summary of other critiques) our political economy, in enabling at least four kinds of engagement, reveals its distinctive and enduring contributions. The first kind of engagement involves the use of the tools of political economy to interrogate policy suggestions. This identifies several contradictions and ambivalences running through the WDR 2008 which result from the Bank's pro-market methodological individualism. The role prescribed by the Bank for the state is inconsistent, with for example the difference between public infrastructure and private goods not clear. While roads and irrigation are for the state to provide, agricultural credit is for the market alone. India's experience shows that relying on markets for financial services, including the privatisation of agricultural banks, has involved a rapid retreat from poor regions and from agriculture (Ramachandran and Rawal 2009). WDR 2008 also argues against food aid and food subsidies. So India's public distribution system – never exceeding 0.99 per cent of India's GDP at its height – has been stripped of its price-stabilising role and is increasingly narrowly targeted, now excluding 71 per cent of agricultural labour in Bihar, 73 per cent in Uttar Pradesh and 52 per cent nationally. Rather than acting as a component of an income/subsistence guarantee, it now intensifies poverty (Swaminathan 2000, 2008).

Another example of inconsistency in the application of the Bank's ideology is revealed in its suggestions for improving returns to smallholders and labour markets in the face of the enormous and growing problem of low returns and rural underemployment (see chapters by Lerche, Devereux, Francis and Heyer in this volume). While core labour rights are called for, the Bank adds that the absence of labour regulation incentivises the informal economy (WDR 2008 Ch. 9: 29). With respect to smallholder agriculture, Ochieng (in this volume) shows that decades of struggles by smallholders together with highest-level ethnicised political patronage were necessary to generate the preconditions needed for a producer-governed organisation. Woodhouse (2009) also shows that the Bank's support of producer organisations rests on evidence from Uganda, where the organisations have been captured by the least poor and supported by a local policy of betting on the strong – thereby revealing that the preconditions for successful producer organisations for the poor are not necessarily there at all.

Secondly, our approach celebrates the importance of history and geography, whereas the Bank is compelled to make large region-wide statements. There is both ambivalence and reductionism about Africa in WDR 2008. The Bank calls for infrastructure and markets, and water control is stressed as being paramount. Yet big dams have been disastrous in Africa (Woodhouse 2009) and the water markets the Bank itself generates are often informal ones and associated with political conflict. The preconditions for successful infrastructural coordination above the level of the household are generally neglected by WDR 2008. While agricultural research led by the CGIAR has been moving towards agriculture-environment relations, international research has neglected labour. African labour productivity shows signs of decline and a tendency towards involution (Woodhouse 2009). Yet our research identifies acute seasonal labour shortages especially for land clearing, irrigation and pest management (see Ellis, Francis and Devereux in this volume).

The same ambivalence characterises WDR 2008's treatment of India. On the one hand it sees India as a sink of agrarian poverty – unable to translate growth in non-agriculture into sustained agricultural development. On the other hand, India is described as 'well advanced' and on a sustained growth path. Kapadia here makes the case, avoided by the Bank, that the one is dependent upon the other.

Thirdly, capitalism is conspicuous by its absence from WDR 2008. It is only since the crisis of the Wall Street financial system that the word has been reintroduced into the vocabulary of the economic academy. Capitalism is not well proxied by 'markets', the 'economy', the 'private sector', 'business' – these terms rob capitalism of its logic(s) and dynamics.

Markets can work for the poor (WDR 2008: 143) but they can also work against the poor, or be irrelevant to them. As allocative mechanisms markets respond to effective demand and where endowments are unequal they differentiate. Markets are very widely expected to bulldoze social institutions which block the free mobility of capital and labour, but this does not happen (Harriss-White 2009; Meagher, in this volume), even in advanced countries (da Corta, in this volume). Regulation is necessary, and in the absence of enforcement – either due to lack of disciplining capacity (Chibber 2003) or due to a deal between the state and top fractions of capital (Dasgupta 2008) – other institutions and practices step into the void and, once there, are extremely hard to remove. Since they are socially constructed they are 'arbitrary' and there is no reason to conclude that either state or social institutions of regulation benefit the poor. Williams's analysis here of cooperative producers' organisations and their modes of control of wage work through the use of prison labour and enforced alcoholism is one example. Other examples abound in the chapters by Ochieng, Francis and Kapadia.

Capitalism has to proceed by competition among firms, but much effort goes into preventing competition (as through quality standards (Ochieng), and other exclusive practices (Prakash)). Capitalist competition cuts costs through exploiting labour (see Lerche and Kapadia), increasing labour productivity, and displacing labour by technological change (Byres 1981) and relentless commodification (Raj, Bhattacharya, Guha and Padhi 1985; Leys 2001).

While the Bank sees smallholder production as a starting point in adverse population-resource endowments, our political economy sees that petty commodity production can be the historical outcome of processes of adverse incorporation into capitalism or 'Global Value Chains' or a new wave of commercial money-lending exploitation and caste-gender oppression. There is a lively debate about whether such production is best conceived as disguised wage labour (Lerche in this volume), or whether – as a result of a different logic (maximising production rather than marginal productivity), and its capacity to be exploited through four markets (rent, interest, inputs and products) rather than one (labour) – petty production is actually distinctively different (Harriss-White 2009).

Finally, our political economy does not shrink from the dialectical, oppositional dynamic of struggle but places it central to its analysis. If the Bank's normative, reasoned suggestions are so obviously beneficial, why have they not been put into practice? What constrains or opposes the Bank's vision for agriculture? The processes causing agricultural impoverishment include things externalised from the Bank's argument. For example, the role of advanced country protection (of cotton, oilseeds and biofuels) is regarded by Bourguignon (Senior Vice-President for Development Economics at the World Bank) as 'a problem in political economy' and not a problem in policy. A political economist would not confine themselves to identifying the problem of agricultural lobbies in advanced countries, but would examine the obstacles to buying off this lobby as an intrinsic component of an agriculture-first strategy which 'alters class relations in favour of working people, frees demand constraints, opens up home markets in the countryside and provides a basis for broad-based productive investment' (Ramachandran and Rawal 2009). It would also go further than the Bank in asking what problems in implementation would be created by this agenda. It would identify, recursively, the political response needed to supply the political and institutional preconditions for the strategies.

For another example, gender (deployed to mean 'women' rather than relations between the genders) is recognised as important, but the Bank does not help the understanding of how women may be empowered in agriculture when all evidence in our book suggests an intensification of patriarchy. The World Bank is silent on other aspects of status identity and their roles as regulators of the economy, but the questions typically asked of 'gender' analysis are relevant to status identity more generally. Education, household bargaining, rights over property, work conditions and wages are all affected by sets of institutions which turn the, more or less, level playing field assumed by Bank-style policy into a mountain range. Indian village-level studies (VLS), only relatively recently sensitised to identity have now revealed incomes of Muslim households at 73 per cent of the incomes of Other Castes and those of Scheduled Castes/Scheduled Tribes at 58 per cent (Ramachandran and Rawal 2009). A development policy informed by political economy would expand its scope to include the conditions under which these aspects of culture can be progressively removed from determining economic chances. Otherwise, policy framed in neutral language will be implemented through these institutions, perpetuating and/or increasing these inequalities.

The long-standing scrutiny of capitalist transformation – struggles of class and status identity pursued through political economy – amply justifies itself in light of the new rural agenda of the World Bank.

The book

Most of the research showcased in this book focuses on poor, vulnerable, politically marginalised, labouring people and their agency. A common thread is a concern with persistent disadvantage. However, the studies in this collection make it clear that one can only understand the predicament of poor people by seeing its connection with social relations in which they are exploited and/or oppressed by the non-poor.

Focusing on the poor, the weak, the vulnerable, implies an interest in labour as much as capital and a recognition that to understand labour one has to study capital as well. To this end, this book uses analytical tools rooted in its historical origins in rural political economy to challenge the division between rural and urban and to shed fresh light on agricultural value chains and agro-processing (tea – Ochieng, Chapter 7; wine – Williams, Chapter 9; opium – Pain, Chapter 10); the politics of collective action against MNCs and fractions of the state, promoting small-scale production through political patronage (Ochieng, Chapter 7) and the control of labour through producer cooperatives (Williams, Chapter 9); the political economy of networked differentiation in industrial clusters (Meagher, Chapter 8); the relations between status differentiation, 'identity economics' and capital accumulation (Meagher, ibid.; Kapadia, Chapter 13; Prakash, Chapter 14; Harriss-White and Vidyarthee, Chapter 15).

The book also examines the social regulation of capital when the state cannot, or chooses not to, enforce its own regulative frame (Meagher, Chapter 8; Williams, Chapter 9 and; Prakash, Chapter 14). It examines capital--labour struggles, regimes of labour control and 'classes of labour' (Lerche, Chapter 4) – in particular the oppressive control over Dalits in India (Heyer, Chapter 11; Gorringe, Chapter 12; Prakash, Chapter 14), and over low-caste women (Kapadia, Chapter 13). Several chapters pursue the implications of socially regulated labour – ethnicised skills and productivity (Pain, Chapter 10); ethnicity and income security (Francis, Chapter 5); gendered labour and wages (Kapadia, Chapter 13); untouchability as an unmeasurable dimension of poverty (Gorringe, Chapter 12). This research also examines how lack of education traps workers (Gorringe, ibid.) and can be used quite deliberately by employers to trap labour in low paying sectors (Williams, Chapter 9).

Several of the contributions have used case material comparatively in building their arguments (Da Corta, Chapter 2; Meagher, Chapter 8; Heyer, Chapter 11; Gorringe, Chapter 12; Prakash, Chapter 14). Others have compared across scales (Lerche, Chapter 4; Francis, Chapter 5; Devereux, Chapter 6; Ochieng, Chapter 7; Kapadia, Chapter 13; Harriss-White and Vidyarthee, Chapter 15). There is also a large-scale comparison that is not addressed explicitly but needs mention here. Despite the record of agricultural growth and superficial indicators of prosperity, long-term agrarian research reveals the extent of capitalist differentiation in India (Ramachandran and Swaminathan 2002; Harriss-White and Harriss 2007; Ramachandran and Rawal 2009), and both differentiation and deterioration of material conditions in Africa (Ellis, Chapter 3; Francis, Chapter 5; Devereux, Chapter 6 in this volume). In India, Heyer (2000) identified a standard-of-living paradox in which the real incomes of the poorest deciles rise but, with aspirations fuelled by rising inequality, expenditure transcends incomes. Households are pitched into unprecedented levels of debt.

In the 1980s, at the height of the Green Revolution and its controversial multipliers, India's rural economy presented a dramatic contrast to the agrarian poverty of Africa. But the intervening years have revealed convergence between India and Africa. India's agricultural economy has faltered in all but a few states (they form a belt in the north from Rajasthan and Gujarat through Madhya Pradesh and Bihar to Chhattisgarh and Jarkhand). The non-agricultural economy in both India and Africa has failed to produce enough alternative employment opportunities to have made this tolerable. India's Ministry of Finance report on agricultural indebtedness and the agrarian crisis (Government of India 2007) argues that a crisis has been developing in Indian agriculture since the late 1980s, with the exhaustion of the Green Revolution seed-fertiliser technology, and the absence of new agricultural technologies to take its place. There has been a drastic decline in agricultural research resources, stagnation in agricultural yields, unprecedented price volatility, reduced policy space to protect against this, the miniaturisation of holdings, mass debt, distress-induced diversification, and casualisation of labour, accompanied by increases in child labour and unsustainable dependency ratios and household forms. Non-agricultural production and non-agricultural activities have failed to provide the quality and quantity of alternative employment that would have made it possible for the agricultural sector to shrink without so much distress. In Africa, too, holding sizes have declined and agricultural yields have fallen increasingly behind. There is much more to compare now than there was a quarter-century ago.

The chapters

Our collection starts with three chapters devoted to big pictures – class, poverty and labour. Da Corta's is a theoretical essay critically comparing the political economy of agrarian change with recent theoretical approaches to the study of poverty which come out of neo-classical economics augmented by social, political and institutional analysis. She suggests a synthesis, bringing Marxist concepts such as capital, class and unfreedom back in. Questions raised by her chapter include whether political economy is still alive and well, perhaps not in development economics or policy analysis, but in development studies, area studies, geography, sociology and anthropology (www.rethinkingeconomies.org.uk/); and whether it is useful to think about all this as a departure from, or as a development of, political economy.

Ellis discusses the larger context in which micro studies are situated, focusing particularly on the interrelationships between agricultural and non-agricultural development with African cases in mind. This is in keeping with a political economy approach which recognises the importance of the macro at the micro level. Ellis builds a currently unorthodox case for progress in rural development through non-agricultural and urban development but acknowledges that this is intimately connected with agricultural and rural development too.

Lerche's essay is concerned with an unorthodox approach to rural class relations in India focusing on 'classes of labour'. Like Ellis's, it traces the move from overwhelmingly agrarian-based class relations, towards a situation where, for most of the rural population, the reproduction of class positions and class relations involves non-agricultural accumulation processes and labour relations. For labour, the overall result of continued processes of flexibilisation, casualisation and/or forced labour-type labour relations is a hierarchy of labour classes, segmented into different types of employment and degrees of self-employment. They are further segmented through social identity: most importantly, gender, caste, religion, locality and language. Lerche focuses on caste and ethnicity to show that this segmentation enables oppressive labour relations, and is part of the reason why pro-labour employment related activities, be it by unions, or NGOs and movements, or even by certain government agencies, have had only a limited impact. In fact, poor labouring groups at the bottom of the employment hierarchy are more likely to seek redress outside labour relations, through caste or locality-based political organisations, and even armed struggle.

Lerche's chapter is linked to Williams's thesis that there is a continuum of contractual arrangements from casual and 'free' to bonded; together with a great variety of routes to cheapen, control and exclude labour – especially so as to make large-scale enterprises (estates and plantations) compete effectively with the super-exploitation of smallholder/petty commodity producing/peasant agricultural labour. It also has implications for the teleology of development. It is not the only chapter to speak of reversion to subsistence and from casual to bonded labour.

With the exception of the final chapter, the remaining chapters on Africa and India (and one on Afghanistan) are all micro studies grounded in detailed empirical material which is used as the starting point for analysis in which the social and political interacts with the economic.

Francis asks what causes poverty in a South African setting, locating this poverty within a macro context in which policies being pursued by the South African government are neither generating additional employment nor redistributing land. She looks at a community in a densely populated rural area in the North West Province in which people cluster around sources of stability in complex households where livelihoods derived from multiple sources are put together. What characterises the majority in the community concerned is their very limited holdings of poor-quality land, the very limited sources of employment locally, and their very limited access to employment on the basis of which to secure better incomes further away. She looks at the strategies deployed to sustain livelihoods, pointing out that they are fragile, vulnerable and barely sustainable. She points out that they are already stretched, and not infinitely stretchable, raising the question of their no longer being sustainable in future.

Devereux looks at the critical role that seasonality continues to play in relation to poverty and inequality in sub-Saharan Africa, and discusses the extent to which social protection policies can play a role in reducing its effects. He shows that seasonality remains an acute problem, impoverishing many of the poorest of all, and that the problem is, if anything, exacerbated by liberalisation. He also shows how seasonality polarises, the relatively less poor benefiting at the expense of the poor. The roots of the problem lie in the isolation, lack of diversification and lack of access to markets that still characterise much of rural sub-Saharan Africa. Its effects were mitigated in the past by state policies which are now being withdrawn. Market processes fail to address the problem. State policies are needed here. However, social protection policies can only play a limited role.

Ochieng gives an account of the gradual increase in participation by small-holders in, and ultimate takeover of, the control and management of a major parastatal, the KTDA, which regulates and processes smallholder tea in Kenya. He shows how conflicts between smallholder tea growers, agri-business and the state in Kenya over the period from the 1960s to the early 2000s drove changes in the balance of power, culminating in the full transfer of ownership to smallholders with the privatisation of the KTDA in 2000. The smallholder struggle was long drawn out but eventually successful in giving smallholders control over the large and dominant enterprise that regulated their production. Ochieng points out the particular circumstances, and political configurations, that made this possible, contrasting it with the case of sugar in Kenya, the outcome for which was very different from that for tea.

Meagher focuses on the role of associations supporting clusters of shoe producers and garment producers in the Igbo heartland of Nigeria. These clusters consist of large numbers of small entrepreneurs producing considerable volumes of output, generating very significant income in the process. Associations have generally been thought to play a positive role in supporting clusters of this kind. She has a more critical view, showing that many of the associations in which shoe producers and garment producers are involved provide very limited support. These include 'home-town' associations, church associations, producers' associations, and savings clubs. She also shows that in this case the associations reinforce inequality and work as economic regulators in different ways for people of different status.

This book has not flinched from examining the role of addictives – alcohol and narcotics (opium) – in rural development, both as commodities and through the impact of consumption. The next two chapters elaborate this neglected theme (but see also Kim 2008 on alcohol). Williams looks at the different ways in which wine producers in South Africa's Western Cape managed to procure both supplies of low-cost labour and support for markets over the period from 1918 to 1988, arguing that wine production would not have been viable in the Western

Cape without state policies to support the supply of cheap labour, and to bolster the market for wine. This is a good example of a general argument that Williams has long espoused: that experience all over the world shows that large-scale producers in agriculture relying on large quantities of hired labour are not viable without state support to lower the cost of labour and/or raise the price of output. Of particular interest in this case are the wine producers' reliance on prison labour for much of the period, and the fact that part of the payment to labour was in wine. Both of these are discussed in some detail in this chapter as is the evolution of the wine-producing regime.

Pain looks at the uneven, and changing, distribution of opium production in Afghanistan in the 1990s and early 2000s, and then focuses on two districts in north-eastern Afghanistan which have been centres of opium production for some time. The irony is that opium is the ideal rural development crop, giving high returns to small producers, over a wide range of conditions. This gives rise to contradictions which he pursues in the chapter. The chapter goes into the political economy of opium production in the two districts on which it focuses, showing the uneven distribution of production both geographically and with respect to class. The key constraints are water, labour and the social organisation of production. Pain concludes that in the second half of the 1990s the production regime favoured the existing hierarchy and the persistence of conflict, whereas in the early 2000s it looked as though the production regime was opening up, spreading the benefits more widely, breaking down the hierarchy, and reducing conflict as well. The chapter ends with the complete cessation of opium production in 2006/2007, and a question mark around its future. The chapter is a strong statement on the irony of the transformatory possibilities of opium production which is anathema to US and other interests in Afghanistan.

Heyer and Gorringe's chapters both look at the role of politics, ideology and culture, as well as changes in material conditions, in breaking the dependency of Dalits at the bottom of the caste and class hierarchy in two different locations in Tamil Nadu, South India, in the 1990s and early 2000s. Heyer's chapter focuses on a group of Dalits, in western Tamil Nadu, where economic development based on industrialisation as well as the modernisation of agriculture has been much stronger, and the ability of Dalits to break their dependency within the agrarian structure has been much more limited, than in the case analysed by Gorringe. Gorringe argues strongly that without political mobilisation changes would have been far more limited, a point borne out by Heyer, in her chapter, which focuses on an area where there has been very little Dalit political mobilisation. Gorringe's chapter focuses on a group of Dalits in central Tamil Nadu where economic development has been mediocre and Dalits have made considerable strides in breaking their dependency within the agrarian structure. These chapters contrast the stronger power of successful capitalists over labour on the one hand, with the weaker power of the less successful capitalists on the other.

Kapadia's chapter looks at the problems of low-paid, low-caste women workers in Chennai, based on interviews with women workers in the slums. She identifies the increasing feminisation of labour in the urban informal sector with globalisation and liberalisation which puts increasing pressure on wages. She links gender discrimination within the household with gender discrimination in the labour market. This is a setting in which a growing acceptance of norms of seclusion both conflicts with increasing pressures on women in poor households to go out to work and decreases their bargaining power in the labour market. All of this applies irrespective of caste or religion. Caste structures the opportunities in the labour market however. Dalit women are found in the worst-paid occupations of all.

Prakash looks at the problems that Dalit entrepreneurs experience, based on a survey in key states across north-central India (Gujarat, Madhya Pradesh, Maharashtra, Rajasthan, Uttar Pradesh and West Bengal), bringing out problems specific to Dalits that make it clear that they are far from competing on a level playing field. He shows just how far-reaching these problems are. Dalit entrepreneurs face problems with respect to credit, which is not readily available within their own kin and caste networks and not readily available from formal sources either. They face problems with respect to markets both as a result of consumer resistance and as a result of hostile competitors using caste as a basis for destroying their position. They face the problem of people not being willing to work for Dalit employers. They face the problem of non-Dalit firms not being willing to supply them with inputs or only being willing to supply them on adverse terms. These problems are wide-ranging and serious enough to explain the relative under-representation of Dalits that Harriss-White and Vidyarthee document below, if not their sectoral differentiation, regional variation and deterioration in numbers. They might provide a starting point for pursuing the explanations of the latter, though.

Harriss-White and Vidyarthee map, for the first time, the distribution of Dalit and Adivasi businesses in India in 1990 and 1998, revealing their uneven incorporation by sector and by region. They show the deterioration in the proportion of Scheduled Caste businesses over a period in which the proportions in all other groups, including Scheduled Tribes, increased. They look for possible explanations of the different patterns in different regions. None of the possible explanations that are currently available from development economics and political sociology explains the patterns at all. They suggest other ways of approaching the question that might produce more satisfactory explanations in future.

These chapters raise many common issues associated with contemporary processes of globalisation and liberalisation. Do they also demonstrate the effectiveness of comparative political economy in analysing contemporary development problems? Da Corta argues that we need political economy to move beyond narrative and association and explore underlying causes, or explanations. How far do the chapters support this claim? Many of the chapters bring out the working of the underlying forces behind capitalist transformation without necessarily using the terms of the classical Marxist tool kit. Williams shows how state support has been necessary to give capital the power to subordinate labour in the wine industry in the Western Cape since at least the last decades of the nineteenth century. In so doing, his case exemplifies the many ways in which the state supports capital and the lengths to which it will go in its struggle against labour. Francis shows that the lack of power of pauperised workers, unable to struggle effectively against capital and the state, can lead to 'biopolitically' unsustainable positions for them. Ochieng shows that the political agency of smallholders confronting the interests of larger-scale capital can be successful when associated with powerful regional political interests. Heyer provides an example of the effectiveness with which caste can be used to support the control by capital of labour, suppressing class struggle. Gorringe provides an opposite example of the use of caste to mobilise labour against capital, and vice versa, with an outcome that was more favourable to labour than in Heyer's case. Kapadia shows capital benefiting from gender norms that support the subordination of female labour. Prakash, Meagher, Pain, and Harriss-White and Vidyarthee all focus on competition between capitalist class fractions, showing how caste, ethnicity, region and sector are deployed to fracture capital precisely in order to protect entry and prevent competition. In some cases (Pain, Prakash), these local structures are seen to stabilise accumulation; in others (Meagher, Harriss-White and Vidyarthee) the reverse.

Taken in their entirety, this collection provides a convincing case that the study of the general process of capitalist transformation requires the revitalisation of a kind of political economy that is undogmatic, specific and empirically grounded in order to understand the tension between the universal and the specific, which gives capitalism its protean forms. Without this political economy, conceptual linkages between the global and the local lack content. Without comparative political economy it is impossible to ascertain from the sheer diversity of capitalism the kind and sequencing of political activity and class struggle and of regulation and protection by the state that will contain its unsustainable excesses.

Bibliography

Basile, E. (forthcoming) 'A Marxist-institutionalist analysis of rural capitalism in South India: the case of a Tamil market town after the Green Revolution', unpublished D.Phil. thesis, University of Oxford.

Byres, T. (1981) 'The new technology, class formation and class action in the Indian countryside', *Journal of Peasant Studies*, 8(4): 405–59.

Chibber, V. (2003) *Locked in Place: State Building and Late Industrialisation in India*, Princeton: Princeton University Press.

Dasgupta, C. (2008) 'State and capital in independent India: from dirigisme to neo-liberalism', unpublished Ph.D. thesis, School of Oriental and African Studies, University of London.

Devereux, S., Scoones, I. and Thompson, J. (2009) 'Critical responses to the World Bank's "World Development Report 2008: Agriculture for Development"', *Journal of Peasant Studies*.

Fernandez, B. (2008), '(En)gendering poverty policy in India: towards a new theoretical framework', unpublished D.Phil. thesis, University of Oxford.

Government of India (2007) *Report of the Expert Group on Agricultural Indebtedness*, New Delhi: Ministry of Finance.

Harriss-White, B. (ed.) (1999) *Agricultural Markets from Theory to Practice: Field Experience in Developing Countries*, Basingstoke: Macmillan.

—— (2003) *India Working, Essays on Society and Economy*, Cambridge: Cambridge University Press.

—— (2008) *Rural Commercial Capital, Agricultural Markets in West Bengal*, New Delhi: Oxford University Press.

—— (2009) 'Globalisation, the financial crisis and petty production in India's socially regulated informal economy', *Global Labour Journal* (forthcoming).

Harriss-White, B. and Harriss, J. (2007) *Green revolution and After: The North Arcot Papers and Long Term Studies of the Political Economy of Rural Development in South India*, QEH Working Paper 146, Oxford: University of Oxford.

Harriss-White, B. and Janakarajan, S. (eds) (2004) *Rural India Facing the 21st Century*, London: Anthem.

Heyer, J. (2000) *The Changing Position of Agricultural Labourers in Villages in Rural Coimbatore, Tamil Nadu, between 1981/2 and 1996*, QEH Working Paper 27, Oxford: University of Oxford.

Heyer, J., Stewart, F. and Thorp, R. (eds) (2001) *Groups, Institutions and Development*, Oxford: Oxford University Press.

Jayaraj, D. and Nagaraj, K. (2006) *Socio-economic Factors Underlying Growth of Silk-weaving in the Arni Region: A Preliminary Study, 2006*, Monograph Series 5, Madras Institute of Development Studies, Chennai.

Kim, Y. (2008) 'The outside and inside meanings of alcohol: changing trends in Indian urban middle class drinking', unpublished D.Phil. thesis, University of Oxford.

Leys, C. (2001) *Market Driven Politics*, London: Verso.

Majid, N. (1998) 'The joint system of share tenancy and self-cultivation: evidence from Sind, Pakistan', *Journal of Peasant Studies*, 25(3): 63–85.

Moore, H. and Vaughan, M. (1994) *Cutting Down Trees: Gender, Nutrition and Agricultural Change in the Northern Province of Zambia, 1890–1990*, London: James Currey.

Ochieng, C. (2005) 'The political economy of contract farming in Kenya: a historical-comparative study of the tea and sugar contract farming schemes, 1963–2002', unpublished D.Phil. thesis, University of Oxford.

Olsen, W.K. (1996) *Rural Indian Social Relations: A Study of Southern Andhra Pradesh*, New Delhi: Oxford University Press.

Pujo, L. (1996) 'Towards a methodology for the analysis of the embeddedness of markets in social institutions: Application to gender and the market for local rice in eastern Guinea', unpublished D.Phil. thesis, University of Oxford.

Raj, K.N., Bhattacharya, N., Guha, S. and Padhi, S. (eds) (1985) *Essays on the Commercialisation of Indian Agriculture*, New Delhi: Oxford University Press.

Ramachandran, V. and Rawal, V. (2009) 'Impact of liberalisation and globalisation on India's agrarian economy', *Global Labour Journal* (forthcoming).

Razavi, S. (ed) (2003) 'Agrarian change, gender and land rights', Special Issue, *Journal of Agrarian Change*, 3(1/2): 2–32.

Rogaly, B. (1997) 'Linking home and market: towards a gendered analysis of changing labour relations in rural West Bengal', *IDS Bulletin*, 28(3): 63–72.

Rogaly, B., Harriss-White, B. and Bose, S. (eds) (1999) *Sonar Bangla? Agricultural Growth and Agrarian Change in West Bengal and Bangladesh*, London: Sage.

Roman, C. (2008) 'Learning and innovation in clusters: case studies from the Indian silk industry', unpublished D.Phil. thesis, University of Oxford.

Ruthven, O. (2008) 'Global value chains in local context: a social relations perspective from South Asia', unpublished D.Phil. thesis, University of Oxford.

Sarkar, S. (2009) 'Limits of politics: dominance and resistance in contemporary India', unpublished D.Phil. thesis, University of Oxford.

Swaminathan, M. (2000) *Weakening Welfare: The Public Distribution of Food in India*, Delhi: Leftword Press.

—— (2008) *Programmes to Protect the Hungry: Lessons from India*, Working Paper No. 70, United Nations, DESA (Department of Economic and Social Analysis), New York.

Williams, G. (1975) 'Taking the part of peasants: rural development in Nigeria and Tanzania' in P.W.C. Gutkind and I. Wallerstein (eds) *The Political Economy of Contemporary Africa*, Basingstoke: Macmillan.

Woodhouse, P. (2009) 'Technology, environment and the productivity problem in African agriculture: comment on the World Development Report, 2008', *Journal of Agrarian Change*, 9(2): 263–76.

World Bank (2008) *World Development Report 2008: Agriculture for Development*, Washington, DC: World Bank. Available online at http://siteresources.worldbank.org/INTWDR2008/Resources/WDR_00_book.pdf (accessed 4 April 2009).

2 The political economy of agrarian change
Dinosaur or phoenix?

Lucia da Corta

A phoenix is a sacred bird, the only one of its kind. At the end of its life cycle it builds a nest that it then ignites. Both the nest and bird burn fiercely and are reduced to ashes. From these ashes, a new phoenix arises with renewed youth and vigour.[1]

Introduction

In this chapter, I discuss how the political economy of agrarian change (PEACH) might enhance research on the causes of chronic poverty and its transformation in rural areas.

The rise and fall of the political economy of agrarian change (PEACH) in mainstream poverty studies

From the mid 1960s through to the mid 1980s, Judith Heyer was part of a general movement which sought to understand rural poverty through a distinctly cross-disciplinary analysis of the political economy of agrarian change and which was firmly rooted in empirical research. In the early 1960s, growth-based theories of agricultural development driven by technical change were promoted as a solution to persistent rural poverty (e.g. Mellor 1967). Yet local observers and village field researchers noted that rural development wasn't working – the numbers of poor grew and some non-poor smallholders, fisherman and pastoralists became poor through loss of assets or common property resources. Bigger farmers appropriated the land of smaller farmers; rural labourers were displaced by machines; capitalist farming depleted scarce water resources and ruined soils; exploitation of the rural poor was intensified through linked credit, labour and commodity markets, and foreign companies continued to extract mineral resources, cheap labour and cheaply made commodities.[2]

It was in this context that many researchers turned to Marxist political economy in order to understand the relationship between economic growth and poverty. Marxist research focused on the ways more powerful classes accumulated by appropriating surplus from less powerful. They were broadly concerned with the influence of productive forces (technical change) and commercialisation on transformations in modes of production (e.g. from feudalism to capitalism), class struggles and associated transformations in rural class structure.[3]

Yet this body of theory did not stand on its own: it was iterated with the PEACH practice of 'muddy footed empiricism' through village studies (Harriss-White and Harriss 2007) and with truly post-disciplinary intellectual approaches developed in comparative political economy seminars and workshops in which anthropologists, sociologists, historians, geographers and political scientists fresh from field research engaged in table-thumping challenges, addressed to political and liberal economists, and vice versa. This unique intellectual environment contributed to new cross-disciplinary theory (e.g. gender–capitalism linkages; commercial capitalisms), method (critical realism) and formed a fertile intellectual ground for the emergence of post-structural ideas in development. Yet just as PEACH began accelerating through its serious engagement with critical and feminist theory in the mid 1980s (see the early research of Razavi; Jackson; Rogaly; and Kapadia, for instance), PEACH, in its entirety, was criticised to destruction in mainstream development studies.

Younger researchers in mainstream development studies today either neglect this very fertile period of thought altogether or refer to this approach, and its research, as the 'old' political economy of agrarian change. This disregard emerges from the attacks on PEACH research, particularly its Marxist variant, in the mid 1980s.[4] In development studies this attack took the shape of a broad methodological critique of structuralist accounts which could:

- mask individual/household mobility,[5] especially the upward mobility of the poor, as it seemed to challenge the teleology of inevitable immizerising proletarianisation;[6]
- obscure poor people's agency, strategies, narratives, identity and thus empowerment;[7] and
- hide endogenous explanations for agrarian institutions – such as sharecropping, tied labour – explained in terms of a risk, asymmetric information and transactions costs logic built on the notion of agency in rational choice theory.[8]

Certainly there were examples of deterministic and mechanistic political economy research especially before the 1980s, but these studies sat alongside richer, non-teleological, historical and cross-disciplinary approaches to PEACH. The latter were substantially more varied, nuanced and self-critical than its 'functionalist, economistic, reductionist' caricature that survives in mainstream development thinking today. While PEACH fell out of favour in the development mainstream, it positively flourished outside it, in more scholarly niches.[9]

The story of the squeeze on agrarian political economy in mainstream development thinking is inextricably linked to the story of the broader squeeze on political economy within economics. Classical economics and political economy, hegemonic in the 1950s, were forced into the category of 'heterodoxy' by Walrasian monetarism, followed later by the new development economics

(NDE) (Byres 2006). Political economy was then forced into the other social sciences, where it was squeezed from the other side by postmodernism – reacting to the hegemony of economics and focusing instead on culture and consumption (Fine 2001). At the same time, the new classical (development) economics colonised the other social sciences and labelled itself the 'new political economy' (Bates 1989). As a consequence, classical political economy was squeezed both within economics and outside, losing its subjects, its subject matter (Fine 2001), its appellation and being re-prefixed 'the old'. This squeeze on political economy also coincided with a major decline in the teaching of the history of economic development and of economic thought (Bagchi 2006: 230).

Chronic poverty

Recent chronic poverty research is firmly situated in the policy-relevant mainstream of development studies. It is concerned with long-term processes of poverty creation and, more recently, the causes of sustained escapes from poverty. This small school born out of the mobility measurement school[10] identified a group of the population in various developing countries trapped below the poverty line for five-plus years and sought to understand chronic or 'structural' poverty (i.e. not transient or stochastic poverty) with a strong focus on assets.[11] They pursued explanations of poverty through cross-disciplinary, Qual-Quant (Q^2) research. The latter combines the econometric analysis of panel data together with qualitative data on livelihood strategies (Ellis 2000) gathered through participatory techniques (Chambers 1997). The concerns of chronic poverty research – understanding long-term, structural, assets-based poverty – have a clear overlap with those of PEACH. Yet chronic poverty research, shaped by highly methodologically individualistic theory developed since the marginalisation of PEACH, has tended to produce results supporting methodological individualism, explaining the cause of chronic poverty in terms of exclusion and the characteristics and experience of the poor. The deeper structural and relational causes of poverty have eluded researchers in this school.

One recent response to these limitations has been the recovery and development of social relational concepts, including domestic relations in the intergenerational transmission of poverty (IGT/I) literature,[12] and social relations in markets, polities and societies in research into adverse incorporation and social exclusion (AISE) (Shepherd 2007; Hickey and du Toit 2007; Wood 2003; Murray 2001; Bracking 2003). Early thinking in AISE research partially recovers PEACH methods for chronic poverty analysis through its social relational-transformational approach, a crucial step forward in this literature (da Corta and Bird 2008). However AISE authors, in common with the Critical Oppositional thinking in this chronic poverty literature,[13] distance themselves from the very concepts which can help specify the economic relational processes which contribute to adverse incorporation into 'the market'. This distance from PEACH leaves the economics of chronic poverty exclusively to NDE models of vulnerability and poverty traps[14] whose endogenous explanations need to be explained 'exogenously'.

In this chapter, I critically examine chronic poverty research, identifying its causal limits and explore what the new social relational concepts can offer (see next section, 'Chronic poverty research'). I then turn to recent PEACH research, arguing for a recovery of PEACH concepts and methods which help explain both the structural causes of poverty and escapes from poverty (see section entitled, 'PEACH research'). I conclude with a case for methodological and conceptual pluralism to guide research on chronic poverty.

Chronic poverty research

Panel studies

Empirical research into chronic poverty usually begins with panel studies, which trace mobility in an individual's or household's economic status over a period of time, enabling a measure of the dynamics and extent of chronic poverty (those poor for longer than five years). Such mobility might be represented in a transition matrix, revealing groups that demonstrate upward mobility, downward mobility or remain stable. Panel studies are also used to explore the causes of mobility, looking at quantitative relationships between economic mobility (based on earnings, expenditure or financial assets) and individual characteristics (e.g. dependency ratios, education, health, livelihood diversification, gender, caste/race, etc.). Causal analysis using panel data alone has been challenged when the characteristics of poor people which are correlated with poverty are confused with the causes of their poverty (Harriss 2007: 2). Moreover, causal processes are hidden when econometrically symmetrical groupings, or received panel periods, replace those that are historically relevant; when binary taxonomies based on above or below the poverty line supplant contextually or conceptually relevant social groupings of actors, and when official space boundaries take the place of those that are contextually relevant.

Proximate cause analysis

In order to put qualitative flesh on panel data skeletons, chronic poverty researchers have gathered qualitative data from a sub-sample of panel individuals focussing on actors' accounts of their upward or downward mobility. One common approach focuses on actors' perceptions of proximate or precipitating causes of their upward or downward mobility in the panel. These proximate causes may then be merged with results of exploratory correlation exercises to identify major 'drivers of downward mobility' and 'drivers of escape'.[15]

Livelihood trajectories: 'snakes and ladders'

This approach has been developed to document sequences of impoverishing or enriching events and livelihood strategies leading to downward mobility (snakes) or upward mobility (ladders) over the life course, lending some insight into causal processes.[16] These studies have illustrated 'double or treble whammies', for example how the need for money to pay for hospital costs can subsequently force a land sale and this can later be followed by loss of earnings through loss of wage work and possibly further asset sales to meet consumption costs (Davis 2006; Kabeer 2004). Conversely, sequential escapes from poverty may also be documented, such as a state loan enabling a labourer to purchase small livestock, fattened and later sold for larger livestock or land (Davis 2006).

This research illustrates two features of the unique assets-based vulnerability experience of being poor which contribute to poverty traps:

1   'Adverse coping' – poor people exposed to frequent crises draw down their productive assets and human capital, and this threatens long-term mobility through:
   • loss of income,
   • loss of buffers, which can make poor people vulnerable to crises and shocks in the future; and
   • downward intergenerational mobility through loss of children's human assets (such as health and education assets, which are often irrecoverable).
2   The extremely constrained choice available to chronically poor people when the need to preserve one asset endangers another. For instance, in order to prevent land or livestock sales, poor people:
   • eat less or overwork, risking future illness and inability to bring in wages;
   • eat less, risking in utero malnutrition, and prenatally depleted human capital;
   • withdraw children from school to work, permanently damaging their human capital.

Exclusion theory

Shepherd (2007) suggests that such adverse coping strategies and intergenerational transmissions of poverty might maintain those asset-poverty traps identified in micro-economic research. Carter and colleagues have identified a subgroup of the chronically poor who have the potential to be non-poor given skills and circumstances, but who lack sufficient assets to 'craft a path out of poverty' (Carter and Ikegami 2007: 1–2). It is assumed that this subgroup is trapped in poverty because their low asset level excludes them from possible growth processes (Carter and Barrett 2006) and this exclusion is compounded by their 'social exclusion' – people below a certain asset threshold are also found to have the lowest social capital.[17]

Problems with chronic poverty research

Understanding asset-based poverty traps and adverse coping sequences is useful, but it is only part of the story. Without explanations incorporating the deeply unequal social relations in which poor people are involved, and the wider political economy, such analyses can be desperately thin. By contrast, PEACH researchers in the early 1980s began to relate vulnerability and poverty traps to social relations in product and labour markets. For instance, PEACH studies of vulnerability and coping during famines and seasonal crises demonstrated how different elite groups benefited from, or even manufactured opportunities for, accumulation through asset grabbing during famine, hoarding grain in order to force price rises or using the opportunity to secure long-term bonded labour contracts, all of which made poor people even more vulnerable to future famines.[18]

These observations echo sentiments in a series of very strongly worded papers commissioned by the Chronic Poverty Research Centre (CPRC) which urge chronic poverty researchers to consider power and the constraints on people's agency through a social relational perspective and also to look at how low-asset poverty traps, low incomes and vulnerabilities are constructed in the first place through political, social and cultural processes.[19]

Theoretical influences on methods and results: $Q^2 = MI^2$

One major reason for the failure to engage in deeper structural causal analysis in chronic poverty Q^2 empirical research is that chronic poverty research has drawn on contra-structuralist, methodologically individualist theory and methods developed since PEACH fell out of favour in the mid 1980s, including:

- an agent-centred version of the *livelihoods strategy analysis* pioneered by Ellis (2000) which tracks over time a household's assets (human, social, and natural physical and financial) and strategies adopted in response to crises and opportunities;[20]
- the *participatory approach* pioneered by Chambers (1997) which centres on poor actors' meanings of poverty, their strategies and their agency;[21] and
- theories that long-term poverty is a result of the asset-based vulnerability experience of poor people and their supposed *economic and social exclusion.*[22]

As a consequence of this highly methodologically individualist (MI) post-PEACH theory, poverty and escapes from poverty are explained in terms of actors' individual characteristics, their independence (rather than relational dependence), their behavioural initiative, strategies and action (agency). This methodological individualism is reinforced several times over in chronic poverty Q^2 research, through the marriage of:

1 MI econometric panel methods, to
2 MI qualitative research based on tracking the lifeworld and livelihood strategies of individuals or individual households within the panel.

Thus $Q^2 = MI^2$ research and this methodological individualism is further reinforced by data gathered through MI participatory methods from a sample of poor people and by analyses shaped by MI endogenous explanatory frameworks of NDE.

For these reasons, the analysis of poverty is methodologically and empirically closed off from wider social relations and macro structural change. As a result, not only can findings of such research can be extremely partial, but also they tend to confirm the post-1980s, post-PEACH MI theory which initially shaped chronic poverty research: poverty being located in the agents' own low-asset/ human-asset traps, their vulnerability, and their adverse coping strategies explained endogenously in terms of their exclusion from economic and social structures. As Harriss (2007) warns, locating the cause of poverty in a person's charac-teristics, strategies and near-universal experience of poverty rather than in unequal relations in the larger political economy profoundly depoliticises poverty.

Why did social relations fall out of the chronic poverty tool box?

Paradoxically, Hulme and Shepherd (2003: 409) explicitly sought to marry individualist poverty dynamics (individual or household mobility) with social structural change, yet in subsequent Q^2 empirical research such relations seem to be neglected. Similarly in Ellis's (2000: 30) original livelihoods framework an individual's assets were very clearly mediated by social relations and institutions. Yet this acceptance of social relations on a rhetorical level has not been translated seriously and consistently into empirical practices in chronic poverty research. I think this reveals a much deeper problem of the erosion of relational theory in development since the demise of PEACH in the mainstream, particularly the neglect of theory and concepts which expose the centrality of social relations to understanding poverty, and which specifically problematise choice and mutuality in the economic relations of poor people.

Social relational concepts and methods: problematising the value of inclusion

In order to address these limitations, researchers at the CPRC under Andrew Shepherd (2007) have been looking into how to put social relations and structure back into long-term poverty studies through the development of new concepts and methods focusing specifically on social relations within households (IGT/I), and adverse terms of incorporation into states, markets and civil society (AISE).

Domestic and intergenerational relations

IGT/I poverty research has recently begun problematising choice in livelihood strategies by recovering feminist research on domestic and intergenerational relations, focusing on how such relations influence timely spending on offspring during crucial stages of childhood which can affect prospects for mobility in adulthood, through the nurturing of human assets (health, physical and cognitive abilities, education), inheritance of productive assets and psychological and social inheritances (Harper, Marcus and Moore 2003). Fresh conceptual territory is being developed through ideas on the intergenerational contract (IGC) or 'bargain' which can be understood as the relationship between different generations which is shaped by norms, rules, conventions and practices structured by gender and age (Bird 2007; drawing on Malhotra and Kabeer 2002). Spheres of economic responsibility might include who receives what spending on education, food and health care; who inherits what assets and in what form (e.g. directly or through dowry to the groom's family); who is responsible for providing for whom and when (including in later life); who is responsible for domestic work, work on own assets or outside paid work;[23] and who controls joint resources.

Bird (2007) suggests that intergenerational contracts often involve decisions for one cohort (e.g. sons, older sons) to do well at the expense of another (e.g. daughters, younger sons) with diverse poverty trajectories for siblings as they mature. As an example, parents might encourage a daughter to work off loans taken in order to fund her brother's ability to stay in school at her own lasting educational expense. This may result in sons becoming educated and landowning and their sisters becoming dependent on landless labouring and their brothers' patronage if widowed or separated (Venkateswarlu and da Corta 2001). Poverty can be reproduced as one set of intergenerational norms is replaced by another: the switch from bridewealth to increasingly higher expected parental payments of dowry among lower castes (as with Sanskritisation in South India) or increased female seclusion can have a devastating effect on longer-term female economic mobility.

While this research focuses on changes in the terms of these contracts over generations within households over time, PEACH research has linked the terms of conjugal and intergenerational contracts to power relations in markets, states and societies which can affect different household members' future mobility. As an example, the bargaining position of subordinate household members vis-à-vis employers can weaken when responsibility for family provisioning is shifted onto them or when they are involved in paying off debt taken by a patriarch (da Corta and Venkateswarlu 1999; Venkateswarlu and da Corta 2001). This can reduce their power to strike against low wages offered by employers (Kapadia 1993) and can diminish their power to 'choose' higher-paid employment (Rogaly 1997). As a result women and children tend to face lower wages and tougher working conditions that reinforce their subordinate position in the home.[24]

AISE research

AISE researchers have also begun to problematise choice in the livelihood strategies of chronically poor people and to question seriously the assumption of the automatic benefit of their inclusion into the economy, state and civil society. Hickey and du Toit (2007) promote the relational concept of 'adverse incorporation' into the state, the market and civil society in order to understand people's poverty. Drawing on the conceptual and methodological research of Colin Murray (2001: 4–5), the authors comment that:

This concept of adverse incorporation, it is argued, captures the ways in which localised livelihood strategies are enabled and constrained by economic, social, and political relations over both time and space, in that they operate over lengthy periods and within cycles, and at multiple spatial levels from local to global. These relations are driven by inequalities of power (Hickey and du Toit 2007: 4).

The concept of adverse incorporation was originally put forth as both an argument and a concept to challenge the widely held view that poverty is caused by social and economic exclusion, by people being left out of development and markets, which the authors note derives from a residualist (or non-relational) understanding of poverty (Bernstein, Crow and Johnson 1992).

Da Corta and Bird (2008) draw on Hickey and du Toit's AISE relational-transformational framework in order to begin to sketch out the range of social relational trajectories which might precede sustained escapes from chronic poverty. As an illustration, changes in the terms of adverse incorporation into:

- *markets* might involve, for instance, the movement from bonded labour relations to attached to free labour relations;
- *polities* can involve shifts in status from clients to citizens;
- *societies, 'communities' or public spaces* (schools, health facilities, etc.) might involve a movement from included but segregated to included, de-segregated, but bullied terms;
- *households* might involve shifts in power in domestic and intergenerational contracts.

Hickey and du Toit make clear that these movements can be partial and complex – for instance the terms of new-found citizenship can continue to be adverse and mediated through a patron's political boss (2007: 12) and similarly free labour can be exploited. Relations can also revert, as we suggest below.

The AISE and IGT/I relational researchers do a great service to chronic poverty research in several ways. The first is that they highlight the need for plural transformative social relational trajectories to help explain longer-term sequenced livelihood strategies and also explain ultimate mobility outcomes.[25] This enables an understanding of the social constraints to livelihood strategies which may force decisions to draw down physical or human assets. This might be sketched as follows:

1   Changes in macro-structural processes or events – whether economic, political, cultural or legal – can improve or reduce the power of different groups.

2   Various social relations (AISE and domestic) are, in turn, contested, challenging or reinforcing authorities, norms and conceptions which support unequal power in social relations, which can improve or reduce the freedom or power of subordinate people.

3   These transformations in social relations can both precede and pose constraints on opportunities for poor people's intergenerational livelihood strategies (including the adverse coping sequences or asset decisions discussed above).
4   The outcome of these strategies determines poor people's ultimate upward or downward mobility.

A second advantage to AISE research is that the authors – together with other Critical Oppositional thinkers such as Murray (2001), Bracking (2003), and Bevan (2004) – respond to a cry for methods for poverty research which are structural, relational, dynamic and transformational (Harriss 2007) without sacrificing critical/postmodern attention to agency, meaning, and ideologies of inequality and oppression. They seek an alternative to the empiricism and positivism of current Q^2 approaches on the one hand and participatory agent focused approaches on the other (Narayan, Chambers, Kaul Shah and Petesch 2000). Their methodological thinking is given a rigour and coherence in much broader ontological arguments for a critical realist social science – an alternative to empirical positivism and pure relativism (which can reduce social science to the interpretation of agents' meanings). Critical realism in Britain is chiefly influenced by the ideas of Roy Bhaskar (1975) and is defined by the belief that there is a world existing independently of our knowledge of it. It seeks to understand the real – regardless of whether we have an understanding of it – which has certain structures, causal powers and susceptibilities to certain kinds of change. This differs from both the actual (e.g. a labourer's potential to labour is actualised when she works) and the empirical, defined as what is observable (Sayer 2000: 12).

The stratified ontology of critical realism is important to understanding gaps in Q^2 poverty analysis. The latter tends to focus on the empirical (econometric analyses of observable characteristics) and the actual (sequenced event analysis) where causation is understood as regularities among sequences of events (a Humean 'successsionist' view of causation). Critical realism challenges the notion that explanation is necessarily equivalent to repeat occurrences under closed conditions and instead focuses analysis on identifying and understanding the causal mechanisms and their tendencies to certain kinds of change – whether or not such mechanisms have been activated and under what conditions (Sayer 2000: 14). As an example, realist structures like capitalism may have certain tendencies to, for instance, production crises and cost/price squeezes (Harriss 1992), proletarianisation (Byres 1981), the control and discipline of labour (Brass 1999), and many other tendencies that affect rural poverty (Harriss-White 2005). But a critical realist political economy not only seeks to understand such mechanisms but also to show how these may or may not be actualised given other social forces – such as gender, politics, race and caste – as well as context, chance and learned behaviour. Moreover, agrarian capitalism evolves. These all result in the great variety of accounts of agrarian change (see the *Journal of Peasant Studies* (*JPS*) and the *Journal of Agrarian Change* (*JAC*)).

Moreover, critical realism recovers for chronic poverty analysis an analysis of underlying realist structures and mechanisms without sacrificing interpretive/

critical attention to agency and meaning. The prefix critical links Bhaskar's realist theory of social science with a critical social science, which Lawson (1997: 158) makes plain: '. . . because social structure is dependent upon human agency, it is open to transformation through changing human practices which in turn can be affected by criticising the conceptions and understandings on which people act'. This might include gender or bondage, for instance. Because critical realist social science identifies and interrogates misconceptions or social ideas and practice causing suffering to its objects of study, Bhaskar (1993) contends that critical realist social science has emancipatory potential (see also Sayer 2000: 156) and thus can enable poverty research to return to the politics of poverty.

A key argument for a critical realist causal or explanatory approach is that it is open, holistic (micro to macro), composed of multiple social and other relational interdependencies, truly plural, and post-disciplinary. Social change is open, contingent and contextually variable – social systems evolve rather than equilibrate (Sayer 2000). These features make critical realism superior to its ontological opposite – the methodologically individualist, endogenous and closed explanatory frameworks found particularly in economics (Lawson 1997) and econometrics. The openness of critical realist methodology is particularly crucial for poverty analysis because open frameworks enable analysis not only of how the objects of its study escape poverty traps[26] but also critically for empirical research to escape from the trap of theory equating poverty with social exclusion. Because the explanatory framework is no longer closed, empirical research can investigate the possibility that poverty is the result rather of inclusion into meso and macro economies, societies and polities.

Recovering PEACH methods without its concepts

Hickey and du Toit (2007), Bevan (2004) and Bracking (2003) and other Critical Oppositional thinkers take us quite far down the road towards methods for explaining chronic poverty. Their methodological thinking coheres with arguments for a critical realist social science. However, Critical Oppositional thinkers have an ambiguous relationship with PEACH. Some distance their approach explicitly; some adopt some PEACH concepts while neglecting others, and some simply omit entirely a discussion of PEACH and its concepts yet heavily reference PEACH scholars. This is an irony because, as we argue below, PEACH scholars together with other post-disciplinary thinking in the 1970s and 1980s helped to forge these critical realist methods: they were critical of positivistic law-guiding science approaches to economic studies of poverty. They also tried to adopt and develop new thinking (not yet discussed as postmodern) on meanings, nuance and sensitivity to lived experience. This PEACH research precedes Critical Oppositional critiques of econometric analysis to poverty research (du Toit 2005; Bevan 2004, 2006) and identification of the variety of social relations which can create poverty (Hickey and du Toit 2006).

Critical Oppositional thinkers on chronic poverty recover PEACH methods without PEACH concepts and materialist dialectics. By using patron–client frameworks instead of class analysis, however, and by neglecting relationships between poverty and unfreedom, class struggle, technical change and processes of capitalist accumulation, such thinkers can seriously hamper their ability to understand those economic processes which contribute to adverse incorporation into 'the market'. This doesn't mean a return to an approach reasoning that 'everything is functional to capital' – if there ever was a time when this predominated – it does mean that this part of the story needs to be rewritten into the analysis of poverty and exploitation. In other words, the 'dark side' of inclusion into capitalisms needs much greater theoretical and conceptual depth. It means recapturing those conceptual 'elephants in the living room' artfully avoided in mainstream discussions about chronic poverty in order to bring in the depth hitherto missing.

PEACH research

PEACH research captures several elements relevant for today's research on chronic poverty. PEACH scholarship shares a methodological and conceptual descent from a nineteenth-century focus on development of capitalism as a post-disciplinary whole. It is based on the critical political economy perspective of Marx, Lenin and Kautsky, an approach which identified and criticised the conceptions upon which capitalisms in different contexts are based, such as the inequalities of class or injustice of property rights. Political economy also has a central focus on power (Harriss-White 1996: 31) and on processes of accumulation.

The caricature of PEACH

The contemporary distancing from PEACH conceptualisations in mainstream thinking might arise from a caricature of PEACH – those tutored in post-structural social theory in graduate school may have been exposed to PEACH only in its critiqued and caricatured form. For instance, Hickey and du Toit (2007) replace a class theoretic with 'analyses of exploitative patron-client relationships from an adverse incorporation perspective'. These authors argue that their AISE methodological framework draws on the strength of the tradition of agrarian scholarship:

- 'without lapsing into the same economistic and reductive tendencies';
- by focusing 'on structural and power relations other than those that shape economic and social class and are as likely to draw on post-structuralist social theorists like Foucault (Bracking 2003) and on actor network theory';
- by capturing 'local history, politics, culture, gender and identity'; and
- by 'considering not only the exploitative aspects of such relationships, but also examining the institutional arrangements and cultural frameworks that make it difficult for clients to leave' (ibid.: 5).[27]

This misrepresents PEACH research, especially the diversification of PEACH in the mid 1980s and its contribution to post-structural thought. The misunderstanding could well be born of a caricature of early PEACH which has its roots in the broader critique of Marxism and structuralism in general in the mid 1980s. The argument at the time was that Marxist research contained tendencies toward teleological and economistic reading of agrarian change: the forces of production (technical change) and commercialisation transform pre-capitalist modes of production to capitalism, thus driving agrarian class structural change in a linear fashion based on differential access to productive assets. The small peasantry are proletarianised or transformed into a disguised proletariat (PCPs) in service to trader capitalists (see Lerche, Chapter 4 in this volume). The state, dominated by the same emergent capitalist elite, supports this progression. Other processes of change – politics, gender, race, caste, biological stages and life cycles, culture, ideology and identity – were understood to be functional to capitalism and its laws (Booth 1985). There was little room for historical contingency and for poor people to use their agency.

A defence of PEACH research and its unique methodological legacy

The critical realist thinker Andrew Sayer (2000) argues with regard to Marxist left social science in general that, while it is true that from the late 1960s to the early 1980s 'much was excluded in those ostensibly all-embracing, all-explaining discourses – notably gender, race, sexuality and much of lived experience; here the rise of feminism, anti-racism and post-colonialism have challenged the old new left to devastating effect' (ibid.: 5). Yet Sayer also argues forcefully that these problems did not reflect research within the Marxist left after the early 1980s, when there were 'reactions against homogenizing and reduction-ist tendencies . . . (marked by) nuance, complexity and sensitivity to local, lived experience' (ibid.: 5). He suggests that this research: 'had to develop more open, context-dependent and plural accounts within which Marxism might have been an important ingredient but no longer a totalizing theory' (ibid.: 5). He contends that: '[m]any reacted to reductionist accounts by shifting to middle range theory and empirical studies, for example from Marxist theories of accumulation to analyses of the institutional forms present in particular capitalist societies.' This meant a 'greater openness to diverse empirical and theoretical influences' (ibid.: 6). He adds that 'all this happened before postmodernism began to be discussed' (ibid.: 6).

PEACH practice: diversity through iteration between theory and village study

I believe that this widening of the PEACH approach was already apparent in the 1970s, and accelerated in the 1980s. Alongside these meta-theoretical and meta-methodological debates was the practice of examining poverty through village studies, which began with Michael Lipton's work in the 1970s. While mechanistic, teleological functionalist accounts and tendencies did exist in the early period of

PEACH, they sat alongside unusually scholarly and meticulous empirical and historical research (involving knowledge of mainstream discipline, local context and language, and Marx). Moreover, research findings were reported and challenged within post-disciplinary intellectual environments, such as the QEH, Oxford comparative political economy seminar led by Judith Heyer, Gavin Williams, Barbara Harriss-White and Megan Vaughan, and similar seminar series run in the UK at the time at SOAS, IDS and UEA. In this intellectual climate it is not surprising that most of the criticisms of Marxist method in PEACH research were posed by PEACH researchers themselves.[28] What emerged from this empirical tradition and post-disciplinary intellectual environment was a collision of Marxist methods – history, class relations, class struggles and transformation (dialectical change) – with concrete village economic, social and cultural reality.[29] The result, I contend, was a largely uncelebrated and open methodology for understanding agrarian change and processes of impoverishment and enrichment. This PEACH methodological legacy spawned a great deal of influential research on the relationship between capitalism, the vulnerabilities it constructs, and poverty (Harriss-White 2005).

Thus, contrary to its caricature:

- PEACH empirical research identified much of the difference and nuance that predated subsequent post-structuralist research.[30]
- PEACH research in India in the 1990s reveals labourers using agency to leave bonded labour arrangements and move into higher-wage off-farm employment driven by complex political, economic and cultural shifts in caste and gender. This is agency 'writ large'.[31]
- Moreover, class relations are found to revert backwards as well as forwards – for instance, petty commodity producers (PCPs) can revert to subsistence peasant production under situations of high price risk (Ellis 2006) and free labourers can become tied labourers (da Corta and Venkateswarlu 1999) or even fully bonded labour (de Neve 2006).
- Shapers and principal drivers of agrarian change have been located in state politics (Ramachandran and Swaminathan 2003; Harriss 1992; Robinson 1988; Rogaly, 1997), caste and culture (Heyer 1992; Kapadia 1993; Scott 1985) and gender (Razavi (ed.) 2002; Chaudhry 1994).
- Understanding gender–class theoretical links have progressed way beyond issues regarding the unvalued domestic productive work of women in peasant households (Deere and de Janvry 1979; Young *et al.* 1981) to the role of gender in structuring labour and product markets (Kapadia and Lerche 1999; Harriss-White 2008; Razavi 2002).
- New theories have evolved on commercial capitalism (Harriss-White 2008; Olsen 1996), unfreedom under capitalism (Rao 2005; Brass 1999), more diverse definitions of agrarian capitalism (Banaji 2002) and multiple transitions in historical contexts (Byres 1996).
- Ideologies and norms supporting exploitative contracts have been investigated through domestic relations (Razavi 2002), in labour and exchange contracts

(Brass 1999; da Corta and Venkateswarlu 1999; Rogaly 1997), at higher meso levels (Venkateswarlu and da Corta 2001) and national and global companies (Venkateswarlu and da Corta 2006).

In short, challenges to PEACH often came from within PEACH and became PEACH. The intention to diversify further is reflected in the 2008 editorial statement (by Johnston *et al.*). This diversification and new theory is contributing to the evolution of critical PEACH method where these critical insights are being linked to Marx's materialist dialectics. PEACH researchers and other political economists and post-disciplinary researchers in the 1970s and 1980s hammered out methods before 'postmodernism' was accepted. It operated on a critical realist basis, often intuitively. Referring to this pluralisation of much broader Marxist empirical research in the 1980s, Sayer argues, 'In some ways, critical realism, with its focus on necessity and contingency rather than regularity, on open rather than closed systems, on the ways in which causal processes could reproduce quite different results in different contexts, fitted comfortably with these developments' (2000: 5).

The Critical Oppositional charge of 'economism' is also out of date. Today the problem is not enough economism. Both chronic poverty research and the Critical Oppositional school in chronic poverty research can be thin on micro–macro dynamic analysis of economic processes.[32]

In summary, Critical Oppositional thinkers both heavily reference PEACH thought (Bernstein, Crow and Johnson 1992; Harriss-White 2005; Murray 2001; Francis 2006) and distance themselves from PEACH. John Harriss (2007: i) calls for a 'dynamic, structural, and relational' method in order to address the causal limitations of chronic poverty research. Critical PEACH methods are all of these without annihilating the material basis of political economy which is crucial to understanding those changing economic relational processes which affect chronically poor people.

PEACH concepts

The literature on PEACH is vast, and because understanding economic processes has perhaps become the biggest weakness in chronic poverty research and Critical Oppositional understandings, we limit ourselves to processes of adverse incorporation into markets and focus on economic processes affecting casual labour – the largest group of the world's chronically poor (Chronic Poverty Research Centre 2005: 72). In India, where more than one-third of the chronically poor live (ibid.), there has been a steady increase in the proportion of the population working as casual labourers (Bhalla, Karan and Shobah 2006: 7). Possibly one-fifth of casual labourers are considered 'forced labour', unable to exit labour contracts, with a much larger percentage regularly moving in and out of unfree, attached labour contracts (Brass 1999). Labour tying is common in agriculture and growing in rural non-agrarian industries (Lerche 2007: 439; and Chapter 4 in this volume). Labour tying is particularly evident among India's 30 million migrant labourers (Shepherd and Mehta 2006).

Moreover, Shepherd, Wood, and Hickey and du Toit frequently refer to adverse incorporation in markets through exploitative patron–client relations, using the example of neo-bonded or forced labour relations. So conceptualisations of tied labour might well be a good place to begin an examination of the relevance of PEACH concepts – such as unfreedom, class, capitalist accumulation and capitalism – to poverty analysis.

NDE and tied labour

One way to explain tied labour and other institutions has been through NDE. This explanatory framework was rooted in the logic of risk, information asymmetries and transactions costs for each actor, in this case, employer and labourer (Bardhan 1984, 1989; Stigltiz 1986). NDE models of institutions recognize that employer and labourer face different conditions (i.e. inequality) but both are better off having made the agreement (Pareto-optimal). This relationship is not seen as exploitative (Stiglitz 1986).

There are problems with these models' contextual assumptions which simply do not apply for many south Asian labour contracts. In the NDE literature, the exchange of labour service for credit is understood to be:

- *voluntary* – labourers voluntarily enter into and remain in such contracts; and
- *mutually beneficial* – labourers benefit from such arrangements by way of insurance (subsistence, employment or wage guarantees); employers are insured against wage uncertainty and/or supply uncertainty (Bardhan 1984).

These assumptions are empirically hard to sustain in much of India: tied wages and prices for tied commodities are often below market prices; labourers and small producers are often forced into such 'agreements' by survival; employment guarantees do not extend beyond the term of the loan, and workers cannot end the arrangement without sacrificing the availability of future loans or encountering ideological and economic sanctions exercised on kinsfolk.[33]

A key problem is the NDE assumption of choice or voluntarism in these arrangements, an assumption which is problematic even with the non-chronically poor,[34] but which is positively irrelevant to the very restricted conditions faced by the chronically poor. If employers propose only 'take it or leave it' offers, then it matters very little that a poor person is able, in theory, to reject such an offer and starve (Rao 2005: 186). The notions that desperately poor people are able to *weigh risks* and to *strategise* seem particularly inappropriate, neologisms born of the post-PEACH discourse of participation/empowerment; and NDE economics often creates a fiction where the neo-bonded relations of a female or child labourer fulfilling loan repayment are labelled 'voluntary', and where adverse coping mechanisms, drawing down productive assets or semi-starving, become a 'strategy'. There is a need for a more appropriate economics to problematise such choice/voluntarism in chronic poverty analysis.

Chronic poverty, Critical Oppositional approaches and labour exploitation

Chronic poverty and Critical Oppositional approaches argue that tied relationships arise out of the need for the chronically poor to manage extreme vulnerability, in severely unequal power and resource contexts. While NDE might argue that a chronically poor person is better off because they received a consumption loan which formal credit institutions would have failed to provide, Critical Oppositional researchers argue that the poor are exploited in these situations and worse off (i.e. not Pareto-optimal), because such patronage relations trap them in poverty, preventing them from accumulating (Shepherd 2007). Labour exploitation is understood through a patron–client or non-class social relational perspective (e.g. clients and patrons or oppressed and elite).

Emergent thinking on tied labour in the chronic poverty literature seems to be an extension of thinking on *adverse coping* understood from the *perspective of poor actors* who need to manage their vulnerability. This idea reflected Wood's Faustian Bargain and Shepherd's suggestion that 'the chronically poor involve themselves in patron-client relations, in which lower earnings are exchanged for greater security, enabling the patron to accumulate capital through the exploitation of the client; the client loses both in terms of his/her agency and also accumulation possibilities' (2007: 18). Shepherd also suggests breaking such clientelistic relations and enabling labourers to enter accumulative trajectories, for example, via opportunities in higher-wage migration (ibid.: 21) or off-farm income.

Problems in this literature arise from the absence of a class theoretic. Firstly, while Shepherd rightly mentions 'accumulation' by the patron, PEACH research takes this further and suggests that such relations arise not merely out of poor people's strategies to manage their own vulnerability, but also that patronage is deployed by capitalists in a very strategic manner in order to *manage the cost and discipline of labour* in the project of capitalist accumulation. In PEACH thinking, such processes of accumulation are also addressed from the *perspective of agrarian capitalists* in order to understand how their own various strategies and vulnerabilities, vis-à-vis other fractions of capital, can affect prospects for labourers.

Moreover, the suggestions that emancipation from patronage and inclusion can both be equated with upward mobility could be confused with their corollary – that clientage and exclusion from markets signifies chronic poverty – thinking which has an enduring hold in development economics. This idea can be found in Sen's ideas of unfree labour (tied relations) in terms of an enforced exclusion from the labour market; 'denied the opportunity of transactions' and hence of obtaining higher wages (1999: 7). PEACH, by contrast, emphasises that, while poor people in such tied labour arrangements are perhaps excluded from the abstract markets of economists,[35] they are thoroughly incorporated into processes of capitalist accumulation.

A related problem is that we have no concepts to analyse the exploitation of labourers once 'free' from exploitative patronage relations. Debt or patronage is merely one of a number of strategies adopted by capitalists to coerce free labour. The problem with the theoretical satisfaction with free labour is encapsulated in Banaji's description of the literature on colonial bonded and other labour arrangements where '(free) wage labour emerges as a veritable Garden of Eden, and markets are shorn of the coercion and sheer exertions of power which are integral to the way they function in reality' (Banaji 2002: 109).

Finally, in Critical Oppositional thinking lifeworld patron–client or other non-class relations are linked to larger 'totalities', such as 'capitalism's pauperising effects' (Hickey and du Toit 2007: 15) or global structures.[36] They rightly seek to pluralise the range of social relations affecting the chronically poor. However, it remains unclear how non-class relations link to meso and macro levels without a materialist analysis of accumulation. The problem is that these analyses tend to be removed from the economic concerns of 'patrons' and the economic processes of accumulation.

Capital and capitalists seem to have no place in this universe – their accumulation processes are invisible, their class struggles and strategies toward managing labour, their vulnerabilities vis-à-vis other fractions of capital and larger national and global class interests are invisible – yet all have direct consequences for the employment and remuneration of chronically poor labourers.

PEACH perspectives on unfree labour

PEACH is much richer than the new Critical Oppositional approach, for it is a critical social relational and transformational approach that does not neglect material change and capitalist accumulation. PEACH often begins with class for a reason – not as merely a description of livelihood chances or as a characteristic – but as a conceptual tool identifying a poor person's social position in processes of production and of capitalist accumulation which can help us understand the mechanisms of poverty creation.

Earlier PEACH theories of tied or unfree labour as part of pre-capitalisms (such as semi-feudalism), based solely on non-economic forms of coercion (e.g. physical force, traditional authority of dominant castes, ideology of clientelism and custom) and/or exclusion from markets, have given way to understanding unfree labour as a form of intensified surplus value appropriation (intensified exploitation) – a strategy deployed by capitalists when they face pressure.

The range of PEACH empirical research suggests that when labourers pose challenges to the terms of their contracts, when capitalists suffer competition (Rao 2005), and profit squeezes (Brass 1999), or pro-labour government intervention (Lerche 2007), capitalists draw on many sources of power in order to control the assertiveness, price and reliability of labour. This includes tying and restructuring labour markets in many different ways (by space, gender, age, race and caste). Employers are found to use:

- economic power in credit markets, but also economic power in other markets (rental is common one);
- political power – such as brokering poor people's right to the whole range of state benefits, to the courts, to police protection;
- social, cultural, religious benefits and 'social' inclusion; and
- physical force.[37]

All of these power relations are also used to exercise third-party sanctions on the kin of a labourer who refuses to work for a particular employer or absconds once tied (for instance, their kin won't be allowed to receive loans or state benefits).

Capitalists also invoke existing and conjured ideologies in order to coerce labour, such as:

- the 'loyalty' of certain labouring families to patrons;
- ideas regarding the sexual, age and caste divisions of labour – such as male, female and caste-based occupations and the valuation of different kinds of labour; and
- reworked oppressive ideas, such as the notion that post-pubescent female labour pollutes fields in order to deter assertive older female labour from coming to fields for work (Venkateswarlu and da Corta 2001).

Indeed, capitalists continue to call on whatever combined local power they have in various economic markets or outside. PEACH research illustrates political economy's unique ability to move beyond the reductionist concept of economic monopoly, to a combined localised power in multiple, linked markets, and power in political, social, health and cultural spheres which together enables employers to pose 'all or nothing' offers.

Capitalists also contend with assertive 'free' labour without tying it in ways which have consequences for chronic poverty. These include mechanising the most assertive/expensive labourers' tasks (usually male, irrigation and ploughing) or replanting to less labour intensive crops (e.g. from paddy to fruit trees) or moving out of farming altogether – all of which create unemployment and lower wages. Other pauperising strategies of capitalist employers include employers' rejection of the infirm, 'those unable to offer their disciplined labour to capital' (Harriss-White 2005), with illness and disability part of a typical working person's life. The private enclosure of common property resources, such as grazing land, together with over-farming and environmental destruction, also have pauperising effects on labour (Jodha *et al.* 2008).

In sum, understanding chronic poverty from poor people's perspectives upwards – their need to manage vulnerability – neglects analysis of patron-capitalists' wider strategies of accumulation (which may well be outside of an actor's lifeworld account of his/her life history). The PEACH literature on unfreedom (a subsection of all of PEACH research) illustrates that tying labour and restructuring the labour market are strategies of capitalists (patrons) designed to manage labour assertiveness, price and supply. Capitalists' strategies toward labour are part of their wider strategies of accumulation, which are often a response to their own vulnerabilities vis-à-vis wider macro pressures, particularly the constant pressures of competition and cyclical profit crises. The latter then translate into permanent pressures on the agency, income and employment of 'free' labour.

PEACH, real markets and real capitalisms

Some PEACH scholars attempt to construct a universal definition of capitalism based on the identification of key features and realist tendencies which work across time and space. However, PEACH practice has always been one of theory and methods informed by empirical, often village-level, studies. I believe the practice of PEACH has always been directed at capturing diversity in real non-canonical capitalisms in various contexts, drawing on Marx's non-teleological method of materialist dialectics together with the pluralisation of this dialectical method in post-1980s research. Thus, PEACH empirical research routinely captures conditions when capitalisms/economies do not conform to abstract markets and capitalisms. It captures conditions when capitalists intensify exploitation when they cannot afford to adopt labour-saving technology; when there are time lags before adoption, or machinery is simply not available for certain tasks (e.g. cottonseed pollination, transplantation); when those extra-economic coercions that theoretically should no longer exist do, and are used together with localised power across several linked markets; and when interlinked markets remain linked, or become re-linked, rather than becoming 'separate' over time as NDE economics predicts.

PEACH goes beyond canonical capitalisms and abstract markets to the analysis of the diversity of real capitalisms and real markets, without losing its focus on economic processes or materialist dialectics. Real capital seeps into the fissures within and between markets, polities, societies and cultures in order to survive relentless and intense competition. PEACH sheds light on, and documents this, through empirical work. It theorises the links between different disciplines and theories (on race, caste and gender) which do not fit into abstract categories or suit dichotomous conceptualisations such as free/unfree, included/excluded or economic/non-economic coercion. This is the essence of cross-disciplinary, cross-relational PEACH research.

Methodological pluralism and a framework for chronic poverty research

Drawing on PEACH research, we can develop a Quant-Qual[3] approach to illustrate the importance of a deeper qualitative approach to accompany panel data analysis as an alternative to Q^2 chronic poverty analyses.

In Figure 2.1 we illustrate how PEACH methods introduce a crucial additional level of analysis to the critical oppositional approach outlined above. This level of analysis includes the multiple layers of capitalist strategies of accumulation and their vulnerabilities to competition and cost crises.

1   The top layer illustrates 'macro structural processes' such as liberalisation, structural adjustment, technical change, demand or supply changes for particular commodities together with political, cultural, and social change, all of which influence opportunities or pressures on successive layers of global, national and local-level capital.
2   Strategies of the latter, in turn, throw up opportunities or pressures (such as specific quality controls, price fixing, etc.) on local, commercial and

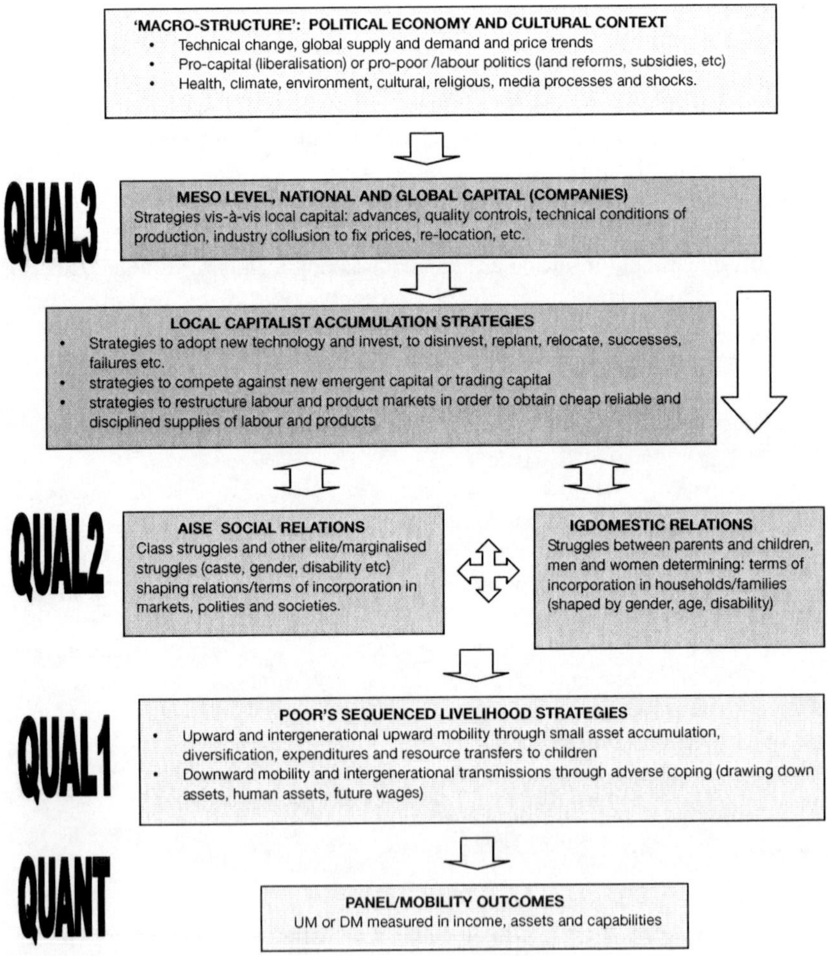

Figure 2.1 Dimensions of PEACH analysis: from Q^2 to Quant-Qual^3

productive capitalists. The resulting changes in profitability, competitive pressures or price squeezes encourage capitalists to adopt various strategies and relations to control chronically poor labourers and smallholders. Macro trends directly affect the agency of poor people. Class struggles ensue in which poor people either win better contractual terms or alternatively lose income and/or suffer unemployment.

3 Class struggles take place alongside, and interact with, other political, social struggles of marginalised groups (AISE relations and domestic relations), shaped further by status identity in terms of age, gender, race, caste, physical impairment, etc.

4 The outcomes of all these struggles set constraints and opportunities for a poor person's livelihood strategies and sequences – greater emancipation, choice and prospects enabling accumulation sequences and greater constraints restricting choice, and triggering adverse coping sequences.

5 All of these affect the final multiple outcomes in panel research.

Theoretical pluralism

This framework can also be used in empirical research to help to explain endogenously theorised, closed models: such as Carter and colleagues' asset poverty traps; Harper *et al.*'s intergenerational human asset poverty traps, and Dercon's model of vulnerability (Adato, Carter and May 2006; Carter and Barret 2006; Harper *et al.* 2003; Dercon 2006). It can also help to explain the reasons why people are forced into the adverse coping sequence found in Q^2 research. All of these can find richer meaning in terms of a dynamic exogenous, methodologically holist and economically relational dynamic approach to poverty, one which also links micro to macro levels. Such an approach is composed of multiple interdependencies. Plural and cross-disciplinary, it enables us to understand why such traps persist and how transformations might be realised. A methodologically pluralist approach to empirical research can also enhance the prospect for theoretical pluralism.

Conclusion: methodological and conceptual pluralism and empowering policy

In this chapter, we have argued that chronic poverty research confronts important limitations arising from the concepts, methods and field research approaches which were developed in the wake of the flawed but sustained critique of political economy in the mid 1980s. While the concepts underlying PEACH research were said not sufficiently to problematise voluntarism, freedom and mutuality in social relations, chronic poverty research methods were methodologically individualist, endogenously explained and closed off from the wider political economy and thus prevented research into poverty resulting from relations of incorporation into economies and societies. Field research methods were informed by actors' lifeworld perspectives, and participatory research such as use of focus groups, which could not always fully address opposing class, gendered and caste interests or the ideologies/norms supporting these inequalities.

Broadening chronic poverty research through a more plural PEACH approach enables the consideration of a wider range of policy possibilities and a more deeply progressive and empowering range of policy responses. For instance, when poverty is theorised as a problem of risk or vulnerability, the solution offered is often insurance/social protection; when it is understood as resulting from unequal gendered, caste or race barriers and relations, the solution is affirmative action. If we understand poverty as a problem of incorporation into the normal workings of markets and of capitalisms, however, then the policy focus turns to the regulation of capital's pauperising effects through pro-labour rather than pro-capital policies. It also means interrogating (and directly lobbying) global and national companies regarding their labour policies (Venkateswarlu 2006).

Political economy, especially PEACH, has been frozen out of economics and squeezed in other disciplines by a postmodern concern with the non-material. Poor people have been disempowered by this. John Harriss (2006a, 2007) cautions researchers that the toleration of inequality and poverty embedded in institutional norms, especially those of legal and political systems, can also pervade the assumptions and research techniques of mainstream poverty analysis. In turn, this cements a particular neo-liberal political perspective on development.[38] Earlier PEACH arguments exposed the ideology underlying research methods and practice of large development institutions such as the World Bank (Heyer, Roberts and Williams 1981). Today, we ignore PEACH and its value for understanding the problems of chronically poor people at the peril of contributing to their disempowerment.

Acknowledgements

I am very grateful for comments from the participants of this workshop and especially for the further comments of Judith Heyer, Barbara Harriss-White, Gavin Williams and Liz Francis. I have also benefited from discussions with CPRC colleagues including Andrew Shepherd, Kate Bird, Karen Moore and Pete Davis and others who have inspired me through their refreshingly interdisciplinary, humble and plural approach to the study of chronic poverty. Thanks also to Gavin Capps for the title and for courage. Mistakes are mine.

Notes

1 The phoenix symbolises immortality. This description is dawn from *Encyclopaedia Britannica* (www.britannica.com/phoenix) and from Wikipedia (http://en.wikipedia.org/wiki/phoenix).
2 See contributions in Heyer *et al.* (1981); Harriss (1983); *The Economic and Political Weekly* and *Journal of Peasant Studies*.
3 Based largely on the ideas of Lenin (1899/1977) and Kautsky (1899/1988).
4 See Booth (1985) and 'PEACH research' section in this chapter.
5 See Shanin (1972).
6 E.g. Cain (1981); Attwood (1979); Harriss (1985); Walker and Ryan (1990).

7 See participatory approach of Chambers (1997); subaltern studies, e.g. Guha and Spivak (1988); and critical theory.

8 See New Development Economics, henceforth NDE, of Stigltiz (1986), Bardhan (1989) and Bardhan and Udry (2000).

9 Such as the *Journal of Peasant Studies* and *Journal of Agrarian Change*.

10 E.g. Baulch and Hoddinott (2000).

11 See Carter and Barrett (2006).

12 See Bird (2007).

13 For ease, I identify a group labelled 'Critical Oppositional': 'critical' because they draw inspiration from Foucault and critical social theory, which is concerned with the human agency–dependent nature of social structure (see Lawson 1997), and 'oppositional' because they are broadly oppositional to capitalism highlighting the need to regulate the pauperising effects of capitalism on the poor, hence tend to be politically progressive (see Lawson 2006 and Bernstein, Crow and Johnson 1992). They tend to be non-economists.

14 For instance, Carter and Barrett (2006); Dercon (2006).

15 See B. Sen (2003); Davis (2006); and Shepherd and Mehta (2006).

16 See Kabeer (2004); Davis (2006); Krishna (2006); Adato, Lund and Mhlongo (2007) for family histories in which events relating to each household member are sequenced and compared.

17 See Adato, Carter and May (2006) for South Africa.

18 See Devereux (1995); da Corta and Devereux (1991).

19 See Francis (2006); Bracking (2003); Harriss (2007); Bevan (2004, 2006); Green and Hulme (2005); Hickey and Bracking (2005); Hickey and du Toit (2007).

20 Ellis's original model clearly contained social relations, but tended to be dropped from empirical applications of his approach.

21 See Narayan, Chambers, Kaul Shah and Petesch (2000); Kanbur and Schaffer (2007).

22 E.g. Carter and Barrett (2006); Dercon (2006); Harper, Marcus and Moore (2003).

23 See also Rogaly (1997: 63–5).

24 See Rogaly (1997) and da Corta and Venkateswarlu (1999).

25 See also Murray (2001); Bagchi *et al.* (1998).

26 See da Corta and Bird (2008).

27 Citing the empirical work of du Toit (2004); and Wood (2003).

28 See, for example, Roseberry (1978); cited in Harriss (2006b: 137) and Hart (1989).

29 See Harriss-White and Harriss (2007).

30 Compare contributions in Heyer, Roberts and Williams (1981) regarding World Bank and other institutional ideologies and practice of rural development with James Ferguson's more recent 'anti-politics machine' research (Ferguson 1990).

31 See, for instance, Ramachandran (1990); the contributions in Byres, Kapadia and Lerche (1999); da Corta and Venkateswarlu (1999); Venkateswarlu and da Corta (2001); Bardhan (1989); Rajasekhar (1988).

32 For instance, there needs to be greater dynamic analysis of the effects of technical change, global commodity prices and rural development policies on the prices faced by poor people, dynamic changes in their wages and staple food prices, days of employment, farm-gate commodity prices, interest rates gathered through the muddied, arduous and expensive empirical approaches of local field study (see Ellis 2006).

33 See da Corta and Venkateswarlu (1999); Venkateswarlu and da Corta (2001).

34 See Byres (2006).

35 See Mackintosh (1990).

36 See Bevan (2004). The explanation for capitalism's pauperising effects draws heavily from analysis of Harriss-White's research on poverty and capitalism (2005), basing this research on nearly four decades of PEACH.

37 Terrorising labouring families, for instance, in Telangana and Bihar (India).

38 See also O'Connor (2006).

Bibliography

Adato, M., Carter, M.R. and May, J. (2006) 'Exploring poverty traps and social exclusion in South Africa using qualitative and quantitative data', *The Journal of Development Studies*, 42(2): 226–47.

Adato, M., Lund, F. and Mhlongo, P. (2007) 'Methodological innovations in research on the dynamics of poverty: a longitudinal study in Kwazulu-Natal, South Africa', *World Development*, 35(2): 247–63.

Attwood, D.W. (1979) 'Why some of the poor get richer: economic change and mobility in rural western India', *Current Anthropology*, 20(3): 495–516.

Bagchi, A. (2006) 'History and development studies', in D. Clark (ed.) *Elgar Companion to Development Studies*, Cambridge: Cambridge University Press.

Bagchi, D.K., Blaiikie, P., Cameron, J., Chattopadhyay, M., Gyawali, N. and Seddon, D. (1998) 'Conceptual and methodological challenges in the study of livelihood trajectories: case-studies in Eastern India and Western Nepal', *Journal of International Development*, 10: 453–8.

Banaji, Jairus (2002) 'The metamorphoses of agrarian capitalism', *Journal of Agrarian Change*, 2(1): 96–119.

Bardhan, P. (1984) *Land, Labour and Rural Poverty: Essays in Development Economics*, New Delhi: Oxford University Press.

—— (1989) *The Economic Theory of Agrarian Institutions*, Oxford: Oxford University Press.

Bardhan, P. and Udry, C. (2000) *Readings in Development Economics*, vol. 1, Cambridge: MIT Press.

Bates, R.H. (1989) *Beyond the Miracle of the Market: The Political Economy of Agrarian Development in Kenya: Political Economy of Institutions and Decisions*, New York: Cambridge University Press.

Baulch, B. and Hoddinott, J. (2000) 'Economic mobility and poverty dynamics in developing countries', *Journal of Development Studies*, 36(6): 1–24.

Bernstein, H., Crow, B. and Johnson, H. (1992) *Rural Livelihoods: Crises and Responses*, Oxford: Oxford University Press.

Bevan, P. (2004) *Exploring the Structured Dynamics of Chronic Poverty: A Sociological Approach*, ESRC Research Group on Wellbeing in Developing Countries WeD Working Paper 06, University of Bath.

—— (2006) *Researching Wellbeing across the Disciplines: Some Key Intellectual Problems and Ways Forward*, ESRC Research Group on Wellbeing in Developing Countries WeD Working Paper 25, University of Bath.

Bhalla, S., Karan, A.K. and Shobha, T. (2006) 'Rural casual labourers, wages and poverty: 1983 to 1999–2000', in A.K. Mehta and A. Shepherd (eds) *Chronic Poverty and Development Policy in India*, New Delhi: Sage.

Bhaskar, R. (1975) *A Realist Theory of Science*, Leeds: Leeds Books.

—— (1993) *Dialectic: The Pulse of Freedom*, London: Verso.

Bird, K. (2007) *The Intergenerational Transmission of Poverty: An Overview*, CPRC Working Paper 99.

Booth, D. (1985) 'Marxism and development sociology: interpreting the impasse', *World Development*, 13(7): 761–87.

Bracking, S. (2003) *The Political Economy of Chronic Poverty*, CPRC Working Paper 23, Manchester: Institute for Development Policy and Management/Chronic Poverty Research Centre.

Brass, T. (1999) *Towards a Comparative Political Economy of Unfree Labour*, London: Frank Cass.

Byres, T.J. (1981) 'The new technology, class formation and class action in the Indian countryside', *The Journal of Peasant Studies*, 8(4): 405–54.

—— (1996) *Capitalism from Above and Capitalism from Below: An Essay in Comparative Political Economy*, London: Macmillan Press.

—— (2006) 'Agriculture and development', in K.S. Jomo and B. Fine (eds) (2006) *The New Development Economics: After the Washington Consensus*, Zed Books: London.

Byres, T.J., Kapadia, K. and Lerche, J. (eds) (1999) *Rural Labour Relations in India*, Special issue, *Journal of Peasant Studies*, 26(2/3) and London: Frank Cass.

Cain, M. (1981) 'Risk and insurance: perspectives on fertility and agrarian change in India and Bangladesh', *Population and Development Review*, 7(3): 435–74.

Carter, M.R. and Barrett, C.B. (2006) 'The economics of poverty traps and persistent poverty: an asset-based approach', *The Journal of Development Studies*, 42(2): 178–99.

Carter, M. and Ikegami, M. (2007) *Looking Forward: Theory-based Measures of Chronic Poverty and Vulnerability*, CPRC Working Paper 94.

Chambers, R. (1997) *Whose Reality Counts? Putting the Last First*, London: ITDG.

Chaudhry, P. (1994) *The Veiled Woman: Shifting Gender Equations in Rural Haryana, 1880–1990*, Delhi: Oxford University Press.

Chronic Poverty Research Centre (2005) CPRC REPORT 2004–5. Available online: www.chronicpoverty.org/cpra-report-0405.php (accessed 30 March 2009).

da Corta, L. and Bird, K. (2008) 'Comparative life history project: research questions and hypotheses', Chronic Poverty Research Centre Working Paper, second draft.

da Corta, L. and Devereux, S. (1991) *True Generosity or False Charity? A Note on the Ideological Basis of Famine Relief Policies*, The Centro Studi Luca d'Agliano, QEH Development Studies Working Paper No. 40, Oxford: University of Oxford.

da Corta, L. and Venkateswarlu, D. (1999) 'Unfree relations and the feminisation of agricultural labour in Andhra Pradesh, 1970–1995', *The Journal of Peasant Studies*, 26(2/3): 71–139.

Davis, P. (2006) 'Poverty in time: exploring poverty dynamics from life history interviews in Bangladesh', paper presented at the Chronic Poverty Research Centre Workshop on Concepts and Methods for Analysing Poverty Dynamics and Chronic Poverty, 23–25 October.

Deere, C.D. and de Janvry, A. (1979) 'A conceptual framework for the empirical analysis of peasants', *American Journal of Agricultural Economics*, 61(4): 601–11.

De Neve, G. (2006) *The Everyday Politics of Labour: Working Lives in India's Informal Economy*, New Delhi: Social Science Press.

Dercon, S. (2006) *Vulnerability: A Micro Perspective*, QEH Working Paper 149, Oxford: University of Oxford.

Devereux, S. (1995) *Theories of Famine*, London: Prentice-Hall.

du Toit, A. (2004) *Forgotten by the Highway: Globalisation, Adverse Incorporation and Chronic Poverty in a Commercial Farming District of South Africa*, Chronic Poverty Research Centre (CPRC), Working Paper 49.

—— (2005) *Poverty Measurement Blues: Some Reflections on the Space for Understanding 'Chronic' and 'Structural' Poverty in South Africa*, Chronic Poverty Research Centre Working Paper No. 55.

Ellis, F. (2000) *Rural Livelihoods and Diversity in Developing Countries*, Oxford: Oxford University Press.

—— (2006) 'Agrarian change and rising vulnerability in rural sub-Saharan Africa', *New Political Economy*, 11(3): 387–97.

Ferguson, J. (1990) *The Anti-Politics Machine: 'Development', Depoliticization and Bureaucratic Power in Lesotho*, Cambridge: Cambridge University Press.

Fine, B. (2001) *Social Capital versus Social Theory: Political Economy and Social Science at the Turn of the Millennium*, London: Routledge.

Francis, E. (2006) *Poverty: Causes, Responses and Consequences in Rural South Africa*, Chronic Poverty Research Centre Working Paper No. 60.

Green, M. and Hulme, D. (2005) 'From correlates and characteristics to causes: thinking about poverty from a chronic poverty perspective', *World Development*, 33(6): 867–79.

Guha, R. and Spivak, G.C. (1988) *Selected Subaltern Studies*, New York: Oxford University Press.

Harper, C., Marcus, R. and Moore, K. (2003) 'Enduring poverty and the conditions of childhood: lifecourse and intergenerational poverty transmissions', *World Development*, 31(3): 535–54.

Harriss, J. (ed.) (1983) *Rural Development: Theories of Peasant Economy and Agrarian Change*, London: Hutchinson University Library.

—— (1985) 'What happened to the green revolution in South India? Economic trends, household mobility, and the politics of an awkward class', DEV Discussion Paper No. 175, Norwich: School of Development Studies, University of East Anglia.

—— (1992) 'Does the "depressor" still work? Agrarian structure and development in India: a review of evidence and argument', *Journal of Peasant Studies*, 19(2): 189–227.

—— (2006a) 'Why understanding of social relations matters more for policy on chronic poverty than measurement', paper prepared for the Workshop on Concepts for Analysing Poverty Dynamics and Chronic Poverty, Chronic Poverty , University of Manchester, 23–25 October.

—— (2006b) *Power Matters: Essays on Institutions, Politics, and Society in India*, OUP: New Delhi.

—— (2007) *Bringing Politics Back into Poverty Analysis: Why Understanding Social Relations Matters More from Policy on Chronic Policy than Measurement*, Chronic Poverty Research Centre Working Paper 77.

Harriss-White, B. (1996) *A Political Economy of Agricultural Markets in South India: Masters of the Countryside*, London: Sage.

—— (2005) *Poverty and Capitalism*, QEH Working Paper 134, Oxford: University of Oxford.

—— (2008) *Rural Commercial Capital: Agricultural Markets in West Bengal*, New Delhi: Oxford University Press.

Harriss-White, B. and Harriss, J. (2007) *Green Revolution and After: The 'North Arcot' Papers and Long Terms Studies of the Political Economy of Rural Development in South India*, QEH Working Paper 146, Oxford: University of Oxford.

Hart, G. (1986) *Power, Labor and Livelihoods*, Berkeley: University Of California Press.

—— (1989) 'Introduction', in G. Hart, A. Turton and B. White (eds) *Agrarian Transformations: The State and Local Process in Southeast Asia*, Berkeley, CA: University of California Press.

Hart, G., Turton, A. and White, B. (eds) (1989) *Agrarian Transformations: The State and Local Process in Southeast Asia*, Berkeley, CA: University of California Press.

Heyer, J. (1992) '"The role of dowries and daughters": marriages in the accumulation and distribution of capital in a South Indian community', *Journal of International Development*, 4(4): 419–36.

Heyer, J., Roberts, P. and Williams, G. (1981) *Rural Development in Tropical Africa*, London: Palgrave Macmillan.

Hickey, S. and Bracking, S. (2005) 'Exploring the politics of poverty reduction: from representation to a politics of justice?', *World Development*, 33(6).

Hickey, S. and du Toit, A. (2006) *Adverse Incorporation, Social Exclusion and Chronic Poverty*, Chronic Poverty Research Centre Theme Paper, Draft, 18 May 2006.

—— (2007) *Adverse Incorporation, Social Exclusion and Chronic Poverty*, Chronic Poverty Research Centre, Working Paper 81.

Hulme, D. and Shepherd, A. (2003) 'Conceptualizing chronic poverty', *World Development*, 31(3): 403–23.

Jodha, N., Ghate, R. and Mukhopadhyay, P. (2008) *Promise, Trust and Evolution: Managing the Commons of South Asia*, New York: Oxford University Press.

Johnston, D., Kay, C., Lerche, J. and Oya, C. (2008) 'From the new editors', *The Journal of Agrarian Change*, 8(1): 3–5.

Kabeer, N. (2004) *Snakes, Ladders and Traps: Changing Lives and Livelihoods in Rural Bangladesh (1994–2001)*, Chronic Poverty Research Centre Working Paper 50, published in association with the Institute of Development Studies, Sussex.

Kanbur, R. and Shaffer, P. (2007) 'Epistemology, normative theory and poverty analysis: implications for Q-squared in practice', *World Development*, 35(2): 183–96.

Kapadia, K. (1993) 'Mutuality and competition: female landless labour and wage rates in Tamil Nadu', *Journal of Peasant Studies*, 20(2): 296–316.

Kapadia, K. and Lerche, J. (1999) 'Introduction', *Journal of Peasant Studies*, 26(2/3): 1–9.

Kautsky, K. (1899/1988) *The Agrarian Question*, trans. P. Burgess, London: Zwan Publications.

Krishna, A. (2006) 'Pathways out of and into poverty in 36 villages of Andhra Pradesh, India', *World Development*, 34(2): 271–88.

Lawson, T. (1997) *Economics and Reality*, Routledge, London.

—— (2006) 'The nature of heterodox economics', *Cambridge Journal of Economics*, 30(4): 483–505.

Lenin, V. I. (1899/1977) *The Development of Capitalism in Russia*, Moscow: Progress Publishers.

Lerche, J. (2007) 'A global alliance against forced labour? Unfree labour, neo-liberal globalization and the International Labour Organisation', *Journal of Agrarian Change*, 7(4): 425–52.

Mackintosh, M. (1990) 'Abstract markets and real needs', in H. Bernstein *et al.* (eds) *The Food Question: Profits versus People?*, London: Earth Scan.

Malhotra, R. and Kabeer, N. (2002) *Demographic Transition, Inter-Generational Contracts and Old Age Security: An Emerging Challenge for Social Policy in Developing Countries*, Institute of Development Studies Working Paper 157, Brighton: IDS.

Mellor, J.W. (1967) *The Economics of Agricultural Development*, Ithaca, NY: Cornell University Press.

Murray, C. (2001) *Livelihoods Research: Some Conceptual and Methodological Issues*, Chronic Poverty Research Centre Background Paper No. 5.

Narayan, D., Chambers, R., Kaul Shah, M. and Petesch, P. (2000) *Voices of the Poor: Crying Out for Change*, New York: Oxford University Press for the World Bank.

O'Connor, A. (2006) 'Global poverty knowledge and the USA: what it has been, why it needs to change', paper prepared for the Workshop on Concepts for Analysing Poverty Dynamics and Chronic Poverty, Chronic Poverty Research Centre, University of Manchester, October 2006.

Olsen, W.K. (1996) *Rural Indian Social Relations*, Delhi: Oxford University Press.

Rajasekhar, D. (1988) *Land Transfers and Family Partitioning: An Historical Study of an Andhra Village*, New Delhi: Oxford and IBH Publishing Co.

Ramachandran, V.K. (1990) *Wage Labour and Unfreedom in Agriculture: An Indian Case Study*, Oxford: Clarendon Press.

Ramachandran, V.K. and Swaminathan, M. (eds) (2003) 'Introduction' in *Agrarian Studies: Essays on Agrarian Relations in Less Developed Countries*, Delhi: Zed Books.

Rao, J.M. (2005) 'The forms of monopoly land rent and agrarian organization', *The Journal of Agrarian Change*, 5(2): 161–90.

Razavi, S. (ed.) (2002) *Shifting Burdens: Gender and Agrarian Change under Neo-liberalism*, Bloomfield, CT: Kumari Press.

Robinson, M.S. (1988) *Local Politics: The Law of the Fishes*, Delhi: Oxford University Press.

Rogaly, B. (1997) 'Linking home and market: towards a gendered analysis of changing labour relations in rural West Bengal', *IDS Bulletin*, 28(3): 63–72.

Roseberry, W. (1978) 'Peasants as proletarians', *Critique of Anthropology*, 3(11): 3–18.

Sayer, A. (2000) *Realism in Social Science*, London: Sage.

Scott, J. (1985) *The Weapons of the Weak: Everyday Forms of Peasant Resistance*, New Haven, CT: Yale University Press.

Sen, A. (1999) *Development as Freedom*, Oxford: Oxford University Press.

Sen, B. (2003) 'Drivers of escape and descent: changing household fortunes in rural Bangladesh', *World Development*, 31(3): 513–34.

Shanin, T. (1972) *The Awkward Class: Political Sociology of a Peasantry in a Developing Society: Russia 1910–1925*, Oxford: Clarendon Press.

Shepherd, A. (2007) *Understanding and Explaining Chronic Poverty: An Evolving Framework for Phase III of CPRC'S Research*, Chronic Poverty Research Centre Working Paper 80.

Shepherd, A. and Mehta, A.K. (2006) 'Chronic poverty in India: an introduction', in A.K. Mehta and A. Shepherd (eds) *Chronic Poverty and Development Policy in India*, New Delhi: Sage.

Stiglitz, J.E. (1986) 'The New Development Economics', *World Development*, 14(2): 257–65.

Venkateswarlu, D. (2006) *Task – and Risk – Mapping Study of Hybrid Vegetable Seed Production in India*, Fair Labor Association.

Venkateswarlu, D. and Corta, L. da (2001) 'Transformations in the age and gender of unfree workers on hybrid cotton seed farms in Andhra Pradesh', *The Journal of Peasant Studies*, 28(3): 1–36.

—— (2006) *The Price of Childhood: On the Link between Prices Paid to Farmers and the Use of Child Labour in Cottonseed Production in Andhra Pradesh, India*, Report Commissioned by the India Committee of Netherlands and Eine Welt (One World) Germany.

Walker, T. and Ryan, J. (1990) *Village and Household Economies in India's Semi-Arid Tropics*, Baltimore, MD and London: Johns Hopkins University Press.

Wood, G. (2003) 'Staying secure, staying poor: the "Faustian Bargain"', *World Development*, 31(3): 455–71.

Young, K., Wolkowitz, C. and McCullagh, R. (eds) (1981) *Of Marriage and the Market: Women's Subordination in International Perspective*, Oxford: CSE Books.

3 Strategic dimensions of rural poverty reduction in sub-Saharan Africa

Frank Ellis

Introduction

For the past forty years, the academic orthodoxy has been that poverty in sub-Saharan Africa (SSA) could be broadly and significantly reduced by raising yields in small-farm agriculture. This orthodoxy is based on some combination of the arguments that:

- most of the poor in Africa live in rural areas;
- the main reason for the prevalence of this rural poverty is the failure to replicate the 1970s Asian Green Revolution in Africa;
- securing strong yield growth in agriculture will generate higher incomes where it matters most – for the small-farm household itself;
- these higher incomes will be spent on locally produced goods and services, thus generating cumulative spirals of increased rural activity and incomes; and
- substantial scope exists to raise yields through the application of new science and technology to African agriculture.

This orthodoxy has undergone something of a renaissance in recent times. It forms the main economic strategy plank in a host of high-profile reports associated with the achievement of the Millennium Development Goals in SSA (e.g. Africa Commission 2005; UN Millennium Project 2005). It is at the centre of the UK's Department for International Development's (DFID) strategic perceptions about the role of agriculture in poverty reduction (DFID 2005).[1] And, of course, it lies at the core of the 2008 World Development Report on agriculture (World Bank 2008). This chapter challenges this orthodoxy, not from the standpoint of a highly theorised set of objections to it (although there are certainly a few of those around in the literature), but rather because it fails in almost all respects to describe real events, trends and outcomes for agriculture and rural poverty in SSA in the past forty years. The chapter argues that efforts to increase yields in Africa have been going on continuously over the past four decades with little to show for poverty reduction; that the Asian Green Revolution was extensively underpinned by government support mechanisms (price supports and input subsidies) that have not been envisaged to play a significant role in the liberalised agricultural markets of contemporary SSA; that SSA economies are relatively small and have limited domestic markets, so that increased food output rapidly translates into falling food prices; that agriculture has represented such a weak and unreliable livelihood platform that most SSA rural families survive or thrive by diversifying into non-farm activities or relying on remittance income; and that farm sizes in SSA are continuously shrinking due to subdivision at inheritance under customary land tenure arrangements.

The chapter further contends that rural–urban interdependencies have been neglected by donors and policymakers in SSA, with little effort being made to improve urban infrastructures, so that towns and cities could form the basis of dynamic economic and social change. It argues that yield growth in agriculture must be taken in conjunction with human mobility as a decisive factor in history explaining rapid and progressive economic and social change. Rural poverty in SSA will sustainably decline only when people leave agriculture to participate in the growth of other sectors, thus creating rising urban demand for food that serves to ensure higher and more stable incomes for those farmers that remain behind.

The chapter proceeds as follows. It considers, first, the dubious legitimacy of the Asia–Africa comparison, set within a critical stance on the overall thrust of the agriculture-led growth hypothesis; second, the limitation that farming as an occupation represents in liberalised markets, post-structural adjustment in SSA economies; third, the prevalence of highly diversified rural livelihoods as an indication of agriculture's inability to generate an adequate living for most people; and, fourth, the considerable underestimation of the positive impact that rural–urban interactions and urban growth could have on rural incomes and poverty reduction.

Agriculture in pro-poor growth and the Green Revolution comparison

The proposition that rises in farm productivity are an essential precursor to overall sustained economic growth and poverty reduction has a powerful intellectual pedigree. Many of the arguments are summarised in a contribution by Peter Timmer that opens with the overarching assertion that 'no country has been able to sustain a rapid transition out of poverty without raising productivity in its agricultural sector' (Timmer 2005: Abstract). Early versions of this proposition essentially saw agriculture as playing an instrumental role in the process of industrialisation of national economies: rises in farm productivity would ensure that agriculture was able to deliver labour, savings and inexpensive food to the growing industrial sector (Johnston and Mellor 1961; Mellor 1966). Later, this position was modified so that the direct poverty reduction effect of rising agricultural productivity, including its linkage and multiplier effects to the rural non-farm economy, became substantive desirable outcomes in their own right (Mellor 1976; Hazell and Haggblade 1993).

The agriculture-led pro-poor growth model seemed to accrue powerful empirical substantiation through the success of the Green Revolution in Asia. Nevertheless, as Timmer himself concedes (2005: 11) it has proved difficult to demonstrate definitively that yield growth in agriculture has been the driving force of non-farm growth and poverty reduction in Asian Green Revolution economies such as India, South Korea, Indonesia, Bangladesh and China. Alternative specifications of econometric models produce varying findings and, for India in particular, quite a body of empirical work challenges the validity of agriculture-led growth propositions (e.g. Karshenas 1995; Foster and Rosenzweig 2004).

The failure of SSA to reproduce the Asian Green Revolution success story of the 1970s (see Figure 3.1) has been attributed to low rural population density, poor rural infrastructure, low proportions of irrigated land, differences in dominant crops grown and an unfavourable policy environment (Johnson, Hazell and Gulati 2003). The last problem was addressed by the international community through conditionalities in structural adjustment programmes (SAPs) during the 1980s and 1990s, and the relative failure of that effort is considered in the next section of this chapter. Policy reform aside, there is a perception that SSA agriculture itself was relatively starved of academic and donor attention during this period (Timmer 2005: 3). Certainly, public expenditure earmarked for agricultural development fell in the 1980s and 1990s (IFAD 2001); however, this does not necessarily mean that the innovation and uptake endeavours of CGIAR (Consultative Group on International Agricultural Research) and national agricultural research centres significantly abated in this period.[2]

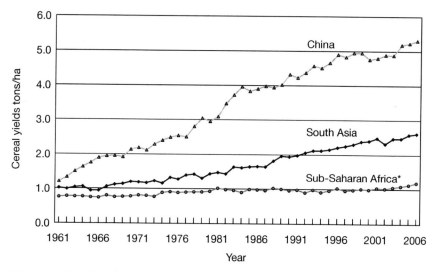

Figure 3.1 Trends in cereal yields sub-Saharan Africa and Asia (1961–2006)

Source: FAOStat – http://faostat.fao.org (accessed 19 August 2007).

Note: * Sub-Saharan Africa (SSA) excludes South Africa.

Whether it is indeed true that SSA agriculture experienced two decades of research neglect at the end of the twentieth century is not, in fact, a trivial point. If it is true, then the case made in a number of recent strategic documents that there is considerable untapped potential for the application of science and technology to SSA agriculture gains some force in its favour. However, if not really the case, then new efforts to achieve sustainable yield increases are not starting from scratch, but are adding impetus to a process that has, in fact, been going on continuously over the past thirty years. This also means, of course, that the scope for a sudden uplift from previous negligible and uneven progress is smaller than is being suggested in some strategic documents.

There are, however, other reasons located at the intersection of policy, market size and globalisation for caution about the prospects for SSA in the 2000s and beyond replicating the experience of the Asian Green Revolution in the 1970s. The principle Asian Green Revolution countries were large, food-deficit countries seeking to achieve food self-sufficiency in the face of unreliable international grain markets. The main era of their Green Revolutions was characterised by rising real food prices in international markets, and domestic economies beginning to undergo rapid urbanisation and industrialisation. Without exception, the Asian Green Revolution economies also had in place in that era comprehensive agricultural support policies, including fertiliser subsidies that in some countries lowered prices to 25 per cent of the international level and were sustained for ten or more years; irrigation investments that were borne entirely by national governments at no cost to beneficiary farmers; price policies that limited output price instability through the operation of floor and ceiling prices and buffer stocks; and demand boosted by publicly distributed subsidised food.

SSA in the 2000s contrasts in almost every respect with that Asian picture. For one thing, SSA comprises nearly fifty mainly small, open economies in an era of globalisation that rapidly transmits international price levels into the domestic sphere. Until an upturn in the mid 2000s, real prices of agricultural commodities had been declining more or less continuously since the 1970s (see Figure 3.2). SSA countries have small domestic markets that veer unevenly between minor surpluses causing uneconomic returns to farmers, and minor deficits causing price rises and food insecurity for their most vulnerable citizens. SSA countries are characterised by the general absence, post-liberalisation, of state-led agricultural support policies and input subsidies, these being replaced by intermittent government initiatives and fragmented efforts to provide farm support services by international and national NGOs. Following market liberalisation, farmers in SSA countries have experienced increased output price risk, uneven market coverage by private traders, spatial price variations reflecting poor market integration, and high price instability.

The failure of SAPs and adverse factors in SSA agriculture

One of the reasons that was considered, at the time, fundamental to the failure of SSA to achieve its own Green Revolution was the policy environment prevailing

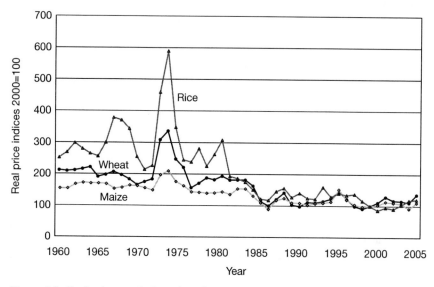

Figure 3.2 Real price trends for selected cereal crops (1960–2005)

Source: UNCTAD, *Commodity Price Statistics* http://stats.unctad.org/CPB (accessed 26 March 2008).

Note: Nominal prices in US$ per metric ton deflated by the unit value index of manufactured goods exports by developed market-economy countries; 2000=100.

in the 1970s, and specifically the pre-eminence of monopoly marketing boards ('crop parastatals') that artificially widened the marketing margin between farm gate and sales prices, extracting surpluses from the rural economy, and immis-erising farmers (World Bank 1981; Bates 1981). Trade and exchange rate policy did not help either; depressing import and export parity prices via overvalued exchange rates and overtaxing export commodities to the further detriment of producers. A considerable research effort centred on the proposition that public policy in agriculture in Africa was detrimental to farm prices and agricultural development (Mellor and Ahmed 1988; Krueger, Schiff and Valdes 1991).

The conditionality clauses in SAPs were designed, in part, to extricate SSA agriculture from these adverse 'state failure' environments. Governments were pressured to eliminate fertiliser and other input subsidies, disband crop parastatals or open them up to private sector competition, eliminate fixed prices or floor prices, reduce export crop taxes, reduce non-tariff import barriers and import taxes, devalue currencies and move to market exchange rates, and facilitate the emergence of competitive private trade in rural areas. Most governments acceded in the end to most of these requests, although often with a lot of foot-dragging and leaving remnants of old regimes still in place, as they still are to this day (see, for example, Cooksey 2005).[3]

The effects of SAPs on farm incomes and outputs should have been positive. That it palpably had more mixed and even detrimental effects is a phenomenon worth attempting to disentangle.[4] Many of the adverse effects seem to have been to do with shocks and sequencing. Currency devaluation and fertiliser subsidy removal tended to be in the vanguard of policy change, and happened very suddenly. The size of devaluations required immediate counteracting measures of monetary and fiscal discipline in order to prevent spiralling inflation. Inflation by itself tended often to cancel out the beneficial effects of devaluation on real farm prices, while monetary tightening caused several-fold increases in interest rates, curtailing the ability of those farmers that had been able to access credit institutions to take on loans. The domestic currency prices of fertilisers doubled or tripled, resulting in all but the wealthiest farmers ceasing to use them at effective levels (or any level at all).

Meanwhile, internal market liberalisation took place in conjunction with trade liberalisation in an era of falling real prices of agricultural commodities in world markets through the 1980s and 1990s (see Figure 3.2). This further reinforced a backdrop of downward underlying price pressures, rather than the buoyant real trends expected as a consequence of liberalisation. Private traders failed to rush into the spaces left behind by receding parastatals. For one thing, they were still impeded by petty barriers-to-entry and trade kept in place by officialdom (licences, taxes, roadblocks); but also the private benefit-cost-ratio of collecting half a pickup truck of maize from a remote village at the end of a terrible dirt road would not in many instances have made much commercial sense.[5]

The argument can also be made that the great liberalisation thrust of the mid 1980s occurred too late to overcome pathological conditions in SSA agriculture that had been set in train during the era of the parastatals. The unreliability of markets in the parastatal era (farmers sometimes failed to be paid for the crops that they delivered, or got paid months in arrears, quite aside from the low real level of prices that they were paid), resulted in a deepening 'food security first' subsistence rationale that the upheavals of liberalisation may have tended to reinforce. If a farm family cannot depend on being able to purchase food at affordable prices during the lean season, then it makes economic sense to retain as much production as required to ensure annual food security. The outcome, however, is low levels of exchange in the rural economy, and therefore little cash in circulation and lack of impetus for broader economic dynamism in rural areas.

The continued high level of subsistence reliance amongst food crop producers was observed for scattered research sites across four countries (Uganda, Kenya, Tanzania and Malawi) in a livelihoods research project entitled LADDER conducted in 2001–2002 (Ellis and Freeman 2004, 2005).[6] The fieldwork covered 1,345 households across 37 villages in 11 districts in the four countries. Some of the evidence on the physical output share of various food crops retained for home consumption rather than sold in the market is reproduced in Table 3.1. It can be seen that subsistence shares for staple foods are routinely above 70 per cent and can, under certain circumstances, reach near enough 100 per cent (maize in Malawi). These are average figures for the whole sample; if disaggregated

Table 3.1 Output share consumed by households, selected crops (LADDER Project)

Subsistence Share %	Kenya n=350	Uganda n=315	Tanzania n=350	Malawi n=280
Bananas	—	73.2	—	—
Maize	90.0	57.9	77.8	96.8
Rice	—	—	60.5	48.2
Millet	95.1	82.4	—	—
Sorghum	89.1	—	60.1	—
Beans	81.8	65.7	59.2	79.2

Source: Sample surveys conducted in 37 villages, 2001–2002.

by relative per capita income levels, the poorest half of the sample exhibit near total non-engagement in the market for their main food crops.[7]

A liberalised agriculture in SSA confronts other difficulties, too. Free agricultural markets are inherently unstable.[8] It is that instability and the routine ruin of farmers to which it gave rise that provided the micro-economic logic underpinning the ubiquitous farm support policies put in place in the industrialised countries from early in the twentieth century, although politics and national security also played their parts. In addition, limited national market size is a factor rarely given sufficient attention. Many SSA countries are more or less self-sufficient in their staple foods in normal years, such that an above-average harvest depresses farm prices and returns to farmers, while a below-average harvest leads quickly to food security difficulties for the most vulnerable.[9] Aside from small country size, limited domestic markets also result from slow non-farm and urban economic growth in most countries, a topic to which this chapter returns, and weak overall per capita income growth in most countries, too.

Finally, any consideration of the scope and limits of agriculture-led poverty reduction in SSA must feature the widespread phenomenon of declining farm size (Jayne *et al.* 2003; Jayne, Mather and Mghenyi 2005). Qualitative research in rural communities invariably reveals that this is the factor that most preoccupies rural families when they look to the future.[10] It arises due to continued rural population growth, customary inheritance practices that subdivide farm land between children in successive generations, the eventual closing of the land frontier in most places,[11] and lack of alternative employment opportunities. Its consequence is a pattern of farm sizes for the bottom income third or so of rural households that is inadequate for generating an agricultural livelihood even in normal or good years.[12] The proportion of rural populations that fall into this deficit group is growing over time.

So liberalisation did not provide a decisive reversal for the parlous state of SSA rural economies towards the end of the 1970s, and there are a number of reasons why this seems to have been the case. Post-liberalisation arguments for utilising agriculture as the main vehicle for SSA poverty reduction are weakened by reference to several facets of farm-based livelihoods in SSA that counteract the potentially beneficial effects of rising yields, if the latter could indeed be sustainably secured. These facets include limited domestic markets, unstable prices in free markets and declining farm sizes. It is perhaps not surprising, then, that SSA small farmers have sought over many years to secure part of their livelihood, and preferably as large a part as possible, from non-farm income sources.

Rural livelihood diversification and its paradoxes

For the purposes of this discussion, rural livelihood diversification simply describes the phenomenon by which small-farm households take up non-farm activities, or rely on non-farm income transfers, for the overall standard of living that they are able to achieve. Diversification in association with small-family farming has been around a long time. The two 'classic' reasons for diversifying – risk and seasonality – have always been pertinent.[13] Non-farm occupations reduce risk by combining activities that have different risk profiles, while they can also ameliorate the labour and consumption smoothing problems associated with seasonality. These reasons are likely to have relevance even in the presence of relatively favourable agricultural conditions and the production of a surplus for the market in normal years.

In SSA, livelihood diversification has come to symbolise a state of affairs arising from reasons distinct from these classic reasons. The difficulties confronting small-farm agriculture in liberalised markets discussed in the preceding section are pertinent. A multi-country research project conducted by the African Studies Centre at Leiden University in the 1990s utilised qualitative and quantitative methods to derive a composite picture of the relative collapse of agriculture as the primary source of rural livelihoods in SSA, and the associated broadening pursuit of non-farm options across the continent (Bryceson 1996, 1999, 2002; Bryceson and Jamal 1997).[14] Key components of this picture are supported by a substantial body of other evidence. Studies of rural income portfolios derived from both large-scale, nationally representative, sample surveys, and from purposive household studies, converge on the once startling figure that, on average, roughly 50 per cent of rural household incomes in SSA are generated from engagement in non-farm activities and transfers from urban areas or abroad; remittances and pension payments being the chief categories of such transfers (Reardon 1997; Ellis 2000; Ellis and Freeman 2004).

There is a great deal of variation around this mean figure at the household level, but less variation than might be supposed when comparing sample evidence across different countries in any particular subregion. A strong positive correlation between the proportion of rural household income obtained from non-farm sources and overall household income per capita has been observed in numerous studies. In relation to this, it is widely found that while diversity of income sources is prevalent across different income classes, the nature of this diversification differs between better-off and poorer households. The better-off tend to diversify in the form of non-farm business activities (trade, transport, shopkeeping, brick making, etc.) or salaried employment, while the poor tend to diversify in the form of casual wage work, especially on other farms, while remaining heavily reliant on subsistence crop production. In other words, diversification associated with poverty and vulnerability tends to occur within agriculture, while that associated with improving livelihoods occurs outside agriculture.

A case study from Tanzania, provided in Table 3.2, typifies diversification findings that are prevalent throughout SSA. It is observed that the average split between own farming and other income sources, for the sample of 344 households, is almost spot on the 50:50 division referred to above as a widespread finding in SSA. The relative dependence on own agriculture declines across the income ranges from 68 per cent for the poorest quartile to 43 per cent for the richest. It is notable that the share of non-farm business income quadruples across the quartiles from 11 to 44 per cent of the income portfolio.

It might be thought that the attention paid by better-off households to non-farm activities would result in the neglect and poor performance of their farming activities. This is not so at all. For all four LADDER country samples, Table 3.3 shows how agricultural productivity per hectare rises steeply across the income ranges. Net farm output per hectare in a series of country samples was between three and six times higher for the top income quartile of households compared to the lowest income quartile.

The interlinked livelihood process conveyed by these two tables is an interesting one: the lower the importance of agriculture in the total income portfolio of the household, the higher the farm productivity realised (Figure 3.3 illustrates this by reference to the Tanzania sample). This emphasises the interdependence between farm and non-farm livelihood components that describe doing well in rural SSA. However, it also points in a broader direction: it seems plausible that

Table 3.2 Income portfolios by income quartile, Tanzania (sample of 344 rural households, 2001)

	Composition of household incomes (%)				
Income sources	*Income quartile*				
	I *n=87*	*II* *n=88*	*III* *n=88*	*IV** *n=81*	*Total* *n=344*
Maize	27.1	21.5	15.1	7.9	12.4
Rice	12.3	14.2	10.3	8.8	10.0
Other crops	23.3	19.9	23.8	11.8	16.3
Livestock	5.0	7.7	6.5	14.1	11.0
Subtotal own agric.	67.7	63.3	55.7	42.6	49.7
Wages	14.6	8.9	9.3	11.0	10.5
Non-farm business	11.5	23.7	29.3	44.0	36.1
Transfers	6.3	4.2	5.7	2.5	3.7
Total	100.0	100.0	100.0	100.0	100.0

Source: Ellis and Mdoe (2003: 1378).

Note: *Seven specialised pastoral households were removed from the top quartile.

Table 3.3 Net farm output per ha, by income quartile, four countries

Country	Income quartile				Ratio IV:I
	I	*II*	*III*	*IV*	
Uganda	131	215	295	487	3.7
Kenya	135	266	358	430	3.2
Tanzania	81	108	156	381	4.7
Malawi	18	44	84	109	6.0

Source: Ellis and Freeman (2004: 18).

farm productivity in SSA rises as a function of household members taking up non-farm opportunities, rather than being the driver of such opportunities as is proposed in much of the agriculture-led growth literature.

The widely observed rural livelihood patterns illustrated by the LADDER project data help to shed light on the dynamics of rural vulnerability in sub-Saharan Africa. The poorest and most vulnerable rural families are those most heavily reliant on agriculture, and most strongly locked into subsistence within agriculture. This is a growing proportion of rural households in food insecure and poorly performing SSA countries. The same category of the rural poor also tends to be dependent on work on other farms in order to cover the deficit in their household food balance. This exacerbates rather than diminishes their vulnerability for two reasons: first, labour on other farms can mean neglect of good cultivation practices on own farms (e.g. Alwang 1999); and, second, work

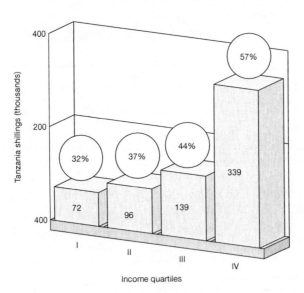

Figure 3.3 Tanzania: rising yields and declining dependence on farming
Source: Based on data reported in Ellis and Mdoe (2003) and Ellis and Freeman (2004).

on other farms proves an unreliable buffer when adverse natural events occur that affect all farms in a geographical zone.

It is clear that livelihood diversification, which involves occupational and geographical mobility away from agriculture, not only provides rural SSA dwellers with greater livelihood security, but also potentially opens up non-farm pathways to improving standards of living. Livelihood diversification is partly predicated on, and itself increases, human capital in terms of experience, skills and willingness to innovate. It generates earnings and remittances that alter the options open to the household by providing it with cash resources that can be flexibly deployed. It contributes to lessening vulnerability by ameliorating risk and reducing the adverse consumption effects of seasonality. The realisation of these positive features can be constrained by public policy environments that are non-facilitating towards small-scale business, and actively discouraging towards mobility and migration.

Rural–urban transitions and poverty reduction

Previous sections of this chapter have proposed that the potential benefits of yield growth in small-farm agriculture in SSA are offset by a number of adverse trends and circumstances, so that in practice little net gain occurs in farm incomes; and, indeed, in the worst cases the adverse factors outweigh efforts to raise yields, so that livelihood circumstances continue to deteriorate despite the best efforts of all concerned to move forward. Undoubtedly, the most lethal combination is failed growth at the macro level (static or declining per capita GDP) combined with these adverse rural trends. This combination severely curtails the non-farm options available, throwing rural households even deeper into excessive reliance on semi-subsistence food crop production. A considerable number of SSA countries persistently or intermittently fall into this category.

Table 3.4 provides rural and urban headcount poverty data for a selection of Southern and East African countries in the late 1990s or early 2000s. Are these data trying to tell us something? Well, yes they are, and that is that with rare exceptions urban poverty levels are very considerably below rural ones. Some of the rural poverty levels are so high in Southern African countries that they are scarcely possible to grasp; however, we do know from what happens when there is a slight disturbance in rainfall patterns that Southern African rural dwellers are indeed among the populations most vulnerable to food deficits in the world. The agriculture-led growth position is that these impoverished populations should be kept in agriculture because yield growth on their farms is an essential precursor to their ability to move out, and this argument has been dominant for the past thirty years.

Strangely, economists, who in all other respects are great believers in the capabilities represented by individual human initiative, have a curious myopia when it comes to what people do for a living in cities. When challenged with the notion of accelerated rural–urban transition in SSA, they will say 'but what will they do there' or 'but there are no visible sources of growth there'. This is,

Table 3.4 Rural and urban poverty data, selected SSA countries (%)

Country	Year	Rural	Urban	National
Kenya	1997	52.9	49.2	52.3
Uganda	2002–03	42.7	14.4	38.8
Tanzania	2000–01*	38.7	17.6	35.7
Malawi	2005	55.9	25.9	52.4
Zambia	2004–05	78.0	53.0	68.0
Zimbabwe	1995–96	76.2	41.1	63.3
Mozambique	2002–03	55.3	51.5	54.1
Lesotho	1993	53.9	27.8	49.2

Source: World Bank (2005) and individual country statistical services.

Note: *The urban headcount figure for Tanzania refers to Dar es Salaam only; the figure for other urban areas was 25.8 per cent.

of course, nonsense as the poverty figures themselves indicate. People have agency, and people's agency when freed from the shackles of unremitting toil on the land, is to find niches in the urban economy where they can get by. Towns and cities become teeming hives of small-scale activity in which people begin to specialise in providing goods and services for others, and purchase goods and services in return. In this process, they develop new outlooks and skills, and down the line they become much more interesting as a potential labour force for larger-scale investments by emerging urban entrepreneurs, and eventually industrialists.

Tiffen (2003) explores a model of rural–urban transitions that ends up by cautiously suggesting that urbanisation has been hindered by policy in SSA, and that urban growth is required to stimulate agriculture and to provide jobs for those who are leaving farming (ibid.: 1343). The interdependency of rural and urban poverty reduction emphasised by Tiffen is central to obtaining a better grasp of the strategic balance between sectors required for accelerated growth and poverty reduction in SSA. For small-farm agriculture to grow and prosper in SSA, rapid rural–urban transitions will have to take place in order to reverse declining farm size, provide a robust domestic market for farm output, increase cash in circulation in rural areas, and take the pressure off over-exploited natural resources.

The proposition is therefore advanced here that failure to grasp the nettle of accelerated rural–urban transition has contributed quite significantly to the spreading rural poverty and intensifying vulnerability of the past several decades in SSA. Ethiopia is a country that exhibits this failure to an extreme. Ethiopia has a population estimated at 70 million people, only 17 per cent of whom in 2005 lived in urban areas. The pro-poor growth strategy of the government, encapsulated in two successive PRSPs (Poverty Reduction Strategy Plans), has been strongly agriculture based, with negligible attention to urban growth or urban infrastructural constraints.[15] In Ethiopia, the state owns the land, and farm families have rent-free access to it and can pass it on to their progeny. Several past land redistributions mean that in the densely settled highland areas farm sizes are in the narrow range of 0.5 to 2 hectares. Farm sizes are shrinking since the rural population is growing at 3 per cent per annum.

Ethiopia follows policies that 'trap people in agriculture'. The capital or rental value of land cannot be realised (say, as a precursor to moving to town) because the land belongs to the state and cash renting is prohibited. There are widespread perceptions in rural Ethiopia from previous state behaviours that if land is left for more than three to four months it will be reallocated by the local administration and the same will also occur if individuals are considered to have moved unduly into non-farm activities (Ellis and Woldehanna 2005). The rate of urbanisation in the country at 6 per cent is considered to be an unwelcome trend, to be contained if possible. However, if this rate is maintained 77 per cent of Ethiopians will still live on the land in 2015, and 15 million more people will need to have been absorbed by the agricultural sector.

Summary and conclusions

A great deal more work needs to be done to get the speculative ideas put forward in this chapter into a shape that would stand up to closer scrutiny. Nevertheless, the outline of a shift in emphasis about what agriculture can do for poverty reduction begins to emerge. In this, rural poverty reduction and urban growth are interdependent, and rural poverty reduction requires a much more rapid rural–urban transition than has been occurring in most SSA countries over the past three decades.[16] This also means investing in urban infrastructures and anticipating the arrival of populations in towns, in order to mitigate the worst horrors of urban squalor. However, there cannot be much worse circumstances than the rural squalor in which very substantial proportions of SSA populations have been mired for the past several decades.

The direction taken by this chapter seems in the end to rest on some core propositions on which a lot more work is required before they can be adequately positioned in debates about development strategy in SSA. These are:

1   that it is human mobility, not yield growth in agriculture on its own, that historically has been the single most decisive factor explaining rapid processes of economic and social change (this is in opposition to the Timmer (2005) principle cited earlier);
2   that agriculture is not a reliable sector on which to base rising prosperity especially in relatively small countries on the world stage unless accompanied by non-agricultural development, because such rising productivity, as can be sustainably secured, is offset by price instability, oversupply in small domestic markets, and declining real prices in international markets;
3   that the notion that poverty reduction is best addressed in the very sectors in which poverty is most acute, virtually an axiom of development policy over the past two or three decades, is flawed because it fails to focus

adequately on supporting growth processes where they actually occur in the economy, and it neglects the interdependence between the farm and non-farm sectors.

Of course, poverty reduction in SSA is not only about interdependent growth processes between economic sectors. Politics and government play important roles. Dysfunctional governance environments can debilitate enterprise and initiative to such a degree that growth processes have little chance to gain momentum before fizzling out in an overwhelming climate of discouragement. The constraints here may be more significant in the urban economy than in the rural economy due to the reliance of urban economic growth on the predictable delivery of urban public services such as electricity, lighting, piped water supplies, mains drainage, and so on. Shifting the balance of the strategic debate in Africa towards what urban growth can do for rural poverty reduction, rather than the reverse, is therefore as much about the political will or capability to get behind such an agenda in SSA cities and towns as it is about the economic merits of the case put forward.

Acknowledgement

Versions of this chapter have already appeared in a number of different guises e.g. Ellis (2005, 2006), although quite a lot of revision has gone into this version. The chapter reflects a research agenda in its early phases of gestation and is therefore somewhat speculative in character. In one way or another it touches on many of the concerns and interests with which Judith Heyer engaged in her distinguished career (for example Heyer 1991; 1996). I am grateful for critical points made during the discussion at the workshop, as also written comments sent to me afterwards by Judith Heyer.

Notes

1 The executive summary of the DFID (2005) policy paper on agriculture is entitled 'Agriculture at the heart of poverty reduction'.
2 Much of the decline in overall expenditure in agriculture can be attributed to the abandonment of fertiliser subsidies and support to parastatal organisations called for in structural adjustment programmes.
3 Interestingly, in just the last two to three years several governments (e.g. Malawi, Zambia) have reintroduced comprehensive fertiliser subsidy regimes, signifying the potential reinstatement of 'big' agricultural policies by the state, along, of course, with their previous ambiguities for policy outcomes.
4 For an excellent case study that does this for a single SSA country, Malawi, see Harrigan (2003).
5 The case where the cost of engaging in a transaction outweighs the benefits of doing so, even when a potential sale could occur, is a particular type of market failure (de Janvry, Fafchamps and Sadoulet 1991). Market failure aspects of post-liberalisation agriculture in SSA have been extensively explored by the Wye research group at Imperial College London (see, for example, Poulton, Kydd and Dorward 2006).

6 LADDER was a cross-country research programme funded by the DFID Policy Research Programme from 2000 to 2004. The research sites were mainly food or mixed food and cash crop areas, selected to represent typical rural livelihoods in the case-study countries. It is, of course, true that some farmers in all countries engage in crop production specifically for the market (i.e. export crops and high-value horticultural crops).

7 Subsistence proportions like this excite little curiosity when mentioned in workshops or conferences, as if it is an unremarkable feature of SSA agriculture that this should be so after forty years of post-independence rural development. Yet, such figures say a lot about the failure to achieve rising standards of living in rural SSA, as well as about the rising vulnerability to food security failure that has characterised many parts of the continent in the early 2000s.

8 This is because farmers can only plan the next season's crop areas by reference to past price patterns, especially the immediately preceding season prices, resulting in oversupply or undersupply in the next season.

9 In economic terms, this food price volatility in the vicinity of national food self-sufficiency occurs due to low price elasticity of demand.

10 This was markedly the case, for example, in participatory work conducted in 31 villages in Ethiopia for a Participatory Poverty Assessment (PPA) (see Ellis and Woldehanna 2005).

11 There remain some exceptions to this inexorable tightening of land supply, notably much of rural Zambia, but in most SSA countries it applies, and within them it applies with particular force to high-potential agricultural zones.

12 The average farm size across 1,295 households across four countries in the LADDER project was near enough 1.5 ha. Between 40 and 50 per cent of households by country sample had farm sizes under 1 ha in 2001 (Cross 2005). Declining farm size can potentially be offset by yield increases or more intensive crop mixes, always supposing that technical and market constraints to these can be overcome.

13 See, for example, Netting (1993) for discussion of these reasons in peasant farming societies in the North as well as the South.

14 This research project, coordinated by the African Studies Centre at Leiden University, was entitled Deagrarianization and Rural Employment (DARE).

15 In the 2002–2006 Sustainable Development and Poverty Reduction Program (SDPRP), urban development was regarded as such a minor cross-cutting issue that it received 2½ pages' attention in the 200-page document (Ethiopia 2002). The second PRSP, the 2006–2010 Plan for Accelerated and Sustained Development to End Poverty (PASDEP), maintains the primary emphasis on agriculture-based poverty reduction (Ethiopia 2006).

16 A similar conclusion is reached in a thought-provoking piece by Stefan Dercon (Dercon 2006) who argues *inter alia* that in an open economy the necessity for pro- poor growth to start in agriculture disappears.

Bibliography

Africa Commission (2005) *Our Common Future: Report of the Africa Commission.* Available online: www.commissionforafrica.org/english/report/introduction.html (accessed 15 March 2008).

Alwang, J. (1999) 'Labour shortages on small landholdings in Malawi: implications for policy reforms', *World Development,* 27(8): 1461–75.

Bates, R.H. (1981) *Markets and States in Tropical Africa,* Berkeley: University of California Press.

Bryceson, D.F. (1996) 'Deagrarianization and rural employment in sub-Saharan Africa: a sectoral perspective', *World Development,* 24(1): 97–111.

—— (1999) 'African rural labour, income diversification and livelihood approaches: a long-term development perspective', *Review of African Political Economy* (80): 171–89.

—— (2002) 'The scramble in Africa: reorienting rural livelihoods', *World Development*, 30(5): 725–39.

Bryceson, D.F. and Jamal, V. (eds) (1997) *Farewell to Farms: Deagrarianisation and Employment in Africa*, Research Series No.1997/10, Leiden, Netherlands: African Studies Centre.

Cooksey, B. (2005) 'Marketing reform? The rise and fall of agricultural liberalisation in Tanzania', in F. Ellis and H.A. Freeman (eds) *Rural Livelihoods and Poverty Reduction Policies*, London: Routledge.

Cross, S. (2005) 'Comparative land tenure issues arising in four countries', in F. Ellis and H.A. Freeman (eds) *Rural Livelihoods and Poverty Reduction Policies*, London: Routledge.

Dercon, S. (2006) *Rural Poverty: Old Challenges in New Contexts*, Global Poverty Research Group Working Paper No. 72.

DFID (2005) *Growth and Poverty Reduction: The Role of Agriculture*, DFID Policy Paper, London: Department for International Development.

Ellis, F. (2000) *Rural Livelihoods and Diversity in Developing Countries*, Oxford: Oxford University Press.

—— (2003) *Human Vulnerability and Food Insecurity: Policy Implications, Forum for Food Security in Southern Africa*, Theme Paper No.3, London: Overseas Development Institute.

—— (2005) 'Small farms, livelihood diversification, and rural–urban transitions: strategic issues in sub-Saharan Africa', in International Food Policy Research Institute (IFPRI), *The Future of Small Farms: Proceedings of a Research Workshop*, Washington, DC: IFPRI.

—— (2006) 'Agrarian change and rising vulnerability in rural sub-Saharan Africa', *New Political Economy*, 11(3): 387–97.

Ellis, F. and Freeman, H.A. (2004) 'Rural livelihoods and poverty reduction strategies in four African countries', *Journal of Development Studies*, 40(4): 1–30.

—— (eds) (2005) *Rural Livelihoods and Poverty Reduction Policies*, London: Routledge.

Ellis, F. and Mdoe, N. (2003) 'Livelihoods and rural poverty reduction in Tanzania', *World Development*, 31(8): 1367–84.

Ellis, F. and Woldehanna, T. (2005) *Ethiopia Participatory Poverty Assessment 2004–05*, Addis Ababa: Ministry of Finance and Economic Development (MoFED).

Ethiopia Ministry of Finance and Economic Development (2002) *Ethiopia: Sustainable Development and Poverty Reduction Program*, Addis Ababa: MoFED.

Ethiopia Ministry of Finance and Economic Development (2006) *A Plan for Accelerated and Sustained Development to End Poverty (PASDEP)*, Addis Ababa: MoFED.

Foster, A.D. and Rosenzweig, M.R. (2004) 'Agricultural productivity growth, rural economic diversity, and economic reforms: India, 1970–2000', *Economic Development and Cultural Change*, 52(3): 510–42.

Harrigan, J. (2003) 'U-turns and full circles: two decades of agricultural reform in Malawi 1981–2000', *World Development*, 31(5): 847–63.

Hazell, P. and Haggblade, S. (1993) 'Farm–nonfarm growth linkages and the welfare of the poor', in M. Lipton and J. van der Gaag (eds) *Including the Poor*, Proceedings of a Symposium Organized by the World Bank and the International Food Policy Research Institute, Washington, DC: World Bank.

Heyer, J. (1991) 'Poverty and food deprivation in Kenya's smallholder agricultural areas', in J. Dreze and A. Sen (eds) *The Political Economy of Hunger, Volume 3: Endemic Hunger*, Oxford: Clarendon Press.

—— (1996) 'The complexities of rural poverty in sub-Saharan Africa', *Oxford Development Studies*, 24(3): 281–97.

International Fund for Agricultural Development (IFAD) (2001) *Rural Poverty Report 2001: The Challenge of Ending Rural Poverty*, Oxford: Oxford University Press for IFAD.

Janvry, A. de, Fafchamps, M. and Sadoulet, E. (1991) 'Peasant household behaviour with missing markets: some paradoxes explained', *Economic Journal*, 101: 1400–17.

Jayne, T.S., Mather, D. and Mghenyi, E. (2005) *Smallholder Farming in Difficult Circumstances: Policy Issues for Africa*, in International Food Policy Research Institute (IFPRI) *The Future of Small Farms: Proceedings of a Research Workshop*, Washington, DC: IFPRI.

Jayne, T.S., Yamano, T., Weber, M.T., Tschirley, D., Benefica, R., Chapoto, A. and Zulu, B. (2003) 'Smallholder income and land distribution in Africa: implications for poverty reduction strategies', *Food Policy*, 28(3): 253–75.

Johnson, M., Hazell, P. and Gulati, A. (2003) 'The role of intermediate factor markets in Asia's Green Revolution: lessons for Africa?', *American Journal of Agricultural Economics*, 85(5): 1211–6.

Johnston, B.F. and Mellor, J. (1961) 'The role of agriculture in economic development', *American Economic Review*, 51(4): 566–93.

Karshenas, M. (1995) *Industrialization and Agricultural Surplus: A Comparative Study of Economic Development in Asia*, Oxford: Oxford University Press.

Krueger, A.O., Schiff, M. and Valdes, A. (eds) (1991) *The Political Economy of Agricultural Pricing Policy, Volume 3: Africa and the Mediterranean*, Baltimore: Johns Hopkins University Press.

Mellor, J.W. (1966) *The Economics of Agricultural Development*, New York: Cornell University Press.

—— (1976) *The New Economics of Growth*, Ithaca: Cornell University Press.

Mellor, J.W. and Ahmed, R. (1988) *Agricultural Price Policy for Developing Countries*, Baltimore: Johns Hopkins University Press.

Netting, R.M. (1993) *Smallholders, Householders: Farm Families and the Ecology of Intensive, Sustainable Agriculture*, Stanford: Stanford University Press.

Poulton, C., Kydd, J. and Dorward, A. (2006) 'Overcoming market constraints on pro-poor agricultural growth in sub-Saharan Africa', *Development Policy Review*, 24(3): 243–77.

Reardon, T. (1997) 'Using evidence of household income diversification to inform study of the rural nonfarm labor market in Africa', *World Development*, 25(5): 735–47.

Tiffen, M. (2003) 'Transition in sub-Saharan Africa: agriculture, urbanization and income growth', *World Development*, 31(8): 1343–66.

Timmer, C.P. (2005) *Agriculture and Pro-Poor Growth: An Asian Perspective*, Center for Global Development, Working Paper No. 63, July.

UN Millennium Project (2005) *Investing in Development: A Practical Plan to Achieve the Millennium Development Goals – Overview*, New York: UNDP.

World Bank (1981) *Accelerated Development in Sub-Saharan Africa*, 'Berg Report', Washington, DC: World Bank.

World Bank (2005) *African Development Indicators*, Washington, DC: World Bank.

World Bank (2008) *World Development Report 2008: Agriculture for Development*, Washington, DC: World Bank.

4 From 'rural labour' to 'classes of labour'

Class fragmentation, caste and class struggle at the bottom of the Indian labour hierarchy

Jens Lerche

Introduction

Employment relations in rural India have undergone major changes in recent decades. Agriculture now requires fewer labour inputs; and the growth of the non-agricultural sectors has created alternative employment opportunities. From the 1990s, new rural and urban employment, often linked to migration, has become an increasingly important income source for former agricultural labourers. Close-knit patron–client relations between low-caste agricultural labourers and their landowning caste Hindu employers have loosened. As pointed out by Heyer and a number of other researchers, this has not always led to free labour relations, but it has, by and large, signalled a change from the rural poor mainly being 'agricultural labour' to their being 'rural labour' (Breman 1996; Byres, Kapadia and Lerche 1999; Heyer 2000).

This chapter continues the investigation of three questions about this rural labour: who the rural labourers are, in what kind of employment relations they are involved today, and what kind of action is taken by and on behalf of the labouring poor. The implications of significant divisions and segmentation among the labouring poor as well as fluidity across some categories of labour will be examined. It will be argued that it is time to conceptualise these labourers simply as 'labour', with no 'rural' or 'urban' prefix, because social segmentation is more important than site. This study focuses on the segmentation of low caste labour. It will be argued that the combination of segmentation and fluidity within the segments identified here impedes work-based social action while making other types of social action, sometimes political and along caste lines, both possible and necessary for the labouring poor.

These issues are wide-ranging, and this contribution can only point out some major aspects and tendencies within the field. Three limitations of the argument need noting at the outset. First, while it is organised around a perspective of class analysis, it concentrates on the 'labour' side of class relations and does not provide a full class analysis of Indian society, let alone an analysis of 'capital'. Second, while it seeks to break down the strict rural–urban distinctions regarding labour, its main concern is the labour that used to be seen as rural. This is because the referents of the argument are a trajectory of studies starting from an agrarian point of departure. Third, there are many, often contradictory, tendencies between and within the regions of India which are acknowledged, but the main contribution of the essay is at the All-India level.

Empirically, this research draws on recent case studies as well as statistical data collected by the Indian National Sample Survey Organisation (NSSO), and the impressive analysis of these data by the Indian National Commission for Enterprises in the Unorganised Sector (NCEUS). It is organised into three sections. The first section identifies the labouring classes in India and the segmentation of these classes into different types of employment and degrees of self-employment. This also involves a methodological/theoretical discussion of how to conceptualise 'labouring classes' in India today. The second section argues that employment is segmented along social lines. The emphasis here is on caste, especially on labour relations involving low-caste labour. The third part focuses on pro-labour actions and movements. It is shown that labouring groups at the bottom of the employment hierarchy are more likely to seek redress outside the immediate labour relation through central policies and sometimes through new types of unions, but also through caste – or locality-based – political organisations. The article concludes with a discussion of these struggles in relation to the ways in which labour relations and the labouring classes are structured.

The Indian labouring classes

Any analysis of labour in India must begin with a clarification of the concept of 'labour'. In major parts of the late-developing world including India, the kind of capitalism that has developed has not led to the universalisation of 'doubly free' labour ('free' to sell their labour power and 'freed' from ownership of the means of production). The development of class-based categories appropriate for the analysis of the actually existing class relations is a long-standing political and analytical challenge. In this context, recent work by Bernstein is relevant. Bernstein's point of departure is that capital today is so dominant that it shapes social and thus class relations in a very direct way, even if not expressed through the dominance of the 'classic' capital–labour relations. He suggests a new concept, 'classes of labour', which includes both classic wage labourers and those who depend indirectly on the sale of their labour power. With this concept he encompasses all those who 'have to pursue their reproduction through insecure and oppressive – and typically increasingly scarce – wage employment and/or a range of likewise precarious small-scale and insecure, 'informal sector' ('survival') activity, including farming; in effect, various and complex combinations of employment and self-employment' (Bernstein 2008: 18). Classes of labour thus can include those who possess some means of production, but who nevertheless share with wage labourers the overall position of being exploited and oppressed – and who, indeed, may alternate between being wage workers and small-scale petty commodity producers, seasonally or throughout their lifetimes.[1]

Rural employment and development

The 'classes of labour' concept provides a useful framework for understanding the fluidity of labour relations for Indian workers of rural origin. This section seeks to identify the labouring classes in India and their segmentation into different types of employment and degrees of self-employment. Several qualitative studies have lent support to the Ministry of Finance's study of agricultural debt (Government of India 2007a): at present, more often than not, agricultural returns are insufficient to keep agricultural labourers and owners of small plots of land remuneratively occupied throughout the year. It is increasingly common for healthy, able-bodied male, rural labourers to migrate seasonally to take up slightly less poorly paid jobs, or jobs providing them with income during the lean agricultural season, and then to return to their villages for harvest work. This migratory work might be agricultural and non-agricultural, or a mixture, depending on the season and on specific local patterns of migration. It may involve self-employment or wage employment. In many households women, together with young and old men, stay in the village throughout the year. They do any available paid work for the landowners and tend any livestock they may possess (e.g. chickens or a single cow), undertake semi-skilled craft activities such as basket-making and rope making for survival, or cultivate (very) small plots of land. In the poorest households even the female members, and often the children of these house-holds as well, migrate. At the very bottom of the labour hierarchy, some households are forced to take out loans during the slack season from labour contractors of migrant labour, or from local landowners, against their future labour input, and so become bonded labourers. This does not necessarily constitute lifetime bondage. Households enter into bondage in very lean years, or when additional expenditure cannot be met (relating to disease, life cycle rituals, etc.). Some households work their way out of it, to become 'free' casual labour again. Geographically, the poor central to eastern parts of India[2] and poverty pockets elsewhere serve as reservoirs of seasonal migrant labour for the rest of the economy (Breman 2007; Breman and Guerin 2009; Guerin 2009; Lerche 1999, 2007; Pitcherit 2009; Srivastava 2005a, 2005b).

The fluidity and variety of positions occupied by labour and labouring households during the year and during a lifetime are important; but so too are the constraints or limits to this fluidity. These limits are best revealed by looking at the overall employment trends in the country. Starting with the sectoral employment pattern, India is still predominantly an agricultural society in employment terms, but less so than it used to be. In the first couple of decades after Independence, more than 70 per cent of the economically active population worked in agriculture and this remained fairly stable until the 1970s. Since then, the proportion of the working population in agriculture has fallen to 57 per cent (Ramaswami 2007: 48).[3] In some states, including those with a highly productive capitalist agriculture and/or a strong non-agricultural economy, the share is significantly lower.[4] The importance of non-agricultural employment for households working in agriculture is also high.[5]

India's agrarian capitalism is well documented and taken as given here. It is less commonly acknowledged that during the last fifty years there has been a significant decrease in land sizes. Between 1982/1983 and 2003 there was a dramatic and accelerating increase in the proportion of farmers owning less than one hectare of land. Today, more than 60 per cent of all landowners fall into this category of 'marginal farmers'. Few, if any, accumulate capital through their agricultural activities. Most marginal farmers are best characterised as de facto wage workers who receive a subsidiary income from the plots of land that they own: more than half of the income of marginal farmers is wage income (NCEUS 2008: 4, 34).[6] These marginal farmers are likely to belong to the 'classes of labour' as defined above, together with most by far of the landless rural dwellers.

Agricultural labourers are either landless or are drawn mainly from the ranks of marginal farmers. According to NSSO figures, the proportion of the economically active population in agriculture whose main income is from agricultural labour hovers at around 40 per cent, with significant swings up and down (from 40 per cent in 1993/1994 up to 42 per cent in 1999/2000 and down to 36 per cent in 2004/2005) (NCEUS 2007: 111–14).[7]

The diminishing importance of agriculture is not just due to the growth of other sectors; agriculture itself is also in crisis, after a decade of the lowest growth rates in agriculture since Independence. During 1994/1995 – 2004/2005, its annual growth rate was only 0.6 per cent (as against, in most years since Independence, between 2 per cent and 4 per cent). The crisis in agriculture is well acknowledged by Indian authorities and is often seen as an outcome, at least in part, of the specific liberalisation policies applied to Indian agriculture from 1991 onwards. The agrarian crisis seems to have intensified already existing processes of land miniaturisation and labour-shedding. Economic growth in the non-agrarian economy from the early 1990s onwards has also not had strong linkages to agriculture (Chandrasekhar 2007; Jha 2006; NCEUS 2008).

However, the aggregate picture disguises very different trends at state and local level. The crisis is much deeper in some parts of the country than in others. States with high growth rates from 1994/1995 to 2004/2005 include the classic Green Revolution states of Punjab, Haryana and Andhra Pradesh, as well as other agriculturally productive states such as West Bengal and, in recent years, Gujarat and some less-developed states. In the period 2003/2004 to 2006/2007, Chhattisgarh, Madhya Pradesh, Orissa and Rajasthan have witnessed remarkably high growth rates (Chand, Raju and Pandey 2007; Government of India 2007b, 2008). The old Green Revolution states are also more dominated by bigger landowners than most other Indian states, pointing to the crisis for small-scale farmers being even greater than shown by the average figures, and to the possibility that large-scale modern agriculture is doing a good deal better than the story told by the All-India averages (NCEUS 2008: 81).

The informal economy and classes of labour

A relative decrease in agricultural employment and the squeezing out of the least-profitable farmers can signify healthy capitalist development. The problem for labour arises when job growth elsewhere is insufficient to provide decent alternative employment. In India, most of the economically active population works in the unregulated or informal economy. Enterprises (including farms) employing fewer than ten people are in practice exempt from labour laws and other regulations. In addition, formal-sector enterprises employ an increasing part of their workforce as contract or casual labour, thus avoiding labour laws and regulations (Singh and Sapra 2007). In line with ILO definitions, these unregulated, unregistered and unprotected enterprises and jobs, both wage employment and self-employment and both agricultural and non-agricultural, constitute the informal economy.

Workers in the formal economy are, in principle, protected by labour law and benefit from social protection entitlements such as sick pay and pensions. They tend to be paid a living wage and to have regulated terms and conditions of work. Informal economy workers have none of these benefits. Even when employed in formal-sector enterprises they will be unprotected, poorly paid and have no social security. In smaller informal enterprises they may also face ruthless oppression which can include physical violence (Breman 1996).

The informal economy accounts for 92 per cent of all economically active workers in India. In the non-agricultural sectors, 72 per cent work in the informal economy, including nearly half of the employees working for formal-sector enterprises in casual contracts and informal labour relations. The employment growth of the 1990s was not only historically low; it was also limited to the informal economy (NCEUS 2007: 4), not the least due to government initiatives which formally extended the reach of the unregulated economy.[8] In fact, the increasing informalisation of labour in India forms part of a long-lasting labour-unfriendly development strategy. From the mid 1970s onwards, the Indian government moved decisively towards what Sundar calls 'hard state policies' and 'authoritarian corporatism' (Sundar 2005). Ever since then, employers and consecutive governments have attempted to discipline labour and restructure production to achieve maximum flexibility and a docile and cheap workforce. Government support for the private sector, anti-union policies and activities by companies have weakened organised labour, and more explicit liberalisation and informalisation policies from the early 1990s onwards have further strengthened the anti-labour hand (Banerjee 2005: 123–5; Datt 2002; Harriss-White and Gooptu 2000: 107; Lerche 2007).

Moving to a more detailed analysis of the informal economy, it is useful to establish a hierarchy of occupational categories. The influential WIEGO network (Women in the Informal Economy; Globalizing and Organizing) suggests that, moving from low to high earnings, occupation types form a hierarchy: from industrial outworkers/home workers to casual wage workers, own account operators (self-employed), informal employees and informal employers (Table 4.1). Women are predominantly found at the low end of this pyramid, while men dominate towards the top (Chen 2008: 21). This is a good starting point. Exploring the classes of labour, the focus here will be on employees and self-employed labour. It is analytically useful first to separate wage labour from the

Table 4.1 Occupational hierarchies in India

Income and power	Occupational categories		
	Wage labour	*Self-employment*	
High	Wage labour with formal contract in formal economy	Self-employed with strong asset base	Self-employed with employees
↑	Informal-sector regular wage labour		
	Casual/unprotected wage labour: manufacturing, services		
	Formal-sector outworkers/homeworkers		
	Casual/unprotected wage labour: agriculture		
↓		Survival self-employed	Unpaid family worker
Low	Bonded labour		

Source: Developed from Chen (2008), NCEUS (2007: 4–7) and Bernstein (2008).

self-employed, and second to keep in mind the fact that many labourers circulate between wage labour and (often agricultural) self-employment, be this seasonally or within a lifetime, and that households may have members straddling the two categories.

The wage labour hierarchy in Table 4.1 covers a wide span of labour relations, ordered by levels of protection of labour, and remuneration. This hierarchy is also a hierarchy of powerlessness, ranging from bonded labour, tied to specific employers through interlocked credit, subordinate social status and labour obligations on the one hand, to more free casual labour relations on the other. The occupation hierarchy encompasses, at the bottom, bonded labour, at the top, wage labourers in the formal sector on proper contracts and protected by labour-related legislation. In between, there are categories such as casual agricultural labour, labour working in informal enterprises, outworkers from formal-sector enterprises and casual workers in formal enterprises. Among the self-employed, there are, in turn, two interrelated hierarchies. One relates to scale and ranges from survival-level self-employment by those who have been unable to find work as wage labour, to those who are self-employed with a strong asset base (e.g. consultants, service providers and capitalist farmers). The other relates to status differences among the self-employed, distinguishing between those self-employed who run a business on the one hand and the household or family members who work for them unpaid on the other.

Figure 4.1 presents the hierarchy of occupations in the labouring classes in India, based on NSSO data. More than half the working population are self-employed; even in the non-agricultural sectors, just under half are self-employed.

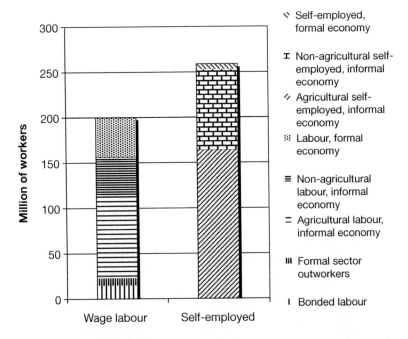

Figure 4.1 Employed and self-employed categories as a proportion of all workers

Source: NCEUS (2007), from NSSO 61st Round 2004–2005; and, for bonded labour, own minimum estimates (Lerche 2007).

Note: 'Agricultural labour, informal economy' adjusted downwards by 1.5 million as 10 per cent of bonded labourers are estimated to be agrarian (division of bonded labour into agricultural and non-agricultural, own rough estimate). 'Non-agricultural labour, informal economy' adjusted downwards by 21.7 million: 13.5 million non-agricultural bonded labourers, and 8.2 million home workers (1999–2000 NSS figures, which are the most recent figures available).

The latest figures (from 1999/2000 to 2004/2005) show that employment growth is mainly driven by self-employment, whereas in the 1990s it was generated by casual labour (Bhalla 2008). It is likely that the data overestimate the number of self-employed: most outworkers/home workers are probably registered as self-employed even though this category is better understood as a type of piece-rate wage labour. Outworkers/home workers exist in many sectors, including bidi making (a country cigarette) and garment production (NCEUS 2007; Mezzadri 2008). It is also not known if the NSSO has counted agricultural workers who are contracted and paid for the harvest of a crop as self-employed workers or as employees. Nevertheless, self-employment is clearly important, even if the precise figures and at least some of the registered growth in self-employment is disputed.

In the occupational hierarchy for wage labour (column one), wage labour employment in the formal economy has highest earnings. This is followed by informal economy employment. Statistical data on average wage earnings and poverty levels as well as case studies of household incomes show that on average non-agricultural labour is slightly less poorly paid than agricultural labour, so non-agricultural labour is set above agricultural labour in the hierarchy.[9] The subcategories of 'outworkers' and 'bonded labourers' have the worst pay and conditions. The numbers of labourers listed as belonging to both these latter categories are likely to be underestimates.[10] Other occupational categories are not enumerated. This includes the important and growing cross-cutting category of seasonal migrant labour (both agricultural and non-agricultural). Reckoned to tally at around 30 million (Srivastava 2005b), they form one of the most disempowered categories of labour. Srivastava estimates that about half are hired through labour contractors, a relationship which often involves advance payments, extreme conditions of work, sometimes physical abuse and very poor and often irregular pay. Many, if not most, migrants working through contractors are bonded labour, with terms and conditions of work, and pay, at the lowest end of the scale, as shown by several case studies, e.g. Breman (2007); Guerin (2009); Guerin *et al.* (2009); Srivastava (2009); Prakash (2009). It needs noting that child labour is not included.

Turning to the hierarchy of the self-employed (column 2), while formal-economy self-employed has highest and most secure earnings, the rest of the vast informal economy is difficult to differentiate. Both agricultural and non-agricultural categories cover a vast range, from surplus-producing self-employed and employers to those engaged in survival activities and unpaid family labour.[11] It is also not known how great a proportion of the self-employed have subsidiary income from wage employment, and vice versa.

Within the labouring classes, there is a straightforward relationship between type of employment and poverty levels. Indian poverty remains abysmally high. According to official figures, in 2004/2005, 28 per cent of the population was below the poverty line, which is set at a near-absolute-minimum calorie intake purchasable with Rs.12 per person per day.[12] In 2004/2005, a staggering 77 per cent of the population were below the Rs.20-per-day line (US$2 in purchasing power parity) (NCEUS 2007: 6; Sengupta, Kannan and Raveendran 2008: 51).

Most poor people belong to households with at least one working member. In keeping with the hierarchy of labour outlined above, the incidence of poverty in the unorganised economy is nearly twice as high as in the organised economy, and higher in agriculture than elsewhere (NCEUS 2007: 24). No official poverty figures exist for outworkers and bonded labourers. However, outworkers are employed because they are cheaper and more flexible than workers based inside firms, and they are thus likely to be poorer. Labour tends to be driven to bonded labour by abject poverty.

Workers below the poverty line are more or less evenly split between the self-employed and the casual labour category, with slightly more being self-employed. Below US$2 a day, self-employed workers dominate in absolute terms while more self-employed than casual labour are well-to-do in relative terms.[13] Among the self-employed, it is not possible to establish a poverty hierarchy in relation to the different types of self-employment. It is likely that those for whom self-employment is due to the unavailability of full-time wage employment will be poorer than labour in wage labour relations. Examples of occupation groups at the foot of the column include basket makers/bamboo product makers, *tendu* leaf collectors, street vendors, cycle rickshaw pullers, rag pickers, bidi rollers and potters (Lerche 1993; NCEUS 2007: 51). Many are disguised wage labourers.

The upper part of the hierarchy of work of the labouring classes is rigid in the sense that it is near impossible for poor people to get access to secure employment in the formal economy or, unless they possess productive assets, to enter the better-off/accumulating self-employed strata. However, there is a great deal of fluidity at the lower end of the labour hierarchy, and between the two main hierarchies, during the life cycle of a labourer, seasonally, and within a household.

Social segmentation among the labouring classes

It is well known that Indian labour markets are segregated along lines of gender, location, religion, ethnicity and caste (see, for example, Harriss-White 2004). Here, the focus is on the caste and ethnic segmentation of the labour market. Groups at the bottom of the caste hierarchy consist of the ex-untouchable Scheduled Castes (SCs, or Dalits), 20 per cent of the population, and the Scheduled Tribes (STs, or Adivasis), 9 per cent (NSSO 2007a: 19). Both groups are greatly discriminated against socially, culturally and economically; something which is reflected in practically all available indicators.[14] They have substantially higher poverty rates than other groups, lower literacy rates, higher infant mortality rates, less access to electricity and so on (Planning Commission 2005; Sengupta, Kannan and Raveendran 2008: 52).

Adivasis are still geographically concentrated in their historic strongholds of the states of the Central Indian Plateau and in the north-eastern states of the country, but there are also Adivasi groups in West and South India. Many Adivasi groups in North-East India have been better able to resist the destruction of their systems of production than the Central Indian groups and tend to be somewhat less poor (Rath 2006). The Adivasis are much more rural than other groups, and they often have access to forest produce and plots of poor-quality land for cultivation. They are also more likely than caste Hindus to undertake wage labour. Throughout India, the Dalit castes have performed menial, degrading and underpaid tasks for the caste Hindus, often in tight-knit but oppressive patron–client relations. The Dalit population is most preponderant in the northern and north-western Indian states, and in Tamil Nadu in the south. They are also more evenly distributed across the rural–urban divide (NSSO 2007a: 20). Both rural and urban Dalits are more likely than any other group to work as wage labourers, and they are less likely than others to be self-employed.

Some Adivasis and Dalits are employed within the government sector through affirmative-action programmes, but nearly all Dalit/Adivasis work in the informal economy: their position in the overall caste hierarchy is an important employment segregator.[15] Within the informal economy, Adivasis tend to be the lowliest employees, followed by Dalits.[16]

Together these two groups form the worst-off segment, with more informal economy Dalit/Adivasi labour below the poverty line than labour belonging to other social groups.[17] Dalits work mainly as unskilled and casual labour, being excluded from skilled work, except those skills and trades that are seen traditionally as polluting and hence left to them – for example carcass and leatherwork – as shown by case studies of employment and labour markets (Breman 2007; Mosse, Gupta and Shah 2005). Within enterprises, a caste hierarchy of labour can often be found, with skills, responsibility, status and pay tending to follow caste lines. It is well documented that Dalit/Adivasi workers are often paid less for the same work as others, and have worse conditions of work (Thorat 2008: 36–7).

Most bonded labourers are Adivasis and Dalits. Migrant workers of low-caste backgrounds are often actively sought out to bond, as they are easier to control and procure on the cheap. Bonded labour dominates in the brick kiln industry, and is common within other sectors such as stone quarries, construction and agricultural labour, especially in harvesting operations. Most bonded labour is from the labour surplus regions of Central India, but disempowered groups of Adivasis and Dalits elsewhere also do debt work (Prakash 2009; Guerin *et al.* 2009; Picherit 2009; Roesch, Venkatasubramaniam and Guerin 2009; Srivastava 2005a, 2005b).

Pro-labour development: policies, class struggle and movements

This section looks at the various types of movements and policy initiatives by and for the labouring classes. It traces how old and new labour organisations have sought to improve conditions and how top–down pro-labour policy initiatives have aimed to influence the conditions of labour without confronting employers directly. It assesses the extent to which such initiatives have benefited those at the bottom of the labour hierarchies. In addition, it is argued that a number of political movements including low-caste political parties and the armed Naxalite insurgency movements active in many tribal areas are also influencing the conditions of the labouring classes, by taking up issues of importance to livelihoods and social oppression, even if these issues are outside the standard arena of labour relations.

Unions and government policies

According to official figures in 2002, only 8 per cent of India's workforce was unionised (Das 2008: 975). Unionisation is at its lowest among casual (informal-ised) labour; and somewhat less extremely low among urban self-employed workers; while regular (formal) workers have unions present in nearly half of their workplaces (NSSO 2007b: iv, 76).[18] Classically unions organised only formal-sector workers, but since the early 1990s all major unions have taken on board the need to organise informal economy workers, with some, limited, success (Sundar 2008: 1069). A leading scholar of labour unions in India describes their standard organising template as involving four steps: a) create special units in the central union to organise informal-sector workers; b) provide legal aid to informal-sector workers; c) demand the constitution of a tripartite council for informal-sector workers and social security measures for the sector; and d) organise demonstrations and hunger strikes to press home the demands (Sundar 2006: 903). The focus appears to be on establishing a regulatory framework for conditions of work and pay, and promoting welfare issues, rather than undertaking more classical grassroots union activities concerning day-to-day conditions of work and pay within enterprises.

By the early 1990s, other organisations were also active in the field. They were often associations which combined aspects of NGO and charity work with union activities for informal economy workers, which might have links with international organisational networks (e.g. StreetNet, WIEGO). They include organisations for the self-employed in the informal economy (e.g. the Self-Employed Women's Association (SEWA) and the National Alliance of Street Vendors (NASVI)), as well as slum movements and new unions (such as the fish workers' union, the National Fish Forum (MFF), and the Adivasi forest workers' association (VIKALP)). In 1995, a coalition of informal-sector unions, the National Centre for Labour (NCL), was set up, providing an umbrella for many of them (Bhowmik 2008; Chowdhury 2003; Sinha 2004; Sundar 2006).

Most of these new organisations focus on welfare issues: night shelters/housing, education, health, pensions, etc. Some also provide micro-credit to self-employed people, or help to organise cooperatives of the self-employed and wage workers. There is less emphasis on the 'classic' union issues relating to terms and conditions of employment (Bhowmik 2008; Sundar 2006). The new organisations often focus on government policy. They campaign for better welfare policies, and they help informal labour to access government schemes and programmes, with some success (Mosse, Gupta and Shah 2005; Agarwala 2006).[19]

There is some tension between the classic labour unions and these new organisations, with the unions resisting encroachment on what they see as their territory, by organisations many of which are not membership based, while others are not restricted to wage employees (Sundar 2006). However, they share a core strategy, not only with each other but also with the left parties in India, intellectuals on the left, and the ILO in India and internationally: namely, to put pressure on the government to regulate crucial aspects of the livelihoods of informal labour. The struggle against employers has been replaced by a struggle to secure improvements from government.

A good deal of legislation exists which, if implemented, would lead to major improvements in the livelihoods of informal labour: the Minimum Wages Act, the Inter-state Migrant Workmen Act, the Contract Labour System (regulation and abolition) Act, the Bonded Labour System (abolition) Act and the Factories Act, to list but a few of the most important laws supposed to regulate labour relations. However, the focus of these struggles has been on legislation and government initiatives to improve other aspects of livelihoods. The reason for this is that, given the present weakness of labour in relation to capital and the near impossibility of taking successful action at the workplace, to seek pro-labour government initiatives in areas not directly challenging capital is the best way forward. In this regard, the Construction Workers Welfare Cess Act (1996) is a celebrated piece of legislation. It set up a welfare fund for construction workers and their families, housing loans, children's education, providing support to accident victims, etc. It is funded by a cess/tax of 1 per cent of the construction cost, payable by construction companies employing ten or more workers and by projects costing more than a million rupees. While it remains far from implemented in most parts of India, there has been some progress in Kerala, Gujarat, Tamil Nadu and Madhya Pradesh (Anonymous 2008a; Agarwala 2006: 433). Workers in other industries such as bidi rolling benefit from similar legislation (Agarwala 2006). However, a case study of the bidi industry shows that only around 30 per cent of formally registered workers are eligible to access the welfare fund and that in order to be allocated resources from the fund labourers often have to pay NGOs a processing fee. Moreover, people other than bidi workers appear to receive benefits from the fund, illegally (Madhavi 2006).

Some Central Indian governments have been more susceptible to pro-labour pressure than others. In 2004, the Congress (I) party formed a government which was dependent on the votes of the left parties. In general, the government continued the existing non-labour friendly policies, but in a few areas some pro-labour and pro-poor initiatives have been taken. The National Rural Employment Guarantee Act (NREGA) passed in late 2005 has been the most important so far. The NREGA guarantees a hundred days of manual employment per rural household per year, paid at the statutory minimum wage (which is very often higher that the actual daily wage paid to rural labourers). The programme has gone from covering a third of all districts in India in 2006/2007 to more than half in 2007/2008, to the whole of India in 2008/2009. Unsurprisingly the programme does not run smoothly, with money being siphoned off to intermediaries in many places. Nevertheless, according to official figures it managed to provide on average forty-three days of work to all households who demanded work in 2006/2007. While this is a good first step it has been very unevenly implemented across regions and states. The four states/groups of states which provided most days of work were Rajasthan, Madhya Pradesh, Chattisgarh and the north-eastern states (Dreze and Oldigez 2009; Mehrotra 2008: 27–8). This geographical concentration is interesting as, apart from Rajasthan, these are some of the states with large Adivasi populations. Altogether 37 per cent of the work went to Adivasis and 33 per cent to Dalits according to official figures (Press Information Bureau 2008). (Forty per cent of work under the NREGA went to women.)

The implementation of the NREGA is not only a technical–bureaucratic issue. The employment guarantee has also become a new battleground, with local movements and activists campaigning for its proper implementation. Some state governments are not engaging much with the programme, while in other cases funds are siphoned off to contractors. Proper NREGA implementation would challenge local economic interests directly (contractors, corrupt government officials, employers paying very low wages) and would challenge employers in general through tightening the labour market for all workers including Adivasis and Dalits. Unsurprisingly, several outspoken NREGS activists have been murdered (Anonymous 2008a, 2008b, 2008c; Khera 2008).

Another piece of legislation to which much campaigning has contributed is the Unorganised Sector Worker's Social Security Bill which was passed in a watered-down, non-mandatory form in 2008 (see Jhabvala 2005; NCEUS 2006). One of the goals was to establish welfare funds for all informal labour, but the bill that was finally passed is unlikely to succeed in this (Rajalakhsmi 2009).[20] Welfare funds are very much in line with present ILO policies (ILO 2004). However, there are also clear limits to what can be achieved through this approach, even if such funds were administered properly. Instead of dealing head-on with the ongoing informalisation of work, they provide a way of making informalisation and casualisation more palatable, by providing a basic social security net for the working poor. They also do not deal with conditions of work, nor abominations such as bonded labour. This fits well into the present union strategy of conceding defeat on the bigger issues, in order to achieve at least some improvements for labour. However, even this limited goal has hardly been achieved with the Social Security Bill.

The Indian trade unions' strategy resembles that of labour unions internationally. Throughout the recent decades of neo-liberal policies, organised labour has lost positions and struggles across the board, and has become significantly weakened, as 'labour-unfriendly regimes' have been established (Silver and Arrighi 2000). Unions have moved away from confrontations with individual employers, towards seeking to achieve goals through political campaigns, legislation and high-level agreements, often centred on the 'Decent Work' campaign by the International Labour Office (ILO) (ILO 1999, 2004; Schmidt 2007). The 'Decent Work' agenda is also a referent in the Indian context, cited by academics and unions alike.

Naxalites and caste based movements

The conditions of Adivasi and Dalit workers encompass other issues than the labour market and welfare issues discussed above. The transformation from precapitalist productive activities to present-day conditions has been painful for the politically disempowered Adivasis. Their livelihoods have been forest-based, relying on common property resources and free access to forest produce resources, both for own consumption and for sale to traders. This way of making a living was already being undermined during colonial times. Parts of their lands were gradually taken over by caste Hindus and non-tribal traders profited from their disempowered condition (Bailey 1957). Since Independence these developments have been exacerbated by major development initiatives utilising Adivasi lands for the benefit of other social interests in India – for example large-scale mining exploiting the rich mineral resources in parts of their lands, the building of hydroelectric and irrigation dams, and the use of hill tracts inhabited by Adivasis as military test ranges. One estimate cited in a recent government report is that between 1947 and 2004, 24 million Adivasis and 12 million Dalits have been displaced by such projects. The discrepancy between the level of investment in such projects and the disregard for the often near-starvation conditions affecting sections of the local population speaks volumes about existing power relations. Judging from government-approved plans, the creation of new special economic zones will encroach even further on their lands in the coming years (Banerjee-Guha 2008; Planning Commission 2008; Rath 2006).

Many Adivasi households still rely in part on forest produce but, as outlined above, they have also become wage labourers, often as seasonal migrants to the more developed parts of the country. To a lesser degree, they have also taken up self-employment outside their forest crafts and trades. Individuals may be engaged in different income-earning activities in a yearly cycle, or during a life-time; households may have several income strands to their bow and communities are engaged in a variety of informal labour activities. Underneath such tactics is the disempowerment which has allowed the encroachment onto Adivasi land, discrimination in the labour market and little by way of government services in many Adivasi areas (Rath 2006).

Several 'mainstream' political movements and government policies aim to improve the livelihoods of Adivasis. However, given the poor track record of mainstream politics with regard to pro-Adivasi development, it is unsurprising that the most effective movement has been the Naxalites, a set of armed Maoist organisations. They control large tracts of mainly Adivasi land in the states of Bihar, Jharkhand, Orissa, Chhattisgarh, Madhya Pradesh and Andhra Pradesh – that is, on and around the Central India Plateau. Naxalite dominance is not without its own problems; the movement is undemocratic internally and its rule is dictatorial. It is said to be corrupt and metes out summary justice. Its overall political programme is vague, but it has succeeded in a de facto transfer of some government-owned land to people (following its slogan 'Land to the Tiller') and in its core areas it has ensured the existence of decent welfare systems – facts acknowledged by a recent official report (Planning Commission 2008). It is only logical to find that the struggle led by the Naxalites against their general disempowerment in, and exclusion from, mainstream society may be as important to the Adivasis as government programmes such as the NREGA.[21]

For Dalits, labour relations are not much better than those experienced by Adivasis. Dalits rarely have land or common property rights and, like the labour relations of the Adivasis, theirs are underwritten by extreme social and cultural oppression. Most recently, their struggle against social oppression has been led quite effectively by the low-caste North Indian party Bahujan Samaj Party (BSP). The political strength of the BSP has led to social changes and some improvements in wages and conditions of work in those parts of North India where local grassroots movements have been able to reap the benefit of their high-level political support. For example, during the late 1990s the BSP government in the state of Uttar Pradesh dealt effectively with local atrocities against Dalits. While the BSP did not deal with labour relations directly, tangible results were achieved by attacking social oppression (Lerche 1999).

Everyday resistance and local labour struggles

Amidst the policy agenda-setting and armed struggles, the local-level 'everyday resistance' against oppression and struggles for higher wages should not be forgotten. For some time the struggles of Adivasi and Dalit rural labour have been documented (see, for example, Byres, Kapadia and Lerche 1999). It has also been pointed out that even low-caste bonded labour, which is arguably the weakest of all classes of labour, has some bargaining power. Given that they tend to be hired by labour contractors, and not by the actual employer, much of their bargaining relates to what the contractor has to offer, namely as large an advance payment as possible. Labourers also argue that it is important for them not to stay with the same employer year on year as that would make them seem 'docile' (Guerin 2009; Pitcherit 2009). Prakash points out that sometimes labour contractor and labourers tacitly work together to raise wages; the contractor would benefit from this as well. Bonded labourers may also seek to organise themselves in unions, although this may lead to their dismissal (Prakash 2009). The cost arising from taking action is also highlighted by Bhowmik (2009) who reports on a case in the tea plantation sector where migrant Adivasi bonded labour took strike action. However, while local labour achieved results through this action, the migrant labour failed. The difficulties involved in collective action at this level are obvious, but so also should be the fact that collective action involving even the most disempowered workers can and does take place.

Conclusion

India's labouring classes have not benefited much from the transformation of the Indian economy away from agriculture. Already, research in the 1990s showed that the old dependency relations of rural labour and marginal farmers on dominant social groups in the countryside had loosened. However, for most of the labouring classes this dependence has been replaced with precarious informalised wage labour or survival self-employment (or combinations), while the income from farming marginal plots has dwindled. Government and capital have rolled back the positions of organised labour and have succeeded in extending the fragmentation of labour as well. This has been achieved through the segmentation of the labouring classes. This segmentation is not primarily along the rural–urban divide. Instead, it is organised through types of employment and/or self-employment and according to social status categories, of which the division between the ex-untouchable Dalit, the Adivasi groups and the rest of caste Hindu society is one. At the same time, the labouring classes are in internal flux, with individuals, households and communities straddling several employment categories at the foot of the labour hierarchies with little chance of moving up the hierarchy unless they acquire assets, which is rare. Both the segmentation and the fluidity in the labour classes make it harder for workers to achieve improved terms and conditions of work and pay. Under these conditions labour action against employers is much less common than it used to be – let alone successful labour action.

The strategies of the new unions have responded partly by acknowledging the importance of the broader 'lifeworlds' of the labouring classes, and by including issues such as housing, education, health and pensions in their fields of activities. They have also moved the activities to the level above the individual employer, seeking to establish labour-related rules and regulations at sector and state level, and seeking to engage government in pro-labour reforms in areas that do not directly challenge its informalisation strategy. These policy changes are in line with policies recommended by organisations such as the ILO and the international trade unions, which now argue explicitly that the old direct confrontational policies by the unions against the employers have outlived their usefulness.

There is, however, an important political space with regard to labour activities which directly addresses employers – and also those on whom many of the formally self-employed depend, such as larger traders etc. The era of major strikes might be over, at least for the moment, but everyday resistance and local-level actions still take place, even involving the most depressed segments of the labour force, with impacts on the conditions of the labouring classes.

Indian government policies such as the NREGS and a proper social security scheme could indeed improve the welfare of labourers in India. The NREGS might even succeed in tightening the labour market somewhat, and through that raise the stakes in labour negotiations. That, however, would require the legislation to be properly implemented. There is no reason to believe that this will happen easily. While electoral politics may lead political parties to propagate such policies, it is unlikely that they will do much to ensure their implementation if opposed by powerful interests at state or district level. The non-implementation of pro-poor policies has been the prevailing pattern since Indira Gandhi proclaimed her 'war against poverty' in the 1970s, and still depends on the balance of power at national, regional and local levels.

The status segmentation such as that between Dalits, Adivasis and other segments of the labouring classes serves only to keep these groups locked into the worst kinds of work. It is based on a segmentation of 'lifeworlds', in which all aspects of their lives are affected by social and cultural oppression. It is hardly surprising that Dalits and Adivasis treated as 'non-citizens' may turn to political groups defending them against their conditions of oppression. So-called extremist movements are not separate from the overall struggle of the labouring classes as they deal with some of the basic building blocks of segmentation of these most exploited classes.

So long as the processes of informalisation and the anti-labour policies persist – including policies working against the interests of the self-employed engaged in survival activities – it will continue to be an uphill struggle to improve the conditions of the labouring classes. Unfortunately, with the segmentation of the labouring classes, it is not easy to see how labour might be able to influence core economic policies of the central and state governments. This makes it important to understand the elements of labour activism in their actually existing struggles, even if they are also shaped along other lines of identity, and even if they seem too small to count.

Notes

1 Banaji (2003) and Linden (2005) have argued in similar theoretical terms to Bernstein.
2 Primarily Madhya Pradesh, Chhattisgarh, Jharkhand, Bihar, Orissa, Eastern Uttar Pradesh and parts of Andhra Pradesh.
3 While, by international comparison, this constitutes a fairly slow move away from agriculture, in India it is nonetheless a significant development, both economically and socially.
4 The five states with the lowest share of employment in agriculture are: Kerala, Tamil Nadu, West Bengal, Punjab and Haryana – ranging from 35 to 50 per cent in 2005 (Kannan 2007: 24). Kerala, Punjab and West Bengal are also the states with the highest Net State Domestic Product from agriculture, while Haryana and Tamil Nadu ranked sixth and eighth on this index (Chand, Raju and Pandey 2007: 2531).
5 It was 38 per cent in 2003 (NSSO figures) (NCEUS 2008: 35).
6 According to NSSO data, 54 per cent of the income of all marginal farmers is from wages, 14 per cent from non-farm business, 6 per cent from husbandry and only 26 per cent from cultivation (NCEUS 2008: 34).
7 These agricultural labour figures raise the issue of the need to approach statistics with caution, even those data generally regarded as reliable. Many field researchers have pointed out that most of the so-called agricultural labourers are, in fact, primarily non-agricultural labourers, even if this is not how they are enumerated. There are also problems resulting from the lack of consensus over the enumeration of discrete jobs: for example, is a labourer hired for a full crop harvest (which may well form her/his main agricultural income) counted as wage labour or as a self-employed contract worker?
8 Government regulations, including labour laws, apply only to units above a certain size. The government extended the regulation-free zone significantly by doubling the size of investments allowed by unregulated units (Rani and Unni 2004: 4579).
9 NSSO data shows that average real daily wage earnings of casual workers are lower in agriculture than in non-agriculture (Unni and Raveendran 2007: 199), and poverty data shows higher levels of poverty for casual workers in the primary sector compared to those in the secondary sector (Bhalla 2008: 16).
10 While official figures exist for outworkers, they are likely to be on the low side (NCEUS 2007: 5). No reliable official figures exist for bonded labour; the figure used here is the minimum estimate by Lerche (2007).
11 Of these, only 'employers' and 'unpaid family labour' have been quantified (3 and 23 per cent of all self-employed, respectively) (NCEUS 2007: 50).
12 These figures are disputed. See Patnaik (2007) for the most radical critique, arguing that, in fact, poverty has probably increased during this period. Moreover, applying the 2008 World Bank upwards adjustment of worldwide poverty figures to India would lead to a poverty figure of 42 per cent for 2005 (Ravallion 2008: 35). These new World Bank estimates are also open to critique (Himanshu 2008).
13 The figures are: below US$1 a day: self-employed 48 per cent, against casual labour 45 per cent; the remainder are regular wage employees. Below US$2 a day, the corresponding figures are 57 per cent and 35 per cent; above US$2 per day the figures are 25 per cent and 10 per cent (Sengupta, Kannan and Raveendran 2008).

14 Muslims are another group suffering from discrimination, but it is outside the scope of the present chapter to analyse the specifics of their position (on discrimination against Muslims, see the report by the Sachar Commiteee (Government of India 2006)).
15 Ninety-five per cent of Dalits and Adivasis work in the informal economy (Sengupta, Kannan and Raveendran 2008: 52).
16 Of the Adivasis working in the non-agricultural sectors, casual workers in the unorganised sector make up a larger proportion than is the case for any other group; Dalits come second. Adivasis also have the highest poverty ratios among unorganised sector workers, followed by Dalits (NCEUS 2007: 21–5).
17 Forty-five per cent of all Dalit/Adivasi informal economy workers are below the poverty line and are disproportionally engaged in the least remunerative work (Sengupta, Kannan and Raveendra. 2008: 53).
18 Seventy-nine per cent of both rural and urban casual workers work in enterprises with no union/association. For self-employed the figures were: rural 80 per cent, urban 63 per cent, total 73 per cent. In 2004/2005, 'only' 53 per cent (both urban and rural) of regular wage workers were employed in enterprises with no unions present (NSSO 2007b: vi, 76).
19 While most such organisations undoubtedly are altruistic, cases have been reported of some new organisations being self-seeking, asking for commissions from labourers in order to provide assistance, and then not delivering it (Madhavi 2006).
20 For example, no time frame exists for its implementation, nor are there any mechanisms for dealing with disputes or complaints. Even more than was the case with NREGA, its implementation will depend on power relations in the specific states (Rajalakhsmi 2009).
21 This said, the armed struggle between the Indian government, local vigilante militias armed by the government and the Naxalites is a serious problem for the Adivasis. It is commonplace that ordinary villagers, who tend to be sympathetic to the Naxalites, are killed by the government side, in fake 'encounters'; see, for example, Saha (2009).

Bibliography

Agarwala, R. (2006) 'From work to welfare: a new class movement in India', *Critical Asian Studies*, 38(4): 419–44.
Anonymous (2008a) 'State apathy towards construction workers', *Economic and Political Weekly*, 43(21): 5.
—— (2008b) 'Struggle for right to employment, state apathy towards construction workers', *Economic and Political Weekly*, 43(31): 6.
—— (2008c) 'NREGA activists who paid with their lives: Narayan Hareka (Orissa)', *Down to Earth*, 17(3). Available online: www.downtoearth.org.in/full6.asp?foldername =20080630&filename=news&sec_id=50&sid=46 (accessed 2 March 2009).
Bailey, F.G. (1957) *Caste and the Economic Frontier: A Village in Highland Orissa,* Manchester: Manchester University Press.
Banaji, J. (2003) 'The fictions of free labour: contract, coercion, and so-called unfree Labour', *Historical Materialism*, 11(3): 69–95.
Banerjee, D. (2005) *Globalization, Industrial Restructuring and Labour Standards: Where India Meets the Global*, New Delhi: Sage Publications.
Banerjee-Guha, S. (2008) 'Space relations of capital and significance of new economic enclaves: SEZs in India', *Economic and Political Weekly*, 43(47): 51–9.
Bernstein, H. (2008) *Agrarian Change in a Globalising World: (Final) Farewells to the Peasantry?*, paper presented at the Journal of Agrarian Change Workshop, SOAS, 1–2 May.

Bhalla, G.S. (2008) 'Globalization and employment trends in India', *The Indian Journal of Labour Economics*, 51(1): 1–23.

Bhowmik, S.K. (2008) 'Labour organisations in the twenty-first century', *The Indian Journal of Labour Economics*, 51(4): 959–68.

—— (2009) 'Unfree labour in the plantation system', in J. Breman, I. Guerin and A. Prakash (eds) *India's Unfree Workforce: Of Bondage Old and New*, New Delhi: Oxford University Press.

Breman, J. (1996) *Footloose Labour: Working in India's Informal Economy*, Cambridge: Cambridge University Press.

—— (2007) *The Poverty Regime in Village India*, New Delhi: Oxford University Press.

Breman, J. and Guerin, I. (2009) 'On bondage: old and new', in J. Breman, I. Guerin and A. Prakash (eds) *India's Unfree Workforce: Of Bondage Old and New*, New Delhi: Oxford University Press.

Byres, T.J, Kapadia, K. and Lerche, J. (eds) (1999) *Rural Labour Relations in India*, Special issue, *Journal of Peasant Studies*, 26(2/3) and London: Frank Cass.

Chand, R., Raju, S.S. and Pandey, L.M. (2007) 'Growth crisis in agriculture: severity and options at national and state levels', *Economic and Political Weekly*, 42(26): 2528–33.

Chandrasekhar, C.P. (2007) *The Progress of 'Reform' and the Retrogression of Agriculture*, Macroscan. Available online: www.macroscan.com/anl/apr07/pdf/Agriculture.pdf (accessed 25 April 2007).

Chen, M. (2008) 'Informality and social protection: theories and realities', *IDS Bulletin*, 39(2): 18–27.

Chowdhury, S.R. (2003) 'Old classes and new spaces: urban poverty, unorganised labour and new unions', *Economic and Political Weekly*, 38(50): 5277–84.

Das, S.K. (2008) 'Trade unions in India: union membership and union density', *The Indian Journal of Labour Economics*, 51(4): 969–82.

Datt, R. (2002) 'Industrial relations – the menacing growth of the phenomenon of lockouts', in R.K. Sen (ed.) *Indian Labour in the Post-Liberalization Period*, Kolkata: K.P. Bagchi.

Dreze, J. and Oldiges, C. (2009) 'Work in progress', *Frontline*, 26(4). Available online: www.flonnet.com/fl2604/stories/20090227260410100.htm (accessed 6 March 2009).

Government of India (2006) *Social, Economic and Educational Status of the Muslim Community of India: A Report*, Prime Minister's High Level Committee Cabinet Secretariat, November. Available online: http://minorityaffairs.gov.in/newsite/sachar/sachar.asp (accessed 18 March 2009).

—— (2007a) *Report of the Expert Group on Agricultural Indebtedness*, Department of Economic Affairs, Ministry of Finance, July. Online. Available online: www.igidr.ac.in/pdf/publication/PP-059.pdf (accessed 18 March 2009).

—— (2007b) *Agricultural Statistics at a Glance*, Department of Agriculture and Cooperation, Ministry of Agriculture. Available online: http://agricoop.nic.in/Agristatics.htm (accessed 19 March 2009).

—— (2008) *Agricultural Statistics at a Glance*, Department of Agriculture and Cooperation, Ministry of Agriculture. Available online: http://agricoop.nic.in/Agristatics.htm (accessed 19 March 2009).

Guerin, I. (2009) 'Corridors of migration and chains of dependence: brick kiln moulders in Tamil Nadu', with Venkatasubramanian, G., in J. Breman, I. Guerin and A. Prakash (eds) *India's Unfree Workforce: Of Bondage Old and New*, New Delhi: Oxford University Press.

Guerin, I., Bhukhut, A., Marius-Gnanou, K. and Venkatasubramanian, G. (2009) 'Neo-bondage, seasonal migration, and job brokers: cane cutters in Tamil Nadu', in J. Breman,

I. Guerin and A. Prakash (eds) *India's Unfree Workforce: Of Bondage Old and New*, New Delhi: Oxford University Press.

Harriss-White, B. (2004) 'India's socially regulated economy', *The Indian Journal of Labour Economics*, 47(1): 49–68.

Harriss-White, B. and Gooptu, N. (2000) 'Mapping India's world of unorganised labour', *Socialist Register*, 2001: 89–118.

Heyer, J. (2000) *The Changing Position of Agricultural Labourers in Villages in Rural Coimbatore, Tamil Nadu, between 1981 and 1996*, QEH Working Paper 57, Oxford: University of Oxford.

Himanshu. (2008) 'What are these new poverty estimates and what do they imply?', *Economic and Political Weekly*, 43(43): 38–43.

ILO [International Labour Office] (1999) 'Decent work', *Report by the Director General for the International Labour Conference 87th Session, 1999*. Available online: www.oit.org/public/english/employment/skills/hrdr/publ/017_2.htm (accessed 9 December 2008).

—— (2004) *Economic Security for a Better World*, Geneva: ILO.

Jha, P. (2006) 'Some aspects of the well-being of India's agricultural labour in the context of contemporary agrarian crisis', *The Indian Journal of Labour Economics*, 49(4): 733–56.

Jhabvala, R. (2005) 'Unorganised Workers Bill: in aid of the informal worker', *Economic and Political Weekly*, 40(22/23): 2227–31.

Kannan, K.P. (2007) 'Interrogating inclusive growth: some reflections on exclusionary growth and prospects for inclusive development in India', *The Indian Journal of Labour Economics*, 50(1): 17–46.

Khera, R. (2008) 'Employment Guarantee Act', *Economic and Political Weekly*, 43(35): 8–10.

Lerche, J. (1993) 'The modernisation of relations of dominance between farmers and artisans in Coastal Orissa', *Sociological Bulletin*, 42(1/2): 85–112.

—— (1999) 'Politics of the poor: agricultural labourers and political transformations in Uttar Pradesh', in T.J. Byres, K. Kapadia and J. Lerche (eds) *Rural Labour Relations in India*, London: Frank Cass.

—— (2007) 'A global alliance against forced labour? Unfree labour, neo-liberal globalization and the International Labour Organization', *Journal of Agrarian Change*, 7(4): 425–52.

Linden, M. van der (2005) 'Conceptualising the world working class', in S. Bhattacharya and J. Lucassen (eds) *Workers in the Informal Sector: Studies in Labour History, 1800–2000*, New Delhi: Macmillan India.

Madhavi, P. (2006) 'Organising the invisible and the informal: a study of unions in the beedi industry in Telangana region of Andhra Pradesh', *The Indian Journal of Labour Economics*, 49(4): 948–54.

Mehotra, S. (2008) 'NREG two years on: where do we go from here?', *Economic and Political Weekly*, 43(31): 27–35.

Mezzadri, A. (2008) 'The rise of neo-liberal globalisation and the "New Old" social regulation of labour: a case of Delhi garment sector', *The Indian Journal of Labour Economics*, 51(4): 603–18.

Mosse, D., Gupta, S. and Shah, V. (2005) 'On the margins in the city. Adivasi seasonal Labour migration in Western India', *Economic and Political Weekly*, 40(28): 3025–38.

NCEUS [National Commission for Enterprises in the Unorganised Sector] (2006) 'Social security for unorganised workers, report', New Delhi: NCEUS, Government of India.

—— (2007) *Report on Conditions of Work and Promotion of Livelihoods in the Unorganised Sector*, New Delhi: NCEUS, Government of India. Available online: www.nceus. gov.in (accessed 17 October 2007).

—— (2008) *A Special Programme for Marginal and Small Farmers*, New Delhi: NCEUS, Government of India. Available online: www.nceus.gov.in (accessed 3 December 2008).

NSSO [National Sample Survey Organisation] (2007a) *Household Consumer Expenditure among Socio-economic Groups, 2004–2005*, NSS 61st Round (July 2004–June 2005) Report No. 514, Ministry of Statistics & Programme Implementation, Government of India.

—— (2007b) *Informal Sector and Conditions of Employment in India, 2004–05 (Part – I)*, NSS 61st Round (July 2004 – June 2005) Report No. 519, Ministry of Statistics & Programme Implementation, Government of India.

Patnaik, U. (2007) *Poverty and Neo-liberalism in India*, Macroscan. Available online: www.macroscan.com/anl/jan07/pdf/Poverty_Neoliberalism.pdf (accessed 6 January 2007).

Pitcherit, D. (2009) '"Workers, trust us!" Labour middlemen and the rise of the lower castes in Andhra Pradesh', in J. Breman, I. Guerin and A. Prakash (eds) *India's Unfree Workforce: Of Bondage Old and New*, New Delhi: Oxford University Press.

Planning Commission (2005) *Report of the Task Force on Development of Scheduled Castes and Scheduled Tribes*, Government of India. Available online: http://planning commission.nic.in/ (accessed 3 April 2007).

—— (2008) *Development Challenges in Extremist Affected Areas*, Report of an Expert Group to Planning Commission, Government of India. Online. Available online: http:// planningcommission.nic.in/ (accessed 2 December 2008).

Prakash, A. (2009) 'How (Un)free are the workers in the labour market? A case study of the brick kilns', in J. Breman, I. Guerin and A. Prakash (eds) *India's Unfree Workforce: Of Bondage Old and New*, New Delhi: Oxford University Press.

Press Information Bureau (2008) 'Extension of NREGA throughout the country need peoples active participation – Dr. Raghuvansh Prasad Singh, Government of India', 1 April 2008 press release. Available online: http://pib.nic.in/release/release.asp?relid= 37029 (accessed 5 March 2009).

Rajalakshmi, T.K. (2009) 'Short on goodwill', *Frontline*, 26(4). Available online: www. flonnet.com/fl2604/stories/20090227260411000.htm (accessed 5 March 2009).

Ramaswami, K.V. (2007) 'Regional dimension of growth and employment', *Economic and Political Weekly*, 42(49): 47–56.

Rani, U. and Unni, J. (2004) 'Unorganised and organized manufacturing in India. Potential for employment generating growth', *Economic and Political Weekly*, 39(41): 4568–80.

Rath, G.C. (2006) 'Introduction', in G.C. Rath (ed.) *Tribal Development in India*, New Delhi: Sage Publications.

Ravallion, M. (2008) 'A global perspective on poverty in India', *Economic and Political Weekly*, 43(43): 31–7.

Roesch, M, Venkatasubramaniam, G. and Guerin, I. (2009) 'Bonded labour in the rice mills: fate or opportunity?', in J. Breman, I. Guerin and A. Prakash (eds) *India's Unfree Workforce: Of Bondage Old and New*, New Delhi: Oxford University Press.

Sahi, A. (2009) 'The jungle justice of the trigger happy', *Tehelka Magazine*, 6(5). Available online: www.tehelka.com/story_main41.asp?filename=Ne070209coverstory.asp (accessed 20 February 2009).

Schmidt, V. (2007) *Trade Union Responses to Globalization*, Geneva: ILO.

Sengupta, A., Kannan, K.P. and Raveendran, G. (2008) 'India's common people: who are they, how many are they and how do they live?', *Economic and Political Weekly*, 43(11): 49–63.

Silver, B.J. and Arrighi, G. (2000) 'Workers north and south', *Socialist Register*, 2001: 53–76.

Singh, N. and Sapra, M.K. (2007) 'Liberalization in trade and finance: India's garment sector', in B. Harriss-White and A. Sinha (eds) *Trade Liberalisation and India's Informal Economy*, New Delhi: Oxford University Press.

Sinha, P. (2004) 'Representing labour in India', *Development in Practice*, 14(1/2): 127–35.

Srivastava, R. (2005a) *Bonded labour in India: Its Incidence and Pattern*, Special Action Programme to Combat Forced Labour, Declaration/WP/43/2005, Geneva: ILO.

—— (2005b) 'India: internal migration and its links with poverty and development', in International Organization for Migration (ed.) *Migration, Development and Poverty Reduction in Asia*, Geneva: IOM.

—— (2009) 'Conceptualizing continuity and change in emerging forms of labour bondage in India', in J. Breman, I. Guerin and A. Prakash (eds) *India's Unfree Workforce: Of Bondage Old and New*, New Delhi: Oxford University Press.

Sundar, K.R.S. (2005) 'State in industrial relations system in India: from corporatist to neo-liberal?', *The Indian Journal of Labour Economics*, 48(4): 917–37.

—— (2006) 'Trade unions and the new challenges: one step forward and two steps backwards', *The Indian Journal of Labour Economics*, 49(4): 895–910.

—— (2008) 'What should Indian trade unions do? An agenda for trade unions at the risk of sermonising!', *The Indian Journal of Labour Economics*, 51(4): 1065–82.

Thorat, S. (2008) 'Labour market discrimination: concepts, forms and remedies in the Indian situation', *The Indian Journal of Labour Economics*, 51(1): 31–52.

Unni, J. and Raveendran, G. 2007: 'Growth of employment (1993–94 to 2004–05): illusion of inclusiveness?', *Economic and Political Weekly*, 42(3): 196–9.

5 Poverty

Causes, responses and consequences in rural South Africa

Elizabeth Francis

Introduction

Recent discussion of the analysis of poverty and livelihoods (see Ellis, Chapter 3 in this volume) draws attention to the limitations of currently dominant approaches to development. Debates about definitions of poverty and its measurement do not much advance our understanding of the causes of poverty. Analysing livelihoods in terms of the assets and strategies of the poor opens up space for taking seriously the priorities, choices and initiatives demonstrated by poor people, but it risks underplaying the constraints thrown up by social relations and institutions that systematically benefit the powerful. It also risks making an assumption that such livelihoods are sustainable. This essay draws on recent attempts to bring power relations into analysis of poverty to discuss the lives of people in a remote rural area in South Africa. It examines causes of, and responses to, poverty and the consequences of those responses. People's responses to poverty in this context appear to be becoming unsustainable and their livelihoods seem increasingly fragile. There is no necessary reason why responses to poverty should be sustainable.

Understanding poverty and livelihoods

Understanding poverty matters because of the scale and depth of poverty to be found in many developing countries. Poverty reduction is now at the core of development policymaking and a key commitment of donor agencies. Progress has been made recently in analysing the causes of poverty and in making sense of the responses of poor people to the pressures that place them in poverty. Some of the most interesting work on these issues has been associated with the UK Chronic Poverty Research Centre (CPRC), or has been engaged in debate with the CPRC (Hulme and Shepherd 2003; Bevan 2004; du Toit 2005a, 2005b; Green and Hulme 2005; Hickey and du Toit 2007; Harriss 2007). Research carried out by the CPRC has been diverse, but shares the premise that studying 'the poor' as a homogeneous category is superficial and misleading, particularly where it is coupled with an assumption that their poverty stems from a lack of integration into the market economy (Hulme and Shepherd 2003). Hulme and

Shepherd distinguish the chronically poor from the transient poor, arguing that the causes of their poverty are likely to be qualitatively different, as are the interventions needed to eliminate their poverty. They offer a definition of chronic poverty based on duration, taking five consecutive years as the criterion. This criterion is driven partly by analytic considerations (five years is considered a significant period of time in most cultures), partly by data availability (many panel studies use five-year intervals for data collection) and partly because there is some evidence that people who are poor for five consecutive years remain poor for the rest of their lives. The criterion is essentially arbitrary (Bevan 2004) and may exaggerate differences between those on either side of the cut-off point. Nevertheless, it is a useful attempt to operationalise a distinction between people who seem to be trapped in poverty from those for whom poverty is a shorter-lived experience and who may have some potential to secure, or even improve their living conditions. This is an important first step in disaggregating 'the poor', though it is also essential to recognise that there are many different ways of becoming, and remaining chronically poor and that an analysis which makes sense in one context, or for one group of people, will not work for another (du Toit 2005b).

What makes people poor? Answers to this question reflect analysts' disciplinary backgrounds, theoretical commitments and political judgements (du Toit 2005a). Many mainstream economists conceptualise the answer in terms of asset endowments, responses to stochastic shocks affecting the household's ability to use these assets (ill health, entitlement failure) and conditions in the local, national and international economies (Baulch and Hoddinott 2000). While these conceptual tools can be powerful, they can easily leave important aspects of poverty-generation unexamined, or even obscured, in generalised analysis of risks, contexts and economic trends. This kind of approach does not deal with the fact that many of the most relevant aspects of the external environment are often shaped by systematic factors, particularly unequal power relations. Thus many of the shocks to which poor people are subject are not best understood as stochastic. They are, instead, subject to a set of conditions that leave them constantly vulnerable (Wood and Salway 2000). Additionally, people's ability to gain access to assets, and their ability to translate them into income, are shaped by the workings of labour and product markets, by their access to skills, information and social networks, by norms governing resource use within and beyond the household and by gendered power relations, again within and beyond households. Household structures and relations – whether households are unitary, cooperative or fragmented – also play an important role in determining resource use (Francis 2000). Sociologists and anthropologists are likely to take such considerations as obvious starting points for an analysis of poverty. The challenge for them is to ground this analysis in an understanding of political economy, at the local, national and international levels (McLaughlin 2002; Bevan 2004; Bryceson 2004; Green and Hulme 2005; du Toit 2005a). Da Corta's Chapter 2 in this volume advocates, similarly, a move away from a concern mainly with the proximate drivers of poverty towards a deeper causal analysis of poverty trajectories and escapes.

One needs to take seriously the need to explore the 'lifeworlds' of poor people while also attempting to understand what she terms the 'realist, structural dimension of the reality of the poor'. This puts the point admirably.

In recent years, many researchers and policymakers have responded to calls for a broader approach to poverty analysis by adopting the concept of livelihoods, by which is commonly meant 'the capabilities, assets (stores, resources, claims and access) and activities required for a means of living' (Chambers and Conway 1992). This definition of the object of study allows one to move beyond a focus purely on assets and income to look at resources more broadly and the relationships which shape their use. Livelihoods research has been carried out through diverse methods and for very different purposes.

One approach to livelihoods analysis, Sustainable Livelihoods (SL), has been adopted by a number of donors and agencies, notably the UK Department for International Development (DFID), OXFAM and UNDP (Scoones 1998; Carney 1998; Carney *et al.* 1999; Solesbury 2003). The SL framework adopted by DFID proposes that people construct livelihoods from a portfolio of assets, which consist of a combination of human, natural, financial, social and physical capital, usually portrayed as an asset pentagon. People's ability to construct livelihoods from these assets is shaped by a 'vulnerability context' and by 'transforming structures and processes' which affect livelihood strategies and, hence, livelihood outcomes. The SL framework has several virtues, in particular the way in which it draws attention to a broad range of resources relevant to livelihoods, the encouragement it gives to policymakers to think cross-sectorally, its emphasis on the impact of institutions on resource use and the attention it pays to the agency of poor people. However, the SL framework also has some serious weaknesses. At the broadest level, this framework runs the risk of making it appear that poor people have more agency than they actually have. This problem applies to both the asset pentagon, with its stress on the strengths of poor people, and to the concept of livelihood strategies, which encourages the assumption that people are typically in a position to strategise, something that is often not the case (Wood and Salway 2000; du Toit 2005a, 2005b) There are other problems with the asset pentagon. Poor people's access to resources is shaped by their relationships with the non-poor and powerful. Thus these 'assets' are not just endowments or attributes. They are inextricably relational and these relations have consequences for people's ability to use their assets (Murray 2001). Finally, the term 'sustainable livelihoods' carries with it the assumption that the livelihoods people construct are sustainable, or, at least, that sustainability is a realistic goal for intervention. These are claims that need to be examined, rather than assumed.

Critiques of the SL framework, and of much livelihoods analysis more generally, therefore suggest a different approach to studying poverty. Bevan advocates a sociological approach, by which she means a focus on the ways in which social actors are located within relationships involving differential power. 'These socially construct a range of diverse interlinked dynamic livelihood structures (including "households") and lifeworlds . . . Taken together these small unequal structures constitute larger unequal social structures (political economies/cultural structures) which must also be seen as dynamically constructed, reconstructed and occasionally destroyed through ongoing interactions among people with differential power' (Bevan 2004: 9). Larger structures themselves constitute and are embedded in global political economy and cultural structures.

Bevan's framework is constructed partly through a critique of the CPRC approach to the analysis of chronic poverty, particularly what she sees as an only partially digested inclusion of 'qualitative' approaches to analysing poverty (Bevan 2004). Green and Hulme (2005) go some way towards dealing with these shortcomings, by advocating exploration of the constraints that close off opportunities for upward mobility and the politically entrenched social relations (at the household, community, national and international levels) that produce chronic poverty. Du Toit calls for a 'fine-grained, critical sociology of chronic poverty' and advocates an analysis of the structural dynamics that 'create marginality, maintain vulnerability and undermine agency for poor people' (2005b: 26). He argues that, while livelihoods analysis can offer such an analysis, the SL framework itself is only a rough schema. It can easily lend itself to a reductionist and ahistorical approach. Instead, du Toit advocates an approach that he considers less abstract than that offered by the SL framework of 'households', 'capitals' and 'vulnerability contexts'. He advocates looking at the 'real, social world in which people – individually and in groups – make their decisions, enter into conflict, or make and break alliances' (2005b: 23).

There is some overlap between this approach and Wood's analysis of the constrained choices made by poor people and the consequences these have for keeping them in poverty (2003). Poor people face chronic risks, which are institutionally and relationally generated, in the form of 'inequality, class relations, exploitation, concentrations of unaccountable power and social exclusion' (Wood 2003: 457). Such risks may force them to make choices that deliver short-term security, at the expense of longer-term reductions in the risks they face. These choices may include over strong reliance on family relations, or allegiance to more powerful people, in ways that perpetuate their dependence.

In a recent paper, Hickey and du Toit have begun to flesh out this approach, drawing on what they argue are the closely related concepts of adverse incorporation and social exclusion, or AISE (Hickey and du Toit 2007). They examine political, economic, socio-cultural and spatial dimensions of AISE. Key political dimensions include forms of clientelism and citizenship that bring about or perpetuate AISE. They relate these to processes of state formation, political organisation and political representation. When looking at economic dimensions of AISE, they emphasise the need to explore the ways in which the operation of markets creates or worsens poverty (laid out in Harriss-White 2005). Markets themselves need to be understood as institutions shaped by power relations. Similarly, Harriss advocates redirecting attention in poverty research to 'the analysis of the social processes, structures and relationships that give rise to poverty' (Harriss 2007), advocating the use of case studies. Harriss, rightly, draws a parallel with earlier poverty research carried out broadly within the political economy of agrarian change (e.g. Bernstein 1977, 1990).

Da Corta's discussion of the historiography of 'old' political economy builds on Harriss's argument. She points out that 'old' political economy is now often remembered in caricature as theoretically led and intellectually rigid, while the reality was quite different, with a plethora of empirically careful and self-critical village-level studies. At its best, this approach powerfully illuminated the links between levels of analysis – between the workings of markets and states and poor people's (highly constrained) responses, as in the case of Murray's research on the impact of migrant labour in Lesotho (Murray 1981). In this kind of work, a central challenge was to understand those responses, not as something to be 'read off' from the social relations of production, but as the results of interplay between those constraints, culturally shaped practices and some, limited degree of agency.

This discussion implies that poverty analysis should pay close attention to what makes poor people vulnerable, with a focus on several analytic levels (principally the household, local, national, international levels) and the links between them. Key issues include:

- power relations (locally, nationally and internationally);
- how labour, product and land markets work;
- the skills, information and social networks to which people have access;
- norms governing resource use;
- household structures and relationships;
- gendered power relations, within and beyond the household;
- the impact of people's responses to the pressures generated by these structures and processes. (Whether or not these responses can give rise to livelihoods that are sustainable is an open question.)

I attempted to take this approach in research I carried out in South Africa in 1999. In retrospect, my treatment of the higher levels of analysis could have been more systematic, though they were important in shaping my understanding of what I observed at the local level.

Poverty in rural South Africa

The remainder of this chapter examines the causes of and responses to poverty in a relatively remote, but densely populated rural area in North West Province, South Africa. Such areas are common, a legacy of population removals to the 'homelands' carried out by the apartheid regime from the 1950s to the 1980s. The characteristics of people living in such areas are in some ways peculiarly South African – very few have access to agricultural land, while older people have access to government pensions – but in many other respects, particularly in terms of reliance on labour migrancy and the prevalence of unemployment, their predicament resembles that of people living in migrant-labour economies across Eastern and Southern Africa (Francis 2000).

Agrarian restructuring, rural development and land reform

The causes of rural poverty in South Africa stem from historically generated power inequalities. These have not been substantially altered by the configurations of power which have emerged since the transition to democratic rule. Taking the long view, one can observe a shift in the class basis of the state, from the infamous alliance between 'gold and maize' (Trapido 1971), to one dominated by an alliance between industrial, financial and mining capital in the 1970s and 1980s, with landowners playing a less important role. In the 1990s, there has been a further weakening of the power of landowners (particularly the small landowners who have been squeezed out of the farming sector by rising real interest rates) and a rapprochement between capital and the small African middle class.

The ANC's 1994 election platform, the Reconstruction and Development Programme (RDP), was in many ways a compromise between its commitment to overcoming some of the most glaring inequalities of the apartheid era and the imperatives of the political settlement which underlay the transition to democratic rule. The RDP did not envisage large-scale redistribution in most sectors, though it did make a commitment to a major land reform. It planned for ambitious programmes of house construction and service provision, as well as making commitments to address 'economic imbalances' and 'democratise' the economy (ANC 1994). The new government made a significant impact on the provision of infrastructure, housing and services to both urban and rural Africans. Racially based restrictions in the labour, housing and land markets were removed and there is now formal equality of opportunity in the education system. The South African government, unusually for a developing country, makes universal pension provision. In 1994, the new government raised African pensions to the same level as that provided for other population groups. Those elderly people (the large majority) who receive a pension thus have a regular source of income, weakening the link between old age and extreme poverty. A small minority of Africans has benefited from opportunities offered by the new dispensation, gaining highly paid jobs in the public and private sectors or taking advantage of support for emerging businesses.

However, the RDP was effectively abandoned in 1996 and replaced by the neo-liberal 'Growth, Employment and Redistribution' programme (GEAR), which aimed to boost jobs and growth through promoting exports and privatisation. This shift of emphasis was intended to stimulate economic growth by making the South African economy more attractive to foreign direct investment, expanding exports and making the public finances more sustainable. It was hoped that these developments would boost employment and, through a trickle-down effect, reduce poverty. GEAR can also be argued to reflect the interests of an emergent African middle class whose interests lie more in capturing the benefits of economic growth than in redistribution to the poor. GEAR has not been successful on its own terms. Gross domestic product grew only very slowly in the late 1990s, though it has increased at a higher rate since 2000. Employment fell during the 1990s and early 2000s and rose slightly only in 2005. Jobs in manufacturing and mining, which have long been central to the livelihoods of many working-class families, mirrored these trends.

The abolition of apartheid restrictions in employment and education has benefited a significant number of Africans, who have moved into higher education, better-paid employment and business. However, these changes have done little to improve the lives of the large majority. Seekings and Nattrass (2005) attempt to delineate the class structure of South Africa, just before the demise of apartheid and in the years immediately afterwards. Because of the extent of unemployment and the small scale of smallholder agriculture, they suggest that the working class was in the middle of the social structure, with the majority of core working-class households, in regular, relatively well-paid employment, situated in the richer half of the population and predominant in urban areas. The poorer half, the marginal working class and those below this category, constituted the majority in rural areas and consisted of farm workers, domestic workers and those without working members, who depended on remittances or welfare payments.

Seekings and Nattrass suggest that, in the last ten years, there have been some changes to this class structure, but there are also significant continuities. Some Africans have experienced rapid upward mobility into the upper classes and income deciles, while urban workers have received rising wages. However, growing unemployment and the stagnation of both the informal sector and smallholder agriculture meant that the numbers of poor people increased considerably, while income inequality remained high, with Gini coefficient estimates ranging from 0.69 to 0.70 for 2000. Income and Expenditure Surveys (IES) carried out by the government Statistical Services (StatsSA) suggest that the Gini coefficient rose between 1995 and 2000, from 0.65 to 0.69 (Seekings and Nattrass, 2005). The trend towards increasing casualisation of the labour force is heightening the insecurity of some of the most vulnerable people.

Official unemployment data and independent poverty estimates confirm these observations. In 2005, the government's Labour Force Survey indicated that unemployment stood at 26.7 per cent of the labour force nationally and 27.4 per cent in North West Province. A further 14.8 per cent of the provincial labour force was classified as 'discouraged workers'. At the national level, the large majority of the latter are women (StatsSA 2005).[1] Meth and Dias's poverty estimates indicate the impact of such high levels of unemployment on income poverty. They suggest that, in 2002, around 22 million people were living in poverty, and that the number living in poverty rose by at least 2 million between 1999 and 2002 (Meth and Dias 2004).[2]

Insecure employment is often accompanied by other kinds of vulnerability, such as shack fires, floods (from building in flood-prone areas), crime, violence, poor agricultural conditions, illness and death (Aliber 2001). Many households also face the loss of prime-age adults through HIV/AIDS. By 2003, 5.6 million of the population were estimated to be living with HIV (UNAIDS 2004). Such insecurities create psychological damage. The South African Participatory Poverty

Assessment revealed the anxiety suffered by the poor about their ability to cope with unpredictable crises and the resignation to poverty felt by the long-term unemployed, their feelings of voicelessness and social exclusion (May *et al.* 1997, cited in Aliber 2001). Certain groups of people are particularly vulnerable to falling into a state of chronic poverty. Rural Africans are particularly vulnerable, especially the 900,000 households in the former homelands lacking access to arable land. People without permanent work, female-headed households, the disabled, the elderly, former farm workers, AIDS orphans and households of HIV/AIDS sufferers, cross-border migrants and the homeless are all vulnerable to chronic poverty.

The distribution of access to critical resources has changed little. In rural areas, most land is still held in the form of large farms, by white farmers. Most rural Africans remain living on small pieces of land in the former 'homelands'. The labour market remains highly segmented, with Africans concentrated in lower-paid and more insecure work. Ownership of capital is still heavily concentrated in a few hands.

There has been a decisive shift in state support away from marginal, food-grain growers and in favour of export-crop producers (Greenberg 2004). In contrast, asset redistribution has been extremely limited and now looks set to favour a small class of African larger-scale farmers (Hall 2004a). The RDP committed the government to an ambitious target of redistributing around 30 per cent of medium- to high-quality white commercial farmland to landless Africans over five years, through a combination of market and non-market mechanisms. A detailed discussion of the land reform programme is beyond the scope of this chapter (see Murray and Williams 1994; Schirmer, 2000; Cousins 2001; Lahiff and Scoones 2001; Hall 2004a). Briefly, the impact on rural poverty has been very limited (Hall 2004a). The programme was dogged by capacity problems and there was no powerful political constituency putting pressure on the Department of Land Affairs (DLA) to speed up the process or remedy its defects. In 2001, in a major shift of goals away from poverty reduction, the DLA introduced a new programme, Land Redistribution for Agricultural Development (LRAD), which aims to promote a class of full-time farmers, operating on a relatively large scale. It has little to offer the rural poor. It is hard to conclude that rural poverty is a serious political priority. Hall argues that LRAD is an example of post-transition pacting between the state, white agricultural capital and a small class of African, larger-scale farmers (Hall 2004a).

Measures to improve tenure for people living and working on commercial farms have often proved counterproductive, contributing to evictions and job losses (Hall 2004a). Tenure reform in the former 'homelands' has been slow. A Communal Land Rights Act, passed in 2004, vests land rights administration in 'communities', either tribal authorities, in the case of much land in the former 'homelands', or in elected land administration committees. The Act was criticised by community representatives consulted at the Bill stage for failing to clarify or support individuals' land rights or to secure rights for unmarried or widowed women. It was also feared that the Act would cause boundary disputes, external and internal to communities. These concerns were not addressed in the Act (Hall 2004b). Such an arrangement renders vulnerable the large numbers of people, often a majority, who have moved into communities from elsewhere and whose relationship with traditional leaders ranges from good, to distant, to hostile. It also strengthens the latter politically at a time when relationships between them and elected local government remain unresolved and, often, tense. This approach to tenure administration is also vulnerable to land grabbing by the powerful (Cousins 2001).

The focus of rural development activity is now moving away from land reform and provision of infrastructure by central government towards an emphasis on local economic development, on local partnerships between government and non-government bodies (in the private and voluntary sectors) and on popular participation in development planning (Pycroft 2000a). The Integrated Sustainable Rural Development Strategy (ISRDS), published in 2000, charges local government with responsibility for promoting rural development. The plan to improve coordination and to try to encourage locally appropriate forms of development may sound attractive, but there are some major problems. Municipalities face severe capacity problems, while most district municipalities lack the ability to raise sufficient revenue locally (Pycroft 2000b). The ISRDS recognises this, but does not envisage putting any more money into rural development. Instead, the government hopes to draw in private-sector funds. Local authorities are expected to compete with one another to attract projects. This puts poor areas, where revenues and local government capacity are weakest, at a severe disadvantage.

North West Province

North West Province contains many such areas. The province consists of the former 'homeland' of Bophuthatswana, together with the white farming areas and industrial towns of the former Western Transvaal. Bophuthatswana was declared 'independent' of South Africa in 1977, under the Presidency of Lucas Mangope. Supposedly an independent Tswana 'nation', 'Bop' remained closely controlled by the South African state and highly dependent on it, financially and politically.

Politics in Bop revolved around patronage, ethnicity and a re-traditionalisation of local political institutions (Lawrence and Manson 1994; Seiler 1999). Potential opposition was repressed and intimidated and civil society barely existed, a legacy that made it difficult to develop more participatory political institutions after 1994 (Seiler 1999). Local government was vested in the chiefs appointed by the Bop government. Local politics revolved around resource access and service delivery. In their pursuit of an agenda of division, the 'homeland' states practised open ethnic discrimination. Non-Tswanas living in Bop faced harassment by the administration and the security forces and discrimination in the legal system (Seiler 1999). Many found it difficult to get access to land, housing and jobs.

From the 1960s to the 1980s, as the South African state implemented forced removals, hundreds of thousands of people moved into the 'homelands'. The largest numbers arrived in the early 1970s (Surplus People Project 1983). Africans without residence rights were forcibly relocated from urban areas and from 'black spot' settlements in white farming areas. At the same time, larger numbers still moved off white farms and into the homelands. Heavily subsidised by cheap credit, commercial farmers switched to more capital-intensive production methods. The overall demand for farm labour fell, while farmers also replaced permanent workers with seasonal, casual labour.[3] Nattrass estimated that 500,000 'full-time' farm workers left the sector between 1960 and 1971 (Nattrass 1981).

In 1994, the homelands were reincorporated into South Africa. This led to rapid political changes, with the introduction of elected provincial governments. There has also been organisational change at lower levels, with the abolition, or reinvention, of homeland development corporations, which had attempted to coordinate and finance 'development' activities, and their replacement by line ministries accountable to provincial and, ultimately, national government. These changes have had marked effects on the local economies of homeland capitals. In Mafikeng, the capital of North West Province, many jobs have disappeared. Factories whose production was subsidised by the apartheid regime have closed, while public-sector employment has been rationalised.

Political power has moved towards Pretoria, as line ministries follow national policy and rely on nationally generated funding. As we have seen, local government is fiscally weak and has weak capacity. The advent of democratic local government has meant that political power at the local level is no longer the sole prerogative of traditional leaders. However, they still control access to welfare payments (through their power to issue identity documents) and have been reinvested with power over land tenure. Official ethnic discrimination has been abolished, but informants in Madibogo village insisted that divisions between long-standing residents and incomers still mattered and still affected people's access to resources controlled by traditional leaders.

So there are continuities with the Bop era, as well as changes. Most important are continuities in the political economy of the relationship between the former homelands and the wider South Africa. These areas are still migrant-labour economies, with a substantial proportion of households depending on remittances. Many migrants have kept strong links to households based in the homelands: bringing back remittances, returning when retired, ill or unemployed and leaving children in the care of relatives. Keeping a secure base from which to migrate or launch different kinds of livelihood-related activities is critically important. Recession and retrenchments, and increasing casualisation of work across the national economy, underline the importance of prioritising security. However, they make it much more difficult for people to rely on migration to deliver secure incomes. There is thus a contradiction at the heart of the relationship between these areas and the rest of the South African economy.

Madibogo

Madibogo village lies 82 km south-west of Mafikeng, the provincial capital. The 1996 Census recorded a population of around 26,000 people, while almost 7,000 were recorded in the neighbouring village of Madibogopan. Like many other rural settlements in the Province, Madibogo saw a rapid increase in population between the 1960s and the 1980s.[4] The village lies beyond daily commuting distance to any major centre of employment and there are few services. Most people who have moved into Madibogo in the last thirty years were allocated a house site, but have no rights over arable land. Long-standing residents have also been affected by land shortage and many of these also have only a house site, with little space for growing crops or keeping livestock. People who do have rights over land often do not work it, as they lack capital equipment. Some lease their land to white or to African farmers.

The Bophuthatswana state discriminated systematically in favour of the well connected, wealthy and well educated, including in the allocation of access to arable land. Formerly white farms that had been added to the 'homeland', and were owned by the state, were leased to those with good political connections and plentiful resources, in an attempt to create a class of larger farmers (Francis 2000, 2002). In the post-apartheid era, such inequalities persisted. In the Geysdorp area, close to Madibogo, landholders who benefited from these leases were given a purchase option in 1999, despite local demands that the land be returned to communal ownership. The farmers had access to NAMPO, the national maize growers' association, which lobbied the DLA on their behalf. Access to the state was thus vital both for their acquiring the land in the first place and in their successful efforts to hold on to the land after 1994. At Geysdorp, there has been no organised opposition to these developments. Stock from nearby villages often stray onto the farms and crop theft is common, but these covert forms of protest have had no political impact. The winners in the transition from apartheid in this area are the articulate, wealthy and well connected.

The new LRAD land reform also targets the well resourced. Many of those who benefited from the old dispensation are thus also benefiting from the new one, while the rest of the rural population has been bypassed by land reform. The adoption at the national level of a development path that does not generate employment for the low skilled similarly leaves them bypassed. The state has adopted 'rural development' as the solution to their predicament, with a remit for this handed to weak and under funded local government. It is difficult to see how this combination of policies could do anything other than lock the large majority of people in Madibogo into continuing, and deepening, poverty. Allocating large farms to wealthy farmers will generate some local employment, but there is no prospect of changes in land, labour or product markets that could open up escape routes from poverty.[5]

Differentiation and poverty

The following discussion is based on research carried out in 1999. I carried out forty-one separate life history interviews with people in forty different households in the villages of Madibogo and Madibogopan and with farmers on nearby state land at Geysdorp. I used a snowball sampling technique, beginning from several different points (members of a group that had applied for land through the redistribution programme, members of a community gardening project, shopkeepers, traders and teachers, local farmers) and then moving on to people with whom they had connections, as employers, employees, friends and acquaintances. I used a unified interview framework that included questions about contemporary livelihoods and interviews lasting around two hours. The households were chosen in order to capture diversities, rather than to construct a statistically representative sample. Interviewees were chosen to reflect diversities in sources of livelihood, apparent income level and income generation source of the household head.[6]

I have argued that poverty analysis should focus on what makes poor people vulnerable, with an emphasis on power relations (locally, nationally and internationally); on how labour, product and land markets work; on the skills, information and social networks to which people have access; on norms governing resource use; on household structures and relationships; on gendered power relations, within and beyond the household, and on the impact of people's responses to the pressures generated by these structures and processes.

People differed markedly in terms of their incomes, the kinds and extent of the insecurities they faced and in their responses to insecurity. There was a chasm between a very small group of larger-scale farmers and business people, and the vast majority. Understanding the few success stories was as important as investigating how the poor survived, or why some poor households found it more difficult than others to put together a livelihood. My sample, therefore, attempted to capture differences in livelihoods, resource access and income levels as follows:

Group 1: Households which experienced substantial income growth since the 1970s, or which have accumulated land, or access to land and/or developed businesses. Their incomes were well over R50,000 per annum [5 households].[7]
Group 2: Households receiving a regular income, in the form of more than one pension, comparably sized remittances or trading incomes [16 households].
Group 3: Households receiving one pension or small but regular remittances [13 households].
Group 4: Households with irregular incomes [6 households].

Two people in the first group were leasing farms on state land at Geysdorp (171 ha and just over 340 ha, respectively); one, a headmaster, had jointly inherited a farm of 450 ha with his five siblings; one owned two shops and ran a small farm; another leased land on a sharecropping basis and had a small transport business. Their incomes were all well over R50,000 a year. All had constructed multiple livelihoods, combining farming with wage employment or running a small business. Some people had put all of their resources and energy into farming, but they were not the most prosperous farmers. Part-time farmers could draw on wages and business profits for their farming operations, rather than having to reply on high-interest loans. This finding underlines the importance of links between farming, labour markets and product markets and is in line with Ellis's analysis of the drivers of rural economies in Chapter 3 in this volume. Why were there so few people in this position? One reason was the paucity of local, well-paid non-farm employment. Another was the difficulty of making a success of non-farm business activity, for a host of reasons, including low purchasing power, domination of the retail sector by large chains that could undercut local competition, poor communications and the fear of crime.

Success in this strategy depended on the ability to mobilise family and kinship networks between sectors and across space and time, reducing the extent to which risks were co-variant – that is, spreading and/or reducing risks overall.

Ladlong Cornelius Masire (born in 1937) had been leasing a 171 ha farm at Geysdorp since 1974. Ladlong was not putting all his energy into crop farming, however. In 1999, for example, he did not farm the land himself, but, instead, had rented it out to a white farmer in return for half of the crop. The land was important to him – the maize it yielded fed his family and provided fodder for their cattle – but it was far from being his only source of income. Ladlong, his father and brother jointly owned 600 cattle that they kept 230 km away, at Kuruman. His brother looked after the cattle and Ladlong travelled there two or three times a month. Their father and mother divided their time between Kuruman and Geysdorp. The family acted like a firm spread across the wide spaces of the Northern Cape and North West Provinces.[8] Ladlong took most of the decisions about running the Geysdorp farm, but, after the harvest, he would take the paperwork to Kuruman to show his brother. The two of them would take the cheques along to the bank. Their father still had the final say about the sale of cattle, however. He commented: 'When you have a family, you should try different places. When you have a family, they shouldn't be clustered in one place, because when they die, they all die. When they are in different environments, trying to make a living, they won't all die at the same time.'

Such a strategy puts a high premium on flexibility, on access to information and on investment in social networks. These attributes are far from being substitutes for labour, skills, capital and access to the state, but they do make it possible to survive. Where they are joined with these resources, the household can prosper. Children and dependent relatives may be called on to manage investments. Such a strategy may spread risk, but it raises problems of labour supervision (see Berry 1986). It can be difficult to discipline kin and they may refuse to be deployed in this way.

People like Ladlong – wealthy, diversifying their livelihood to accumulate resources – stood out. For most people, constructing a livelihood was a difficult business, a matter of managing from month to month on a pension, hoping that a daughter would bring groceries when she next visited, or finding ways to juggle the money needed to buy the next meal with the need to save a little capital to use in trading the following week. As Ellis argues, livelihood diversification can be for growth or for survival.

This major contrast between wealthy farmers and the rest should not obscure the very real differences in life circumstances and livelihood strategies in the rest of the population, the most important of which was the contrast between people with some kind of regular income and those, the poorest of the poor, without this. Twenty-nine people in the sample lived in households with a regular income. Sixteen of these (Group 2) were receiving two pensions, regular remittances or a regular income from trading, underlining the importance of access to employment and pensions as a protection against poverty in rural areas. Such people could feed themselves, and even save a little, but they lacked the resources needed to trade on anything other than a very small scale. Those who did attempt to trade – mainly in cooked food – operated in a market that was close to saturation. Like their better-off counterparts in business, informal traders faced a market that had been largely captured by major retail chains.

Group 3 had lower, but still regular incomes. Some were pensioners, again emphasising the importance of pensions in weakening the link between old age and extreme poverty. Some were receiving small amounts of money from spouses, parents or children living and working elsewhere. Thus, the most important protections against falling into deep poverty came from sources outside the area, from urban employment and from the state's system of social protection.

What made the difference between just about managing, albeit at a low level, and a constant battle to survive, was a predictable source of income. The poorest households (Group 4) had no regular source of income. People retrenched or unable to find work might easily find themselves in this position. Illness, death and work injuries lay behind other people's fall into poverty. Several had been victims of violence. A rise in the number of dependants in a household could also put it under severe strain. Child-fostering and, increasingly common, the return of adult children to live at home, could push a household into deeper poverty. Inability to access welfare payments, through lack of knowledge of the welfare system, or poor relations with traditional leaders who issued the necessary documentation, could prevent people from gaining the resources they needed to deal with these difficulties.

How poor people respond to poverty

Poor people's responses to poverty are shaped by their institutional environment, by the social relations in which they are enmeshed and by the repertoire of culturally shaped practices available to them. They are often forced to prioritise a search for security and predictability over income maximisation. In the absence of access to better-paid work, insecurities explain the attraction of low-paid work, such as farm labouring, which at least offers the prospect of a predictable food supply (farm labourers are often paid partly in sacks of grain).[9] Because of their lack of access to capital, even those who did have access to arable land might choose to let others sharecrop it, rather than farm it themselves. Others sent children to live as dependent, semi-servile herders, with better-off households.

Institutionally generated insecurities also contributed to people's giving priority to maintaining a rural base, from which some household members could move back and forth in search of work, often over long distances. These movements made household composition fluctuate markedly. Such a response may also be explained by a long-standing repertoire of cultural practices. The widespread occurrence of such practices suggests that stable, nuclear families are not the norm in rural South Africa.[10] Thus, people living together may not consider themselves a nuclear family and co-residence may itself be a temporary phenomenon. Children may be distributed among a number of households and move between them (Russell 2004: 42). Household membership may therefore fluctuate greatly, even over short periods. However, this should not obscure the fact that such households usually revolved around one or more people who provided a stabilising base. Complex households were part of the repertoire of culturally shaped practices available, providing a means of surviving in the very precarious situation in which many people found themselves. Clustering around someone with a stable source of income was thus another response to the pressures of poverty. This person might be a grandparent, whose pension was a vital resource, or a younger person receiving remittances from a spouse, parent or sibling.

Lydia Akanyang Tshatsha stood at the centre of one such cluster, in Madibogo. Her father, William Motseki Tshatsha, had been working as a mechanic in a dairy in Klerksdorp, 170 km away, for the last thirty-five years. There were seven children, four sons and three daughters, the youngest of whom was twenty. Lydia herself, now forty, had worked in the dairy for a few years in the early 1980s, and then, escaping a violent husband, worked in a hotel near Springs, on the East Rand, for five years. She came back to Madibogo when her mother died. Her father told her to do this, because there was nobody else to look after the family. Lydia was the stable centre of the household. Her two youngest sisters and her youngest brother, all still at school, lived with her, as did her four children. Another brother, Edwin, had left his three children in Lydia's care a year previously, when his relationship with his partner broke down. The youngest of these children, now four, alternated between the Tshatsha household and that of her mother. Edwin himself had worked as a miner in Rustenberg until two years previously, when he lost his job. He moved to Mafikeng and found work in a shop for five months, but then lost that job and came home for seven months. He had left for Klerksdorp two months previously, hoping that his father could help him find work in the dairy. William's relationship with his children had deteriorated since their mother died. For the first six months 'he took care of us properly', bringing money regularly and sending milk to sell on pension day. Lydia used some of the money to buy chickens, which she slaughtered, stored in the deep freeze and sold on pension day. She also tried selling cooked food, but selling chickens paid better. Then William began a relationship with another woman. He still brought R300–400 home every month, but this was not enough money to trade with.

Lydia was thus responsible for ten other people, in a situation which seemed to have been forced on her by her father. The family's position had become increasingly difficult, vulnerable to unemployment (Edwin's experience) and unable to exert much leverage over a distant father. For these reasons, the family had moved from Group 2 into Group 3. Only Lydia's father's resources were keeping them out of Group 4.

It was difficult to tell whether household instability was increasing. The growing difficulty of finding work was forcing people to move frequently, apparently more often than in the past. There was a striking contrast in this regard between the life histories of older people, who often remained in the same location, and job, for long periods, and younger people, forced to move back and forth between Madibogo and various towns in the region as they looked for work. The contrast between Lydia's father's employment history and that of his son, Edwin, reflects this change. Many such households were female-headed, de facto or de jure. Women in de facto female-headed households were in a structurally weak position, often lacking discretion over resource use, as appeared to be the case for Lydia. Women in de jure female-headed households might have more autonomy, but suffered from lack of access to a spouse's income. In this, their predicament resembled that of women in migrant-labour economies across Southern and Eastern Africa (Francis 2000).

Other complex households consisted of people looking after their siblings' children, pensioners looking after grandchildren, or living with their unemployed adult children and their offspring. Many of these households had come into being through marital breakdown, or from unemployed young adults' inability to set up households on their own. People living in complex households faced several challenges. For older people, the most common of these was the challenge of maintaining their authority over, and getting access to, the wage incomes and labour power of the next generation. People who were fostering children had to negotiate the delicate issue of how such children would be supported when their parents sent little or no money for their upkeep, as seemed to happen quite often.

Modiegi Johanna Mokoatsi and her husband were both receiving pensions. They had provided a stable base and material support for two generations of relatives. As well as her own children, Modiegi had brought up the two sons of her unmarried sister. Now these men, Ishmael and Abraham, had children of their own. Abraham's wife had gone off to work at Stella, 40 km away. He used the house in Madibogopan as a base, leaving his three children with Modiegi while he did a series of insecure, badly paid and short-term jobs on farms and construction sites. He usually returned empty-handed, but Modiegi found it hard to imagine sending the children away.

Modiegi and her husband's pensions placed them in Group 2, enabling them to act as the pivotal point in a complex household where the younger adults were often working elsewhere. Rather than gaining access to remittances, however, *they* were supporting the children. Kinship is still a safety net for such children, but it is being stretched tight by the pressures of unemployment and insecurity. It cannot be assumed to be an indefinitely available resource. Fostering of children and adults' mobility between kin, while an accepted part of a 'culturally specific rubric', must rest, ultimately, on a material base. People with nothing to offer cannot assume that such a rubric will provide support for them indefinitely. Particularly worrying is the impact of unemployment and insecurity on young people's ability to form households, or, indeed, make any kind of long-term plans, as can be seen in the case of 'Teacher', whose circumstances placed him in Group 3. Teacher stood at the centre of a household of young people, unable either to find a stable job or start a household of his own.

Herbert Modisakoma, or 'Teacher', as he was known, was the eldest of Ruth Modisakoma's seven children. Although he was thirty-two, he was still living in the family house in Madibogopan with two of his sisters, a brother and a nephew. His mother, Ruth was away in Johannesburg, working as a maid. Teacher's father, who had a little business doing construction work in Johannesburg, had died in 1992. Ruth's job was their main source of income and she sent them money every month, sometimes R200, sometimes less. One of Teacher's sisters, a woman of twenty-seven, had gone to live with her mother in Johannesburg after falling ill. It was her small son who was living in the house with Teacher. One of his brothers was living in Mafikeng, looking for work after losing his job as a security guard in the Department of Works. Another brother, who was still at school, was living with relatives nearby. The family had no land.

Teacher had left school in 1985, when he was in Standard 5. He tried many different ways to earn a living, but he had never managed to find regular work. After looking for work in Mafikeng, he decided to come back to the village and found casual work on white farms nearby, cutting wood and loading it onto trailers. This brought in about R150 each time. Teacher would try to earn some extra money by persuading the farmer to give him some of the wood, which he then sold in the village. It was hard work and, after two years, he had had enough. 'The job was weakening me and I wasn't getting much out of it.' So he left for Johannesburg, finding a place to live with relatives. He never found a permanent job. He fitted carpets and did some gardening, but the piece jobs dried up, so he decided to come home. 'I felt I was a burden to the people I was living with.'

People with building skills could sometimes find contracts locally, though it was very difficult to make a steady income. When he returned to Madibogopan, Teacher was taken on by a man who did building work. Then he decided to start working for himself. He and two other men occasionally managed to find building work locally.

While these different responses to poverty raised their own, particular challenges – maintaining good relations with distant relatives who might, or might not, be providing support; fulfilling obligations to look after younger siblings, grand-children and more distant kin – some problems could undermine any attempt at strategising. Ill health and disability were recurring themes in the life histories of people in Group 4, as can be seen in the case of Florence Mosadi Moroka.

Florence Mosadi Moroka was twenty-three. She and her husband, Ishmael Onkokame Mphothe, aged forty, lived in a cramped house in Madibogopan with their three children. All of Ishmael's brothers and sisters died of illness. Florence, her brother and sister all had epilepsy. She had never been able to look for work, while Ishmael lost the only steady job he had held, in Mafikeng, when he contracted asthma. He came back to Madibogopan and, for a year afterwards, worked on a new school building. They married in 1994. Afterwards, he started doing seasonal work, weeding and harvesting, but he didn't manage to find another regular job. He heard that there were building jobs going in Rustenburg, but when he got there he discovered that he was supposed to pay a R500 tip to the person who was doing the hiring. Since he didn't have the money, he didn't get the job. Then he tried unsuccessfully to get a job building a new village hall next to the Chief's house in Madibogopan. Florence commented: 'the people who do the hiring practice a kind of apartheid. If they don't know you, they don't hire you.' Florence was unsure whether her epilepsy would entitle her to disability benefit. Besides, she could not apply for it because she did not have an identity card, though she had twice tried to apply for one. The first time, she missed the people. The second time, she was told to produce her parents' marriage certificate. Florence's family was too fragmented for her to be able to meet this demand. Her parents were divorced and neither of them lived in the village. Her mother, a domestic worker, was living 40 km away in Stella. Florence's father was a miner in Kuruman (230 km away) and was sometimes away for as long as four months.

Florence and Ishmael had no land. They used to own four cows, but these died in the 1992 drought. They had three chickens. The only income they could hope to get was from the weeding and harvesting work that Ishmael did for a local white farmer. In 1999, Ishmael weeded crops from February to May and he expected to start harvesting in June. He was paid R10 a day and given the money at the end of the week. He also received some sacks of grain, at harvest time.

The most vulnerable people were those, like Florence and Ishmael, without access to a secure source of income and who could not reduce their insecurity by constructing multiple livelihoods, whether because of disability or ill health, or inability to leave children unattended. There are now more and more such people because of the impact of HIV/AIDs. The South African Department of Health reported an antenatal prevalence rate for HIV in 2006 of 29 per cent in North West Province (which is similar to the national prevalence rate) and a rate of 23.6 per cent in the Central District of the Province, in which Madibogo lies (Department of Health 2007). Social marginality can compound the effects of disability. Other vulnerabilities might seem to be the result of contingencies (illness, death, a quarrel in the family), but these could often be traced back to poverty and insecurity.

To summarise, Madibogo was deeply stratified between a tiny minority with access to the state and to capital and a large majority who lacked these advantages. In this much larger group, people with access to a regular income were able to survive and some could add to this income through a little small-scale trading. They also, often, provided a stable base from which other family members could move around in search of work and with whom they could leave their children. Those without these advantages found themselves in a precarious position, often relying on casual work or occasional remittances, but these were often jeopardised by ill health.

The general trend of national policymaking, which systematically favours the highly skilled and those involved in high-value export sectors, suggests that the latter, highly insecure group will continue to grow. Land reform is now relevant to people in Madibogo only insofar as new, large-scale farmers can provide employment. Rural development is in the hands of institutions with capacity problems and which are financially weak. The key question is therefore whether responses to poverty built on constant movement in search of temporary work are sustainable. Complex households come into being through marital breakdown and/or unemployment among young people unable to form separate households. Russell (2004) rightly underlines how common child fostering and residential instability are in the region, but the sustainability of such arrangements rests on the willingness of kin to foster migrants' children, often with no financial support, and to make their own incomes available to migrants in the periods when they are at home and unemployed. It is difficult to see how this willingness can continue indefinitely.

Some key themes from this case study are:

- the importance of multiple livelihoods (most people gain an income through some combination of remittances – from employment – or casual work). This accords with Ellis's findings in the LADDER project (Ellis, Chapter 3 in this volume);
- the impact of unemployment, financially, in terms of people's increasing need to move around in search of work and in terms of their ability to form and sustain households;
- high levels of dependency – in some households, like those of Lydia Tshatsha, dependency levels are very high and there are just too few incomes supporting too many dependents;
- the role played by pensions in staving off extreme poverty and underpinning complex households;
- the strains put on obligations people recognise towards kin – kinship should not be seen as infinite resource; ultimately, fulfilment of obligations to kin needs a material base.

All of these themes are shaped by power relations, within and well beyond households. The large majority of people in Madibogo have been left behind by a national political transition that has reconfigured political power towards a small, African elite and, in rural areas, has constructed new alliances between this elite and commercial farming capital, particularly exporters. Government adherence to a neo-liberal growth strategy also has little to offer the rural poor. Poverty at the local level is largely caused by these wider processes. People's responses to these processes depend on the material and social resources available to them. These include access to pensions and repertoires of culturally shaped practices, themselves also shaped by power relations within complex households.

Policy implications

The scale of unemployment and poverty in South Africa has prompted calls for a pro-poor distributional regime, including a basic income grant (BIG), which would providing a minimum income for all those not currently receiving a grant or pension (Samson and Standing 2003; Seekings and Nattrass 2005). Proponents argue that a BIG would be both politically acceptable and economically feasible; politically feasible because there is widespread acceptance that the depth of the unemployment problem warrants intervention and economically feasible because the degree of income inequality means that it would be possible to finance the BIG by a large increase in indirect taxes (Le Roux 2002, cited in Seekings and Nattrass 2005). A BIG could make a significant difference to the lives of the poor and make some of the responses to impoverishment outlined above more endurable. However, the levels of support envisaged (R100 a month) would not do more than make life in continued poverty sustainable. A BIG could not tackle 'the constraints that close off opportunities for upward social and economic mobility' (Green and Hulme 2005). Devereux (Chapter 6 in this volume) argues that cash transfers should be accompanied by policies which promote and diversify rural livelihoods at the local level and activism to redress inequalities and injustices in international trade regimes. But there is also a need to change policy at the national level, in order to create the jobs needed to support both the urban population and their rural dependents. Seekings and Nattrass argue that intervention to tackle unemployment requires a new social accord to bring about labour-market reform and policies to create new jobs (Seekings and Nattrass 2005). Such an approach is vulnerable to the charge that it sidesteps the deep power inequalities that have shaped the current distributional regime (du Toit 2005b). However, the alternative on offer is not widespread asset redistribution. Rather, it is continuation of policies that have generated slow, jobless growth.

Conclusions

This chapter examines recent attempts to analyse poverty and the responses of poor people to the pressures that place them in poverty. It identifies a set of key issues for poverty analysis and attempts to show how these can be put to work to understand poverty in a rural area of South Africa. I argue that the approach taken by many mainstream economists leaves important aspects of poverty-generation unexamined, or even obscured. Like da Corta, I advocate an approach which attempts to understand what makes poor people vulnerable, with a focus on the links between the power relations which generate impoverishment and people's responses to impoverishment. In the case study, I discuss the political economy of post-apartheid South Africa, in order to account for the developments in the national economy which are the economic drivers of poverty – and responses to poverty – at the local level (these are principally unemployment, extremely limited land reform and the equalisation of the state pension between races). My case study from Madibogo shows the depth of inequality in this rural area, the critical importance of multiple livelihoods to both the well off and those trying to avoid a fall into extreme poverty. Such livelihoods have become increasingly hard to construct, because of the dearth of regular employment, either locally or within the wider region. Consequently, people looking for work are increasingly mobile and their residential arrangements are correspondingly unstable. While complex households appear to be part of a repertoire of culturally available practices in rural South Africa, the erosion of material resources caused by unemployment is putting the relationships on which they are premised under strain. Rural livelihoods in Madibogo look increasingly unsustainable. Widening safety nets through social security payments may stave off the worst aspects of people's predicaments, but they need to be accompanied by action to stimulate employment.

Acknowledgements

The research on which the case study is based was carried out as a collaborative project with Colin Murray and Rachel Slater, of the University of Manchester, under the title 'Multiple Livelihoods and Social Change', funded by the UK Department for International Development. The project involved comparative research on poverty, livelihoods and social differentiation in North West Province and the Free State, South Africa. I should like to thank Ben Mosiane and Nancy Moilwa, of the University of the North West, who assisted me in the research, and staff at the North West Province Department of Land Affairs.

Notes

1 'Discouraged workers' are not included in the unemployment statistics. Discouraged workers did not take active steps to find employment in the month prior to the survey, but professed a desire to work. Kingdon and Knight (2001) argue that there is strong evidence to support the contention that the latter should be included in unemployment statistics.
2 Meth and Dias used a variant of the headcount method to estimate the number of people falling into the bottom two expenditure classes (R0–399 and R400–799 per household per month), using the September 2002 Labour Force Survey (StatsSA 2003) and the 1999 October Household Survey (StatsSA 2000).
3 De Klerk (1984) and Marcus (1989) give overviews of the impact of agricultural restructuring on employment in the commercial farming sector in this period.
4 It is not possible to give accurate population data to track changes over time. Pre-1994 population data, including the 1991 Bophuthatswana Population Census, are highly unreliable, while the 1996 and 2001 Censuses were also problematic (see endnote 5). Breutz, a government anthropologist, surveyed the area in the mid 1950s and estimated that Madibogo then had a population of about 2,000, while there were 1,800–2,000 people living in Madibogopan (Breutz 1955). In 1983, the Surplus People Project estimated that 20,000 people were living in Madibogo (Surplus People Project 1983), while the 1991 Bophuthatswana Census recorded 22,000 in Madibogo (Bophuthatswana 1993). The 1996 Population Census recorded 26,327 people in Madibogo and 6,817 in Madibogopan (StatsSA 1998).
5 Cf. Green and Hulme (2005: 876): 'Frameworks based on the understanding of poverty reduction as linearly increasing household income or consumption through economic growth are unlikely to generate development policies and mobilize public action that can adequately tackle the underlying causes of poverty. Conceptualizing deprivation in terms of chronic poverty, exploring the constraints that close off opportunities for upward social and economic mobility, and analysing the politically entrenched social relations (household, community, national, and international) that work to produce

the effects that constitute the experience of chronic poverty provides a potential means for deepening understanding and guiding action.'
6 I also conducted interviews dealing with the local and regional institutional context with Paramount Chief Phoi at Madibogo, the chief at Madibogopan, their headmen, local councillors, other local political activists, members of local community-based organisations (CBOs), officials in the Central District Council, the provincial Departments of Land Affairs, Agriculture and Local Government and Planning, and the National African Farmers' Union.
7 In March–May 1999 (the time of fieldwork), R1 was worth approximately £0.67. R50,000 was, therefore, around £33,500.
8 See Ferguson's (1999) description of a similar family 'firm' in rural Zambia.
9 See Sender (2002).
10 Russell stresses the importance of agnatic kinship idioms in shaping people's responses to the pressures of poverty in South Africa, arguing that it is a reworked 'tradition', a 'culturally specific rubric' (Guyer and Peters 1987) and one of many such traditions by which people impose a 'comforting continuity' in the interpretation of their lives (Russell 2004).

Bibliography

Aliber, M. (2001) 'Study of the incidence and nature of chronic poverty and development policy in South Africa: an overview', Chronic Poverty Research Centre Background Paper No. 3. Available online: www.chronicpoverty.org/pdfs/sa.pdf (accessed 15 January 2006).

ANC [African National Congress] (1994) *The Reconstruction and Development Programme*, Johannesburg: African National Congress.

Baulch, B. and Hoddinott, J. (2000) 'Economic mobility and poverty dynamics in developing countries', *Journal of Development Studies*, 36(6): 1–24.

Bernstein, H. (1977) 'Notes on capital and peasantry', *Review of African Political Economy*, 10: 60–73.

—— (1990) 'Taking the part of peasants?' in H. Bernstein, B. Crow, M. Mackintosh and C. Martin (eds) *The Food Question: Profits versus People?*, London: Earthscan.

Berry, S. (1986) *Fathers Work for Their Sons: Accumulation, Mobility and Class Formation in an Extended Yoruba Community*, Berkeley: University of California Press.

Bevan, P. (2004) *Exploring the Structured Dynamics of Chronic Poverty: A Sociological Approach*, ESRC Research Group on Wellbeing in Developing Countries Working Paper 06, University of Birmingham.

Bophuthatswana, Republic of (1993) *Population Census*, Mmabatho: Central Statistical Service.

Breutz, P.L. (1955) *The Tribes of Mafeking District*, Department of Native Affairs, Ethnological Publications No. 32, Pretoria: Government Printer.

Bryceson, D. (2004) 'Agrarian vista or vortex: African rural livelihood policies', *Review of African Political Economy*, 102: 617–29.

Carney, D. (ed.) (1998) *Sustainable Rural Livelihoods: What Contribution Can We Make?*, London: Department for International Development.

Carney, D., Drinkwater, M., Rusinow, T., Neefjes, K., Wanmali, S. and Singh, N. (1999) *Livelihoods Approaches Compared*, London: Department for International Development.

Chambers, R. and Conway, G. (1992) *Sustainable Rural Livelihoods: Practical Concepts for the 21st Century*, IDS Discussion Paper No. 296, Brighton: IDS.

Cousins, B. (ed.) (2001) *At the Crossroads: Land and Agrarian Reform in South Africa into the 21st Century*, Cape Town/Johannesburg Programme for Land and Agrarian Studies, National Land Committee, University of the Western Cape.

De Klerk, M. (1994) 'Seasons that will never return: the impact of farm mechanization on employment, incomes and population distribution in the Western Transvaal', *Journal of Southern African Studies*, 11: 84–105.

Department of Health, South Africa (2007) *National HIV and Syphilis Antenatal Prevalence Survey 2006*. Available online: www.doh.gov.za/docs/reports-f.html (accessed 28 August 2007).

du Toit, A. (2005a) *Poverty Measurement Blues: Some Reflections on the Space for Understanding 'Chronic' and 'Structural' Poverty in South Africa*, Chronic Poverty Research Centre Working Paper No. 55.

—— (2005b) *Chronic and Structural Poverty in South Africa: Challenges for Action and Research*, Chronic Poverty Research Centre Working Paper No. 56.

Ferguson, J. (1999) *Expectations of Modernity: Myths and Meanings of Urban Life on the Zambian Copperbelt*, Berkeley: University of California Press.

Francis, E. (2000) *Making a Living: Changing Livelihoods in Rural Africa*, London: Routledge.

—— (2002) 'Rural livelihoods, institutions and vulnerability in North West Province, South Africa', *Journal of Southern African Studies*, 28(3): 531–50.

Green, M. and Hulme, D. (2005) 'From correlates and characteristics to causes: thinking about poverty from a chronic poverty perspective', *World Development*, 33(6): 867–79.

Greenberg, S. (2004) *Post-apartheid Development, Landlessness and the Reproduction of Exclusion in South Africa*, University of Natal, Centre for Civil Society, Research Report No. 17. Available online: www/nu.ac.za/ccs (accessed 15 January 2006).

Guyer, J. and Peters, P. (1987) 'Conceptualizing the household: issues of theory and policy in Africa, introduction', *Development and Change*, 18(2): 197–214.

Hall, R. (2004a) 'A political economy of land reform in South Africa', *Review of African Political Economy*, 100: 213–27.

—— (2004b) *Land and Agrarian Reform in South Africa: A Status Report 2004*, Programme for Land and Agrarian Studies Research Report No.20, University of the Western Cape. Available online: www.oxfam.org.uk/what_we_do/issues/livelihoods/landrights/downloads/land_agrarian_reform_%20sa_status_report_2004.pdf (accessed 15 January 2006).

Harriss, J. (2007) *Bringing Politics Back into Poverty Analysis: Why Understanding Social Relations Matters More for Policy in Chronic Poverty Than Measurement*, Chronic Poverty Research Centre Working Paper No. 77.

Harriss-White, B. (2005) *Poverty and Capitalism*, QEH Working Paper No. 134, Oxford: University of Oxford.

Hickey, S. and du Toit, A. (2007) *Adverse Incorporation, Social Exclusion and Chronic Poverty*, Chronic Poverty Research Centre Working Paper No. 81.

Hulme, D. and Shepherd, A. (2003) 'Conceptualizing chronic poverty', *World Development*, 31(3): 403–23.

Kingdon, G. and Knight, J. (2001) *What Have We Learned about Unemployment from Microdatasets in South Africa?*, Department of Economics, Centre for the Study of African Economies, University of Oxford. Available online: www.csae.ox.ac.uk/resprogs/usam/social%20dynamics%20paper.pdf (accessed 15 January 2006)

Lahiff, E. and Scoones, I. (2001) *The Politics of Land Reform in Southern Africa*, Cape Town: Programme for Land and Agrarian Studies, Sustainable Livelihoods in Southern Africa research briefing, University of the Western Cape.

Lawrence, M. and Manson, A. (1994) 'The dog of the Boers: the rise and fall of Mangope in Bophuthatswana', *Journal of Southern African Studies*, 20(3): 447–61.

Le Roux, P. (2002) 'Financing a universal income grant in South Africa', *Social Dynamics*, 28(2): 98–121.

Marcus, T. (1989) *Modernising Super-exploitation: Restructuring South African Agriculture*, London: Zed Books.

May, J., Attwood, H., Ewang, P., Lund, F., Norton, A. and Wentzal, W. (1997) *Experience and Perceptions of Poverty in South Africa*, synthesis report for the SA-PPA, Durban: Praxis.

McLaughlin, B. (2002) 'Proletarianisation, agency and changing rural Livelihoods: Forced Labour and Resistance in Colonial Mozambique', *Journal of Southern African Studies*, 28(3): 511–30.

Meth, C. and Dias, R. (2004) 'Increases in poverty in South Africa, 1999–2002', *Development Southern Africa*, 21(1): 59–85.

Murray, C. (1981) *Families Divided: The Impact of Migrant Labour in Lesotho*, Cambridge, Cambridge University Press.

—— (2001) *Livelihoods Research: Some Conceptual and Methodological Issues*, Chronic Poverty Research Centre Background Paper No. 5.

—— (2002) 'Livelihoods research: transcending boundaries of time and space', *Journal of Southern African Studies*, 28(3): 489–509.

Murray, C. and Williams, G. (1994) 'Editorial: land and freedom in South Africa', *Review of African Political Economy,* 61: 315–24.

Nattrass, J. (1981) *The South African Economy: Its Growth and Change*, London: Oxford University Press.

Pycroft, C. (2000a) 'Integrated development planning and rural local government in South Africa', *Third World Planning Review*, 22(1): 87–102.

—— (2000b) 'Democracy and delivery: the rationalization of local government in South Africa', *International Review of Administrative Sciences*, 66(1): 143–59.

Russell, M. (2004) *Understanding Black Households in Southern Africa: the African Kinship and Western Nuclear Family Systems*, Centre for Social Science Research Working Paper No. 7, University of Cape Town.

Samson, M. and Standing, G. (eds) (2003) *A Basic Income Grant for South Africa*, Cape Town: University of Cape Town Press.

Schirmer, S. (2000) 'Policy visions and historical realities: land reform in the context of recent agricultural developments', *African Studies*, 59(2): 143–67.

Scoones, I. (1998) *Sustainable Rural Livelihoods: A Framework for Analysis*, IDS Working Paper 72, Brighton: IDS.

Seekings, J. and Nattrass, N. (2005) *Class, Race and Inequality in South Africa*, New Haven: Yale University Press.

Seiler, J. (1999) 'Bophuthatswana: a state of politics', in J. Seiler (ed.) *Transforming Mangope's Bophuthatswana: Towards Democracy in North West Province*, Johannesburg: *Daily Mail* and *Guardian*.

Sender, J. (2002) 'Women's struggle to escape rural poverty in South Africa', *Journal of Agrarian Change*, 2(1): 1–49.

Solesbury, W. (2003) *Sustainable Livelihoods: A Case Study of the Evolution of DFID Policy*, ODI Working Paper No. 217, London: Overseas Development Institute.

StatsSA (1998) *Population Census, 1996.* Available online: www.statssa.gov.za (accessed 18 January 2006).

StatsSA (2000) *October Household Survey 1999.* Available online: www.statssa.gov.za (accessed 18 January 2006).

StatsSA (2003) *Labour Force Survey September 2002.* Available online: www.statssa. gov.za (accessed 19 January 2006).

StatsSA (2005) *Labour Force Survey 2005.* Available online: www.statssa.gov.za (accessed 18 January 2006).

Surplus People Project (1983) 'Forced removals in South Africa', *The Transvaal*, 5, Cape Town: Surplus People Project.

Trapido, S. (1971) 'South Africa in a comparative study of industrialisation', *Journal of Development Studies*, 7(3): 309–20.

UNAIDS (2004) *Report on the Global AIDS Epidemic* Available online: www.unaids.org (accessed 20 January 2006).

Wood, G. (2003) 'Staying secure, staying poor: the "Faustian Bargain"', *World Development*, 31(3): 455–71.

Wood, G. and Salway, S. (2000) 'Introduction: securing livelihoods in Dhaka slums', *Journal of International Development*, 12(5): 669–88.

6 Seasonal food crises and social protection in Africa

Stephen Devereux

Introduction

Seasonality has always been an important contributor to hunger and poverty in rural Africa, but it has consistently received inadequate analytical and policy attention. Not only does seasonality generate short-term hunger and seasonal food crises, it is also responsible for various 'poverty ratchets' that can have irreversible long-term consequences for household well-being and for productive capacity in rural areas. Because seasonality is predictable and repetitive, rural households and communities have developed complex behavioural responses to buffer its worst effects. But since many 'coping strategies' involve the transfer of assets (including labour) from poor to richer households at less than full value, seasonality is a polarising mechanism that is economically and socially stratifying. In such contexts, safety nets or social protection mechanisms are needed, to correct or compensate for market failures until appropriate forms of economic development makes these interventions redundant.

This chapter brings together two old agendas – seasonality and 'coping strategies' in rural Africa – with one new agenda – social protection. There are several justifications for making this connection. First, although seasonality was well described and understood decades ago, the problems that seasonality creates have not gone away – in some respects they are more severe now than ever. For instance, agricultural liberalisation reforms reintroduced seasonal food insecurity, by dismantling policies that had been initiated by governments to counter seasonality's adverse consequences. Secondly, although the fundamental causes of seasonal hunger need to be tackled at source, the social protection agenda offers effective policy ideas (such as demand-driven 'employment guarantee schemes' and index-linked cash transfers) to mitigate the immediate consequences of seasonality. Thirdly, however, social protection to date has paid too little attention to seasonality and its implications for food insecurity and rural poverty.

The empirical evidence on seasonality, coping strategies and social protection on which this chapter draws comes from fieldwork that I either conducted or led in Ethiopia, Ghana, Malawi and Namibia over a period of almost twenty years. These studies included:

- Ghana 1988/1999: doctoral fieldwork on household responses to a seasonal food crisis in a millet-farming district;
- Namibia 1992/1993: a national survey that enumerated the responses of farmers and pastoralists to a regional drought;
- Malawi 1999, 2001/2002 and 2006/2007: a survey of household responses to an exchange rate devaluation in 1999; a survey of household efforts to survive the famine of 2001/2002; evaluations of seasonal cash transfer programmes in 2006 and 2007;
- Ethiopia 2006: an assessment of how farming families in four highland regions survived the hungry season.

The next section of this chapter ('Seasonality') describes the process of seasonality in rural Africa and its implications for household food security. The section entitled '"Coping" with seasonal food crises in Africa' discusses household responses to seasonal food insecurity and food crises, often misleadingly labelled 'coping strategies', in four African countries. The 'Social protection responses to seasonality' section critically examines public responses to seasonality in agricultural production (input provision), rural labour markets (public works) and food prices (food supply management, price subsidies and cash transfers). The final section concludes.

Seasonality

Seasonality is an under-reported food and health crisis that impoverishes and kills Africans every year, though its severity and duration vary across households and over time. In rain-fed farming systems, where smallholders depend on a single rainy season for most of their staple food needs, the annual 'hungry season', or *soudure*, can last from a few weeks to several months, depending on the extent of self-sufficiency in food production achieved in a given year. The rhythm of rural life in much of Africa is entirely dictated by this seasonal calendar, but the success or failure of self-provisioning agriculture is determined by the unpredictable behaviour of the weather. The mechanism is as repetitive and relentless as the calendar. Smallholders prepare their plots while waiting for the rains to start; they plant their seeds; then they pray that the rains will be adequate and well distributed through the growing season, during which they weed their fields and watch the skies. If the rains are well behaved, their harvest will be good – ideally, enough grain to fill the granary for the coming year – but if the rains are low or erratic, harvests will be poor and the subsequent hungry season will be long and hard – granaries will be depleted sooner and food prices will start rising earlier and more sharply.

Communities most vulnerable to seasonality are rural and derive their livelihoods predominantly from farming. Their farming is 'subsistence-oriented' but they are not 'subsistence' farmers, because they rely on diversified sources of income and because they do not achieve self-sufficiency in most years. They practise low-input, low-output agriculture, using hoes or ploughs rather than tractors and combine harvesters, and their yields are low (typically one-third or less of the potential yield of their plots). Unpaid family labour dominates rather than hired labour. The level of commercialisation, as proxied by the proportion of crop production that is marketed, is low. Their vulnerability derives from a number of sources, including:

- their dependence on a single unreliable source of food and income – rain-fed agriculture – in a context where rainfall is erratic and unpredictable;
- the weakness of rural markets for food, assets and employment;
- inadequate roads, transport systems, telecommunications and other rural infrastructure.

All of these are exacerbated by widespread poverty from household to national levels. Seasonality is a mechanism that perpetuates poverty and retards efforts to escape from it. The direct relationship between seasonality and poverty can be measured through panel surveys that reveal how sensitive poverty headcounts are to the time of year that rural households are interviewed. The Ethiopia Rural Household Survey tracked 1,400 households during the 1994/1995 agricultural year. In the 1994 pre-harvest hungry season, the income poverty headcount was 34 per cent, but this fell to 27 per cent around harvest time and returned to 35 per cent in the 1995 pre-harvest months (Dercon and Krishnan 1998).

Supply and price seasonality in grain and labour markets was well documented by the early 1980s (Seaman and Holt 1980; Chambers, Longhurst and Pacey 1981). Grain prices in unimodal rainfall systems with weak local markets are often extremely variable, reflecting the fact that the single farming season results in a highly skewed availability of locally produced grain in local markets at different times of year. The seasonal pattern of food price variability is entirely predictable, even if the magnitude is not. Grain prices are lowest immediately after the main annual harvest, when supplies are high and demand is low. When the rainy season begins some months later, prices of staple foods start to rise either steadily or sharply, peaking a month or so before the next harvest is due, then fall back as the new produce arrives in the market.

Seasonality also creates a tension within self-provisioning households between what Pierre Spitz (1980) labelled the 'forces of retention' (the need to retain food for subsistence consumption) and the 'forces of extraction' (the need to dispose of food production to meet non-food needs), which explains why deficit food producers with inadequate alternative sources of cash are forced into the seemingly irrational behaviour of selling food for low prices at harvest time, only to buy the same food back for consumption later in the season, when prices are high. This behaviour has been observed during hungry seasons in northern Ghana (Shepherd 1981) and during the 2001/2002 famine in Malawi (Tiba 2005). Even in the less isolated and more commercialised agrarian economy of India, seasonality persists as a significant problem (Olsen 1996).

The adverse consequences of seasonality on the well-being of rural people living in the tropics have also been well understood for decades (Chambers, Longhurst and Pacey 1981; Gill 1991; Ulijaszek and Strickland 1993). Seasonality arises from the production of only one or at most two harvests each year, which has two implications for rural livelihoods: (1) annual household income depends crucially on the size of the harvest, and a single failed harvest can destitute a poor family with limited savings and assets; (2) families with undiversified livelihoods must survive from one harvest to the next on produce harvested only once or twice each year. The situation is compounded by seasonality in health and nutrition: many killer diseases are concentrated in the rainy season (e.g. malaria, diarrhoea, typhoid), when hunger and under-nutrition have already compromised the body's immune system.

The causal linkages between seasonality and hunger were documented by one colonial administrator in northern Ghana as long ago as 1911:

> No-one who has been stationed in FRA FRA at the end of the dry season can fail to be struck with the food difficulty. At the end of every dry season there is a FOOD-SHORTAGE ... There is said to have been a famine in FRA FRA fifteen or sixteen years ago, when children were sold for a calabash of corn or a goat.
>
> (Webster 1911: 1, 5)

In the late 1980s, when I conducted fieldwork in nearby Bawku District, the correlation between rainfall, food prices and malnutrition remained just as evident. The main rainy season in northern Ghana is June through August (Figure 6.1a), which is also the hungry season when grain prices peak in local markets and under-nutrition rates follow (Figure 6.1b). Millet prices can be seen rising steadily from January through July, then collapsing as early harvesting starts. Child malnutrition rates in 1988 started rising in April, as if tracking food prices with a time lag, and fell back slightly but remained high from August onwards – rises in malnutrition take longer to reverse than do rises in food prices.

These adverse consequences of agricultural seasonality are not confined to northern Ghana. We found a similar situation in Malawi, for instance, in 2004/2005. Maize prices and child malnutrition rates are both low during the post-harvest months (May through October), but then start rising together, peaking during the annual hungry season (January–February) before falling around the new harvest (March–April). Figure 6.2 illustrates this relationship, with admissions to a Nutrition Rehabilitation Unit (NRU) in central Malawi as a proxy for child malnutrition.

A survey of farming households in four highland regions of Ethiopia showed that seasonality is gendered. Eighty-six per cent of 960 households interviewed reported suffering a food shortage during 2005/2006, but the prevalence was higher among female-headed (97 per cent) than male-headed (81 per cent) households (Devereux *et al.* 2006b: 19). Disaggregating this indicator by month reveals that food insecurity is experienced most intensely during the mid-year months of June through August – the peak months of the main rainy season – and is least severe around the turn of the year, following the main annual harvest in October–November. Figure 6.3 also illustrates that female-headed households consistently reported higher levels of food shortage.

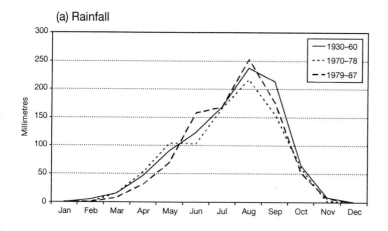

(a) Rainfall

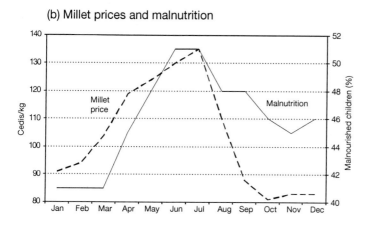

(b) Millet prices and malnutrition

Figure 6.1 Rainfall, grain prices and malnutrition in northern Ghana, 1988
Source: Devereux (1992).

Despite this unequivocal evidence of a close and generally adverse relationship between seasonality and well-being outcomes in rural Africa, there is little evidence that policymakers are even aware of seasonality. Very few policies or plans are seasonally disaggregated, for instance, and school calendars are notoriously insensitive to the cycles of rural activities (which might influence when parents can afford fees or when they are likely to withdraw children from school to assist on the farm). Table 6.1 provides a rare exception to 'seasonality blindness'. Following a poor harvest in 2005 and not long after the devastating famine of 2001/2002 (see below), the Malawi Vulnerability Assessment Committee (MVAC) forecast the number of Malawians 'at risk', and their 'missing food entitlements', for the 2005/2006 agricultural year. Two key features of Table 6.1 are the steady

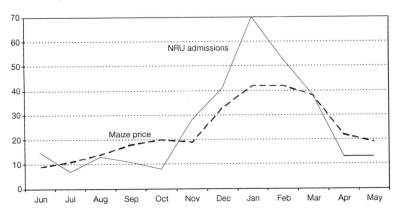

Figure 6.2 Maize prices and NRU admissions in central Malawi, 2004/2005
Source: Devereux *et al.* (2006a: 62).

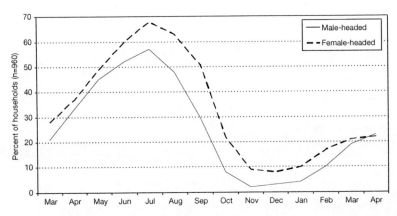

Figure 6.3 Self-reported food shortages in rural Ethiopia by month, 2005/2006
Source: Devereux *et al.* (2006b: 66).

Table 6.1 Seasonal progression of 'missing food entitlements' in Malawi (2005/2006)

Season	Population affected	Per cent of national population	Missing food entitlement (MT)
April–June	1,571,600	13.8	21,100
July–September	2,883,500	25.3	46,400
October–December	3,993,300	35.0	76,000
January–March	5,500,000	48.2	335,400

Source: Malawi Vulnerability Assessment Committee (June 2005: 20).

increase in the proportion of the population expected to be 'at risk' from season to season (starting at 13.8 per cent after the harvest and peaking at almost half the population during the hungry season), and the exponential increase in 'missing food entitlement' as granaries were expected to be depleted on farms across the country. These seasonally disaggregated data allowed humanitarian actors to plan their interventions in a phased manner and to scale up relief assistance during the critical pre-harvest months of early 2006.

The persistence of seasonality as a cause of food insecurity and premature mortality in Africa is shocking, both because it has been well described and understood for at least a century (as noted above) and because effective remedial policies have been available for almost as long (as discussed below). The failure of 'adverse seasonality' to fade away over time also reflects a deeper failure of development in countries where poverty remains widespread, and markets and institutions remain fragmented and weak.

'Coping' with seasonal food crises in Africa

> Africans do not starve, they 'cope'.
> (Seaman 1993: 27)

Seasonality results in an annual food crisis of varying intensity for deficit farming households, who respond or 'cope' with varying degrees of success, depending on the severity of the hungry season, each household's set of assets or 'entitlements to food', and the effectiveness of household and community 'coping strategies'. During every hungry season, poor farming families experience hunger and loss of assets, and many will end the agricultural year more impoverished and vulnerable than ever. Conversely, their wealthier neighbours might well end the year better off than before, since they profit from the transfer of assets from the poor at low prices – one person's 'coping strategy' is another person's accumulation opportunity.

Self-provisioning farmers start each agricultural year not knowing if they are facing the promise of a feast or the threat of famine. If the rains are good then yields will be reasonable, grain supplies in local markets will be adequate and prices will remain affordable throughout the year. The family may not need to buy food at all, if they manage to retain enough grain. But if the rains are inadequate, harvests throughout the area will be below average and 'scarcity prices' will peak when the family runs out of stored grain and becomes market-dependent for food. Smallholder families will then resort to a range of 'coping strategies' such as selling livestock and other assets, or searching for casual employment. But their effective demand for food will be curtailed by falls in asset prices and wage rates, precipitated by excess supplies of assets and labour on local markets. These terms of trade declines between asset values or wages and food prices have been labelled a 'price scissors movement' by Jeremy Swift (Swift and Hamilton 2001) and an 'exchange entitlement decline' by Amartya Sen (1981). An example comes from fieldwork in Ghana in 1988, where the terms of trade between grain and livestock doubled or halved every few months. In January, an adult goat could be exchanged for 33 kg of millet, but in July grain prices were peaking, livestock prices had collapsed and a goat was worth just 15 kg of millet (Devereux 1992). Similarly, during the 2001/2002 famine in Malawi, households incurred an average loss of 53 per cent on 'distress sales' of assets that they sold or exchanged for food (Devereux *et al.* 2003).

How smallholders respond to seasonality can be understood through the lens of famine 'coping strategies'. Shortages of food force self-provisioning smallholders into adopting a range of behavioural responses which can be categorised in various ways, for instance:

1   *rationing consumption* by reducing portions or skipping meals, for adults and/or children;
2   *diversifying diets* by consuming cheaper and/or 'inferior' foods;
3   *reducing expenses* by cutting spending, withdrawing children from school, and so on;
4   *acquiring cash or food* by selling assets, migrating for work, borrowing or begging.

All of these strategies are adopted by households facing seasonal food stress, and they are also adopted, but with more intensity and on a larger scale, during a famine. In terms of intensity, there are qualitative distinctions within each strategy – rationing can be mild, moderate or life-threatening; a loan can be taken interest-free from a friend, at a subsidised rate from a microfinance institution, or at usurious rates from a moneylender. In terms of scale, seasonal hunger typically affects a minority of poor households within rural African communities (or it might affect the majority but relatively mildly), while a famine affects entire districts or regions to a catastrophic extent, reducing even affluent families to destitution and starvation. In other words, within rural communities the behaviour of poor households during a hungry season is almost indistinguishable from generalised responses to famine.

The ability to cope with food stress is determined by each household's economic and social assets, and seasonality exacerbates economic and social differentiation. Two rural families affected by a comparable food deficit will be at different stages on the continuum of 'coping strategies', and the further a family is forced to proceed along the continuum the more serious and long-lasting are the consequences. In his fieldwork in northern Nigeria, Michael Watts found that coping sequences reflect increasing 'commitment' of household resources and 'irreversibility' of consequences. Only the poorest class of households in Watts's survey resorted to desperation measures during a food shortage in 1973/1974 – such as selling farmland or migrating. A few rich households bought grain and sold some livestock, but none sold their labour (a strategy adopted by 94 per cent of the poor) or assets (51 per cent of the poor) (Watts 1983: 440).

This fact – that seasonality is unequalising because the poor adopt responses to food deficits which differ qualitatively and not just quantitatively from those

Table 6.2 Household responses to food deficit in northern Ghana (1988/1989) (in %)

Strategy	Poorest 25 per cent	Richest 25 per cent
Rationed food consumption	93	22
Used off-farm income	78	63
Bought inferior foods	59	4
Relatives or friends helped	59	4
Borrowed/mortgaged crops	56	22
Sold livestock	52	48
Postponed debt repayment	52	15
Ate seeds reserved for planting	33	0
Sent children to relatives	22	0
Postponed a funeral	7	0
Whole household migrated	4	0

Source: Devereux (1992); sample size = 110 households.

adopted by the rich – was confirmed by my fieldwork in Ghana. Seasonal food crises occurred frequently in northern Ghana during the twentieth century, usually triggered by erratic weather (droughts or floods) and/or pest attacks (locusts or armyworms). In 1988, a combination of drought and armyworms resulted in 67 per cent of households in the worst affected district harvesting no millet or sorghum at all. This immediate shock to local food supplies was exacerbated by rapidly rising food prices in local markets some months later (as shown in Figure 6.1) – the classic indicator of a seasonal food crisis.

Table 6.2 summarises coping strategy adoption rates by the poorest and wealthiest quartiles from a sample of 110 households that I interviewed several times during the twelve months between the 1988 and 1989 harvests. The overall pattern reflects adherence to the principles of sequencing by 'irreversibility' and 'level of commitment' identified by Watts (1983). The ranking of responses reflects increasing distress. Strategies that do the least damage were adopted first, while strategies that have potentially devastating consequences for household livelihoods and future viability were deferred to last. Note that some responses to food deficit in Table 6.2 are 'normal' livelihood activities – in particular, selling the off-take from livestock enterprises and using off-farm income to buy food – which explains why these are the only responses that were adopted to roughly the same extent by the richest and the poorest households.

Seasonality affects poorer households more severely, and has longer-term consequences. All eighteen responses recorded in northern Ghana (not all shown in Table 6.2) were deployed by households in the poorest quartile, while those in the richest quartile deployed nine – not because the rich had fewer options (on the contrary), but because their strategies were more effective or lucrative. Rich families survived this hungry season with no lasting damage to their physical or economic health. One wealthy farmer-trader sold a cow to buy all the millet his family needed, but his poor neighbour had to sell several guinea fowl, search for casual labour and mortgage next season's groundnut crop to raise the same amount of cash. Far fewer wealthier households rationed food consumption, borrowed, sought help from relatives and friends or postponed debt payments, and no rich household migrated, ate seeds reserved for planting, or postponed a funeral.

In fact, the gap between the richest and poorest families actually widened because of the polarising impact of this food crisis. There is one crucial feature that the literature on 'coping strategies', with its presumption that food crises are 'Malthusian levellers', overlooked. Hungry seasons and famines can be economically stratifying: rich people can (and do) profit from the distress of others. The converse of impoverishment is accumulation, and food crises accentuate inequality and differentiation within affected communities. In Watts's Nigerian study, while poorer households were buying grain, borrowing cash, and selling their labour and land, wealthier households were selling grain, lending cash, hiring labour and buying land (Watts 1983). Similarly, in northern Ghana in 1988/1989, when poor families were forced to decapitalise, it was their wealthier neighbours who bought up their land rights and exploited their labour. Grain and labour markets were especially stratifying, as they are wherever agricultural seasonality is pronounced. Wealthier households bought grain in bulk at low prices at harvest time, to store for later consumption or profitable resale. Poorer households, buying grain in small quantities later in the agricultural year, paid high prices, which pushed them closer to destitution.

Rural labour markets offer both opportunities and threats for poorer households. 'Off-farm income' for the poorest quartile in Table 6.2 is dominated by casual labour, especially weeding other people's fields, which helps to fill the hunger gap before the next harvest but has several disadvantages. First, working on other farms competes directly with own farm production, so smallholders are forced to allocate their scarce labour resources between earning food for today and growing food for tomorrow – a 'seasonal poverty trap'. Secondly, casual agricultural labour (known as *ganyu* in Malawi, where it is equally important) is economically and socially stratifying, because it redistributes labour from poorer to richer households on extremely unfavourable terms – a day's work for a plate of food – and divides communities into those who offer work and those who beg for work. A visible indicator of these polarising resource transfers in Ghana was the iron roofing that wealthy farmer-traders put up on their brick houses, as if oblivious to the hunger in neighbouring mud-and-thatch compounds.

No starvation deaths were reported in northern Ghana in 1988/1989. A few years later, in 1992, Southern Africa suffered a disastrous rainy season that triggered a major food crisis. Cereal production in the region collapsed to 38 per cent of the five-year mean, 20 million people were declared to be 'at serious risk' of starvation, and more than a million cattle died (Eldridge 2002: 79). Partly thanks to a prompt and effective response – including a trebling of cereal imports into the region – but largely due to the coping capacities and resilience of affected people, a mass mortality famine was averted.

In Namibia, pastoralists in central and southern districts were as badly affected as crop farmers in northern districts, because they suffered a double decline in their ability to access food. First their animals died in large numbers, and second, livestock prices collapsed due to excess supply and deteriorating quality of animals offered for sale. A survey of drought-affected pastoralists recorded a dramatic 'exchange entitlement decline' of 53 per cent due to livestock deaths, and a further 21 per cent due to livestock price declines and maize price rises. The total loss of household entitlement to food derived from livestock in semi-arid districts exceeded two-thirds (69 per cent) of pre-drought value (Devereux and Næraa 1996).

Nonetheless, no famine deaths were reported in Namibia, due to a combination of public action (a Drought Relief Programme that included free food distribution, public works and fodder subsidies) and the effective deployment of 'coping' strategies by drought-affected families (Table 6.3). Namibia's social pension, which transfers cash every month to all citizens over sixty years old, was another extremely important factor, and the predictability of this source of income throughout the crisis period probably explains why the proportion of households adopting strategies such as rationing and borrowing was lower than in Ghana. However, the sequence of adoption (as proxied by their prevalence) is familiar: austerity measures (consumption rationing and cutbacks in expenditure) are preferred to measures that deplete economic and social assets (borrowing, selling livestock, requesting assistance from relatives and friends), which in turn precede strategies that have permanently damaging consequences for household viability (whole household migration, selling key productive assets).

Alongside the data from Namibia in 1992, Table 6.3 provides comparable data on adoption of the identical 'coping strategies' in Ethiopia's famine-prone highlands in 2006, following a good rainy season and an 'average' harvest (Devereux *et al.* 2006b). The two sets of figures are strikingly similar. The sequencing is almost identical – except that Ethiopian farmers sold livestock before borrowing or collecting wild foods, rather than after – and rates of adoption for most strategies are systematically lower in Ethiopia, which is understandable

Table 6.3 Household responses to food deficits in Namibia (1992) and Ethiopia (2006) (%)

Strategy	Namibia 1992	Ethiopia 2006
Rationed food consumption	64	76
Reduced non-food spending	40	28
Borrowed food or cash	37	13
Collected wild foods	36	14
Sold livestock	34	22
Relatives or friends helped	27	10
Migrated to find work	8	10
Sold other assets	6	5

Source: Namibia: Devereux *et al.* (1993: 40); sample size = 830 households; Ethiopia: Devereux *et al.* (2006b: 20); sample size = 960 households.

given that Namibians were struggling to survive one of the worst food crises in living memory in 1992, whereas Ethiopians in 2006 were enjoying a relatively good harvest. But the most striking figure in Table 6.3 is for food consumption rationing, which was actually higher in Ethiopia than in Namibia. This can best be explained by putting the two groups of households surveyed in context.

Namibian farmers and pastoralists are not used to shortages and hunger. Namibia is a wealthier country than Ethiopia and rural households own more assets, including social capital in the form of networks of people to approach for loans or donations. Ethiopian farmers have been subjected to repeated shocks that have undermined their assets and eroded the stock of social capital within highland communities. So Ethiopians facing even a 'normal' seasonal food gap have fewer reserves to draw down, and are inclined to protect what assets they still own by going hungry. Namibians with more diverse asset portfolios were better placed to protect their consumption by following 'normal' livelihood activities, such as converting livestock off-take into food. The fact that at least three-quarters of rural Ethiopians are going hungry every year (assuming this finding is generalisable) provides powerful evidence for one argument of this chapter, that agricultural seasonality is a household-level food crisis even in the best of years. The tolerance by national and global policymakers of persistently high levels of chronic and seasonal hunger in Ethiopia confirms Bradbury's notion of the 'normalisation of crisis' (Bradbury 2000).

Further evidence on 'adverse seasonality' and the limitations of 'coping' with crisis comes from the Malawi famine of 2001/2002, a complex humanitarian disaster that was triggered by erratic weather which reduced the national maize harvest by two-thirds, but was compounded by failures of government and international donors to intervene to bolster food supplies and prevent maize prices spiralling to unaffordable levels. In contrast to Namibia's well-organised Drought Relief Programme, food aid was delivered too late to prevent this avoidable tragedy. No official mortality statistics were published, but estimates from two surveys put the number of deaths in the range of 46,000 to 85,000 (Devereux *et al.* 2003; Devereux and Tiba 2007: 145), making this a far graver crisis than either Ghana in 1988 or Namibia in 1992.

Table 6.4 displays the responses adopted by affected Malawians during the famine, which began with dietary adjustments and searching for work as early as September 2001, when granaries started being depleted. By January the food crisis was peaking and more damaging strategies were adopted, including withdrawal of children from school and borrowing from moneylenders at 'katapila' rates – two for one, repayable within one month. This illustrates the point made earlier about differing intensities of 'coping strategies'; in the absence of functioning financial markets in rural Malawi, moneylenders charge exploitative interest rates. Harvesting of 'green maize' in March provided the first relief from hunger, and the famine was effectively over when a reasonable harvest was secured in April 2002 – followed by the belated arrival of food aid.

One of the arguments of this chapter is that hungry seasons and famines in rural Africa should be understood as food crises that differ mainly in their severity and

Table 6.4 Household responses to famine and seasonality in Malawi (%)

Strategy	Famine (2001/2002)	Hungry season (1999)
Rationed food consumption	100	91
Ate inferior foods	100	89
Did extra casual labour	88	59
Sold or bartered assets	84	15
Postponed ceremonies	73	0
'Immoral behaviours'	71	0
Migrated to find work	39	12
Reduced non-food spending	19	33
Borrowed food or cash	9	7
Relatives or friends helped	3	39

Source: Famine: Devereux *et al.* (2003: 52); sample size = 1,200 households; Hungry season: Devereux (1999); sample size = 104 households.

frequency. Empirical support for this assertion derives from a comparative analysis of both events in Malawi. In 1999, a study of 'coping strategies' in southern Malawi recorded household responses to 'normal' seasonality. All of the behavioural responses to the 1999 hungry season were adopted (more intensively) during the famine three years later, but not all the responses to famine were required during the 'normal' hungry season. One indication that hunger in 2001/2002 was worse than in 1999 is higher levels of adoption; for instance, 84 per cent of households surveyed sold or bartered assets in 2001/2002, but only 15 per cent of households sold assets for food in 1999. A more powerful indicator of the severity of the famine is that several extremely unusual survival strategies were recorded in 2001/2002 (e.g. stealing and begging) that were not mentioned in 1999 (Devereux 1999). The famine period was characterised by a breakdown of social norms, with people in the worst affected communities resorting to transactional sex, stealing maize and vigilante violence against alleged thieves on an unprecedented scale. Respondents labelled these responses 'immoral behaviours'. They would have been inconceivable in the 1999 hungry season, when social cohesion still prevailed and 39 per cent of households received informal support from friends and neighbours – compared to only 3 per cent of communities in the famine year, when very few families had food to share.

This discussion has demonstrated that the impoverishing consequences of seasonal food crises, and the sequencing of household 'coping strategies' reported from six studies in four countries over eighteen years, display a remarkable consistency and continuity, despite covering a diversity of socio-economic and agro-ecological contexts. Seasonality is always and everywhere detrimental to the poor, and socially polarising – wealthier people can exploit weak markets and profit from seasonal hunger. Poorer families balance the imperative to survive until the next harvest against the imperative to protect their longer-term livelihood viability, and they do this by trading off the economic, social and nutritional costs of alternative behavioural responses. Subverting expectations that households facing food deficits will liquidate their assets to protect food consumption, all six surveys find that austerity measures are an immediate response and that retaining scarce household assets is prioritised, even at the cost of going hungry. Comparative data from Malawi and Ethiopia reveal that chronically food-insecure families respond to seasonal food gaps in the same way that entire affected populations attempt to survive famines.

Having considered how rural Africans affected by seasonality strive to 'cope' through their own efforts and resources, the next section of this chapter examines public responses to seasonality and food crises in Africa.

Social protection responses to seasonality

Seasonality is responsible for a range of detrimental impacts to well-being, and to rural productive capacity, so it requires a range of policies to tackle and eventually eradicate the problems that seasonality brings. Conventional rural development is the most effective cure, but this requires accelerated public investments in agricultural research and extension services, and in off-farm employment opportunities. Market integration to reduce price fluctuations is crucial, and this requires improvements in rural roads, transport and communications infrastructure. Governments also need to pursue consistent input supply and output marketing policies, and the private sector should be supported (perhaps even subsidised) to extend credit and insurance services to self-provisioning rural families.

These interventions will reduce the impacts of seasonality, but they will take time and resources. In the short term, social protection can help to reduce some of the polarisation and undermining of productive capacity that results from seasonality and food crises. Poor rural people need to be protected against the consequences of seasonality when their own resources and responses prove to be inadequate, and this is where social protection can play a key role. Social protection has been defined as 'public and private initiatives that provide income or consumption transfers to the poor, protect the vulnerable against livelihood risks, and enhance the social status and rights of the marginalised' (Devereux and Sabates-Wheeler 2004: 7). In the context of the annual hungry season and seasonal food crises, relevant interventions include transfers to smooth consumption and safety nets against shocks. This section examines several examples of these: food supply management, food price subsidies, public works programmes and seasonal cash transfers. Seasonal food insecurity can also be reduced by boosting food production (reducing the need for safety nets and social transfers), so this section also considers policies that enhance access to inputs for poor farmers.

'Adverse seasonality' can be modelled as a series of market failures, starting with input markets (unavailability or unaffordability of agricultural inputs), and including financial markets (lack of credit and savings facilities for farmers facing seasonal cash-flow constraints), labour markets (seasonally skewed availability of rural employment), food markets (sharp commodity price fluctuations between seasons) and asset markets (collapsing exchange value of assets sold when food is scarce and expensive). Household responses to seasonality, or 'coping strategies', are ineffective because poor farmers operate in informal markets that are vulnerable to precisely these market failures: efforts to raise money for food are thwarted by low prices offered for assets, low wages paid to labour, and high interest rates charged for loans. The result is a series of 'exchange entitlement failures' (Sen 1981), which leave the rural poor simultaneously hungry and impoverished.

In this context of predictable seasonal hunger, multiple market failures and an inability to 'cope', public action is clearly needed. Social protection has the potential to redress 'seasonal market failures', or at least to provide compensation to people adversely affected until other measures succeed in reducing poverty, strengthening household resilience and correcting for market failures. But the rapidly evolving social protection agenda is surprisingly reticent on the subject of seasonality. Until the 1980s, African governments used a range of institutions and policies specifically to address seasonality, including input and food price subsidies and grain reserve management. These mechanisms were abolished or weakened by the liberalisation agenda, which asserted that markets rather than governments should be responsible for delivering household and national food security. In reality, the private sector failed to fill the vacuum left by retreating parastatals, and market-dependent deficit food producers were once again exposed to the full consequences of weak or missing markets, which culminates in several months of avoidable hunger every year.

This section examines the evolution of social protection and related public responses to seasonality in Africa. This discussion is limited to interventions that have a 'social protection' emphasis, so a range of 'developmental' interventions – such as adoption of cash crops, or investment in non-farm employment – are not considered here. The discussion is organised around three selected dimensions of seasonality – agricultural production, rural labour markets and food markets – while recognising that many other sectors and interventions also require urgent policy attention.

Responses to food production seasonality: input supplies

Interventions to address seasonal food gaps in farming households can focus on either end of the food system: promoting production by increasing crop yields, or protecting consumption with food or cash transfers when on-farm plus off-farm incomes are inadequate. This section focuses on subsidised input provision to deficit food producers as a form of 'productivity-enhancing safety net' (Devereux 1999). During the 1980s, input subsidies were abolished across Africa under the neoliberal reform agenda, though some countries resisted for several years, fearing the food security consequences. A range of alternative approaches to channelling inputs to small farmers has since been implemented. Two options discussed here are free input distribution (supported by international donors in Malawi) and loans for inputs (supported by international NGOs such as Sasakawa Global 2000).

Agricultural liberalisation and public sector reform processes in Africa were accompanied by drastic cutbacks in agricultural research and extension services, which contributed to declining food production per capita and rising food insecurity. In many countries, NGO projects replaced the Ministry of Agriculture as the main provider of inputs and advice to smallholder farmers. Sasakawa Global 2000, for instance, delivers fertiliser and seeds on a revolving loan basis, with repayment made in kind after harvest. The objective is to promote self-sufficiency by alleviating seasonal input constraints. 'At planting time, usually referred to as "hunger" season, the urgent need to purchase grain to feed the family conflicts with cash for production, i.e. purchase of inputs and hiring of labour' (Sasakawa Global 2000 1989: 4). Although yields often increased and the threat of exclusion from further input loans led to high repayment rates, Global 2000 has been heavily criticised. First, the imperative to recover produce to replenish the revolving fund created incentives to register 'progressive' farmers – in Ghana, extension officers were instructed to look for 'productive, hard-working farmers', and they lost some salary for every bag of produce they failed to collect (Devereux 1992) – so outreach to the poorest and most food insecure farmers was limited. Secondly, revolving funds are vulnerable to covariate shocks such as drought, which compromise the fund's capital base. Thirdly, punitive action against (involuntary) defaulters discouraged many farmers from registering for Global 2000 – in Ethiopia, some farmers were imprisoned when a failed harvest left them unable to repay.

In Malawi, donors assumed a leading role in the agricultural sector after food security deteriorated following structural adjustment reforms of the 1980s and 1990s, which included a Fertiliser Subsidy Removal Programme, the closure of 'unprofitable' social markets run by the Agricultural Development and Marketing Corporation (ADMARC), and repeated currency devaluations, all of which undermined smallholder access to fertiliser and seeds. As productivity declined and seasonal and chronic hunger intensified, the donors turned their attention to restoring access to inputs. Instead of revolving loans (the Global 2000 model) or subsidies (which were politically out of favour in the 1990s, though they are currently enjoying a renaissance), donors led by the UK Department for International Development (DFID) opted to support the free distribution of agricultural inputs.

Between 1998 and 2002, free fertiliser and seed packages were given to Malawian farmers every year, at first on a universal basis (the 'Starter Pack' programme) but later restricted to one-third of farming households (the 'Targeted Inputs Programme'). Starter Packs added 100,150 kg of maize to each farmer's harvest and up to 400,000 tonnes to the national harvest, substantially reducing seasonal food deficits at both national and household levels (Levy 2005). The Targeted Inputs Programme added only 3–4 per cent to smallholder maize production in 2001, compared to a 16 per cent contribution achieved by the Starter Pack in 1999. The Government of Malawi blamed the donors, who cut their funding of free inputs following a bumper harvest in 2000, for exacerbating the food crisis of 2001/2002, but variations in rainfall were probably the main determinant of both good and bad harvest outcomes. Levy (2005) argues that the Starter Pack's crucial food-security impact was on food prices, and hence on access to food, rather than on food production. By extending the months of self-provisioning in deficit farming households, pressure on weak food markets was reduced and prices remained affordable through the hungry season. In 2001/2002, however, weather shocks and the scaled-down Targeted Inputs Programme caused granaries to be depleted early, precipitating sharp rises in maize prices and triggering famine.

Responses to rural labour market seasonality: public works

The best-known 'social protection' response to rural unemployment or under-employment is public works programmes. Labour markets in rural Africa have been described as thin, weak, even non-existent. Seasonality of rural employ-ment opportunities was discussed earlier – most demand for casual labour is agricultural and therefore competes directly with own-farm labour requirements, while chronically food insecure households are often labour-constrained. In northern Ghana during the post-harvest 'slack season', young men migrate to cocoa farms in the south looking for work. In this context, well timed public provision of employment would seem an appropriate response to labour market failures. Yet public works programmes have a chequered history in Africa. Public works have been implemented as an emergency relief measure, as a seasonal food-security programme, and as a rural poverty alleviation mechanism, always with mixed results.

Ethiopia is currently (2005 to 2009) implementing Africa's largest public works programme, reaching close to 8 million people. The Productive Safety Net Programme (PSNP) is essentially an extension of earlier employment-based safety nets in Ethiopia, since 85–90 per cent of beneficiaries are enrolled on the labour-intensive Public Works component and only 10–15 per cent of labour-constrained families receive free food or cash from the Direct Support component. (The Ethiopian government is resistant to social welfare, which it believes is unaffordable and causes dependency.) The PSNP was conceptualised as a way of addressing chronic food insecurity by delivering predictable transfers during the hungry season for three to five years, rather than continuing to respond on an ad hoc basis with annual emergency appeals. By paying workers in cash rather than food, and by selecting infrastructure projects that benefit participating communities directly, the PSNP aims simultaneously to protect household food consumption, to stimulate production and markets, and to create productive assets of lasting value, thereby enabling poor and vulnerable households to 'graduate' out of food insecurity and dependence on food aid.

An evaluation after the first year of the PSNP found that most public works projects undertaken were appropriate and environmentally sustainable. But the majority were of low quality – due to inadequate technical skills of implementing staff and inappropriate construction materials – and financially unsustainable, because no funds were allocated for maintenance (Government of Ethiopia 2006). This complaint is heard about public works programmes almost everywhere. During the drought of 1991/1992, for instance, the government of Namibia launched a national Food-for-Work programme to deliver food aid and construct rural infrastructure such as feeder roads and community water-points, but due to a failure to provide follow-up funding or to establish local maintenance committees, most of this infrastructure deteriorated rapidly once food transfers to programme participants ceased (Devereux 2001).

In terms of addressing food consumption and labour market seasonality, a survey of PSNP participants found that seasonal food shortages in highland Ethiopia are most acute between May and September, while most public works employment in 2005 was provided between April and September (Figure 6.4). Although this appears to represent an almost perfect synchronicity between household food insecurity and a social protection response, this intervention was not well timed, for two reasons. First, since the hungry season is also the farming season, public works competed directly with on- farm demand for labour. Public works should be provided during the slack season, not the hungry season. Secondly, since public works payments were invariably late and erratic, earnings from public works hardly addressed seasonal hunger in PSNP households at all (Devereux *et al.* 2006b).

Malawi is another African country with long experience of public works. Since the 1990s, public works have been implemented in Malawi for various purposes, including to deliver food aid during emergencies, to generate employment opportunities during the hungry season, to build community infrastructure, to provide independent income to women, and, most recently, to ensure access

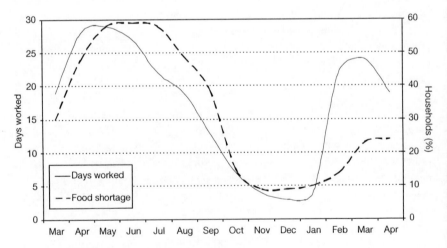

Figure 6.4 Public works employment and food shortage in Ethiopia, 2005/2006

Source: Devereux *et al.* (2006b: 68).

to fertiliser and seeds through 'inputs-for-work'. Several challenges faced in Malawi have wider relevance to global public works debates; these include payment levels and gender quotas.

Cash-for-work wages or food-for-work rations in Malawi (and elsewhere) are typically set slightly below local market wage rates, for self-targeting purposes. This raises ethical questions and can be self-defeating, because the net nutritional benefit of the cash or food transferred is reduced by the amount of energy expended on the works, and most participants are already undernourished. Instead, decent wages should be paid to achieve real impacts on well-being, to enhance dignity rather than stigmatise participants, and to give rural workers bargaining power with informal employers who might otherwise exploit them. Ravallion (1990) found that the Employment Guarantee Scheme in Maharashtra, India, had the unexpected benefit of allowing workers to challenge the monopsony power of employers and negotiate for higher wages, and Kaluwa and Masanjala (2007) found the same effect derived from 'emergency cash transfers' in rural Malawi.

Finally, gender quotas on public works are a further source of controversy in Malawi. The Malawi Social Action Fund targets women and female-headed households, on the grounds that 'female-headed households make up a dispropor-tionate share of the poorest' (MASAF 2004: 16), but this has been criticised for ignoring the reality of poor women's lives. Rural women in Malawi are already overburdened with domestic and community responsibilities, as well as farming and other livelihood activities. Requiring time-constrained women to work long hours for below-market wages, on public works projects that demand heavy manual labour, is hardly gender-sensitive.

Public works programmes are falling out of favour in Africa, as new social protection instruments are preferred that are seen as more progressive and less controversial, such as cash transfers. However, seasonal underemployment persists as a source of vulnerability throughout rural Africa, motivating some form of labour market intervention. One model that merits serious consideration is India's National Rural Employment Guarantee Act (NREGA), which has a decisive advantage over conventional public works because it is demand-driven and guaranteed, rather than supply-driven and discretionary (see Lerche, Chapter 4 in this volume). Every rural Indian household has the right, underpinned by legislation, to claim 100 days of work each year at close to the minimum wage from their local administration. This is precisely the guaranteed seasonal safety net that public works programmes (including the PSNP in Ethiopia) aim at but fail to provide. The NREGA in India responds to demands for work at times of the year when there is no work, not to demands for food at times of the year when work is plentiful.

Responses to food price seasonality

Seasonal food price rises are a direct cause of hunger and premature mortality in rural Africa, making this a logical entry point for social protection. Food price inflation was blamed by one expert witness to the UK Parliamentary Inquiry into the 'Humanitarian Crisis in Southern Africa' for contributing to the 2001/2002 famine in Malawi: 'if you had stabilised the price of maize in 2001 in Malawi no crisis would have occurred' (IDC 2003: EV67). Two responses to food price seasonality are possible: managing food supplies, and stimulating effective demand. Supply-side approaches try to prevent prices from rising, by controlling food availability through open market operations or legislation. Demand-side approaches compensate people adversely affected by price rises, with handouts of food aid or cash. Examples of both come from Ghana and Malawi.

Food supply management has a long history in Africa. The British colonial administration of the Gold Coast frequently banned exports of cereals from the Northern Territories during the 1930s and 1940s, arguing that local farmers sold too much of their produce after harvest, then went hungry when supplies were scarce later in the year. (At least since the Irish Famine of the 1840s, commercial export of staple food out of deficit areas, for resale in more lucrative markets elsewhere, has been a feature of many food crises.) During the 1946 famine, a relief intervention was launched, with the administration purchasing food from surplus regions in southern Ghana and selling it at low prices in the north, while banning exports of grain out of the affected districts. 'A bad harvest in 1945, followed by the delayed harvest this year, produced famine conditions . . . The Government purchased 150 tons of maize in Ashanti and sold it at cost in the worst affected districts . . . Prices reached unprecedented levels . . . Livestock prices slumped following a glut on the market' (Department of Agriculture 1947: 9). 'There is no doubt that the ban on exports of grain from the Northern Territories was of assistance to the natives of North Mamprusi in keeping prices down' (Mamprusi District Administration 1947: 8).

After independence, export bans fell out of favour but the government of Ghana continued to use open market operations to shift food supplies from surplus to deficit regions, through a parastatal – the Ghana Food Distribution Corporation (GFDC) – which was mandated to protect household food security. The GFDC bought rice, millet and sorghum in surplus regions to the south and sold it in northern markets throughout the hungry season, at purchase prices plus a mark-up to cover storage and transport costs.

Governments also manage food supplies by maintaining national grain reserves: holding buffer stocks until supplies are scarce, then releasing grain on to the market or distributing it as food aid, to dampen price rises. Malawi has maintained a sizeable Strategic Grain Reserve (SGR) for decades, but management of buffer stocks is notoriously difficult, and mismanagement of the SGR was another factor that contributed to the famine of 2001/2002. In late 2000, following two bumper harvests, the IMF advised the government of Malawi to sell off the fully stocked SGR and replenish it to a lower level. But the 2001 harvest was poor and the parastatal managing the SGR was unable to buy maize locally, so the grain reserve was empty precisely when it was most needed. Food prices soared and thousands of Malawians died while their government had no capacity to intervene (Devereux and Tiba 2007).

Alternatively, governments can intervene to control prices through legislation and subsidies. Until the 1980s, pan-seasonal and pan-territorial prices were gazetted throughout Africa and defended with government subsidies. Floor prices guaranteed a reasonable income for poor farmers at harvest time, and ceiling prices ensured that food remained affordable to poor consumers during the hungry season. Governments argued that these policies protected vulnerable citizens against market failures, but 'Washington consensus' proponents argued that these government actions were causing market failures by discouraging traders. Price controls and subsidies were phased out under agricultural sector reforms that were enforced through conditionalities. But the assumption that private traders who had been crowded out by government parastatals would fill the gap in agricultural input and output marketing proved to be mistaken in many countries. Instead, poor families were exposed to the full consequences of erratic weather, seasonality and failures of input, credit and commodity markets.

Agricultural liberalisation in the 1990s was followed in Malawi by a series of food crises after 2000. Public action has been dominated by ad hoc humanitarianism – food aid and food-for-work. Instead of this conventional approach to augmenting food supplies in food insecure households, in 2005/2006 and 2006/2007 the NGO Concern Worldwide delivered 'emergency cash transfers' in response to localised crop failures in central Malawi. Unusually, recognising that the purchasing power of cash would be compromised by rising food prices, the monthly transfer was adjusted to reflect food price movements in local markets, to maintain a constant entitlement to food throughout the hungry season. In effect, Concern underwrote the seasonal price risk facing market-dependent deficit farmers. The cash transfers did smooth consumption, as intended. Monitoring surveys found that meals per day stabilised in beneficiary households but fell steadily throughout the hungry season in non-beneficiary households. The cash transfers also enabled beneficiaries to meet a range of non-food needs, including groceries, health and education expenses, debt repayment, investment in farming – even asset accumulation (e.g. purchasing poultry) while avoiding damaging coping strategies such as 'distress sales' of assets for food.

Both these interventions were implemented for just four to five months, but this type of intervention has potential as a seasonal social protection measure even in non-crisis years, if calibrated to the severity of the season and numbers of people affected. The crucial innovation is index-linking the transfer level to local grain prices, which protects rural households against hungry season price spikes where food supplies are constrained. Another important advantage is that cash stimulates demand for food, providing incentives to local farmers and traders (assuming they are able to respond) – unlike imported food aid, which discourages production and trade. Over time, cash transfers could contribute to stabilising supplies, integrating markets and smoothing food prices across seasons. On the other hand, cash transfers alone are not enough. They address the symptoms rather than the causes of seasonal food crises. Unless markets respond favourably to injections of cash, it could be argued that cash transfers are simply underwriting market failures.

Conclusion

Comparing experiences of seasonality and famine from fieldwork in rural communities in several African countries over almost twenty years allows a number of robust conclusions to be drawn:

1   Seasonality continues to be a major contributor to poverty and food insecurity in rural Africa.
2   Household responses to hungry seasons and food crises are remarkably similar across very diverse contexts.
3   Poor households 'cope' with the hungry season in ways that are highly reminiscent of famine 'coping strategies'.
4   Wealthier households deploy fewer 'coping strategies' than poorer households because they have more options and their strategies are more effective.
5   Although the hungry season lasts only a few months each year, it inflicts permanent damage on the physical health and economic viability of poor and vulnerable families.
6   The annual hungry season acts as a polarising mechanism, with food-insecure households transferring resources, including their labour, to wealthier households at undervalued prices.

Even communities that are well adapted to seasonal cycles have to deal with the consequences of seasonality. Their resilience depends on the severity of each hungry season and the resources on which each affected household can draw. Some coping strategies, such as using off-farm income or selling off-take livestock to buy food, are simply applications of normal livelihood activities by self-provisioning farmers to bridge seasonal food deficits. These strategies are adopted at little long-term cost, but when they are exhausted more drastic means of accessing food must be found, such as selling productive assets or taking high-interest loans. It is these 'abnormal' strategies that impoverish food-insecure families and polarise rural communities, as the gap widens between those who are depleting their assets and those who acquire these assets at bargain prices.

Public interventions should aim both to reduce the impact of seasonality and to protect vulnerable households against the adverse consequences of seasonality. Seasonal food insecurity among self-provisioning farmers (paradoxically, one of the groups most vulnerable to seasonality in rural Africa) can be reduced by boosting agricultural production to shorten the hungry-season food gap. In this respect, the abolition of input subsidies across Africa in the 1980s looks decidedly short-sighted, and the range of options for enhancing farmers' access to inputs considered in this chapter – free input distribution, input loans, even the reintroduction of subsidies – all deserve serious consideration, without undermining the emergence of private-sector input markets. Alternatively, rural public works can provide an effective employment-based safety net, but only if (1) employment is offered during the slack season, rather than during the hungry season when labour is most needed on the farm, and (2) public works is demand-driven and guaranteed by the state – as with the National Rural Employment Guarantee Act in India – rather than supply-driven and at the discretion of donors and international NGOs.

Social protection has grown rapidly within development policy since the late 1990s and is credited with achieving notable successes in terms of risk management and even poverty reduction, but it has its limitations. Compensating food-insecure people for developmental failures with targeted handouts of cash, food or fertilisers is a palliative measure that tackles the symptoms but not the root causes of seasonality. For example, poor people can be protected against seasonal food price rises by providing wage employment or free cash to buy food (ideally index-linked to maintain constant purchasing power) or with free food (to avoid having to buy food). Alternatively, governments can intervene at the level of the food system, by controlling food supplies and prices through grain reserve management and food price subsidies. But the most effective solution to seasonally inflated food prices is neither handouts nor government interventionism, but economic development that integrates markets, smoothes inter-seasonal price variability, and provides financial mechanisms to manage price variability when it occurs.

Acknowledgement

My thanks to Judith Heyer, whose expert supervision of my doctoral thesis over several years was matched by her diligent and patient efforts to improve this chapter over several drafts.

Bibliography

Bradbury, M. (2000) 'Normalizing the crisis in Africa', *Disasters*, 22(4): 328–38.

Chambers, R., Longhurst, R. and Pacey, A. (eds) (1981) *Seasonal Dimensions to Rural Poverty*, London: Frances Pinter.

Department of Agriculture (1947) *Report on the Department of Agriculture for the Year 1946–47*, Accra: National Archives of Ghana.

Dercon, S. and Krishnan, P. (1998) *Changes in Poverty in Rural Ethiopia 1989–1995: Measurement, Robustness Tests and Decomposition*, Working Paper Series 98(7), Centre for the Study of African Economies, Oxford: University of Oxford.

Devereux, S. (1992) 'Household responses to food insecurity in northeastern Ghana', unpublished D.Phil. thesis, University of Oxford.

—— (1999) *"Making Less Last Longer": Informal Safety Nets in Malawi*, IDS Discussion Paper 373, Brighton: Institute of Development Studies.

—— (2001) 'Transfers and safety nets', in S. Devereux and S. Maxwell (eds) *Food Security in Sub-Saharan Africa*. London: ITDG Publishing.

Devereux, S. and Næraa, T. (1996) 'Drought and survival in rural Namibia', *Journal of Southern African Studies*, 22(3): 421–40

Devereux, S. and Sabates-Wheeler, R. (2004) *Transformative Social Protection*, IDS Working Paper 232, Brighton: Institute of Development Studies.

Devereux, S. and Tiba, Z. (2007) 'Malawi's first famine: 2001–2', in S. Devereux (ed.) *The "New Famines"*, London: Routledge.

Devereux, S., Rimmer, M., LeBeau, D. and Pendleton, W. (1993) *The 1992/3 Drought in Namibia: An Evaluation of Its Socioeconomic Impact on Affected Households*, SSD Research Report 7, Windhoek, Gamsberg Macmillan and Social Sciences Division: University of Namibia.

Devereux, S., Chilowa, W., Kadzandira, J., Mvula, P. and Tsoka, M. (2003) *Malawi Food Crisis Impact Survey: A Research Report on the Impacts, Coping Behaviours and Formal Responses to the Food Crisis in Malawi of 2001/02*, Institute of Development Studies and Zomba Centre for Social Research, Brighton: University of Malawi.

Devereux, S., Mvula, P. and Solomon, C. (2006a) *After the FACT: An Evaluation of Concern Worldwide's Food and Cash Transfers Project in Three Districts of Malawi*, External evaluation report, Brighton: Institute of Development Studies.

Devereux, S., Sabates-Wheeler, R., Mulugeta, T. and Hailemichael, T. (2006b) *Ethiopia's Productive Safety Net Programme (PSNP): Trends in PSNP Transfers Within Targeted Households*, Report commissioned by DFID Ethiopia, Brighton and Addis Ababa: Institute of Development Studies and Indak International.

Eldridge, C. (2002) 'Why was there no famine following the 1992 Southern African drought? The contributions and consequences of household responses', *IDS Bulletin*, 33(4): 79–87.

Gill, G. (1991) *Seasonality and Agriculture in the Developing World*, Cambridge: Cambridge University Press.

Government of Ethiopia (2006) *Productive Safety Net Programme: Summary of the Public Works Review Findings for SNNPR, Oromia, Amhara and Tigray Regions*, Addis Ababa: Ministry of Agriculture and Rural Development.

IDC [International Development Committee] (2003) *The Humanitarian Crisis in Southern Africa, Third Report of Session 2002–03*, London: House of Commons.

Kaluwa, B. and Masanjala, W. (2007) *The Impact of the Dowa Emergency Cash Transfer (DECT) Project on Local Labour Markets: Results from Surveys*, Zomba: Chancellor College.

Levy, S. (ed.) (2005) *Starter Packs: A Strategy to Fight Hunger in Developing Countries? Lessons from the Malawi Experience 1998–2003*, Wallingford: CABI Publishing.

Malawi Social Action Fund (MASAF) (2004) 'Evaluation of the "Improving Livelihoods through Public Works Programme", ILTPWP', Lilongwe: MASAF.

Malawi Vulnerability Assessment Committee (MVAC) (2005) 'Malawi Food Security Monitoring Report: June 2005', Lilongwe: MVAC.

Mamprusi District Administration (1947) *Mamprusi District Annual Report*, Tamale: National Archives of Ghana.

Olsen, W. (1996) *Rural Indian Social Relations*, Oxford: Oxford University Press.

Ravallion, M. (1990) *Reaching the Poor through Rural Public Employment, a Survey of Theory and Evidence*, World Bank Discussion Papers 94, Washington DC: World Bank.

Sasakawa Global 2000 (1989) *Annual Report, Upper East Region: 1988*, Ghana: Bolgatanga.

Seaman, J. (1993) 'Famine mortality in Africa', *IDS Bulletin*, 24(4): 27–32.

Seaman, J. and Holt, J. (1980) 'Markets and famines in the Third World', *Disasters*, 4(3) 283–97.

Sen, A. (1981) *Poverty and Famines: An Essay on Entitlement and Deprivation*, Oxford: Clarendon Press.

Shepherd, A. (1981) 'Agrarian change in northern Ghana: public investment, capitalist farming and famine', in J. Heyer, P. Roberts and G. Williams (eds), *Rural Development in Tropical Africa*, London: Macmillan.

Spitz, P. (1980) *Drought and Self-provisioning*, Working Paper, Food Systems and Society, Geneva: United Nations Research Institute for Social Development (UNRISD).

Swift, J. and Hamilton, K. (2001) 'Household food and livelihood security', in S. Devereux and S. Maxwell (eds), *Food Security in Sub Saharan Africa*, London: ITDG Publishing.

Tiba, Z. (2005) 'A new type of famine with traditional response: the case of Malawi, 2001–2003', unpublished Ph.D. thesis, School of Oriental and African Studies, University of London.

Ulijaszek, S. and Strickland, S. (eds) (1993) *Seasonality and Human Ecology*. Cambridge: Cambridge University Press.

Watts, M. (1983) *Silent Violence: Food, Famine and Peasantry in Northern Nigeria*, Berkeley: University of California Press.

Webster, H. (1911) *Food Supply in Fra-Fra*, Accra: National Archives of Ghana.

7 The political economy of contract farming in tea in Kenya

The Kenya Tea Development Agency (KTDA), 1964–2002

Cosmas Milton Obote Ochieng

Introduction: Contract farming: instrument of rural development or exploitation?

Contract farming has always generated controversy over its social and economic implications. In the United States, concerns have been raised because of asymmetrical market information between agribusiness and individual farmers, among other factors influencing the bargaining power between them (Roy 1972). These concerns have dogged contract farming in the United States since the late nineteenth century when problems of monopsony and oligopsony by food processors and marketers prompted Congress to enact a series of laws aimed at increasing the bargaining power of farmers and providing legal frameworks through which contract farming disputes could be resolved. Such laws include: the Capper Volstead Act of 1922, which exempted agricultural cooperatives from anti-trust laws in order to increase the power of cooperative bargaining associations; the Sugar Act of 1934 which established farmer bargaining associations for sugar beet growers; the Agricultural Marketing Act of 1937; the Agricultural Fair Practices Act of 1967; the Uniform Business Code; and the Perishable Agricultural Commodities Act. All of these provided legal frameworks for resolving disputes over contracts, bargaining over prices, and enabling farmers cooperatively to process agricultural products (Key and Runsten 1999). As recently as 2001, sixteen State Attorneys General in the United States drafted for state legislation a Producer Protection Act designed to protect farmers from perceived exploitation by agribusiness firms. Senator Tom Harkin of Iowa introduced similar legislation in the United States Senate in 2001, despite claims by opponents who argued that such legislation would reduce the competitiveness of the grain and livestock industries which rely largely on contract farming, and that it was impossible to write long-term contracts that meet all contingencies (Boehlje *et al.* 2001).

Partly because of the rapid expansion of contract farming in recent years and partly because of relatively underdeveloped institutions, concerns about the social and economic implications of contract farming in the developing world have been more diverse and perhaps more urgent than in the industrialised world.

Contestation over the degree to which contract farming can be viewed as a dynamic partnership between smallholders and agribusiness benefiting both without undermining the rights of either, or the degree to which it can be seen as an asymmetrical relationship prone to exploitation, pervades the literature on contract farming in developing countries. Contract farming in the developing world dates back to the 1940s–1960s. The earliest examples of contract farming schemes in developing countries include the Compañía Chilena de Tobacco in Chile (1940s), the Federal Land Development Authority (FELDA) rubber and palm oil schemes in Malaysia (1956), the Gezira Irrigation Scheme in Sudan (1920s) and the Kenya Tea Development Authority tea scheme in Kenya (1964). The evolution of contract farming in developing countries around the middle of the last century was occasioned by a combination of political and economic factors. In Latin America, the period following the Second World War was characterised by import-substitution industrialisation (ISI) policies and national-istic pressures that made foreign ownership of land and plantations untenable. At the same time, the market for fruits, vegetables and other agricultural produce in nearby North America was increasing rapidly, and lower wages in Latin America made it a competitive source of production relative to North America. Consequently, multinational food processors set up contract farming projects in Latin America. The companies received support from Latin American govern-ments that favoured the ISI model of development and viewed contract farming as a means of achieving self-sufficiency in food production. The companies were also warmly received by local owners of capital who stood to gain from the fusion of international and domestic capital through joint ventures (Key and Runsten 1999).

In Asia and Africa, the political and economic pressures occasioned by the decolonisation process provided the initial motivation for contract farming. The FELDA scheme in Malaysia, for instance, was a public project that was intended to settle new lands and to create a prosperous export-oriented Malay peasantry (Glover and Kusterer 1990) much like the Kenya Tea Development Authority (KTDA) in Kenya which was initially established to promote a petty-capitalist African agricultural bourgeoisie capable of absorbing potentially rebellious land-less Africans as wage labourers and making the country less dependent on external assistance (Ochieng 2005). Since the 1980s, however, the growth of contract farming in the developing world has been driven by a combination of agrarian reforms, neo-liberal policies, and changes in the organisation of major agro-industrial firms and food-processing chains, particularly the strategy of subcontracting or outsourcing (Korovkin 1992).

Proponents of contract farming generally contend that it is a mutually beneficial institutional arrangement that introduces smallholders to modern technologies and managerial skills, high-value crops, lucrative markets, credit and regular cash flows while enabling agribusiness firms to access land and labour relatively cheaply, reduce political risks through 'indigenisation' and produce goods of high quality and quantity (Williams and Karen 1985; World Bank 1981). Opponents counter that contract farming can be an exploitative relationship in which, due to their command of markets, control of credit facilities and technical skills and political influence, agribusiness firms exercise disproportionate power in bargaining. They use this to exploit smallholders by:

- shifting market and production risks to smallholders through low prices (Bernstein 1996; Dinham and Hines 1983; Little and Watts 1994; Porter and Phillips-Howard 1997; Lappe and Collins 1977);
- shifting the burden of quality and quantity standards to smallholders through labour practices and husbandry techniques that utilise smallholder labour more intensively (longer hours) and extensively (unpaid household/family labour) (ibid.);
- restricting smallholders' rights to alternative uses of their land and labour, thereby reducing them to wage workers (Clapp 1994; Dinham and Hines 1983; Lappe and Collins 1977);
- encouraging poor husbandry practices like mono-cropping, deforestation, and production and processing practices which create pollution, leading to environmental degradation (ibid.);
- increasing socio-economic differentiation among the peasantry either by excluding small-scale and poorer farmers or by disintegrating the peasantry through the creation of a peasant capitalist class, which then works against the interests of rural peasant farmers (Korovkin 1992; Little and Watts 1994).

In its transformation from a top-down bureaucratic public–private partnership contractual arrangement in the early 1960s into a farmer-owned and controlled contract farming enterprise in 2000, the KTDA faced many of these opportunities and challenges. At various points in time, the scheme's potential as a vehicle for rural development was challenged and fears rose that it could turn into an instrument for smallholder exploitation. As will be shown, there were complaints that the contract shifted the burden of quality to smallholders through stringent husbandry practices that included the relatively labour-intensive harvesting of two leaves and a bud (compared to the less intensive four or three leaves and a bud plucking practised by multinational tea companies). There were also complaints that the contract sought to exclude poorer farmers in favour of those that were relatively better off. These complaints were countered by claims that the contract was exposing smallholders to modern technologies, access to premium markets for tea (as a result of the high standard of husbandry practices), regular cash flows and general improvements to their economic welfare. How the KTDA navigated through these competing views and possibilities to emerge as a technically efficient, economically viable private enterprise owned and controlled by smallholders, against significant opposition from multinational competitors and the state at various points in time, is the subject of this chapter.

The KTDA case study is unusual in the outcome of its contract farming arrangement but not unusual in its initial design or composition of actors. It is not often that one finds a major agribusiness in the hands of smallholder farmers. Equally, it is not often that one finds privatisation succeeding in transferring ownership to small growers, rather than larger-scale interests. Similar contracts or schemes, most notably the sugar schemes in Kenya, with the possible exception of Mumias Sugar Company, produced opposite outcomes, in spite of fairly similar beginnings. Empirical studies of contract farming in rice, tomato and bananas in Africa, Asia, Latin America and the Caribbean support the proposition that few contracting schemes in the developing world would have come to fruition without some state or public assistance (Grosh 1994; Korovkin 1992; Little and Watts 1994; Raynolds 2000; White 1997). Even where contracting occurs between private firms and growers, the role of the state is still significant for many of the conditions under which contracting becomes favourable to both growers and agribusiness are usually mediated by the state. For instance, the state commonly supports contract farming by donating land, providing concessionary financing and subsidies, building the infrastructure, regulating markets and prices, enforcing contracts, and controlling the space for political contestation through collective action (ibid.).

The KTDA shares much in common with many of the state-sponsored or -mediated contract farming schemes in Africa and elsewhere in the developing world. Where it differs from many of these schemes is in its transformation into a large-scale technically complex and financially sound private-sector enterprise wholly owned and managed by smallholders. This chapter examines this transformation and argues that contract farming by itself is neither inherently good nor bad. The extent to which it becomes efficient and equitable depends upon the socio-economic and political structures and relationships in which it is embedded. Contract farmers like any other smallholders/small farmers are prey for whatever socio-political predators are present in particular national or local contexts. Contract farming reflects the relative socio-economic and political bargaining strengths of the parties involved. Socio-economic and political bargaining strength is a function of prevailing socio-economic and political structures and relationships, particularly the relationship between the state and smallholder farmers, and the relationship between the state and agribusiness. Socio-political predators may be present within the state, agribusiness or smallholder communities.

The privatisation of the KTDA and the processes under which it came about contrasts sharply with conventional privatisation programmes in Kenya and elsewhere in Africa. For instance, a similar attempt by smallholders in contract farming schemes in sugar to have the Moi state privatise parastatal sugar companies wholly and exclusively to smallholder farmers, as was the case in the tea sector, failed. This even after a coalition of sugar-cane smallholder farmers and members of parliament from Nyanza and Western Provinces had forced the passage of the Sugar Act 2002, which explicitly provided for 50 per cent of the shares in these factories to be transferred to smallholder farmers on their privatisation. In the event, only 30 per cent of the shares were reserved for smallholders during the privatisation of Mumias Sugar Company in 2002, the only parastatal sugar company to have been privatised in Kenya so far. This was in complete disregard of the provisions of the sugar law enacted in 2002.

Similarly, in the 'booming' horticultural crops sector, the Kenya government has encouraged relatively more market-led contract farming arrangements. These have resulted increasingly in the exclusion of relatively poor smallholders in favour of relatively large-scale farmers. Ochieng (2005) has attributed this to the politics of patron-clientelism based on an ideology of ethnic competition that has informed the policy biases in favour of certain commodities, regions and smallholders in Kenya.

The Kenya tea development agency, 1960–2002

Can smallholder farmers become sole shareholders of a company with a gross annual turnover of US$350 million? Can such a company maintain its position as one of the world's leading tea corporations in this age of a few powerful integrated supply chains? Conventional private-sector logic would present sceptical answers to these questions. Such logic has long viewed a majority of the African population – the rural poor – as non-entrepreneurial, non brand- and value-conscious, irrational and inefficient (for critiques of this view, see Schultz 1964; Moser 1978; de Soto 2000; Prahalad 2005). The predominant private-sector logic in Africa has constrained rural development by consigning a majority of the African population (the rural poor) to the 'informal economy'. In spite of this logic, in 2000 the Kenya government succumbed to smallholder pressure and privatised the Kenya Tea Development Agency (KTDA), putting it wholly and exclusively into the hands of smallholder tea farmers. Against the predictions of the conventional private-sector logic, the KTDA not only maintains the brand name and reputation of the Kenyan teas associated with the formerly state-owned corporation, but continues as one of the largest tea companies in the world.

Origins and early years of the KTDA

The KTDA was founded in 1960 as the Special Crops Development Authority (SCDA) with a mandate to promote smallholder participation in cash crops such as tea and pineapples. Its name was changed to the Kenya Tea Development Authority (KTDA) in 1964, after which its mandate was confined to the development of smallholder tea in Kenya. The name was changed again to the Kenya Tea Development Agency (KTDA) following its privatisation in 2000.

Prior to the establishment of the SCDA, tea was grown as a plantation crop, legally restricted to white colonial settlers and multinational tea companies such as Brooke Bond, George Williamson and James Findlay. Africans grew tea illegally, processing and selling it domestically as 'sun-dried tea' – so called because it was processed by drying green tea leaves in the sun. The legal ban on Africans growing tea was lifted when the Swynnerton Plan was introduced in 1954.

Tea is Kenya's third largest foreign exchange earner. In 2006, it accounted for over 20 per cent of the country's foreign exchange earnings (Republic of Kenya 2006). Kenya is the second largest exporter of black tea in the world, amounting to 18 per cent of global tea exports in 2001 (TBK 2002). The country's competitiveness in the global tea markets is a measure of KTDA's success. In 1954 (before there were any smallholder tea exports), Kenyan teas commanded prices 14 per cent below the average London auction price. By 1971, as smallholder production caught up with multinational tea production on estates/ plantations, Kenyan teas commanded prices 6 per cent above the London average. This leadership in quality has been maintained ever since (Leonard 1991; Lichts Tea Monthly various). In 1964, 19,000 Kenyan smallholders cultivated 4,700 ha of tea in eleven districts, producing about 2.8 million kilos of green leaf. By 2002, the numbers had grown to 360,000 smallholders growing tea on 85,000 ha of land in twenty-eight districts, producing over 700 million kilos of green leaf per year (Ochieng 2005). In 2002 the KTDA accounted for 60 per cent of all tea produced in Kenya, and provided direct and indirect employment to some 2 million people (Ochieng 2005).

The KTDA was founded on two general principles – commercial orientation and social development. The Working Party that had recommended the establishment of the KTDA had been adamant that for it to be successful it had to be a commercially oriented, self-financing entity, even if it was legally constituted as a parastatal company (Colony and Protectorate of Kenya 1960). Subsection 19 of the KTDA Order empowered it to impose a levy on growers as part of its drive to be self-financing. The Working Party had also emphasised social development objectives, namely the creation of an African agrarian 'middle peasant' class of tea growers. Throughout its history, the KTDA, together with the state (as guarantor of KTDA and provider of rural infrastructure and of policy incentives) and smallholders (as contract farmers supplying land and labour), has struggled with the problem of how best to balance these twin objectives. The pursuit of this 'balance' has engendered continuous contestations between the KTDA, the state and smallholder tea farmers. These contestations have resulted in the following outcomes among others:

- the form of industrial organisation initially adopted for the contract scheme
- the inclusion of smallholder representatives on the KTDA board of directors (1960s)
- the vertical integration of KTDA (1970s)
- the introduction of grower shareholding (1960s through the 1990s)
- privatisation (2000).

The rest of this chapter examines the contestations leading to these outcomes. These contestations are the key to understanding the way in which smallholder ownership and control were gradually established within the KTDA. For the purposes of this chapter, the contestations leading to the five outcomes above are discussed under three broad categories:

1 contestation over multiple controls on grower behaviour
2 vertical integration and
3 privatisation.

Contestation over multiple controls on smallholder behaviour and smallholder representation in the KTDA contract scheme

At the outset, the KTDA was designed to ensure effective control of smallholders through monopoly and monopsony and through administrative powers. The 'early' KTDA owned and controlled by the state in conjunction with multinational tea companies contrasts sharply with the 'latter-day' KTDA owned and managed by smallholder farmers following privatisation. In the early 1960s through the 1980s, the KTDA was the only legal source of smallholder planting material and the only legal buyer of smallholder green leaf. It determined who could grow tea, where tea could be grown, using what husbandry practices, and what levies could be charged. It was empowered to inspect, grade, accept or reject smallholder green leaf (Steeves 1975; Ochieng 2005). The role of smallholders was initially limited to supplying land and labour and following husbandry techniques designed by KTDA's extension officers. The government ran the scheme in conjunction with multinational tea companies (such as Brooke Bond, George Williamson and James Findlay) that served as KTDA's managing agents. It also provided rural infrastructure, especially 'feeder' roads into tea growing areas.

It would take nearly three decades of smallholder contestation of KTDA's monopoly, monopsony and administrative powers (and their inherent impacts on efficiency and equity) for the multiple controls on grower behaviour to be substantially relaxed. The working party that had recommended the formation of the KTDA had argued that strict control of smallholders was necessary in order to secure low production and processing costs, high-quality tea, commercially adequate quantities and high tea prices. In other words, it was necessary to secure the economic and financial viability of the smallholder project (Colony and Protectorate of Kenya 1960). Others have shown that many of the controls on smallholder behaviour were unnecessary on such grounds (Steeves 1975; Ochieng 2005, 2007). Rather, they were influenced by the interests of the multinational tea companies, which had a complex relationship with the smallholder project that was both competitive and cooperative. This complex relationship engendered continuous contestations between the state, agribusiness and smallholders within the scheme. The very first contestation occurred over smallholder representation within the KTDA.

Smallholder representation within the KTDA management structure had been a late addition to the smallholder tea project. It evolved in reaction to the formation of the Central Province African Grown Tea Association (CPGTA). The CPGTA had been formed by a group of smallholder tea farmers in Central Province to fight for their interests in the SCDA. The SCDA had been created following the success of two pilot smallholder tea schemes established in 1956 and 1958 respectively – the Central Province African Grown Tea Marketing Board and the Nyanza and Rift Valley Provinces Tea Marketing Board. The pilot schemes had been heavily subsidised by the colonial state, keen to undermine peasant rebellion through economic incorporation (Leonard 1991: 126). Smallholders who started tea growing under the pilot projects experienced declines in their returns following the shift from the pilot scheme to the SCDA with its self-sufficiency objectives. It was this situation, coupled with the burden of multiple controls on grower behaviour, that led to the formation of the CPTGA (Steeves 1975: 154–5; Ochieng 2005: 188–93).

The CPTGA took exception to the multiple controls on grower behaviour. It demanded arrangements similar to those that had existed under the pilot schemes as well as a greater management role for smallholders within the scheme. The CPTGA felt that the tea industry was driven by the interests of the multinational companies at the expense of smallholders. It sought increased smallholder representation and participation to correct this imbalance (Leonard 1991: 126–9). The SCDA and the colonial authorities viewed the CPTGA as a serious threat to the smallholder project. By criticising the 'self sufficiency' design of the SCDA, it undermined smallholder recruitment to the tea project.

It was against this background that, in 1962, the SCDA moved to institutionalise smallholder representation and to co-opt the CPTGA. In 1962, the government gave the SCDA powers to 'set up Regional Boards or Committees consisting of members and officials of the Authority and such other persons associated with them as it considers desirable to advise the Authority in carrying on its functions' (Steeves 1975: 22). The SCDA quickly established committees so that representatives for each district could be nominated to represent smallholders on provincial boards. The committees were supposed to be two-way channels of communication – of grower grievances and recommendations to the SCDA and of SCDA policies to growers. The SCDA system of grower representation had elected grower representatives from the divisional and district levels (divisional and district tea committees, respectively) on the provincial (provincial tea boards) and the national boards (SCDA board of directors).

By 1964, when the SCDA was renamed the KTDA, an autonomous smallholder representation structure outside the KTDA had been destroyed and replaced with semi-autonomous representation embedded in the organisational structure of the KTDA. From this point on, internally institutionalised smallholder representation within the KTDA took three forms:

1   elected representation through divisional and district tea committees, provincial tea boards and the KTDA board of directors;
2   shareholding in the factory companies, and
3   elected representation on the boards of the factory companies.

Following the institutionalisation of grower representation within the KTDA's management structure, each tea-growing district came to have a District Tea Committee (DTC), comprising a majority of elected farmer representatives. The DTCs served to convey farmer complaints to the KTDA and KTDA's policies to farmers. An examination of the minutes of the meetings of DTCs in the 1960s[1] indicates that DTC meetings were often lively, with farmers raising questions about a whole range of issues, including low producer prices, high levies, inadequate leaf plucking and collection hours, the conduct of KTDA staff, and husbandry practices. These were minuted and sent to KTDA District Agricultural and Tea Officers, Provincial Tea Officers, Provincial Tea Boards and the KTDA board of directors. KTDA board of directors meetings always tabled and discussed minutes of DTCs. The DTCs made the KTDA management at all levels aware of the wishes and complaints of smallholders in particular districts. The KTDA in turn used the DTCs as avenues for communicating its policy to smallholders.

Each of the five tea-growing provinces had a Provincial Tea Board (PTB). PTBs comprised elected farmer representatives (majority), the Senior Tea Officer (STO), Provincial Director of Agriculture (Vice-Chair) and the Provincial Commissioner (Chair). The DTCs elected farmer representatives to the PTBs. The PTBs in turn elected grower representatives to the KTDA Board. At least one of the PTB farmer representatives would be a member of the KTDA board of directors. The KTDA General Manager and the Chief Technical Officer (CTO) also sat on the PTBs as members. The PTBs functioned more or less as the DTCs. They conveyed farmer grievances to the KTDA and KTDA policies to farmers. Invariably, the complaints and policy issues discussed at the PTBs were similar to those expressed at the DTCs, judging from a sample of minutes of the meetings of the Central, Rift Valley and Western Provinces' PTBs in the 1970s (Ochieng 2005). Farmers often complained about both 'macro' issues which could only be resolved at the national board level, such as high service charges, low producer prices and tea plucking and collection times, and 'micro' issues such as tea roads, location of leaf buying centres and factories, and conduct of local KTDA staff (Ochieng 2005).

The law (formally known as 'Order') establishing the KTDA vested policy-making and overall management functions in its board of directors. The KTDA board consisted of eighteen members: nine members representing smallholders, the Permanent Secretary in the Ministry of Agriculture, the Director of Agriculture, the Chairman of the Tea Board of Kenya, a representative of the Commonwealth Development Corporation (CDC) as long as CDC loans were outstanding, a representative of any other lender who in the opinion of the minister was a substantial lender as long as that lender's loan was outstanding (no other lender apart from the CDC and the World Bank was thus appointed), the General Manager of the Authority (appointed by the Board), a Chairman appointed by the Minister for Agriculture and three other members appointed by the Minister for Agriculture. The composition of the board of directors was intended to bring together as wide an intra-industry representation as possible.

The presence of smallholder representatives, comprising half of the board – some if not all of them members of the PTBs – ensured that the KTDA had direct contact with smallholder representatives at the highest levels of management. With high-level government representation on the KTDA board and on the PTBs and DTCs, this meant that the state had similar contact with smallholders and was kept aware of their concerns. An examination of sample DTC, PTB and KTDA board[2] minutes indicate that this was the greatest strength of this internally institutionalised form of smallholder representation. It allowed direct contact between smallholders, KTDA, the government, the CDC and multinational companies in a decision-making environment. As will be shown shortly, however, this does not mean that this form of representation delivered substantial results for smallholder tea farmers in critical areas. The asymmetrical power relations between the various players (state, business, farmers), including most notably the 'veto' powers exercised by the World Bank and the CDC in the 1960s and 1970s, meant that although farmer representatives constituted half the board, their interests could be suppressed by the board. This was replicated in the lower organs of management that had farmer representatives (Ochieng 2005).

While established to provide grower representation in policymaking and management, the DTCs and PTBs effectively became KTDA's instruments of control over smallholders. The KTDA head office regarded them as advisory bodies that were there to provide legitimation for the KTDA. They were not expected to participate in policy and personnel decisions, although many DTCs initially contested this interpretation and made forays into the employment of field and factory staff and several policy and personnel areas. This forced the KTDA board to issue a board paper in 1964 (KTDA Board Paper 121) outlining the powers and duties of the DTCs. It stated that the KTDA viewed the DTCs and the PTBs as purely advisory bodies. Until well into the 1990s, when these structures were abolished (and replaced by alternative structures known as 'Zonal Centres'), the KTDA followed the policy set out in this board paper on the roles of smallholder representative organs (Steeves 1975; Ochieng 2005).

Where KTDA's interests were closely aligned with smallholder interests (for example in the introduction of tea plucking on Saturdays in 1966), these management organs appeared to advance smallholder interests. Where these interests were not closely aligned, asymmetrical relationships between the state, business and producers in the partnership ensured that the KTDA utilised these organs in attempts to resist smallholder pressure for the advancement of their interests. An examination of key KTDA board papers and minutes indicates that, in all the cases where farmer interests were threatened by KTDA policy, the tea committees (DTCs and PTBs) supported KTDA policy. Examples include:

- the introduction of the much contested Development Charge (minutes of KTDA board meeting of 10 November 1966; KTDA Board Paper 40/70);
- the introduction of Grower Financed Planting (KTDA Board Paper 15/1966);
- the credit contraction scheme of the mid 1960s (Steeves 1975).

Although smallholder representation within KTDA management structures at various levels was of limited immediate value to them from the 1960s through the 1990s (Ochieng 2005), continued contestation over the substance of these forms of representation led to the advancement of smallholder interests over time. KTDA's initial stringent controls on smallholder behaviour had two lasting impacts. First, by forcing smallholders to observe a higher tea husbandry standard than multinational tea companies (through stringent legal requirements), it enhanced the competitiveness of the smallholder tea industry over the multinational tea companies. The KTDA has maintained this position since its inception (Leonard 1991; Lichts various). Secondly, smallholder representation catalysed the smallholder push for policy, organisational and managerial reforms that ultimately led to smallholder acquisition of the company.

An early contestation in this respect was the resistance by 'lower strata' farmers to calculated efforts by the government, the multinational tea companies and the KTDA to exclude them from the contract farming arrangement. From 1960 through 1963, in keeping with the objectives of the Swynnerton Plan,[3] the SCDA (predecessor to the KTDA) adopted as its general social development ideology the creation of African agrarian 'middle peasants' in the tea sector (Steeves 1975). Almost anyone willing to participate in the smallholder project could do so through a widely accessible credit scheme, low initial deposits and minimum starting requirements. However, from 1964 onwards there occurred a marked shift in the KTDA from developmental concerns (focusing on widespread participation of smallholders farmers) to commercial considerations (focusing on middle- to upper-strata farmers that could afford to pay their way through the scheme). This was mainly due to pressure from KTDA's lenders, the World Bank and the CDC, and its managing agents (Brooke Bond Liebig, James Findlay and George Williamson (Ochieng 2005)). Consequently, there was a rapid contraction of credit throughout the 1960s, and it was abolished completely in 1972 (Steeves 1975). A Grower Financed Planting Scheme was introduced, targeting relatively well-off farmers who could afford to participate in the scheme without credit.

KTDA argued that lower-strata farmers with less than 0.8 ha of land were too poor to be helped (Ochieng 2005). While in the initial years the KTDA did not have any stipulation about the minimum area of land that one had to have to participate in the scheme, following this shift in orientation it demanded that those contracted into the scheme have a minimum of 0.8 ha, not all of it devoted to tea. The argument was that smallholder tea would be economically viable only if complemented by alternative economic activities, particularly food crops. Those with smaller pieces of land would not benefit from the scheme and would constitute a potentially liability to the agency. While there is some validity in this argument, Ochieng (2005) has argued that the expansion of the smallholder scheme constituted a near-existential threat to the multinational tea companies in the 1960s–1970s in the light of efforts then being made to impose production and export quotas on tea-producing countries. The multinational companies feared the impact of such a quota with the increasing competitiveness of the KTDA and the overwhelming national support for the smallholder tea sector. Ochieng points to the introduction of vegetative propagation (VP) methods during the KTDA's Third Plan (1968–72) to dismiss the claim that the shift from a developmental to a commercial orientation was necessitated purely by efficiency considerations.

VP provided the KTDA with a good opportunity to expand planting at substantially lower costs. VP involved replacing seedlings (planted in KTDA nurseries) with cuttings from 'mother bushes' and was much cheaper (than nursery seedlings). However, instead of lowering the cost to growers of planting material as a result of this technical innovation, the KTDA increased the minimum VP units required for first-time participants and already recruited smallholders (with 5 units for new farmers (3,500 tea stumps) and 3 units (2,100 tea stumps) for old farmers). The KTDA also introduced an additional levy known as the Development Charge, the cost of which was higher than that of the planting material and had to be paid by every farmer regardless of where they obtained their planting material. The overall effect of these changes was to increase the cost of participation in the scheme with a view to excluding lower-strata farmers. Despite the introduction of the cost-lowering VP method in the mid 1960s, by 1970 the cost of participating in the smallholder project was over ten times (in real terms) that during the period 1960–63 (Steeves 1975).

In spite of this, the lower-strata farmers were determined to participate in the scheme and found ways to do so. The credit contraction policy forced farmers across the country from 1964 onwards to start acquiring and planting tea plants illegally, relying on friends and relatives to purchase tea plants on credit, rather than having to pay cash for them (Steeves 1975). It also forced them to subdivide family land units without informing the KTDA, and to rely on 'middlemen' buying planting material from the KTDA and selling to others. These farmers were aided by KTDA field officers who neglected to enforce the strict KTDA rules. By the early 1970s, the KTDA reckoned that there were more farmers planting tea illegally than legally. It granted an amnesty to all illegal planters and formally re-absorbed lower-strata farmers into the scheme (Steeves 1975). It also scrapped the Grower Financed Planting Scheme.

In spite of the socio-economic differentiation (and other differences, including ethnic and regional) between smallholder tea farmers, they had colluded to prevent the exclusion of poorer farmers from the scheme, and, by extension, the transfer of the scheme to relatively wealthy or large-scale farmers. This is largely because socio-economic differentiation between the so-called 'lower strata' farmers and average smallholders was minimal, while the threat posed by Grower Financed Planting was quite significant to a majority of smallholders. The fact that the Grower Financed Planting Programme threatened the credit scheme alienated many smallholders who felt that the measures being directed at lower-strata farmers could one day be directed at them (Steeves 1975). After fighting off the Grower Financed Planting Programme, KTDA smallholders turned their attention to fighting for broad-based participation within the scheme, particularly some degree of smallholder control or influence over decision-making and management – something more than the advisory role the KTDA had assigned them. This contestation is perhaps best represented by the contestation over vertical integration.

KTDA's vertical integration

The 1970s were characterised by conflicts within the KTDA between the state, smallholders, the KTDA, the multinational tea companies, the World Bank and the CDC. Particular issues of conflict included producer prices that were perceived by farmers to be low, and service charges and managing agency fees that were regarded as excessive or exploitative (Swainson 1980; Ochieng 2005). By the early 1970s, these complaints had caught the attention of a section of Kenyan members of parliament (MPs), notably Martin Shikuku and Joseph Seroney who raised the issue of smallholder welfare within the KTDA, during a parliamentary debate on the CDC loan for the fourth KTDA Development Plan in 1974 (Swainson 1980).

Until 1973, the KTDA functioned largely as a leaf collection and extension service. The processing/manufacturing, marketing and retailing functions of all but one of the factory companies (Ragati) were performed on its behalf by its managing agents (Swainson 1980). With the KTDA expanding rapidly in the 1970s, the managing agency contracts became subjects of contestation. Farmer representatives on the KTDA board and the KTDA General Manager Charles Karanja became increasingly dissatisfied with the commissions charged by the managing agents as recorded in the board paper on Factory Management of 1973:

> With increased factory capacities above the initial expections [sic] the remunerations to the Managing Agents have become very attractive and the existing Managing Agents would be expected to have interest in managing all factories. With the increase in the number of factories to 53 and if the present policy of employing Managing Agents is continued, the present Managing Agents would be overloaded and unable to handle the work. However, most of them would be prepared to expand their organisations to cater for the increased work if they were to be given the Management. This extra commitment will finally be borne by smallholders. The cost to smallholders would be considerable.

The Board Paper concluded that, to avoid this extra cost, the KTDA should take over the management of its factory companies.

There was also internal discontent with the rate at which the multinational companies were proceeding with the Africanisation process, especially at the level of the factory managers. By 1973, in nearly fifteen factory companies owned by the KTDA, there was only one African factory manager. These were the reasons that prompted the two MPs to table a motion in parliament calling for the KTDA to be turned into a public liability company and its activities decentralised to give smallholders greater say in its affairs (Ochieng 2005). The motion was defeated but the 1970s continued to witness significant 'expression of voice' by MPs on behalf of smallholders demanding changes in the corporate governance of the KTDA. In the mid 1970s, this 'coalition' between smallholders, the KTDA General Manager and a section of MPs succeeded in forcing the Kenyatta state to fundamentally alter the relationship between the KTDA and the multinational tea companies.

In 1973, following a presentation by the KTDA General Manager Charles Karanja of a board paper on the merits of the KTDA taking over the management of any new factory companies established by it, farmer representatives on the KTDA board voted to empower the KTDA to move into factory management and tea processing. The other representatives on the board, led by the CDC, voted against the move (Leonard 1991; Ochieng 2005). The government, represented by the Permanent Secretary, Ministry of Agriculture and the Director of Agriculture, also voted against the proposal. This meant that only Karanja, the General Manager, voted with the nine farmer representatives. This was a majority vote but, under the KTDA Order, the CDC and the World Bank held veto powers over major changes in policy, so a 'no' vote by the CDC meant that the matter could not proceed further unless cleared by the Minister for Agriculture.

The World Bank, the CDC and the multinational tea companies argued that manufacturing, marketing and retailing functions were technically demanding and that rushed Africanisation could jeopardise the future of the entire small-holder project. By this time, Naftali Wachira (the former CPTGA President) had been running Ragati Tea Factory successfully for three years. Charles Karanja and smallholder representatives on the KTDA board were convinced that it was time the KTDA moved into factory management, marketing and retailing. With consensus lacking on the board, the matter was referred to the Minister for Agriculture, Jeremiah Nyagah. Under the law establishing the KTDA, the minister had extremely wide powers over its affairs. On the advice of his perma-nent secretary and the Director of Agriculture, the minister sided with the CDC and the World Bank.

This should have been the end of the matter, for the law establishing the KTDA did not provide for appeal against the decision of the minister. However, Karanja hailed from the same constituency as President Kenyatta and used this personal relationship to take the matter directly to the president. He met the president in the presence of the Minister for Agriculture and argued that the KTDA had matured and had the right to process and market its own teas, adding that this would be a practical and visible implementation of the Africanisation programme. The minister repeated the reservations of the World Bank, the CDC and the multinational companies. President Kenyatta overruled his minister and gave his personal approval for the KTDA to move into tea manufacturing, processing and marketing, and, from 1974 onwards, the KTDA took over processing functions in its new factory companies. Vertical integration accelerated Africanisation within the KTDA. By the end of the 1970s, all senior posts within the KTDA were held by Africans (Leonard 1991: 138). It also enabled the KTDA to con-solidate its position in the Kenya tea industry, and reduce costs and increase profit margins by capturing upstream and downstream profits (Ochieng 2005).

Privatisation of the KTDA

In spite of vertical integration from 1974 on, smallholders continued to exercise limited ownership and management rights within the KTDA. The law establishing the KTDA empowered it 'to establish, acquire and operate processing factories, and to promote and subscribe to shares in any company incorporated in Kenya for the purpose of processing or marketing tea' (The Agriculture Act, KTDA Order, Section 19 (f), 1963). Pursuant to this power the KTDA established and subscribed to shares in its factory companies (totalling fifty-three by 2004). Each of the factory companies has always been an independent entity, registered as a limited-liability company under the Companies Act, Chapter 486 of the Laws of Kenya. The first such factory companies (Chinga and Mataara) were established in the early 1960s as joint ventures between the KTDA, the CDC and multinational tea companies (Ragati was the only early factory to be established with the KTDA as the sole shareholder). Subsequent factory companies were modelled on these except that, with the evolution of time, the concept of joint venture disappeared as either the KTDA repaid loans or smallholders bought the so-called 'founder shares' (Ochieng 2005: chapters 5–6).

The establishment of the factory companies was premised on the understanding that the ownership and management role of growers would eventually be dominant (Board Paper 123/1964). Consequently, they were set up on the basis that, whereas initially the KTDA and its joint venture partners would provide part of the equity to supplement the loans contracted for the construction of the factory companies, they would divest their interests and allow smallholder subscription for the equity once the loans were repaid. The share capital of the companies was accordingly divided into two: founder shares and grower shares. Founder shares were issuable only to entities that founded the factory companies. Depending on the history of particular factory companies, these shares have been allotted to the CDC, James Findlay, George Williamson, Brooke Bond and, in every case, the KTDA, given its statutory role in founding the factory companies (Ochieng 2005). Grower shares were only issuable or transferable to bona fide licensed growers, or to cooperatives or other corporate organs of such growers whose holdings were served by the particular factory company and the KTDA. In theory at least, this restrictive classification of shareholding was meant to ensure that smallholders played a dominant ownership and management role in the factory companies that processed their tea.

KTDA Board Paper 123/64 recognised that smallholders would be motivated to acquire shares in the factory companies, partly to get some sense of ownership and management control and partly as a result of dividends and appreciation of shares. It also acknowledged that the prospect of management control was a long way off and that smallholder say in the affairs of the factory companies would be limited to general meetings and 'possibly the right to appoint an additional director' (KTDA 1964: 3). The KTDA attitude to smallholder shareholding made the entire scheme unattractive. Although smallholders were allowed to buy shares in KTDA factory companies from the mid 1960s, by 1982 only about 10 per cent of smallholders (15,000 out of a total of about 140,000) owned shares in the sixteen KTDA factory companies that allowed shareholding (Lamb and Mueller 1982). This was mainly because there was no market for the shares (being restricted to tea smallholders or smallholder tea organisations only) and the dividend from the factory shares (fixed at no more than 8 per cent annual averages over an eighteen-year period) was unrelated to the financial performance of the factory companies. The KTDA management held the view that the first priority of the factory companies was to pay their creditors and not their shareholders (KTDA 1964).

An argument can be made that, as a parastatal, the KTDA was not obliged to pursue the 'shareholder profit objective' and that the 'developmental objectives' of the smallholder project outweighed commercial considerations. Nonetheless, this would not explain the tight grip that the KTDA had over the factory companies, and its unwillingness to treat smallholder shareholders as part owners of the factory companies. Prior to privatisation the factory companies operated as extensions of the KTDA management structure (Mahihu 1990), although legally they were autonomous entities. The KTDA routinely failed to contact the respective factory boards on major investment decisions directly affecting them. Moreover, KTDA headquarters procured virtually all goods and services required by the factory companies it managed without consulting them.

Smallholders were a minority on factory company boards and the factory companies were subordinate to the KTDA. While smallholders viewed the factory companies as opportunities for them to own and participate more actively in the smallholder tea project, the KTDA management (encompassing the government, the CDC – up to 1985 – and multinational tea companies) used shareholding as a device for creating an illusory sense of ownership among smallholders. In spite of vertical integration from the 1970s, smallholders continued to exercise limited ownership and management rights within the KTDA. They continued to press for greater ownership and management rights throughout the 1970s and 1980s, albeit relatively passively as the national space for political contestation became more restricted in the 1980s (Ochieng 2005). With increased space for political contestation following the reintroduction of multi-party politics in the early 1990s, they renewed this pressure.

In November 1994, a political grouping of Central and Eastern Province MPs named the Coffee and Tea Growers Parliamentary Association (CTGPA) was formed under the chairmanship of the then Democratic Party Chairman, Mwai Kibaki (currently the third president of Kenya). CTGPA took up the tea small-holders' 'cause' by advocating smallholder tea boycotts as a means of forcing policy change within the smallholder tea sector. This aggressive approach by the CTGPA facilitated the formation of a splinter smallholder representative body calling itself the Kenya Union of Small-Scale Tea Owners (KUSSTO). Backed by CTGPA, KUSSTO operated outside the KTDA smallholder representation structure and sought to effect change in the smallholder sector through protests, demonstrations and boycotts rather than through the institutionalised form of representation within the KTDA, which they viewed as compromised (Ochieng 2005).

KUSSTO wanted an independent smallholder body outside the official structure of the KTDA, the withdrawal of the KTDA from the direct management of factory companies and the privatisation of the KTDA to smallholders (Ochieng 2005: chapter 6). In a coincidental confluence of interests, this time between smallholders and segments of international capital, in 1992 the World Bank and the IMF pushed through the Public Enterprises Reform Program (PERP) in Kenya. PERP was a policy condition that sought to enhance the role of the private sector in the economy by shifting responsibility for production and delivery of products and services from the public to the private sector, reducing the demand of public enterprises on the exchequer, improving the regulatory environment and broadening the base of ownership (Republic of Kenya 1994: 1). It did not specifically target the KTDA initially because the agency had long been regarded as one of the few efficient state-owned enterprises in Kenya, but it validated the calls for KTDA's privatisation. By this time, the cooperative relationship between the government and the World Bank in particular had turned antagonistic as the Moi government tried to stall the aid conditionality-led push for nationwide political and economic liberalisation (Ochieng 2005).

The government resisted calls for privatisation of the KTDA until 1996 when it launched KTDA's privatisation blueprint, scheduling it for privatisation by 2000. When it did succumb to privatisation, the Moi state opted to privatise the KTDA in a manner that suited its politics of patron-clientelism based on an ideology of ethnic competition.[4] Instead of a competitive bidding process or public floatation of shares through the Nairobi Stock Exchange, which had been the medium of choice for previous privatisations of state-owned enterprises (for example Kenya Airways in 1996), the government restricted the sale of KTDA shares to smallholder tea growers only. Ochieng (2005) has argued that the Moi state's decision to finally privatise the parastatal wholly and exclusively to smallholders in June 2000 was influenced by a number of factors, including policy conditionality, smallholder collective action and favourable political economy considerations. The government's insistence that KTDA shares be sold only to smallholder tea farmers, with farmers subscribing for shares only in factory companies where they delivered green leaf, meant that President Moi could protect the interests of his core ethnic constituency on the west of the Rift Valley. Moreover, the earlier relative insulation of the KTDA from political interference, and its operational and financial autonomy (by this time it relied neither on the state nor on donors for financial support), meant that the government had a limited financial stake in it. These factors combined to make its privatisation relatively less painful to the Moi government, both politically and financially (Ochieng 2005).

The transfer of the KTDA into the hands of smallholders was thus aligned with the long-term interests of Moi's political and ethnic constituency. Where this type of privatisation was at odds with Moi's politics of patron-clientelism based on an ideology of ethnic competition, as was the case with sugar (grown in Nyanza and Western Provinces, long the bedrock of opposition politics in Kenya), the Moi state rejected the exclusive transfer of ownership to smallholders. In June 2000, the KTDA became a private enterprise, wholly owned by smallholder tea farmers through their respective factory companies. The KTDA was de-linked from the state through its exemption from the State Corporations Act and the aforementioned measures. It now came under the Companies Act.

Full management and ownership rights had finally come to smallholders. The now smallholder controlled KTDA retained its role as managing agent of the 'KTDA factory companies'.

These changes altered the relationships between smallholders on the one hand and the government and the KTDA on the other. The government's role was diminished, limited to regulatory rather than 'executive' or 'administrative' functions. The KTDA effectively became a managing agent of the KTDA factory companies under the ownership of smallholders. Elected smallholder representatives took charge of management and policymaking, especially at factory company levels.

In sum, after privatisation, the control of the KTDA, both over the factory companies and over smallholders directly, was severely undermined. The KTDA was now owned and controlled by its factory companies. The factory companies were in turn wholly owned and controlled by smallholder farmers. The factory companies assumed greater roles in husbandry, extension, leaf collection, transportation and processing activities. Where previously the KTDA provided extension, transport and processing services, now it provided only financial, engineering, information technology, marketing, insurance and warehousing services (Ochieng 2005). Privatisation also presented new challenges to the KTDA. While smallholders enhanced their ownership and management rights through shareholding, privatisation subjected the KTDA and factory companies to corporation taxes for the first time in its history. This had the effect of reducing its annual profits, or payments to smallholders, by as much as 35 per cent (Ochieng 2005).

Conclusion

This chapter has traced the evolution of the KTDA from a top-down autocratic organisation dominated by the interests of foreign capital (the World Bank, the CDC and multinational tea companies) in the early 1960s into a private company owned wholly and exclusively by smallholders in 2000. The chief forces that led to this outcome included patron–client politics based on an ideology of ethnic competition; competing interests between foreign capital and elements of 'domestic' capital; smallholder collective action; and coincidental confluence of interests between smallholders and ethnically factionalised but dominant elements of the state during the Kenyatta and Moi regimes. The socio-economic and political structures and relationships under which contract farming in tea in Kenya was embedded under the Kenyatta and Moi regimes favoured the gradual transformation of the KTDA into a vibrant private enterprise wholly owned and controlled by smallholder farmers.

It has been shown that, in spite of policy biases that favoured the tea sector, tea-growing regions and smallholder farmers, it still took nearly four decades of sustained contestation to transfer substantive ownership and managerial control of the KTDA from the state, the CDC, the World Bank and multinational tea companies into the hands of smallholder tea farmers. Coincidental confluence of interests between smallholders and ethnically defined factions of the state played a critical role in helping advance smallholder interests at critical points in time due to the preponderance of patron–client politics based on an ideology of ethnic competition. It was this coincidental congruence of interests or the prevailing socio-economic and political structures and relationships between the state, agribusiness and smallholders that ensured the evolution of a fairly democratic and broad-based smallholder ownership and control of the KTDA while maintaining its high technical and managerial expertise. Whether this is sustainable in the absence of competing interests (as was represented by the state and multinational companies) is too early to tell. There have been recent complaints that smallholder control over the factory companies is compromising technical and managerial expertise through lack of competitive recruitment practices. Some MPs even tried to sponsor a motion calling for the deprivatisation of the KTDA on efficiency grounds. Whether this represents an effort by large-scale interests to regain control of the company and how smallholders will fight off this potentially new round of contestation is an empirical question. However, that certain interests of a segment of the smallholder population (tea growers) coincided with the interests of ethnically defined factions of the Kenyatta and Moi states at certain points in time did not constitute a fundamental or sustainable alignment of interests that could be justified by Michael Lofchie's (1989: 189) assertion that Kenya's government, was 'one of farmers, by farmers and for farmers'. Where interests of some segments of smallholders did not coincide with the core political and economic interests of ethnic factions of the state, as was the case in contract farming in sugar cane, the outcome was remarkably different (see Ochieng 2005).

The KTDA case study is thus unusual and must be viewed within Kenya's political economy under the Kenyatta and Moi regimes. Both Kenyatta and Moi hailed from predominantly tea-growing regions (Central and Rift Valley Provinces respectively), while sugar for example is predominantly grown in Nyanza and Western Provinces, which have long formed the bastion of opposition politics in Kenya. This case study demonstrates both the 'agency' and ability of small-holders to contest agricultural policy making and management (through short term coalitions if necessary) but also the vulnerability of smallholder interests to manipulation by competing interest groups or coalitions including factions within the state. It also demonstrates that neither the state, agribusiness nor smallholders are 'homogeneous'. The sometimes divergent interests within these groups can constrain their relative influence in contractual relationships. This chapter thus suggests that contract farming can play a positive or negative role in rural development, depending – at least in part – on the socio-economic and political relationships and structures under which it is embedded. This chapter also confirms that, contrary to conventional opinion, smallholder farmers may be poor but that does not necessarily mean that they are not efficient, entre-preneurial, brand- or value-conscious.

This essay emanates from a doctoral thesis that was inspired by Heyer's early work on Kenya (Heyer 1976, 1981). It examines the political economy of the tripartite relationship between the state, agribusiness and smallholders in contract farming in tea under the Kenyatta and Moi regimes (1963–2002) to shed light on some of the conditions under which contract farming can be an effective instrument for rural development. The present study supports the critical findings of Heyer's early work (1976, 1981), most notably that the Kenyan development model was characterised by policy biases in favour of certain commodities and regions at the expense of others. However, as this case study has shown, even among the 'favoured' crops, regions and smallholders, the pursuit of smallholder interests was still subject to significant contestation. Although the present study does not focus on crops, regions and smallholders that were less favoured by policy biases in Kenyan agriculture under Kenyatta and Moi regimes, the protracted, drawn-out conflicts between the state, agribusiness and smallholders over the transformation of the KTDA into an institution capable of advancing substantive smallholder interests gives some indication of the constraints facing rural development in Kenya. Heyer's early work also pointed to political economy factors that later researchers would confirm – neither the Kenyan state, agribusiness nor smallholders were 'monolithic or 'homogenous'. Rather, there existed conflicting interests within and between these principal actors in Kenyan agriculture. The Kenyan state was ethnically factionalised based on an ideology of ethnic competition (Bates 1989); there existed significant variations and contestations within the agribusiness sector, including notably contestations between 'foreign' capital or multinational companies and 'domestic' capital or indigenously owned firms (Ochieng 2005); and there was significant socio-economic differentiation (besides differentiation based on ethnicity, geographic location and gender) among smallholder farmers (Ochieng 2005).

Notes

1   See for instance minutes of Nyeri DTC meeting on 5 September 1970; minutes of Kirinyaga DTC meeting on the 15 January 1966; Kisii DTC meeting 19 January 1966 (in Ochieng 2005).
2   KTDA board meetings on 13 January 1966, 14 April 1966, 27 June 1974, 9 August 1976, 26 November 1976 and 13 January 1977 (in Ochieng 2005).
3   The 'Plan to Intensify the Development of African Agriculture in Kenya' (1954–1959), popularly known as the Swynnerton Plan, was formulated in reaction to the Mau Mau war for independence (1952–1956). It had twin political and economic objectives. The political objective was to ensure political stability by creating a class of yeomen African farmers whose prosperity it was hoped would absorb potentially rebellious landless Africans as wage labourers. The Plan sought to promote the establishment of private property rights in land as a basis for providing economic incentives for productivity increases in smallholder agriculture. It also sought to improve African commodity protection through the provision of technological and other support services. The Swynnerton Plan is considered the foundation of many institutional innovations in Kenya agriculture that were put in place in the second half of the twentieth century.
4   Tea is predominantly grown in Rift Valley, Central, Eastern and parts of Western and Nyanza Provinces. Rift Valley provided the bedrock of support to the Moi regime.

Bibliography

Bates, R. (1989) *Beyond the Miracle of the Market: The Political Economy of Agrarian Development in Kenya*, Cambridge: Cambridge University Press.

Bernstein, H. (1996) 'The agrarian question in South Africa', special issue, *Journal of Peasant Studies*, 23(2): 1–304.

Boehlje, M. *et al.* (2001) 'The producer protection act: will it protect producers?', *Purdue Agricultural Economics Report*, West Lafayette: Purdue University.

Clapp, R. (1994) 'The moral economy of contract', in P. Little and M. Watts (eds) *Living under Contract: Contract Farming and Agrarian Transformation in Sub-Saharan Africa*, Madison: University of Wisconsin Press.

Colony and Protectorate of Kenya (1960) *Reports of the Working Party set up to Consider the Establishment of an Authority to Promote the Development of Cash Crops for Smallholders and of the Working Party set up to Consider the Financial Implications of the Proposed Authority*, London: HMSO.

de Soto, H. (2000) *The Mystery of Capital: Why Capitalism Triumphs in the West and Fails Everywhere Else*, New York: Basic Books.

Dinham, B. and Hines, C. (1983) *Agribusiness in Africa*, London: Earth Resources Research.

Glover, D. and Kusterer, K. (1990) *Small Farmer, Big Business: Contract Farming and Rural Development*, London: Macmillan.

Grosh, B. (1994) 'Contract farming in Africa: an application of the New Institutional Economics', *Journal of African Economies*, 3(2): 231–61.

Heyer, J. (1976) 'Achievements, problems and prospects in the agricultural sector', in J. Heyer *et al.* (eds) *Agricultural Development in Kenya: An Economic Assessment*, Nairobi: Oxford University Press.

—— (1981) 'Agricultural development policy in Kenya from the colonial period to 1975', in J. Heyer *et al.* (eds) *Rural Development in Tropical Africa*, London: Macmillan.

Key, N. and Runsten, D. (1999) 'Contract farming, smallholders and rural development in Latin America: the organisation of agro-processing firms and scale of outgrower production', *World Development*, 27(2): 381–401.

Korovkin, T. (1992) 'Peasants, grapes and corporations: the growth of contract farming in a Chilean community', *Journal of Peasant Studies*, 19(2): 228–53.

Lamb, G. and Mueller, L. (1982) *Control, Accountability, and Incentives in a Successful Development Institution: The Kenyan Tea Development Authority (KTDA)*, Working Paper No. 550, World Bank.

Lappe, M. and Collins, J. (1977) *Food First: The Myth of Scarcity*, London: Institute of Food and Development Policy.

Leonard, D. (1991) *African Successes: Four Public Managers of Kenyan Rural Development*, Los Angeles: University of California Press.

Lichts, F.O. (various) *World Tea Markets Monthly*, July 2001.

Little, D. and Watts, M. (1994) (eds) *Living under Contract: Contract Farming and Agrarian Transformation in Sub Saharan Africa*, Madison: Wisconsin University Press.

Lofchie, M. (1989) *The Policy Factor: Agricultural Performance in Kenya and Tanzania*, Boulder: Lynne Rienner Publishers.

Mahihu, E. (1990) 'Report of the Committee to Probe and Restructure Kenya Tea Development Authority', presented to President Daniel Arap Moi, April.

Moser, C. (1978) 'Informal sector or petty commodity production: dualism or independence in urban development', *World Development*, 6(9): 1041–64.

Ochieng, C. (2005) 'The political economy of contract farming in Kenya: a historical-comparative study of the tea and sugar contract farming schemes, 1963–2002', unpublished D.Phil. thesis, University of Oxford.

—— (2007) 'Development through positive deviance and its implications on agricultural policy making and public administration in Africa: the case of Kenyan agricultural development, 1930–2004', *World Development*, 35(3): 454–79.

Porter, G. and Phillips-Howard, K. (1997) 'Comparing contracts: an evaluation of contract farming schemes in Africa', *World Development*, 25(2): 227–38.

Prahalad, C.K. (2005) *The Fortune at the Bottom of the Pyramid*, Saddle River, NJ: Wharton School Publishing.

Raynolds, L. (2000) 'Negotiating contract farming in the Dominican Republic', *Human Organisation*, 59(4): 441–51.

Republic of Kenya (1994) *Public Enterprises Reform Programme*, Nairobi: Government Printer.

Republic of Kenya (2006) *Economic Survey*, Nairobi: Government Printer.

Roy, P. (1972) *Contract Farming and Economic Integration*, Illinois: Interstate Publishers.

Schultz, T.W. (1964) *Transforming Traditional Agriculture*, New Haven: Yale University Press.

Steeves, J. (1975) 'The politics and administration of development: the Kenya Tea Development Authority (K.T.D.A)', unpublished Ph.D. thesis, University of Toronto.

Swainson, N. (1980) *The Development of Corporate Capitalism in Kenya, 1918–1977*, London: Heinemann.

TBK [Tea Board of Kenya] (2002) Annual Report.

White, B. (1997) 'Agro industry and contract farmers in Upland West Java', *Journal of Peasant Studies*, 24(3): 100–136.

Williams, S. and Karen, R. (1985) *Agribusiness and the Smallscale Farmer: A Dynamic Partnership for Development*, Boulder: Westview Press.

World Bank (1981) *Accelerated Development in Sub-Saharan Africa*, Washington, DC: World Bank.

8 Networking for success

Informal enterprise and popular associations in Nigeria

Kate Meagher

Introduction

In informal as in rural economies, understanding processes of social and economic change poses a daunting challenge. Formal structural changes and policy initiatives are constantly cross-cut by local cultural, kinship and political dynamics that disrupt intended outcomes and mystify the majority of development economists. What has made the work of Judith Heyer stand out is her meticulous attention to these informal dynamics, and to the complex ways in which they shape rural society. Her use of detailed fieldwork and fine-grained analysis to trace individual and collective strategies that defy formal structural categories has inspired generations of students frustrated by what Polly Hill (1986) called 'the poverty of development economics' – myself included. A key lesson arising from Heyer's work is that the study of inequality and social change in rural and other informal economic contexts requires attention, not just to large-scale structural factors such as ethnicity, caste and class, but to more fluid social forces such as migration, religious conversion or local gender politics that shape struggles to forge alternative channels of access and advancement.

Drawing on this approach, I will consider how social ties of community, religion, class and gender interweave to create incipient structures of economic differentiation among small firms in a south-eastern Nigerian town. The analysis will focus on the role of popular associations, which serve as an important site for micro-entrepreneurs to consolidate or restructure business and livelihood networks eroded by the upheavals of economic restructuring. New pressures of liberalisation, mass unemployment and rapid informalisation have disrupted existing organisational arrangements embedded in ethnic and occupational identities, encouraging a shift to alternative strategies for shoring up or diversifying livelihood networks. Participation in popular associations has become a key mechanism through which individual producers attempt to restructure their enterprise networks, creating new channels of opportunity and exclusion. As such, associations operate at the interface of structure and agency, providing a lens into the social dynamics of accumulation, differentiation and marginalisation in the fluid institutional environment of informal enterprise and economic restructuring. In the process, the focus on associational participation addresses the concern expressed by Lucia da Corta (Chapter 2, in this volume) for identifying the deeper structural processes that shape individual agency, allowing some to chart trajectories of 'escape', while others are dragged down by 'poverty traps'.

A great deal of ink has been spilled on the role of popular associations in economic development. Debates focus on whether popular associations tend to foster or to frustrate the emergence of more efficient forms of collective organisation. Rural sociologists of the 1960s and 1970s saw 'voluntary associations' as critical to the formation of developmentally oriented values (Redfield 1960), while the more recent fascination with social capital represents popular associations as nurseries of trust, civic engagement and economic efficiency (Putnam 1993). In a similar vein, scholars of small enterprise clusters have been keen to emphasise the role of local clubs and associations in strengthening collaborative relations and economic efficiency among clustered producers. However, development economists and more critical political scientists have been less sanguine about the developmental tendencies of popular associations. They suggest that in unequal and ethnically divided societies, associations may reinforce social divisions, fostering ethnic fragmentation and differentiation rather than cooperation (Englund 2001; McCormick 1999). Rather than fostering economic efficiency, Sara Berry (1993: 271) argues that the participation of African small producers in networks and associations, particularly in times of economic stress, leads to 'a high degree of mobility of people and resources, but little tendency for institutions to develop into stable frameworks for collective action, resource management or the consolidation of capital and knowledge.'

In this chapter, I will examine the individual networking strategies and structural implications of associational participation among small-scale informal entrepreneurs in the town of Aba in the Igbo heartland of Nigeria – an area noted for the rapid growth of its informal manufacturing activities, as well as for high levels of associational participation. I will focus on two large informal manufacturing clusters in Aba, a garment cluster of over 2,000 firms and an artisanal shoe cluster of over 11,000 firms (Meagher 2006). The analysis will begin with an examination of the social history of the two clusters, with attention to the structural underpinnings of identity, class and gender, and the weakening of collective community-based enterprise networks in the context of economic restructuring. This will be followed by a consideration of the varied ways in which participation in local associations has been used to restructure informal economic networks, through individual strategies of reinforcing or breaking ascriptive ties, or building new ties to fill gaps in livelihood networks. Patterns of associational participation reveal individualised processes of agency that fragment rather than reinforce collective entrepreneurial networks. Three distinct networking strategies are evident, described here as embedding, disembedding and diversification, which reveal underlying structural forces shaping patterns of agency. The chapter is based on fieldwork conducted in Aba between October 1999 and September 2000. Detailed fieldwork data are used in conjunction with regression analysis to trace the ways in which structural histories shape individual strategies, and the ways in which individual strategies in turn aggregate into new structural outcomes.

While the social setting for this analysis is urban rather than rural, the Igbo people of south-eastern Nigeria retain rural hometown identities, despite long residence in towns. Severe land shortage since pre-colonial times has led to high levels of urban migration, but the majority still come to town as migrants and return regularly to their rural homes to reaffirm local allegiances. Ongoing land shortage, together with an inheritance system in which the land passes to the eldest son, ensures a steady supply of migrants to the towns to take up the few jobs available, but mostly to engage in culturally embedded systems of small-scale entrepreneurship which have developed over the centuries as the principle solution to agrarian constraints. Effectively, this analysis captures from the other side of the rural–urban nexus some of the themes of diversification, migration, socio-cultural influences and class formation that have come up in Judith Heyer's recent work on rural India. A key point of contrast is that, rather than creating a class of landless labourers, land scarcity in Igbo society has generated a highly developed system of migration and small-scale entrepreneurship.

Informal manufacturing in Aba: a brief institutional history

Igbo society provides an ideal environment for examining the role of associations in the development of informal enterprise. A stateless society in pre-colonial times, the Igbo are renowned for their small-scale, self-help forms of social, political and economic organisation, which even today are manifest in a myriad of hometown associations, credit societies, occupational associations and social clubs (Harneit-Sievers 2006; Brautigam 1997). The Igbo are also famous for their success in the informal economy, owing in large part to strong communal economic institutions, such as hometown-based credit networks, trade associations and an unusually effective apprenticeship system (Forrest 1994; Silverstein 1983). Since the imposition of Nigeria's Structural Adjustment Programme in 1986, the Igbo town of Aba has gained a reputation across Nigeria as a centre of informal manufacturing (Dike 1997). 'Aba-made' has become a widely used Nigerian expression for cheap, low-quality products. While structural adjustment initially stimulated the growth of informal manufacturing by shifting demand from imports to cheap local manufactures, it is the indigenous economic institutions of Igbo society, rather than the liberalised economic environment of adjustment, that has underpinned the dynamism of informal manufacturing in Aba.

The informal shoe and garment clusters constitute Aba's largest and most dynamic informal enterprise clusters. Both clusters emerged in the late colonial period as the occupational niche of migrants from particular Igbo communities outside Aba. The shoe cluster was founded by migrants from the poor, particularly land-scarce community of Mbaise in central Igboland, while the garment cluster was pioneered by migrants from the more prosperous trading and agricultural communities of Old Bende in eastern Igboland. Because of the comparative poverty and lowly social status of Mbaise migrants, and the arduous and unmechanised character of the activity, informal shoe production is regarded as a 'poor man's business'. By contrast, informal garment production is regarded as a respectable occupation owing to the higher social status of Bende migrants and the mechanised character of the activity, which tends to create higher educational and capital barriers to entry. The disreputable and physically demanding character of informal shoe production has militated against the entry of women. While nearly half of firm heads in the informal garment cluster were women, informal shoe producers were all male, and it was rare to find women working in the cluster even as apprentices or family labour.

Both clusters are dominated by very small firms. Garment firms averaged 4.4 workers including the firm head, while shoe firms averaged only 2.4 workers. Despite the small size of firms, these two activities have generated impressive levels of employment and income. By the year 2000, the garment cluster employed over 12,000 people, while the shoe cluster employed a remarkable 46,000 people. The two clusters had a combined annual turnover of nearly US$200 million. Rapid growth has been facilitated by the embeddedness of these enterprise clusters in informal Igbo trading networks that have expanded the distribution of Aba manufactures across West, Central and even Southern Africa in response to growing demand for cheap goods from structurally adjusted African consumers. Impressive as they appear, these figures conceal significant inequalities among firms. In the year 2000, garment producers in the most successful 25 per cent of the cluster enjoyed an average monthly turnover nearly fourteen times that of those in the bottom 50 per cent, and employed more than five times as many workers. In the shoe cluster, divergences were less extreme. Shoe producers in the top quartile had five times the turnover of those in the bottom half of the cluster and employed twice as many workers.

Despite high overall levels of employment and income generation, both clusters were characterised by high levels of economic informality. The majority of the firms involved are unregistered, do not pay many of their required taxes, fail to observe basic official labour and factory regulations, and, in many cases, operate in residential areas not zoned for commercial or industrial activity. A few formal-sector firms operate in and around these clusters, but have comparatively little interaction with the bulk of clustered firms. Operation outside the formal regulatory framework has required the development of alternative structures of business organisation. Firms in these clusters have depended on hometown-based institutions of credit, apprenticeship and trading networks to organise access to markets and resources. These are embedded in a 'Pan Igbo' institutional framework of cooperation among economically specialised Igbo hometown groups.

Since the mid 1980s, structural adjustment has contributed to the dramatic expansion of these clusters, which has tended to overwhelm the regulatory effectiveness of hometown-based economic networks and institutions. High levels of unemployment in the country have triggered rapid entry into both activities, intensifying competition and eroding relations of trust in credit, apprenticeship and marketing networks. The influx of new entrants has also radically altered the communal and class composition of the clusters. At the level of communal identities, rapid entry has diluted the dominance of the founding migrant communities, weakening the regulatory role of hometown-based networks and associations in labour control, debt collection and reputation-based sanctions. In some cases, new entrants have been drawn in from closely related Igbo communities as well as from Igbo groups specialising in the trading side of the activity. These communally and occupationally linked entrants, along with the founding communities, all benefit from a degree of socio-cultural and occupational embeddedness within the activity. Such producers can be said to belong to 'advantaged communities' in their respective activities, owing to their historical experience and extensive communal contacts within the business. There has also been a growing influx from a wider range of Igbo and even non-Igbo groups lacking embedded knowledge or close communal connections within these activities. These comparative outsiders can be said to belong to occupationally 'disadvantaged communities' within the respective clusters.

At the level of class composition, high unemployment has triggered the penetration of better-off, often middle-class entrants into the informal economy. In informal manufacturing, traditional entrants from rural, artisanal or petty commercial backgrounds were being joined by new entrants with backgrounds in formal-sector employment or indigenous business classes. New patterns of class participation have introduced additional structures of advantage and disadvantage. Informal entrants from more privileged class backgrounds, although often forced into informal manufacturing by adverse circumstances, have economic advantages over those from rural or informal sector backgrounds. These include higher levels of education and stronger ties to more resourced and better-connected social groups. With respect to gender, patterns of advantage and disadvantage have been more subtly affected. Women have always made up a significant proportion of garment producers, owing to a traditional division of labour in which women sew for women. However, men have begun to encroach on the more lucrative dimensions of women's tailoring, while there has been a greater feminisation of labour in the production of men's and children's clothes. There has also been a limited feminisation of labour in the shoe cluster, but heads of enterprises have remained exclusively male.

These changes have played themselves out in distinctive ways in Aba's shoe and garment clusters. The more prosperous communal origins of the garment cluster, combined with a communal reputation for tailoring skills, and the higher capital requirements associated with the purchase of sewing machines, have allowed Bende migrants and other historically advantaged communities to maintain their prominence in the activity. By the year 2000, 77 per cent of informal garment producers originated from occupationally advantaged communities, including 44 per cent who originated from the Bende area itself. This suggests a potential for high levels of communal cohesion and cooperation. By contrast, only 38 per cent of shoe producers came from advantaged communities, and only 14 per cent from the founding Mbaise community. Poverty, a reputation for poor skills, and low capital-based barriers to entry (owing to a reliance on simple hand tools) gave Mbaise migrants and related communities little competitive advantage in informal shoe production, making it easier for new entrants from other communities to establish competitive firms. As a result, the majority of shoe producers came from a disparate range of Igbo and even non-Igbo communities with no socio-historical connection to shoe production, creating a greater risk of organisational fragmentation in a highly competitive and informally regulated activity. Despite increased communal fragmentation, economic precariousness, and a constant influx of new firms, survival rates were high. Seventy per cent of firms in the garment cluster, and 63 per cent in the shoe cluster, were over five years old, more than 30 per cent of firms in each cluster were more than ten years old, and each cluster had a small percentage of firms that was more than twenty-five years old.

Owing to differences in the social status of the two activities, the entry of advantaged classes was higher in the garment cluster than in the shoe cluster. By the year 2000, 26 per cent of informal garment producers and 18 per cent of informal shoe producers came from formal sector and business backgrounds rather than from farming or petty commercial backgrounds that have traditionally made up the informal sector. In the garment cluster, women made up a significant share of entrants from advantaged class backgrounds, since tailoring was considered a respectable occupation for middle-class women trying to bring in additional income. By contrast, informal shoe production was not considered respectable for men or women, but some educated actors were forced into the cluster by hard times. These drastic changes in social composition created increasingly wide variations in the social networks available to particular producers. New patterns of associational participation reflect efforts to enter new markets, gain access to new sources of credit or more reliable labour, or just to fill gaps in crumbling business and livelihood networks.

Associational life among Igbo informal manufacturers

Although they belong to the less advantaged sections of society, informal manufacturers in Aba were typically involved in a range of local associations, including hometown unions, religious societies, producers' associations, savings clubs, and a range of social clubs, friendship societies and private-sector associations. Few of the associations common among Aba's informal manufacturers were formed as a result of state initiatives to promote 'civil society' (Guyer 1994). The majority are a product of local initiatives, grounded in local forms of organisation, and operate without state support. While many of these associations are of comparatively recent origins, they have considerable regulatory power in the small-scale socio-cultural framework of Igbo society. But the dense network of associational ties thus created does not provide quite the degree of popular empowerment that one might suppose.

The character of the associations joined by informal manufacturers is quite varied. Some, such as hometown unions, have come to be regarded as mandatory within the moral framework of Igbo society, despite colonial efforts to make them voluntary. Others, such as producers' associations, are more subject to individual choice, despite the efforts of association executives and market officials to make them compulsory. Some of these associations combine informal producers with more advantaged members of society, while others, such as social clubs, are limited to people of the same socio-economic level. Many of the associations involved are formally registered, at least at the local government level, while others remain purely informal. In short, the 'voluntary associations' of informal entrepreneurs are not necessarily voluntary, and not necessarily informal.

This variety of associations provides a dense web of ties that foster opportunities for building and strengthening business linkages, mobilising resources and exchanging information, as well as linking informal producers across communal lines. However, the capacity of local associations to foster trust and economic efficiency is often limited by the social and economic marginality of informal producers. Low social status, limited education and constraints of time and resources influence the types of associations informal producers are able to join, and their access to benefits within them. Workers in informal enterprises also join most of the same associations, with the exception of producers' and business associations and social clubs, but their degree of marginalisation within these associations is even greater than in the case of informal producers.

Patterns of associational participation

Overall, Aba's informal manufacturers were found to belong to an average of 3.6 associations across a range of communal and cross-community organisations (Table 8.1). On the whole, shoe producers participated in more associations than garment producers for reasons that will be discussed below. The two most important types of associations in both clusters were hometown unions and religious societies, to which the majority of informal producers belonged. While the popularity of these associations appears to indicate a prevailing commitment to particularistic loyalties, they have come to represent more progressive forms of civic engagement. In the face of state withdrawal, hometown and religious associations increasingly mobilise members around issues of economic and infrastructural development rather than around more parochial concerns.

Table 8.1 Rates of participation in various types of popular associations (% of firms)

Cluster	Home-town unions	Religious societies	Producers' associations	Savings clubs	Local social clubs	Formal private-sector associations and business clubs	Avg. no. of associations per person
Garments	63.9	85.2	6.6	39.3	9.8	6.6	3.0
Shoes	81.7	77.5	83.1	49.3	18.0	5.6	4.2
Average	73.5	81.1	47.7	44.7	14.0	6.1	3.6

Source: 2000 fieldwork.

Note: N = 132.

Hometown unions in particular have become increasingly important agencies of infrastructural and social welfare provision in the face of declining state involvement. They can also be important sites for business contacts and access to loans within advantaged communities. These functions are not so much independent of the state as complementary to it. Igbo hometown unions are officially registered and have strong connections with the state through incorporation into official community development strategies and through links with their elite sons in government. Thus, hometown unions serve as a conduit for state resources and a gateway to wider political connections.

Participation in the village union of one's home community, requiring an annual return visit to the village, is considered mandatory for all adults (which usually means after marriage). Non-participation is sanctioned by social disapproval and various degrees of ostracism. However, involvement in hometown unions has become increasingly problematic for those with limited resources. The increased social welfare and infrastructural responsibilities of hometown unions, and their growing role in political mobilisation, have led to higher and more frequent levies on members. At the same time, assistance from better-off members to more needy townsmen has declined, hardening lines of class differentiation within local communities. Despite the strong moral sanctions against withdrawal, hard economic times and the contradictory demands of evangelical Christianity have begun to erode commitment to hometown unions.

By contrast, participation in religious societies has been rising in the face of economic pressures and the proliferation of Pentecostal or 'prosperity' churches. This is particularly marked in Abia State, where Pentecostal and evangelical churches far outweigh the established churches. The sheer profusion of religious sects in the area is remarkable. Within a sample of 132 informal producers, 26 different denominations were represented, 20 of them Pentecostal sects. Since the 1980s, these sects have spread rapidly in Nigeria and have proven particularly attractive to members of the middle and aspiring middle classes who have lost out in the process of economic restructuring. In Aba, prominent sects include Deeper Life Bible Church, Assemblies of God, Christian Partnership Mission and the non-Christian sect of Eckankar, all of which are global organisations, with branches in the United States.[1] The attraction of these churches appears to be both moral and strategic. Pentecostal churches promote an ethic of moral rectitude, frugality and economic advancement, as well as creating new social boundaries based on religious purity rather than communal identity. They also link members into global religious networks which facilitate access to overseas contacts, scholarships, travel to international church conventions, and other resources outside the framework of state connections and influence.

Where hometown unions and established church associations reinforce communal embeddedness, Pentecostal religious associations tend to encourage disembedding from community-based ties, and re-embedding in new, more global and professionally oriented organisational networks. From this perspective, the higher participation of garment producers in Pentecostcal rather than hometown associations appears strange, given the comparative prominence of the founding community. By contrast, the preference of shoe producers for participation in hometown associations would be expected to reinforce their communal fragmentation and socio-economic disadvantage. The reasons for this unexpected twist will be explored below.

Producers' associations and savings groups represent the second most prominent types of association. Both of these represent organisations with more specifically economic goals that unite members across both religious and community lines. While participation levels are highly uneven, they average just under one-half of producers across the two clusters. Participation in producers' associations is particularly uneven, with only one producers' association in the garment cluster, representing fewer than 10 per cent of producers. By contrast, more than 80 per cent of shoe producers are members of producers' associations, despite, or perhaps because of, their diverse community origins. Producers' associations provide basic regulatory services within the clusters, including dispute resolution, security and contributions for the burial of members.

Savings clubs, which account for 40–50 per cent of producers in the clusters, refer to arrangements in which an independent operator collects regular contributions from an otherwise unconnected clientele. These institutions only facilitate savings, and do not grant loans. Although these savings clubs date from colonial times, they have become particularly popular in the past decade owing to the high level of bank failures triggered by numerous reforms of the banking sector from the early 1990s. South-eastern Nigeria appears to have suffered disproportionately from the spate of bank failures, severely shaking local confidence in the banking system. A number of informal producers indicated that they had previously used bank accounts, but had reverted to informal savings groups because the banks were too unreliable. Unfortunately, participation in savings groups has also been weakened by declining earnings and greater dishonesty of savings group operators. Many producers participated in contribution clubs embedded in their hometown unions, church groups or social clubs, which were seen as more reliable.

Finally, social clubs and formal private-sector associations show the lowest levels of participation, averaging less than 20 per cent of informal producers overall. Local social clubs refer to groups organised around socialising with peers, also known as friendship societies or 'committees of friends'. These groups may unite peers from the same home area or occupation, or they may cross-cut community and occupational boundaries, depending on the objectives and social contacts of the participants. They can be an important means of mobilising resources or information for business needs, but tend to be highly segregated along socio-economic and educational lines. It is striking that the participation of shoe producers in social clubs is nearly twice as high as that of garment producers, despite the former's less advantaged socio-economic and educational status.

Formal private-sector associations and business clubs also reflect pronounced class divisions (Silverstein 1983: 292). They involve a range of social organisations with national as well as international links to formal-sector business interests. These include national private-sector organisations, such as the Manufacturers'

Association of Nigeria (MAN), the Aba Chamber of Commerce (ACCIMA), the Nigerian Association of Small and Medium-Scale Industrialists (NASSI), as well as national and international associations of businessmen and professionals, such as the Full Gospel Businessmen's Fellowship and the Rotary or Lions' Clubs. All of these associations have branches in Aba. Derisory levels of participation among informal shoe and garment producers, averaging only 6 per cent, reflect the persistence of strong class divisions between formal- and informal-sector operators, despite the growing penetration of middle-class operators into both clusters.

The majority of formal private-sector associations preserve class boundaries through legal requirements and relatively high membership fees. Some, such as MAN and ACCIMA, have explicit requirements that the businesses of members must be formally registered. These institutional barriers are reinforced by social barriers, which discourage participation of producers who feel their educational level, command of English (the language of education in Nigeria), mode of dress or financial capacity to bear entertainment costs might lead to embarrassment. Questions regarding why producers decided against participation in these associations were generally met with embarrassed and vague answers. The handful of informal producers in the sample who participated in private-sector associations did so only at the lowest level. One was a member of NASSI and the remainder were members of the Full Gospel Businessmen's Fellowship, which is popular among traders and tends to be less educationally exclusive.

The economic role of local associations

Despite high levels of participation in local associations among informal manufacturers, the direct economic advantages of participation were limited. Over 40 per cent of garment producers, and nearly 70 per cent of shoe producers, maintained that local associations offered no advantages for enterprise development. At best, they provided limited social welfare assistance in response to family emergencies or burials. Among the minority who felt that associations contributed to the development of their businesses, the main benefit centred on the role of associations in attracting customers. Small producers found associations a useful way of advertising their businesses, and tailors and shoe producers often wore their own best wares to church or to important meetings in order to interest potential clients.

Among the better skilled and connected, membership in associations could bring production contracts to supply ceremonial wear for burials, weddings or associational functions. The downside of these forms of assistance was that concessional prices were expected for any business obtained through associational ties. Moreover, associational membership was only useful for attracting business if there were not too many others in the same activity within the association. This meant that belonging to a hometown union in which shoe or garment producers were well represented was a mixed blessing.

In some cases, associations could provide a useful source of business contacts. References from local notables or well-connected businessmen within one's association were an important means of guaranteeing credit or obtaining contracts with companies or parastatals. However, interviews with producers suggested that loans, references and even useful business contacts were rarely available to small informal producers. They tended to be reserved for more influential or successful association members. Business loans were sometimes mobilised through social clubs, though interest rates were not necessarily concessional. Rotating credit groups were normally used only as means of savings, and most producers maintained that the funds generated were insufficient for business purposes.

In addition to being intermittent and limited, the forms of business assistance available though associations were largely side effects of membership, rather than associational objectives. Popular associations were unable to offer more structured forms of assistance to local businesses because their own projects consumed the bulk of their resources. Providing infrastructure for their local communities, building churches, raising funds for local or religious ceremonies, and responding to pressing social welfare demands left little in the way of funds or organisational slack for providing assistance to a profusion of small businesses. In fact, the growing responsibilities of popular associations for social provisioning transformed them into an increasing financial drain on members rather than a source of economic assistance. As one garment producer put it, 'Associations don't help you with money, they demand it!'

While membership dues remained fairly modest, the increasing financial demands of local associations manifested themselves in a growing array of levies and emergency contributions. Members' standing in a given association was strongly influenced by the ability to contribute lavishly on such occasions. Including dues and special levies, average annual contributions amounted to roughly two months' wages for a skilled worker in both clusters. The cost of participation varied significantly according to social status. Successful garment producers reported levies and extra contributions of nearly twice as much as their poorer colleagues, while better-off shoe producers contributed more than ten times as much as their less successful counterparts. The time demands of associational membership were also a significant constraint on participation. Time commitments for participation in associations averaged 19 hours per month in the case of garments, and 16 hours per month for shoes. This excluded burials and ceremonies, which often took participants out of town. The majority of producers in both clusters feared heavy participation in associations would run down their business. Those with more resources and social authority could defray the pressures of associational time commitments by sending someone to represent them at less important meetings or ceremonies, or by leaving trusted workers in charge of the business in their absence. Poorer producers, who lacked such control over labour, faced fines and social censure for non-attendance at meetings. This forced them to restrict associational participation in order to minimise the drain on time and resources.

Associations and popular agency: embedding, disembedding and diversification

Among Aba's informal shoe and garment producers, voluntary associations appear to offer a very uneven source of 'social capital'. In fact, flows of information and resources generated by associational participation appear to reinforce rather than counteract structures of advantage emanating from the formal economy. Communal, gender and class divisions embedded in associational structures, combined with the economic pressures of associational participation, clearly limit the extent to which popular associations are able to compensate for structural disadvantages in the wider society.

This becomes glaringly obvious when the focus is shifted from particular types of associations, to the social factors governing overall participation rates in voluntary associations. Regression analysis of the influence of identity, class, gender, age and religion on associational participation in the two clusters revealed that structurally advantaged producers tended to join a greater number of voluntary associations than their less advantaged counterparts (Table 8.2). Producers aged thirty or more from advantaged class backgrounds tended to participate in more associations than younger, lower-class producers. By contrast, women and members of evangelical churches participated in fewer associations than men and members of mainstream churches. In short, senior male producers from established churches and advantaged class backgrounds – in other words, the local establishment – were the most active participants in voluntary associations. Once these social factors were taken into consideration, differences in associational participation between the shoe and garment clusters became statistically insignificant.

While popular associations tended to reinforce structural disadvantage among informal producers, they also created space for popular agency. Patterns of associational participation were not only a product of economic constraints

Table 8.2 The relationship between structural disadvantage and levels of participation in local associations (linear regression)

Factors	Unstandardised beta coefficient	Significance
(Constant)	3.52 (.41)	.000
Shoe sector (ref. Garment)	.64 (.38)	.090
Age 30+ (ref. below 30)	.75 (.29)	.011
Women	−1.19 (.44)	.002
Advantaged community	−.49 (.31)	.115
Advantaged class[a]	.67 (.34)	.053
Evangelical membership	−.60 (.29)	.038
R*[b]	.245	
N	129	

Source: 2000 fieldwork (second small-firm survey).

Notes
a Those from formal sector or medium-/large-scale commercial backgrounds.
b Dependent variable: the number of associations to which a small producer belongs.

on membership; they were found to reflect strategic choices about the types of networks that various categories of producers wished to build or reinforce. A closer examination of the patterns of associational participation revealed that, far from being trapped by their structural disadvantages, informal producers exercised considerable agency in deciding which associations to join in order to maximise economic advantages or fill gaps in business networks. Three different strategies of associational participation were identified, which can be described as embedding, disembedding and diversification.

Hometown associations and embedding strategies

Associational strategies based on strengthening communal embeddedness centred on participation in hometown unions. Interestingly, the appeal of this strategy was shaped, not by membership in artisanally advantaged communities, but by a particular configuration of class, gender and communal characteristics. In fact, regression analysis showed that producers from artisanally advantaged communities were considerably less likely to participate in their hometown unions (Table 8.3). Women were also found to be less likely to join hometown unions than men, owing to their very limited power within them. Those with junior secondary education or more, and those below the age of thirty, were also associated with a lower probability of membership. By contrast, producers from advantaged class backgrounds showed a very strong propensity to join hometown unions – indeed, they were found to be over four times as likely to join as producers from disadvantaged class backgrounds.

On the whole, these findings corroborate earlier indications that older male members from advantaged classes tend to monopolise benefits within hometown associations, to the disadvantage of women, youth and those from disadvantaged classes. In short, participation in hometown unions reflects a strategy of collaboration with the establishment in the hope of access or assistance. The following case from the shoe cluster illustrates the interplay between identity and class in networking strategies based on hometown unions.

Mr Chukwuma, an indigene of Mbaise, is a well-established producer of women's shoes. He is from a trading background and his father is also a village chief. After completing primary school in the early 1970s, he was apprenticed to a townsman. In 1978, he started up his own business with substantial capital given to him by his family. Now the head of a thriving business with three apprentices and three temporary workers, Mr Chukwuma has built up his business through active participation in a range of associations. These include both his village and his town unions, a Catholic Church association, his local shoemakers' association and a savings club. He says his hometown union has been a useful source of business contacts and customers, while his church group sometimes helps with loans. Strengthening his embeddedness in the communal and religious establishment has provided the resources and contacts to diversify his business networks. None of Mr Chukwuma's workers are relatives or townsmen – he prefers to use friendship ties and business contacts as a means of selecting workers. Ties with suppliers and customers are also largely through pure business relations. In addition to selling to traders who distribute across West, Central and North Africa, Mr Chukwuma also gets significant business from formal-sector firms and boutiques. His business networks involve many traders who are non-Mbaise, and even non-Igbo. In fact, Mr. Chukwuma complains that the concentration of Mbaise producers in the shoe cluster is a disadvantage, since it exposes him to too many demands for assistance from struggling townsmen.

In the above case, the producer's advantaged class background afforded him better access to capital and contacts within his hometown union than most of his fellow producers – something he has used to advance himself occupationally by diversifying his business networks, and distancing himself from his less advantaged townsmen.

Evangelical religious associations and communal disembedding

Producers who find themselves marginalised within the framework of hometown unions have had to seek alternative networking strategies in their quest to 'get ahead'. Evangelical religious associations have played a central role in the creation of alternative networks of social advancement. This is not to suggest an absence of spiritual motivation in conversion to evangelical sects, but to indicate that spiritual impulses to convert tended to arise within a particular socio-economic framework. Exhortations of religious purity discourage members of strict evangelical sects from participating in any other types of associations, especially hometown unions, owing to their involvement in the consumption of alcohol and connections with ancestral shrines and 'idol worship'. Steeped in a Weberian ethic of piety, industry and frugality, Nigeria's Pentecostal churches not only address the spiritual anxiety induced by the punishing economic circumstances of structural adjustment; they provide a normative framework for the conservation and concentration of resources, rather than their dissipation through levies and ceremonies of a range of hometown, occupational and friendship associations. In Aba, 33 per cent of producers in the garment cluster, and 10 per cent of producers in the shoe cluster adopted a disembedding strategy based on exclusive participation in their religious associations.

As Table 8.4 indicates, participation in evangelical exit strategies was shaped by two key factors: gender and class. Women and producers from disadvantaged class backgrounds were over five times more likely to join exclusive evangelical religious societies than men or producers from advantaged class backgrounds. These factors are the opposite of those found to promote participation in hometown unions, suggesting that religious exit strategies were a response to the exclusion experienced by skilled but structurally disadvantaged small producers within the framework of hometown unions. This explains why garment producers, who had a high proportion of women and members from disadvantaged classes, were especially prone to participation in religious exit strategies.

An examination of producers' social histories reveals that evangelical exit strategies were also accompanied by a strong commitment to artisanal values of skill and quality. Where not associated with membership in artisanally advantaged communities or higher levels of education, a skill-based orientation was often indicated by other factors in a producer's history, especially the tendency to enrol in additional apprenticeships in the same activity in order to obtain more specialised production skills, as the following example illustrates.

Mr Esiobu is a middle-aged producer of men's shirts from Okigwe, a disadvantaged community in the garment cluster. Hailing from a rural farming background, Mr Esiobu never had an opportunity to go to school. He came to Aba in 1972 to train as a tailor. He first trained in sewing general men's wear, then, in order to improve his skills, did a second apprenticeship with a tailor who specialised in shirts. After completing his second apprenticeship, Mr Esiobu worked for his master as a journeyman to earn some start-up capital, and also worked as a bricklayer. He started his own business in 1976 and worked extremely long hours to get established – sometimes going three to four days on end without sleep. This regime affected his health, and he was forced to leave the business after two years. He turned to trading shoes, which he continued to do until his trading business collapsed in 1987. At this point, Mr Esiobu felt called back to tailoring and relaunched his shirt business in 1988.

During his absence from tailoring, Mr Esiobu became a member of Deeper Life Bible Church. He now belongs only to his religious society and to no other association. He claimed the hometown union did not help businesses, but just imposed levies to build things for the village. Participation in Deeper Life has reduced his economic liabilities, contributing to the growth of his business. Through skill and hard work, Mr Esiobu has developed good contacts with traders and boutiques, and builds up his distribution networks on the basis of reliability, quality and the use of a complementary card. He once had an order of over one thousand shirts through an indirect contract from the Nigerian Shipping Council. He recruits most of his workers through customers on the basis of his reputation, selecting them for their skills and paying higher than the going rate in order to keep them loyal. However, Mr Esiobu's lack of education has limited his ability to gain access to Deeper Life occupational networks in the garment sector. In contrast to more educated converts, Mr Esiobu has not found Deeper Life connections a useful source of workers, since those offered to him lacked adequate education (most parents in the church would not send an educated child to train with an uneducated tailor). His lack of education also limits his ability to get contracts, forcing him to source such work via better-connected middlemen for less than the going rate.

While this case study supports the contention that withdrawal into religious societies was favoured by ambitious producers with a strong artisanal orientation, it also indicates that education is critical to the ability to reap the full benefits of evangelical religious networks. While the producer profiled above was able to reduce his social liabilities by joining an exclusive religious group, he was not able to tap into a significant level of new social capital. By contrast, a moderately successful shoe producer with secondary school education was far more successful in tapping into evangelical networks to further his business. He obtained much more skilled labour through Deeper Life contacts, and his longest-standing customer was a Deeper Life member from Lagos, who brought him considerable business and granted credit when needed. Gender could also influence the ability to benefit from evangelical networks, but poor women's economic opportunities were better in evangelical than in hometown networks. For a producer even to contemplate withdrawal into evangelical networks, however, his or her skills and occupational values must be strong enough to warrant the risky strategy of cutting oneself off from the social welfare assistance of hometown associations.

Diversification strategies: religious conversion and social clubs

A final set of strategies involves efforts to use associational participation to diversify social networks rather than to concentrate them. In contrast to disembedding strategies, diversification represents a risk-averse strategy oriented toward increasing connections to various groups in order to maximise options for access and assistance. Diversification strategies were found to involve two main practices: conversion to evangelical churches without withdrawal from hometown unions, or participation in social clubs.

Diversification strategies based on evangelical conversion involved producers whose skills and education were above average, but who, for a variety of reasons, were unwilling to cut themselves off from community networks altogether. This strategy was found among about one-quarter of shoe and garment producers. In general, religious diversification strategies were used to compensate for critical weaknesses in one's social networks, without cutting off any options.

In some cases, religious conversion acted as a mechanism for bonding with the main artisanal groups in a cluster. In both the shoe and the garment clusters, membership in evangelical churches was prominent among comparatively skilled and successful producers who were not from the original artisanal community. In some cases, conversion occurred some time ago, often well before structural adjustment. Many of the producers involved were from important trading communities, making it undesirable to sever hometown connections, since strong trading links were useful to the individual enterprise as well as to the cluster as a whole. A more prevalent strategy was to use religious diversification to maximise limited advantages in the face of economic insecurity. In such cases, evangelical conversion was a fairly recent response to contemporary social and economic upheavals, and constituted a purely personal rather than a collective networking strategy. Recent evangelical converts were characterised by higher-than-average levels of skills and/or education, but tended to suffer from serious capital constraints and weaknesses in their social networks. These weaknesses, often accompanied by heavy family responsibilities, made it too risky for them to sever ties with their home communities, which were a critical social welfare fallback in times of trouble. The story of Mrs Ubah, a widow of advantaged class background, exemplifies the pressures and strategies involved.

Mrs Ubah is a women's tailor from an advantaged class, but disadvantaged community background in Abia State. Her parents were employed in the formal sector and put their daughter through secondary school. Mrs Ubah finished secondary school in the late 1970s, after which she married, and came to Aba in 1985. By 1987, one year after the onset of structural adjustment, Mrs Ubah decided to take up tailoring to help make ends meet. She served a two-year apprenticeship with a tailor to whom she was directed by friends, and started up her own business in 1989 with capital from her family. Somewhere along the line, her husband died, leaving Mrs Ubah to support the family with her tailoring business. She is now the head of a household of eight and has been struggling to keep things together. Part of this struggle has involved her conversion to the Pentecostal Covenant Mission, although she still maintains membership in her husband's village and hometown associations as well. Mrs Ubah has built up her labour, supply and distribution networks largely through a combination of business and personal relationships. She currently has one employee and one apprentice, obtained through customers and a former apprentice rather than through kinship or hometown ties. She sews largely for individual customers from various parts of Nigeria, who linked up with her through relatives and previous customers. Mrs Ubah finds that her church meeting is a particularly useful source of customers and business contacts, though not of loans or contracts from companies.

Although educated and reasonably skilled, the producer described above lacks both the strong artisanal socialisation and the occupational networks that characterised the Deeper Life members profiled in the previous case studies. Mrs Ubah's economic orientation was driven by livelihood rather than occupational concerns. While widening networks of assistance, evangelical diversification also increases the demands on a producer's time and resources. Converts face the resource demands of regular church collections and levies in addition to those of their hometown unions. For evangelical diversification to facilitate economic advancement, converts would have to be in a position to invest significantly in evangelical as well as hometown networks, both systems in which status is heavily influenced by the generosity of contributions. In diversifying their networks, more economically insecure converts broaden their contacts, but most spread their resources too thin to reap any significant business gains.

A completely different diversification strategy concerns participation in social clubs and friendship societies. This strategy involves an attempt to diversify ties through investment in friendship networks, which create links across community lines, or across various lines of business. Unlike religious diversification strategies, which encourage an ethic of modesty and frugality, participation in social clubs revolves around an ethic of lavish hospitality. Among Aba's small manufacturers, social clubs built relations of trust, mutual assistance and exchange of information among peers through social activities such as hosting each other with food and drink, and spending as lavishly as possible at each other's ceremonies (marriages, baptisms, burials, etc.). Social clubs were often a means of strengthening links among townsmen in other businesses, or of maintaining ties formed in secondary (or junior secondary) school. Some social clubs also hosted seasonal festivities, such as Christmas parties, in which displays of wealth and generosity were aimed as much at creating important social and business contacts with guests from outside the group as they were at maintaining ties within the group.

For some producers, social clubs were an important means of pooling resources for loans, particularly among those whose community- and class-based connections provided little alternative access to such resource pools. At the same time, the ability to participate in such clubs required enough in the way of surplus resources to meet entertainment obligations without obvious strain. As a result, social clubs were favoured by producers who were successful enough to engage in economic displays among their peers, but lacked the class contacts, skill levels and social disposition to advance themselves through hometown or religious associations.

Unsurprisingly, given these motivations, participation in social clubs was heavily concentrated among older, better-off producers from disadvantaged communities, and was almost twice as high in the shoe cluster as in the garment cluster. Established producers from disadvantaged communities tended to have more capital than connections or skills, making social clubs a more effective method of strengthening occupational networks. This situation was particularly pronounced in the shoe cluster, where non-advantaged communities predominated, occupational professionalism was more weakly developed and profits could be high for those with capital and passable skills. The strategy of network diversification through investment in friendship ties is illustrated by the case of Mr Wilfred, an enterprising non-Igbo shoe producer from Delta State.

Mr Wilfred, a producer of ladies' and children's shoes, has been in the business for sixteen years. His father was a farmer and was unable to fund Mr Wilfred's education beyond the primary school level. Originally, Mr Wilfred had come to Aba to train as an electrician, but his master ran into economic problems and sent him back to his village. Not wanting to hang around, Mr Wilfred returned to Aba to train as a shoemaker under a friend of his. His family gave him a little capital to start up with, but he had to work as a labourer to build up his capital to a viable level. Difficult economic times forced him to move shop several times during his first years in business, but through hard work and reliable performance, he managed to build up strong credit and customer networks. In 1994, he was among the shoemakers forced by police to move to the newly constructed shoe production zone known as Bakassi, at the edge of Ariaria market. The facilities were very poor, with no electricity, no paths between the stalls, and no security for people's goods.

Mr Wilfred now does comparatively well at the lower end of the market but is against the kinds of sharp practices and use of inferior materials common among younger producers. He supports a household of nine and belongs to six associations, including an Anglican religious association and three social clubs. One of these involves friends from his home area, another involves shoemaker friends, and another involves friends in other lines of business. Involvement in these associations is largely for social purposes, but they can also be helpful for business. One of his social clubs gives loans large enough for business purposes, based on internal contributions. Some of the members of another club have brothers who are shoe traders, and these traders have become his customers. However, participation in so many associations requires a significant commitment of time and resources. Mr Wilfred must attend meetings as well as ceremonies, especially for the fellow members of his social clubs. Membership fees, levies and contributions consumed N30,000 (US$300) in 2000. Mr Wilfred intends to stay in shoe production for another five years, and then to move into another activity more suitable for older men, such as trade.

Conclusion

The high levels of associational participation characteristic of Igbo society have done little to promote the development of a more collaborative informal institutional environment for small-scale enterprise. Indeed, the thick web of associational life in which informal actors are embedded appears to reinforce rather than moderate tendencies toward social fragmentation and intense competition over access to resources. Rather than creating a basis of trust and collective action, associational strategies appear to be geared largely to the pursuit of personal or sectional advantage.

The embedding and disembedding strategies associated with hometown unions and exclusive evangelical societies reflect tactics of group closure that seek to maximise class or skill-based advantages in ways that marginalise weaker fellow producers. Groups with more limited advantages in human and social capital turn to diversification strategies in an effort to widen their portfolio of ties with better-off members of society, though in ways that tend to dissipate rather than focus resources. The poorest producers, unable to afford the risks of closure or the costs of diversification, remain marginalised within these associational networks by the same lack of skills and resources that marginalise them in the formal economy. They join very few associations and rely largely on ascriptive membership in hometown and conventional religious associations when they do.

Ultimately, associational participation appears to have more to do with strategies for linking up with more powerful and successful groups than with strengthening collaborative relations or popular agency within the clusters. Not only do these strategies tend to dissipate resources in the service of diverse associational goals, as Sara Berry (1993) argues in other African contexts, but they also make small producers vulnerable to the powerful interests with which they strive to forge ties. Despite the appearance of agency afforded by associational strategies, informal producers seem more like flies than spiders in the web of associational life.

Notes

1   Deeper Life has an office in Montgomery, Alabama; Overcomers and Christian Partnership Mission both have branches in Texas; Assemblies of God runs its activities out of Springfield, Missouri; and Eckankar has a temple in Chanhassen, Minnesota.

Table 8.3 Logistic regression of propensity to join hometown associations

Variable	Odds multiplier	Significance
Shoe sector (ref. Garment sector)	.94	.926
Women	.20	.020
Youth (ref. 30 years and over)	.44	.087
Advantaged class	4.58	.021
Advantaged community	.37	.054
JSS education+ (ref. primary or less)	.40	.080
Constant	16.39	.000
Model improvement	28.52 (6 df)	.000
Total N	129	

Source: 2000 fieldwork (second small-firm survey).

Table 8.4 Logistic regression of propensity for exclusive membership in religious associations

Variable	Odds multiplier	Significance
Garment sector	2.80	.091
Women	5.31	.008
Disadvantaged class	5.27	.026
Constant	.021	.000
Model improvement	23.89 (3 df)	.000
Total N	131	

Source: 2000 fieldwork (second small-firm survey).

Bibliography

Berry, S. (1993) 'Coping with confusion: African farmers' responses to economic instability in the 1970s and 1980s', in T.M. Callaghy and J. Ravenhill (eds) *Hemmed In. Responses to Africa's Economic Decline*, New York: Columbia University Press, pp. 248–78.

Brautigam, D. (1997) 'Substituting for the state: institutions and industrial development in eastern Nigeria', *World Development*, 25(7): 1063–80.

Dike, E. (1997) *Structural Adjustment and Small-scale Industrial Entrepreneurs in Southeastern Nigeria*, Geneva: United Nations Research Institute for Social Development.

Englund, D. (2001) 'The politics of multiple identities', in A. Tostensen, I. Tvedten and M. Vaa (eds) *Associational Life in African Cities*, Uppsala: Nordiska Afrikainstitutet, pp. 90–106.

Forrest, T. (1994) *The Advance of African Capital: The Growth of Nigerian Private Enterprise*, Edinburgh: Edinburgh University Press for the International African Institute.

Guyer, J.I. (1994) 'The spatial dimensions of civil society in Africa: an anthropologist looks at Nigeria', in J. Harbeson, N. Chazan and D. Rothchild (eds) *Civil Society and the State in Africa*, Boulder, CO: Lynne Rienner, pp. 215–30.

Harneit-Sievers, A. (2006) *Constructions of Belonging: Igbo Communities and the Nigerian State in the Twentieth Century*, Rochester, NY: University of Rochester Press.

Hill, P. (1986) *Development Economics on Trial: The Anthropological Case for the Prosecution*, Cambridge: Cambridge University Press.

McCormick, D. (1999) 'African enterprise clusters and industrialization: theory and reality', *World Development*, 27(9): 1531–51.

Meagher, K. (2006) 'Social capital, social liabilities, and political capital: social networks and informal manufacturing in Nigeria', *African Affairs*, 105(421): 553–82.

Putnam, R.D. (1993) *Making Democracy Work: Civil Traditions in Modern Italy*, Princeton, NJ: Princeton University Press.

Redfield, R. (1960) *Peasant Society and Culture*, Chicago, IL: University of Chicago Press.

Silverstein, S. (1983) 'Sociocultural organization and locational strategies of transportation entrepreneurs: an ethnoeconomic history of the Nnewi Igbo of Nigeria', Graduate School, Boston, MA: Boston University.

9 Free and unfree labour in the Cape wine industry, 1838–1988

Gavin Williams

Sociological enquiries start from questions or puzzles. My puzzles began in a discussion with the late Johann Hamman at a conference in Wageningen in 1989 (Williams 1991). How did agricultural labour markets work in the wine industry in the absence of pass laws to control and canalise labour to meet the needs of farmers and mining companies? This led to further questions. How did a producers' cooperative rather than a state marketing board regulate the industry? What were the relations between the regulation of markets for wine and the forms of labour?

Unfree to free labour

The wine industry was built on slave labour. When the rule of the Dutch United East India Company ended in 1795, its successors were soon persuaded that slavery was indispensable for the life of the economy (Worden 1989: 31). After the abolition of the slave trade in 1808 and the opening of the British markets to Cape exports from 1813, wine production 'necessarily involve[d] the more intensive exploitation of the existing labour force' (Rayner 1986: 7–8).

Ordinance 50 of 1828 placed 'Hottentots [Khoi] and other free persons of colour' in a position of equality before the law (Macmillan 1968: 211–12). They could no longer be made to carry the passes that had been imposed in 1809. This would allow the Khoi immediately, the freed slaves after 1838, and the Coloured labourers in the future, a degree of mobility. Farmers would continue to look for ways to get around the free status of Coloured farm workers, to control farm workers and to prevent them from 'deserting' their employers.

On Emancipation Day, 1 December 1838, freed slaves deserted the wine and wheat estates 'to escape the bonds of farm labour' (Ross 1986: 82). They went to towns, villages or mission stations or wherever they could find a space. The first task for landowners was to get workers back onto their farms.

The 'options open to the former slaves themselves were limited' (Dooling 2007: 117). They were denied land and legally prohibited from squatting. They needed money and somewhere to live. Farmers could attract workers by paying advances and by providing wine rations. To keep workers, farmers provided small plots of land, and lodging, conditional on the availability of the tenants and their wives to provide labour. Farm worker households gained a measure of autonomy, but within the farm economy rather than separate from it.

Colonists pressed the government to legislate what they could not compel, making 'idle persons, thieves and vagabonds . . . seek for service' (Mason 2003: 170). Successive 1841, 1856 and 1875 Masters and Servants Laws were designed to force free workers back into service on farms under the authority of their masters and of the colonial government.

After Emancipation, farmers and the government created an array of institutional arrangements in response to the unwillingness of freed slaves, and of free Khoi, men and women, to be available for work on farms under their direct authority and at the least possible cost. Some were enshrined in laws to tie servants to contracts and subject their attitudes and behaviour to the moral and legal authority of their masters. Others were extra-legal: the allocation of land for cultivation and offers of wine. The needs for such arrangements indicate the scope for rural households to maintain a degree of autonomy from the domination of landowners.

Prices, regulation and wages

In 1860, the Anglo-French Trade Treaty removed the Cape's tariff advantages. The wine industry had to find its own market within the Cape Colony. The market for wine was dependent on the rises and falls of diamond prices and production. The extension of the railways and the diamond fields opened up a new and lucrative Cape market for wine farmers. They shared in the long international depression from 1884 to 1894 and drew some benefit, though less than might have been expected, from the South African War (1899–1902).

Production expanded from 25,000 to 35,000 leaguers per annum between 1865 and 1875 and reached 48,000 leaguers in 1893.[1] The median price of 'inferior', which was most wine, was £9 per leaguer between 1870 and 1907, but it varied between £24 during the first diamond boom in 1874 and £4 during the international depression of 1884–94. It collapsed completely to 7s 9d (3/4d a gallon) when the supplies of wine and brandy glutted the market in 1889 (Cape of Good Hope 1878: Q7, Q10; Scully 1990: 106).[2] The discovery of gold on the Witwatersrand in 1886 did not come to the rescue of Cape wine farmers as Zuid-Afrikaansche Republiek tariffs shut them out of the Rand market (van Onselen 1982: 51–67). Brandy found new buyers during the South African war. The price of wine reached £16 per leaguer at the end of the war but the market could not be sustained.

The diamond industry reduced the supply and increased the wages of labour at the same time as it increased the demand for wine. The possibility of finding work elsewhere made labour more expensive and also constrained the ability of farmers to exercise authority over their workers. Schemes to recruit European workers from Europe failed because the workers could not be kept on the farms; plans to import Africans because farmers paid too little. Farmers had to fall back on their local labour force (Constantia Association 1895–1900; Scully 1986: 4; Harries 2005: 99–100).

Between 1870 and 1909, wages paid by the day in the Paarl and Stellenbosch districts were typically between 1s and 1s 6d per day. Cash wages paid monthly to resident workers were between 15s and 20s (7d to 9d per day). Between 1870 and 1877, in response to changes in the fortune of diamonds, wages in pence changed in line with the price paid for wine in pounds the previous year. They then diverged, to the advantage of workers, between 1878 and 1901 (Scully 1990: 61). Farmers could not make up for low prices during the depression years by reducing wages proportionately. Wages went up briefly when there was a rapid increase in the demand for labour in the Colony. But when prices fell, wages did not go down very far with them.

From 1905, the primary concern of farmers was to raise the prices they received for their very ordinary wine. The Ko-operatieve Wijnbouwers Vereeniging van Zuid-Afrika (KWV) was formed in December 1917 with the aim of buying up the entire vintage and thereby fixing the price at which wine was bought by the manufacturing wholesalers. This proved unsustainable. But Act 5 of 1924 gave the KWV the statutory authority to fix the minimum price at which wine could be sold for distilling and to determine the price received by producers (van Zyl 1993: 21–56; Vink, Williams and Kirsten 2004: 229–31).

The KWV's right to fix prices for distilling wine partially protected farmers from changes in demand after 1924. The success of regulation undermined itself by encouraging farmers to plant high-yielding vines in the newly irrigated districts to produce more and more wines of poor quality. Production expanded from 116,000 to 326,000 leaguers per annum (at 20° proof spirit) between 1924 and 1940 (Drew 1937: Tables 1, 2, 5, 9; Swart 1944: Tables 3, 9). In 1925, the KWV set the price for farmers at just over £4, in line with the lowest levels during the depression of the nineteenth century, and to distillers at just below £8. In 1932, the KWV had to reduce its price to producers to £3 3 6d (Drew 1937: 39; Vink, Williams and Kirsten 2004: 231–3).

Regulation breeds more regulation. The Wine and Spirits Control Act 23 of 1940 empowered KWV to set an annual minimum price for 'good wine'. In 1960, it set in place a system of quotas. It controlled who could plant which grapes where, but then set the overall level ahead of the expansion of cultivation into new areas. Fixed minimum prices discouraged competition and facilitated the concentration of control of wine markets by Stellenbosch Farmers Winery (SFW), owned by South African Breweries (SAB), and of markets for spirits by Distillers, part of the Rembrandt empire. In 1979, they amalgamated, together with KWV, to form Kaapwyn, which controlled 85 per cent of the market in wine and all the market in spirits. It left SAB as the sole manufacturer and supplier of malted beer (Deacon 1980; Fridjhon and Murray 1985; van Zyl 1993: 226–43; Competition Board 1982).

Quantity continued to get priority over quality; standardisation over differentiation. Consumption of wine was segregated by race. Only in 1954 did the production of ordinary 'table' wines exceed that of fortified wines. Between 1954 and 1988, total production increased from 506,000 to 1,015,000 leaguers per annum (KWV 1971: Table 1.1; 1997: Table 5.1).

As long as farmers produced wine for sale by the leaguer without discriminating by quality, they had little incentive to undertake the costs involved in changing their methods of production. Consequently, the priority of each farmer was still to maximise yields and to reduce cash outlays, particularly the cash costs of employing labour and building houses. Between 1960 and 1988, changes in legislation and consumer tastes in the 1970s and 1980s encouraged farmers to begin to plant higher-quality varietals,[3] which made it possible for the industry to take advantage of the opening of international markets in the 1990s.

Free labour

Free labour does not simply present itself on the doorstep of its own accord. It must be obtained, managed and kept. How this can be done and on what terms depends on the intersections of labour markets and the institutions which govern them. The supply of and demand for labour are never sufficient unto themselves.

Evidence to successive official commissions and committees between 1925 and 1975 showed that labour relations and social conditions remained, in many respects, much as they had been in the nineteenth century. Hours were always long 'from sunrise to sunset'; counting breaks for meals (and wine), eleven hours in the summer and nine in the winter (Meaker 1944–45: 67).

Between the world wars, the rate at which the production of wine increased ran far ahead of the growth in the employment of Coloured workers on farms in the Cape (van den Berghe 1995: 203–5, Tables 20–22). What is remarkable is not that labour was scarce but that enough labour power could be found and made to work hard enough to plant all those vines and harvest all those grapes. After the First World War, the producer prices for wine were no better and generally much worse than they had been in nineteenth century. But money wages had more or less doubled. Wages may only have kept more or less in line with inflation but prices fell far behind and never caught up.[4]

Workers needed money and somewhere to live. Wine farmers needed to recruit labour throughout the year so that, even when they were paid by the day, their workers could expect to receive an income through the year, supplemented by wages paid to women and children at harvest. Cash wages could not easily be lowered beyond a certain level. Supplemented by rations, they were a meagre but integral part of families' subsistence incomes.

Farmers could dismiss workers and deprive their families of their houses. But workers could find other jobs, and housing, and alcohol, within the district. Young men might look for better-paid and less onerous work further afield. Farmers typically agreed to fix wages for the season in accordance with levels that had become customary over the years in their districts (Perold 1916: 22; Wilcocks 1934–5: 1/249, 4/697; Theron 1975: Appendix Tables 9–12). This was an effective way to keep wages from rising but not to force wages down below the accepted level.

Farmers gave credit to workers to keep their services and so that workers could meet immediate expenses or exceptional needs, as for example at times of illness (Meaker 1944–45: 650; Theron 1975: 51). Loans from farmers created relations of personal as well as financial dependence. The money earned by men's wives and children from domestic and seasonal work was essential to provide the families' cash income.[5] Women were paid about half to two-thirds as much as men.[6] Resident workers received about half the wages of those who were paid by the day. Allocation of a house typically entailed the worker's wife and even children providing seasonal labour or working in the master's house.

Workers' residential accommodation, garden plots and food rations were both integral costs of the farming enterprise, and necessary components of the incomes of farm workers' families.[7] The costs were, in effect, deducted from wages. To whom it was a cost and to whom it was a benefit depended on which way round one looked at it.

The 'deplorably poor' 'housing conditions of labourers on farms' were, said the Wilcocks Commission in 1937, a 'distinct menace to the Coloured farm population' among whom there was a high incidence of 'respiratory diseases and especially pulmonary tuberculosis' (Drew 1937: 121–2). Professor Cruse testified to the Commission that:

> In so many houses you find only one room . . . With infectious diseases isolation is impossible . . . When there is rheumatism or TB these are harmful . . . I have never seen any [sanitation facilities] on farms. Any doctor will know diseases spread much more easily. To erect a shower bath you must have a pipe leading to the shower but a cheaper system is the bucket arrangement.
> (Wilcocks 1934–5: 3/1028–9)

Farm workers had poor access to doctors and the means to pay for them (Drew 1937: 101; Meaker 1944–45: 650). At Worcester in 1934, there were twelve hospital 'beds for females and 4 for males . . . also an outside shed which is sometimes used.' There were nine rooms elsewhere for VD, TB, chronic and incurable cases. 'They have only a coloured boy to feed them. They have no nursing facilities whatever' (Wilcocks 1934–5: 1/335).

Witnesses to the 1945 Coloured Liquor Commission included prominent academics, doctors, district surgeons, magistrates, police officers, Coloured school teachers and artisans. They all linked appalling housing to health, and particularly to the high incidence of TB and VD, and both with access to, and the provision of, alcohol to farm workers (Meaker 1944–45: 31, 160, 491–2, 1471). Uys's and du Toit's fieldwork in Lynedoch (Stellenbosch district) and in Tulbagh in 1946 illustrated the variations in the nature, sizes and qualities of housing. Houses were still erected on clay or soil and sanitary facilities barely existed (Uys 1947; du Toit 1947; and see, for 1956, Viljoen 1957: 74, Table XXX). Farmers had pared down the cost of housing to a minimum.

The combination of increasing wine production, economic expansion in the Cape, and the implementation of the policy of excluding Africans from the Western Cape under the terms of the 1950 Native Laws Amendment Act strained the ability of farmers to recruit free labour. Africans made up 12 per cent of regular farm workers in 1968. When African men were employed, either as regular or seasonal workers, they were paid similar wages to Coloured workers. Farmers' associations began in the 1960s to turn the influx control laws round to enable them to recruit African workers on contract directly from the Transkei. But farmers found that they were unable to 'track down' and prosecute 'deserters' (Kok 1973: 84–5) when they broke their contracts, and migrant workers themselves were not willing to take up just any type of work (Louw 1969: 85; Komitee van Ondersoek 1973–74; Theron 1975: Appendix Table 7).

At the behest of the Boland Agricultural Union, the government set up an Interdepartmental Committee of Inquiry into the Availability of Coloured Farm Labour in the Western Cape in 1973, to investigate housing, educational and health services, and wages, as ways to keep Coloured workers on the farms (Komitee van Ondersoek 1973, 1973–1974, 1974).

Studies conducted between 1970 and 1974 showed that cash wages had risen since the 1940s, but so had producer prices and urban wages.[8] Wine farmers continued to reduce the movement of workers among farms by conforming to the wages and conditions offered by their neighbours.

Wine farmers had made more use than others of contract, casual and prison labour and were most likely to want to employ more. Some had built more houses. Fewer had improved conditions of service to keep or attract workers as compared with farmers elsewhere. Living conditions on farms had improved since the end of the war but only to a limited degree. Most houses still had two or three rooms. A majority still had no ceilings. Most floors were now of cement but many were still on bare ground. Indoor latrines, bathrooms, water supplies and electricity were the exception. Less than half had their own latrines and a majority had no bathrooms to use at all.[9] The substance of farmers' claims to provide housing was modest.

Medical facilities had expanded but farm workers still depended on employers, clinics and part-time district medical officers for access to medical care (Komitee van Ondersoek 1974: 3–25). Nutrition was poor, and the incidence of alcoholism, and of TB, still extremely high. In 1966, the agricultural unions finally accepted a scheme for the government to subsidise the building of new houses on farms. The take up was low. Farmers unions complained that the costs of building a house to the required standard and supplying water and electricity were too demanding; that farmers were expected to provide their own labour; that the loans (R800) were insufficient; that the interest rate was too high; and that the procedures were too cumbersome. Farmers unions proposed that the government provide more funds for farm schools and boarding facilities to encourage workers to stay on the farms but the Committee did not regard this as a priority (Kaaplandse Landbou-Unie 1973; Komitee van Ondersoek 1973: 1–18, 1974: 3–25).

Farms offered workers low wages, poor conditions and limited opportunities for their children. Few were able to take part in any social activities beyond the farms. Most responded to the 1974 survey that they preferred to work on farms because they were used to it or could not expect to find an alternative (Theron 1975: 59–60, 70–79). There was a fairly high turnover of labour on individual farms: about one worker in ten per year. But most workers stayed in employment on the same farm or within the same district. Some moved towards the Cape to get better wages and be closer to urban labour markets. Some returned from towns to find work and housing.[10]

The Cape Province Agricultural Union observed that 'Coloureds had freedom of movement to seek work in other areas of the country,' creating a scarcity of labour in the industrial areas of the Western Cape, and a consequent 'pull [*trekkrag*] on Coloured labour in the surrounding country [*platteland*] areas' (Komitee van Ondersoek 1974: 46, 59). The Committee firmly insisted that it could not force Coloureds to stay on the platteland or be prohibited from entering the towns and that farmers would have to look to improving the standards of living of workers (Komitee van Ondersoek 1974: 52–3).

What farm workers of all ages had in common was their lack of education. In the 1974 study, 43 per cent of farm workers were below thirty years of age (Theron 1975: 41, Appendix Table 21). Barely half had any education at all. Few farm workers had gone beyond Std. IV (the sixth year). Nor had this changed noticeably between 1946 and 1983.[11] This had the dual effect of workers being tied to the farms and wanting schooling for their children. In many respects, workers and their households were trapped on the farms. This was still insufficient to satisfy the needs of the wine farmers.

The Rural Foundation was set up in 1982 with financial support from prominent farmers, the KWV, the Christian Adenauer Foundation, and the government, to promote community development. It took control of the agenda of social reform. Its strategy was to begin from elite farmers who would be the model for and attract others. Within a modernising economy, social 'upliftment' was to have material benefits which would assure reluctant farmers of the prudence of the programmes (*Wynboer* 1986: 43; Coetzee 2008; Groenewald 2008). Its funding did not see out the end of apartheid (Ewert and du Toit 2005).

Free labour was always expensive. It was, and is, the most costly item in the production of wine. It was difficult to push wages down. Under the regulatory regime in place until it began to unravel in the 1990s (Vink, Williams and Kirsten 2004), prices were set for farmers and there were few incentives to raise quality and thus income. Consequently, farmers spent as little as possible on housing and other amenities for workers. They recognised the need for better housing, health facilities and access to schools to keep workers on the farms, but looked to the government to meet the costs.

Unfree labour (1886–1988)

If sufficient free labour was not forthcoming, a source of unfree labour had to be found to make up the shortage.

Buitenverwachting in the Constantia Valley, in 1886 was probably the first farm to benefit from a system of convict labour. 'The entire farm was built by prison labour' (Mentz 1960: Evidence, G.A. Louw, 11 May). Its owner was one of a close elite of families among the elite Constantia grape and wine farmers, who inherited prestigious historical farms and used their claims to social standing and political connections to capture and to keep the largest allocation of prisoners available to farms. From 1920, the Union Department of Prisons extended the supply of prisoners from mines, railways and docks to wine farmers in the Boland. The going rate was 1s 6d per day (Department of Prisons 1920–25). From 1932, farmers employed short-term prisoners on a 'sixpenny' (per day) basis, which gave way in 1947 to a 'ninepenny' scheme. The money was paid out to prisoners on their release. This arrangement was replaced in 1959 by the hiring out of prisoners on 'parole' (Viljoen 1957: 88; Wilson 1975: 147; Goussard 2002: 33,

43–52). Prisons supplied labour to farmers and cut labour costs by a half or more of the prevailing wage rate.

The closing of Wynberg prison in 1959 meant that more farmers would each have to depend on a limited number of prisoners from Pollsmoor. An interdepartmental committee revealed the dependence of large-scale farmers on prison labour, and the claims of the Constantia elite to be entitled to their 'quotas' of convicts, and the consequent enhancement of their land values. Together five Constantia families employed 62 full-time workers and had a daily allocation of 120 convicts plus warders. Most respondents made do with a single span of six convicts. They would not, they said, be able to manage if the supply of prison labour was reduced or even withdrawn (Mentz 1960).

There were only a handful of wine farmers at Constantia. Boland wine farmers needed a more far-reaching solution. One of the ways to solve the problem was to extend the employment of prison labour. In 1953, prominent Boland wine farmers cooperated with the Department of Prisons to take part in a more ambitious scheme, which provided an additional and regular supply of labour that was cheap, plentiful, and unable to leave the farm.

Farmers' associations invested in buildings to accommodate prisoners and staff. The return on the investments was their entitlement to hire labour in proportion to their shares in the prison. The first three outstations in the Western Cape were built in the historic wineland areas around Paarl, and at Rawsonville, the area that produced the most wine. By 1960, there were thirteen farm prisons extending across all the wineland districts (Goussard 2002: 69–129). In 1974, almost one-third (30/95) of the sample of farmers in the core wineland areas in the study for the Theron Commission employed prison labour. Convicts thus made up almost one-fifth (19 per cent) of the regular workforce, and a larger proportion of the workforce of those who hired them (Theron 1975: 15, 27).

Prison conditions varied from tolerable if unhygienic to appalling, compounded by gang violence, harsh discipline and, if need be, suppression of riots. Time spent on farms must have been a relief for most prisoners (Goussard 2002: 101–12, 124–8).

The economics of hiring prisoners from regular prisons were simple. They were cheaper than free workers. Farm prisons were more complicated. They were large enterprises, generally housing between 300 and 500 prisoners. In 1954, they were reckoned to cost about £250,000, or £500 per prisoner (Goussard 2002: 106, 113, 119). If they were not occupied to capacity, new prisoners had to be drafted in from another source. Convicts were not employed as seasonal workers but formed part of the core labour force. In the summer, they had to be fetched from the prison at 7 a.m. and returned by 5 p.m.; this made their working day two hours shorter than the working day of the free worker. The overall cost of a 'unit' of prison labour was probably about 45c per day as against 75c for a free wage worker in 1964; and R1 as against R2, just after the price of prison labour was raised in 1975.[12]

The differences between the direct cost of free and of prison labour increased over time, with the scarcity of labour and with inflation. Similarly, the cost of renting a 'unit' of prison labour as shown in Table 9.1 relative to the prices

Table 9.1 Changes to the weekday rental for prisoners

Year	1953>	1961>	1964>	1975>	1980>	1982>	1987
1s 9d	18c	15c	25c	30c	40c	R1.32	

Sources: Mentz (1960: 3); Goussard (2002: 72, 82).

paid to producers for distilling wine diminished from 1953 to 1986. Farmers thus became more dependent on prison labour the more politically unsustainable it became. The government shocked farmers on 1 April 1986 when it announced the imminent end of the system. It was terminated in 1988 (Komitee van Ondersoek 1973–74; Goussard 2002: 107, 111, 115, 122).

Like slavery, prison labour requires its own justifications. Constantia farmers simply took the view that labour was scarce, the supply of prison labour was being reduced, but they wanted to go on getting their share, or their business (and even their historic farm) would collapse (Mentz 1960).

The prison farm system attracted more positive support. It was initiated by leading farmers, acting for the public good of their own communities. It created opportunities for rehabilitation – and was certainly an improvement on breaking stones – as well as saving the state money, making labour cheaper for farmers, and bringing members of the farming community into closer touch with one another. Farmers emphasised their generally fair treatment of, and good relations with, the prisoners (Goussard 2002: 107, 111, 115, 122). International criticism sharpened the responses of prominent farmers to attacks on the good faith of those who participated in the system. Defensive arguments do not preclude, though they may obscure, constructive intentions.

Prisoners are clearly not slaves. Farmers owned slaves but hired prisoners by the hour. Convicts can be put out to work but their sentences are limited in time. There are also analogies between prison and slave labour. Slave owners had to house and feed their slaves. Prison outstations housed and largely fed the workforce. Prisoners are clearly not free workers. Their labour power is not freely available in the marketplace nor are they free to take it somewhere else. Farmers did not exchange wages for labour power but invested in shares from which they derived their right to hire convicts. Farmers expected compensation for losing their property rights when prison labour was abolished. Prison labour must make moral sense to those involved. The defence of prison labour, as of slavery, involved naturalising unfree labour as a normal way to secure labour and as indispensable to the rural economy.

Providing the dop (1838–1988)

The dop (or tot) system, the daily provision of alcohol to farm workers by their employers, and its effects on alcoholism, foetal and child health, domestic violence and TB, are even now the greatest scandal and embarrassment to the wine industry.[13]

As a regular practice of giving wine for seasonal work, the tot (dop) seems to have come into its own after 1838. Farmers needed to get workers to the farms and to compete for labour during harvesting and shearing. Once workers had been employed, they needed to be kept from deserting when farmers most needed them. The tot system was fully established by 1866 and by the end of the century the system seems to have embedded itself in the rural economy and society (Scully 1990: 56). The 1890 (Maasdorp) Cape Liquor Commission reported that:

> It seems that custom so enforces this practice that employers of labour are generally forced to yield to it, in order to obtain a necessary amount of labour ... The first drink is taken in the very early morning on an empty stomach. This at once starts the craving for the stimulant, which is taken in a greater or less degree throughout the day. There is no discretion used by the farmer. The young labourer of 17 years of age is at once initiated into the habit on his arrival ... These labourers are thus taught at an early age the love of the taste of wine.
>
> (Maasdorp 1890: 22–3)

Farmers' spokesmen explained that 'workers are in a hot climate and sweat for the whole day in the open air ... and drink 2 bottles of white wine a day, we don't think this is too much' (Maasdorp 1890: 23). They kept this refrain up for the next eighty-five years.

The evidence to the 1918 (Baxter) Select Committee of the Cape Parliament, the 1926 (Roos) Select Committee, the 1937 Wilcocks Commission, the 1944 Coloured Liquor Commission and the 1952 (Malan) Select Committee repeated the same observations:

> Drunkenness is at its height in these parts, chiefly as a result of the tot system. The coloured man drinks himself drunk, and his condition makes the wife desperate. And she takes to drink too, and the children are born with the desire for drink. (Roos 1926, cited in Wilcocks 1934–35: 7/713)
>
> What seems to me the worst part of the whole thing is that it takes a young boy and deliberately trains him to need 5 tots. After a few years he forms a habit he will probably never be able to lose ... I have no difficulty in getting families. I pay 6d per day extra instead.
>
> (Baxter 1918, cited in Wilcocks 1934–35: 3/699)

> The Coloured man [*jong*] will do anything to get an extra dop in his hands. He will work himself to death. I have myself heard that the farmer says to his people [*volk*]: Come and work for another hour, and then I'll give you an extra [*dop*].[14]
>
> (Meaker 1944–45: 883)

The Liquor Act 30 of 1928 explicitly allowed farmers in the Cape to supply to their employees 1½ pints (0.8 litres) of unfortified wine per day at intervals of no less than two hours. It was illegal to provide alcohol as remuneration for work. The limit easily becomes the norm. It also came to be regarded by workers as their entitlement. Farmers offered tots to workers in order to recruit them.

This meant that they were part of the workers' wage and could not be otherwise (Wilcocks 1934–5: 3/900, 4/412; Uys 1947: 36; Malan 1952: 376; KWV 1959; Malan 1960: §99).

The 1937 Wilcocks Commission simply recommended the abolition of the system; the 1945 Meaker Commission that it be abolished within three years (Wilcocks 1937: 26; Meaker 1945: 13, 21). The KWV sustained its close connections with MPs from wineland constituencies of both white parliamentary parties (Wine and Spirit March 1937, September, October 1938). Neither recommendation bore legislative fruit.

The KWV proposed to the Malan Commission of Inquiry that, far from being restricted, the system should be 'applied throughout the Union of South Africa' (KWV 1959). These ideas were then followed through by the Commission itself: 'the farmer should be at liberty to determine in his own farm without disruption whether to continue this practice, to alter it or to dispense with it altogether.' It recommended: 'That all references to the so-called "tot system" [and consequently any restrictions] be removed from the 1928 Liquor Act.' (Malan 1960: 11). The 1963 Liquor Act officially 'abolished' the 'dop system' (KWV 1975: 2), by not prohibiting farmers from giving wine to their workers or the KWV from supplying the wine!

The dop continued to be ubiquitous but not universal on wine farms. The 1974 survey for the Theron Commission, whose report was published as Theron (1976), found that 86 per cent of farmers (82/95) provided wine, mostly daily; a majority during the working day. Most farmers (74/95) were against the complete abolition of the dop. Most Coloured workers favoured abolition; a clear majority of those who received wine would have preferred higher wages instead (Theron 1975: 67–75, Appendix Tables 53–8).

The KWV and the South African Temperance Alliance (SATA) rehearsed the same arguments repeatedly to commissions of enquiry, parliamentary select committees, and conferences.[15] The dop became the symbolic test for both sides in the opposing campaigns on the wider issues of the liberalisation of liquor laws.

The cause of temperance, and most particularly the immediate need to abolish the dop, was insistently and consistently put by spokesmen for the missions, and particularly the local Coloured elites. They were schoolteachers, artisans and ministers of religion. Magistrates, senior police officers, administrators, members of parliament and Stellenbosch University professors, and the National Council of Women, all testified that the dop system led to and exacerbated the drunkenness which was so prevalent in the towns of the Western Cape.[16] Only farmers and their representatives took a contrary view.

From 1890 to 1975, the wine industry maintained support for the dop with a mixture of their own experiences, innovative proposals, poor reasoning and contradictory arguments. Farmers provided only 'light wine', by which they meant that it was not 'sweet' (fortified). It was typically about 11.5 per cent (Baxter 1918: 226, 229; Meaker 1944–45: 312–35). The dop is a long-established institution. It does not intoxicate the worker. 'The dop is given . . . not as part of the wage but . . . primarily because it is a means of nutrition and refreshment' (P.P. du Toit,

MP in the House of Assembly, cited *Wine and Spirit* 1937: 3034). Providing wine made the worker physically fitter and stimulated him to greater effort. Farm labourers form habits of temperance and are taught learn to drink wine in moderation. Indeed, farm workers receiving tots were generally a sober class of people. Farmers would not tolerate employees who were incapable of doing their work nor allow drunkenness among their 'neighbours' on their farms. Labourers should be allowed to consume some of the wine they had produced.

Anyway, they said, farmers had no choice; they could not recruit workers unless they provided dop, even if they offered better wages. Prohibition would make it even more difficult to prevent workers leaving for the towns. The dop was a benefit and not part of the wage: in 1959, it cost only 4d per day (6 per cent of the cash wage) and made up only 4 per cent of the crop; in 1974, 2.5 per cent. An increase in wages instead of the dop might cause workers to work for fewer days or spend the increase on drink. Labourers got drunk in canteens and in the towns (at weekends) and not on the farms. Abolition would create a market for illicit liquor on the farms themselves. KWV wanted the liquor laws to be liberalised to allow the sale of light wines to 'natives' and in cafés and groceries, and to reduce constraints on the purchase of liquor by Coloured women and men.[17] The Boland Landbou-Unie explained in 1973 'in the evening after work, when the workers receive their wine, they have the opportunity to discuss their problems with their boss [*baas*]' (Bolandse Landbou-Unie 1974). The KWV stated more bluntly that the dop improved the farmer's control over the worker, and provided 'an incentive to take on extra bits of work' (KWV 1975: 3.2.1.2).

SATA systematically exposed the KWV's arguments. The dop was in the interests neither of farmers nor of labourers. SATA drew on physiological evidence that the dop intoxicated workers and weakened them physically. Alcohol acts initially as a stimulant and the dop increased workers' ability to tolerate it. It also made them want more – hence their preference for cheap fortified wines at weekends. By increasing wages, farmers could recruit all the labour they needed and, if they agreed to eliminate the dop, they would not need to use it to compete for labour. Those farmers, mainly from Stellenbosch, who did not provide the dop and had improved conditions, did not find it difficult to recruit labour and altered the lives of, and created opportunities for the education of, women and children on farms.[18]

From the 1980s, the Rural Foundation began to act against the dop system. It became unacceptable to give dop to workers during the day, even though workers might be allowed to take home some wine 'which they shared with their family' (Frans Malan, Chairman of the Rural Foundation, cited Die Burger 1988). Giving dop to workers began to be antithetical to the dominant cultural practices and material interests of wine farmers. Once international markets were open to South African producers, overseas retailers began to insist that exporters conform to Fair Trade and Ethical Trade Agreements. KWV made no direct response until Nelson Mandela addressed them in 1996, and even then it evaded the issue (Lourens Jonker, Chairman of the KWV, *Wynboer* 1996a,b). The system declined but it did not go away. Nor could its social, physiological and medical consequences soon be brought to an end. It was part of a pattern of alcohol dependence, with terrible consequences among a significant section of the farming community (London, Sanders and Te Water Naude 1998; Te Water Naude *et al.* 1998).

Why would farmers and their spokesmen have continued for so long to provide such poor reasons to justify a system in which their workforce were under the influence of liquor throughout the working day and in many cases completely drunk at weekends? First, let us take the arguments seriously. The industry's main contribution to alcoholism is not the dop (KWV 1959, 1975). It is the sale in towns to Coloureds of cheap semi-sweet and fortified wines, which made up 96 per cent of the market for wine in 1970 and 88 per cent in 1978 (*Wynboer* 1977). Abolition probably would have brought illicit selling of alcohol onto the farms. But that assumes that workers are dependent on alcohol in the first place. People can work at a persistent level of alcohol consumption and then not do so without it. To the dependence of farm worker families on farmers for their income and housing is added dependence on alcohol. Farmers for their part found that they had to provide the dop if they were to recruit and retain workers. Once the system was established, it was difficult to turn round. As with prison labour, it became, as the KWV explained in its submission to the Malan Commission in 1959, 'quite natural and normal that the Coloured worker, just like his employer, should consume and enjoy wine' (KWV 1959).

The question remains: why not pay higher wages and provide better housing and other facilities. The dop is cheap; whether it was supplied from the farmers' own cellars or bought back from KWV. Wages and housing are expensive and have to be paid for in cash. Dependence on the dop did not ensure the loyalty of workers to individual employers but it did keep them available for farm labour within the rural districts.

The dop was one part of a set of accepted institutional practices that responded to the limits of the abilities of the masters to recruit labour under conditions for workers and their households that farmers were able and willing to offer. These institutions were not just a matter of the price of labour but of maintaining the status and the property rights of farmers and their authority to run their farms in the ways they chose, which became integrated into an established way of life. Above all else, prohibition of the dop system interfered with the unilateral authority of the farmer over his farm and his people (*plaasvolk*).

Changing the system was not only a response to political circumstances and legal requirements. Nor can the dominant institutions of rural society be explained only in terms of instrumental calculation. It depends, and continues to depend, on changes in the social relations and respective expectations of farmers and workers and thus in the moral economy of the *platteland.*

Puzzles and solutions

In the nineteenth century, farmers' incomes depended on changes in the international economy. At the end of the First World War, they set up the KWV to manage supply and to keep fluctuations in the wine market at bay, with some measure of success. The system of regulation provided a market for wine sold by the leaguer at an assured price, in which the production of quantity overrode any considerations of quality. The KWV could, within limits, set the price of wine in the interests of farmers collectively but individually each farmer had to produce as much as he could as cheaply as possible.

Since the former slaves left the farms after Emancipation in 1838, wine farmers have had to persuade workers to go back to work on the farms and to stay there. Workers needed money and places to live; farmers needed workers to plant, tend and harvest their vines.

Farmers always found enough workers to plant, tend and harvest their vines, at a price they were willing to pay.[19] Farmers could limit rises in cash wages but it was more difficult to reduce wages when prices fell. They had to find other ways to reduce or at least contain costs. Providing housing was an important way to recruit, to retain and to control labour. Building houses, maintaining them, and providing basic facilities cost money. Hence, the appalling state of most farm housing. Farmers asked government for subsidies to enable them to build houses for their workers but then complained that the costs of doing so were too high.

Farmers relied in the first instance on resident farm workers, their wives and children, daily-paid, seasonal and contract workers. They needed to keep their labour force from being pulled into the mines, railways, docks and industries. Workers and their wives could move from farm to farm but most stayed within the farming district. They and their children were kept to farm life by familiarity, by social networks, by dependence on farmers for cash wages, housing and other 'benefits' and daily rations of wine and, most of all, by their lack of education. 'Free workers' are not free to seek employment as they choose; their ability of dispose of their labour is constrained by complex sets of conditions.

Farmers could always reduce their costs by employing convicts. But there were not always enough to go round. Faced with increasing competition for labour, accentuated by apartheid policies in the 1950s, farmers invested in their own system of prison labour. Large-scale farmers who initiated the system and rented the most convicts could best afford it and were most in need of workers.

Prisoners made up a substantial part of the regular labour force on Western Cape wine farms between 1960 and 1986. They did not replace free workers but supplemented their labour at the margins. By reducing demand, they brought down the price that farmers needed to pay for free labour. Unfree labour is not separate from but is a complement to free labour (Corrigan 1977).

A political economy of material interests goes a long way to explain the formation and persistence of forms of unfree and free labour and the conditions for buying, renting or purchasing it. Farmers defined their own social status by their place in the farming 'community' and their authority over their farms and over those who lived on them. Status groups (Weber 1998) defining themselves by social honour, political influence or racial exclusion can always find arguments to justify their material interests. But this does not take us far enough. People give meanings, both instrumental and moral, to their intentions, justifications and actions. These are not separate from but integral to the complex relations of social production.

Notes

* All translations from Afrikaans are the author's own.

1   1 leaguer = 127 gallons = 577.3 hectolitres. Leaguers of wine were measured at 20° proof spirit (i.e. 11.5% alcohol) until 1980 when South Africa changed to the international standard of 10% alcohol by volume (AV).

2   £1 = 20s; 1s = 12d; £1 = 240d.

3   The area devoted to seven premium varietals – Crouchen Blanc (Cape Riesling), Cabernet Sauvignon, Pinotage, Sauvignon Blanc, Chardonnay, Shiraz and Merlot – increased from 3 per cent in 1970 to 7 per cent in 1979, to 12 per cent in 1988 and to 19 per cent in 1996 (*Wynboer* 1972: 14–15; KWV 1981: Table 1.4.2; 1997: Table 4.1).

4   Evidence on wages between 1916 and 1960 can be found in Perold (1916: 22); Wilcocks (1934–5; 1/340, 3/896, 4/409, 694); Wilcocks (1937: 76); Meaker (1944–45: 67, 1066 Meaker (1945: 46); Uys (1947: 45); du Toit (1947: 57); Malan (1952: 328); van den Berghe (1995: 229); Viljoen (1957: 27); Mentz (1960, Evidence); Beyers (1971: 228); *Wynboer* (1983), the retail price index on Union of South Africa (1960).

5   The mean cash income of the household head (R465) was estimated in 1974 as 65 per cent of the mean household cash income of R700 (Theron 1975: Appendix Tables 37–8).

6   Wilcocks (1934–35: 3/96, 4/40); Uys (1947: 45) for 1946; Viljoen (1957: 96) for 1956; Mentz (1960, Evidence) for 1960; Komitee van Ondersoek (1973: 20) for 1972.

7   They were variously calculated as a percentage of total income in 1956 at 37 per cent (Viljoen 1957: 26); in 1972 at 46 per cent (Komitee van Ondersoek 1973: 20); in 1974 at 26 per cent (Theron 1975: Appendix Table 37–8).

8   Evidence on wages between 1960 and 1974 is to be found in Beyers (1971: 228); Cilliers, Groenewald and Stuart (1972: 330); Komitee van Ondersoek (1973: 20); Komitee van Ondersoek (1973–74: 28 October 1974); Komitee van Ondersoek (1974: 34–7); Theron (1975: 13–29), on price indices, in Republic of South Africa 1970, 1980, 1990.

9   Louw (1969: 94); Groenewald (1972: 194–216, 344–5); Theron (1975: 15–29, 63–6, Appendix Tables 14–15, 40–52).

10   In 1974, 122 workers of 1,496 (8.2 per cent) left farms in the core wine-growing districts (Theron 1975: 19–24). Also Uys (1947: 20–25); Viljoen (1957: 101, 103); Louw (1969: 93–5); Groenewald (1972: 108–30).

11   Wilcocks (1934–45: 1/323–8); Wilcocks (1937: 76); Meaker (1944–45: 521, 875, 181); Groenewald (1972: 103–5); Theron (1975: 41–2, Appendix Table 22); *Wynboer* (1983: 35).

12   Viljoen (1957: 97–8); Horrell *et al.* (1973: 40); Theron (1975: 18, 28); Goussard (2002: 79, 81, 85).

13   The dop was measured roughly in the tins from which it was dispensed. From 1928 to 1962, the legal dop was a maximum of 1.5 pints (0.85 litres) a day to be given out at intervals of up to five times a day. Each dop would be 0.3 pints (0.17 litres) of wine at 11.5 per cent alcohol and 20 per cent proof spirit.

14   Head Constable H.C. Stafford, Paarl. In this context, *jong* and *volk* are everyday, but demeaning, terms.

15   Baxter (1918: 218–37); Wilcocks (1934–5: 3/698–732); Meaker (1944–45: 99–102, 167–208, 302–3, 931–74).

16   Wilcocks (1934–35: 1/105–106, 116–118, 124, 136–144, 272, 274, 280–94; 2/204–206, 233–2583/105; 3/698–732, 899, 1033; 4/273); Meaker (1944–45: 1–2, 51–71, 168–207, 318–36; 497–505, 892–5, 973–9).

17   Wilcocks (1934–35: 3/698–732); Meaker (1944–45: 923–42); *Wine and Spirit* (1950: 19–20); Malan (1952: 45–8, 299–312, 335–6); KWV (7 Nov. 1975).

18   Wilcocks (1934–35: 1/305; 3/348–50, 698–732); Meaker (1944–45: 248–350, 923–42); *Wine and Spirit* (1950: 19–20); Malan (1952: 45–6, 90–91, 229–36).

19   This was emphasised to me by Joachim Ewert.

Bibliography

Baxter, W.D. (1918) 'Report of the Select Committee on Drunkenness in the Western Cape', *Cape Provincial Council*, S.C., 7–18.

Beyers, J.P. (1971) 'Farm labour in a demarcated area of the Western Cape', unpublished Ph.D. thesis, University of Cape Town.

Bolandse Landbou-Unie (1973) Getuienis aan *Die Kommissie van Ondersoek na Aangeleenthede rakende die Keurlingbevolking* (Voorsitter: Prof. E. Theron), dated 28 May, 1973, Box File 15. University of Stellenbosch Library.

Cape of Good Hope (1878) *Statistical Record*.

Cilliers, S.P., Groenewald, C.J. and Stuart, O.D.J. (1972) 'Die invloed van strukturele kenmerke van boerderyeenhede in die Stellenbosse distrik op die aanbod van landbouarbeid', *Humanitas, RSA*, 3(3): 325–35.

Coetzee, J. (4 August 2008) Interview, Vriesenhof, Stellenbosch.

Competition Board (1982) *Investigation into Restrictive Practices in the Supply and Distribution of Alcoholic Beverages in the Republic of South Africa*, Report no. 10.

Constantia Association (1895–1900), *Minute Books*, Cape Archives A1947, 3/2.

Corrigan, P. (1977) 'Feudal relics or capitalist monuments: some notes on the sociology of unfree labour', *Sociology*, 11; reprinted in *Social Forms/Human Capacities* (1990), London: Routledge.

Deacon, I.B. (1980) 'The South African liquor industry – structure, conduct, performance and strategies for future action', unpublished DComm thesis, University of Stellenbosch.

Department of Prisons (1920–25) *Annual Reports*, Pretoria.

Die Burger (1988) 11 July.

Dooling, W.M. (2007) S*lavery, Emancipation and Colonial Rule*, Durban: University of KwaZulu Natal Press.

Drew, H.C. (1937) *Report of the 'Wine Commission*, UG 25, Pretoria: Government Printer 2680.

du Toit, J.N. (1947) 'Plaasarbeiders, 'n sosiologiese studie van 'n groep plaasarbeiders in die distrik van Tulbagh', unpublished MA thesis, University of Stellenbosch.

Ewert, J. and du Toit, A. (2005) 'A deepening divide in the countryside: restructuring and rural livelihoods in the South African wine industry', *Journal of Southern African Studies*, 31: 315–32.

Fridjhon, M. and Murray, A. (1985) *Conspiracy of Giants: The South African Liquor Industry*, Johannesburg: Divaris Stein.

Goussard, Y. (2002) 'Die gebruik van gevangene arbeid in die Wes-Kaapse landbou', unpublished MA thesis, University of Stellenbosch.

Groenewald, C.J. (1972) ' 'n Sosiologiese ondersoek na die aanbod van landbouarbeid n Wes-Kaapland', unpublished M.Litt. en Wys thesis, University of Stellenbosch.

—— (6 August 1986) Interview, Stellenbosch.

Harries, P. (2005) 'Making "Mozbiekers": history, memory and the African diaspora at the Cape' in B. Zimba, E. Alpers and A. Isaacman (eds) *Slave Routes and Oral Tradition in Southeastern Africa*, Maputo: Filsom Entertainment.

Horrell, M. *et al.* (1973) *A Survey of Race Relations in South Africa*, Johannesburg: South African Institute of Race Relations.

Kaaplandse Landbou-Unie (1973) *Die plaasbevolking en arbeiders in Suid-Afrika*, Pretoria: State Archives Deposit, K301, 6/2.

Kok, T.F.L. (1973) 'Bantoe plaasarbeid in die landbou-distrik van Stellenbosch', unpublished MA thesis, University of Stellenbosch.

Komitee van Ondersoek (1973) *Tussentydse verslag van die tussendepartementele komitee van ondersoek na die beskikbaarheid van kleurlngplaasarbeid in groter wes-Kaapland,* Pretoria: State Archives Deposit, K301, 6/2.

—— (1973–74) *Ondersoek na kleurlingplaasarbeid in wes-Kaapland,* Pretoria: State Archives Deposit, K301, 5/1: Schalk van der Merwe aan SE H. Schoeman, LV, Minister van Landbou, 22 March 1974.

—— (1974) *Tweede en finale verslag van die tussendepartementele komitee van ondersoek na die beskikbaarheid van kleurlngplaasarbeid in groter wes-Kaapland,* Pretoria: State Archives Deposit, K301, 6/2.

KWV [Ko-operatieve Wijnbouwers Vereeniging] (1959) *Verdere Memorandum deur die K.W.V. opgestel vir indiening by die [Malan] Kommissie van Ondersoek na die Distribusie van Drank en die Verkooppryse daarvan,* State Archives Deposit, K301 5/3. 3

—— (1971) *A Survey of Wine-growing in South Africa, 1970-71,* Paarl: KWV.

—— (1975) *Die voorsiening van wyn aan plaasarbeiders deur hul werkgewers, Memorandum vir voorlegging aan die Kommissie van Ondersoek.* Getuienis. University of Stellenbosch Library, Boxfile 15.

—— (1981, 1997) *SA Wine Industry Statistics,* Vols 5, 21.

London, L., Sanders, D. and Te Water Naude, J. (1998) 'Farm workers in South Africa – the challenge of eradicating alcohol abuse and the legacy of the dop system', *South African Medical Journal,* 88: 1092–5.

Louw, P.G. (1969) ' 'n Ondersoek na arbeidsprobleme vir wynboere in wes-Kaapland', unpublished MA thesis, University of Stellenbosch.

Maasdorp, C.G. (1890) *Report of the Liquor Laws Commission,* Cape of Good Hope, G'1–90.

Macmillan, W.M. (1927; reprint 1968) *The Cape Coloured Question: An Historical Survey,* Cape Town: A.A. Balkema.

Malan, A.I. (1952) *Report of the Select Committee on the Subject of the Liquor Bill,* House of Assembly, June 1952, Parow: Cape Times.

—— (1960) *Report of the Commission of Enquiry into the General Distribution and Selling Prices of Intoxicating Liquor,* Pretoria: Government Printer.

Mason, E. (2003) *Social Death and Resurrection: Slavery and Emancipation in South Africa,* Charlottesville: Duke University Press.

Meaker, R. (1944–45) Evidence to *The Cape Coloured Liquor Commission of Inquiry,* Pretoria: State Archives Deposit, K38 E5/39.

—— (1945) *Report of 'The Cape Coloured Liquor Commission of Inquiry',* Pretoria: Government Printer.

Mentz (1960) *Interdepartementale komitee oor gevangenisarbeid in die Kaapse Skiereiland,* Report, Evidence, and Appendices, State Archives Deposit, K122 E5/40.

Perold, A.I. (1916), 'Viticulture in South Africa', *International Review of the Science and Practice of Agriculture,* 7: 1–30.

Rayner, M.I. (1986) 'Wine and slaves: the failure of an export economy and the end of slavery', unpublished thesis, Duke University.

Republic of South Africa (1970, 1980, 1990) *Bulletin of Statistics,* Pretoria: Government Printer.

Roos, A. (1926) *Report of the Select Committee on the Liquor Bill,* House of Assembly, Cape Town.

Ross R. (1986) 'The origins of capitalist agriculture in the Cape Colony: a survey', in W. Beinart, P. Delius and S. Trapido (eds) *Putting a Plough to the Ground: Accumulation and Dispossession in Rural South Africa,* Braamfontein: Ravan Press.

Scully, P. (1986) 'Stellenbosch District c.1970–1910', *Western Cape Roots and Realities* (seminar series), Centre for African Studies, University of Cape Town.

—— (1990) *The Bouquet of Freedom: Social and Economic Relations in the Stellenbosch District, South Africa c1870–1900*, Cape Town: Centre for African Studies.

Swart, H.C. (1944) 'Prys en produksiebeheer in die Wynbou van Suid-Afrika', unpublished MSc thesis, University of Stellenbosch.

Te Water Naude, J., London, L., Pitt, B. and Mohamed, C. (1998) 'The dop system around Stellenbosch – results of a farm survey', *South African Medical Journal*, 88: 1102–5.

Theron, E. (1975) *Die sosio-ekonomiese posisie van die Kleurling plaasarbeiders. Getuenis aan die Kommissie van Ondersoek na aangeleenthede rakende die Kleurlingsbevolkingsgroen*, evidence, Theron Commission, Boxfile 18, University of Stellenbosch Library).

—— (1976) *Report of the Commission of Inquiry into Matters Concerning the Coloured Population Group*, RP 38, Pretoria: Government Printers.

Union of South Africa (1960) *Union Statistics, 1910–1960*, Pretoria: Government Printer.

Uys, A. (1947) 'Plaasarbeiders, 'n sosiologiese studie van 'n groep plaasarbeiders in die distrik van Stellenbosch', unpublished MA thesis, University of Stellenbosch.

van den Berghe, E.-N. (1995) 'Farm labour relations and the regional economy of the Western Cape', unpublished Ph.D. thesis, University of Cambridge.

van Onselen, C. (1982) 'Randlords and rotgut, 1886–1903', in C. van Onselen *Studies in the Social and Economic History of the Witwatersrand, 1886–1914, vol. 1: New Babylon*, Harlow: Longmans.

van Zyl, D.J. (1993) 'KWV: 75 jare', bound typescript, University of Stellenbosch Library.

Viljoen, P.J. (1957) 'Plaasarbeid in wes-Kaapland', unpublished MComm thesis, University of Stellenbosch.

Vink, N., Williams G. and Kirsten, J. (2004) 'South Africa', in K. Anderson (ed.) *The World's Wine Markets: Globalization in Practice*, London: Routledge.

Weber, M. (1998; 1st edn 1948) 'Class, status, party (1921)', in H.H. Gerth and C. Wright Mills (eds) *From Max Weber: Essays in Sociology*, London: Routledge.

Wilcocks, R.W. (1934–35) *Evidence to the Commission of Inquiry Regarding the Cape Coloured Population of the Union*, University of Stellenbosch Library.

—— (1937) *Report of the 'Commission of Inquiry Regarding the Cape Coloured population of the Union*, Pretoria: Government Printer.

Williams G. (1991) 'Capitalism, peasants and land in Africa: a comparative perspective', in S. Mathlape and A. Muenz (eds) *Towards a New Agrarian Democratic Order: A Reader on the South African Land Question*, Amsterdam: South African Economic Research and Training Project.

Wilson, F. (1971; 2nd edn 1975) 'Farming 1866–1966', in M. Wilson and L.M. Thomson (eds) *The Oxford History of South Africa*, Oxford: Oxford University Press.

Wine and Spirit (1937) 'Die dopstelsel voor die parlement', March: 3032, 3034, 3041.

—— (1950) 'Manifesto re the use of alcoholic liquor in SA', May: 19–20.

Worden N. (1985) *Slavery in Dutch South Africa*, Cambridge: Cambridge University Press.

Wynboer (1972) 'Wingerdstatistiek', Febuary: 14–15.

—— (1977) 'Suid Afrikaanse landswyne onder soeklig' (G. Boonstra), February: 28-30. 33; March: 45, 47, 49; April: 19–52.

—— (1983) 'Die plaasgemeenskap in Wes-Kaapland' (G. Kotze), June: 30–7.

—— (1986) 'Landelike Stigting', July: 43.

—— (1996a) 'Madiba by die wynboere', June: 14–16.

—— (1996b) 'Wat is die dopstelsel?', August: 3.

10 The Opium 'Revolution'

Continuity or change in rural Afghanistan?

Adam Pain

It's only in practical matters that one may look for signs of progress. Ideas are always changing . . . but who is to say that one is better than another? It is material things that progress as can be clearly seen. I hope that you'll forgive me if I mention opium but really one has to go no further to find progress exemplified. Opium, even more than salt, is a great source of revenue of our own creation and is now more productive than any except land revenue. And who pays it? Why John Chinaman . . . who prefers our opium to any other. That is what I call progress.

(Farrell 1973: 471)[1]

Introduction

Opium has a track record and its production and trade has been central to geopolitics for centuries. There is more than a degree of irony that a crop that old and new empires – the British in India, the Americans in South-East Asia – did so much to globalise should come back to haunt them.[2] Opium is not new to Afghanistan – the country was officially exporting from 7 to 20 tons a year in the 1940s, to both the United States and Germany. According to reports from farmers in Badakhshan, they were selling opium directly to a state trading company based in the provincial capital well into the 1950s and 1960s. But there is no doubt that since the 1990s, and particularly since 2001, the cultivation of opium has dramatically expanded (see Table 10.1 below), both because of and despite the barrage of counter-narcotics measures that have been directed against it.

The reasons why this expansion should have taken place and what it tells us about the problematic nature of state building in Afghanistan and the reconstruction effort is not the central issue of this chapter. The attempts to moderate this 'irrepressible' market for a truly globalised commodity driven by a largely Western demand (which remains unaccountable for its effects (Goodhand and Sedra 2007)), by focusing on the supply side have been frankly bizarre and fascinating. The contingency of place and context which can have opium variably as a legal commodity in one country – see the photographs of opium poppy growing in front of the Didcot power station in Oxford[3] – while that very same state is seeking to repress it in a second country on the grounds that it is illegal, verges on the theatre of the absurd. The notion of legality itself in Afghanistan – with a state that has acute problems of legitimacy and where its de facto existence depends on non-sovereign forces – is a problem of its own.

There is no doubt that eight years on from 2001 the Afghanistan state building project is in deep trouble (Suhrke 2006; Goodhand and Sedra 2007) highlighting 'the limitations of an orthodox development model' as a state-building modality (Goodhand and Sedra 2007: 57). None of the transitions to security, a political settlement and strong socio-economic development have been achieved and, if anything, the condition of Afghanistan may be worse than it was in 2001, although different. There is varied opinion as to the reasons for this state of affairs – the limitations of the original Bonn Agreement (5 December 2001), the confounding of a war on terror with a state-building project, the creation of a rentier state through excessive aid (Suhrke's 'more is less' argument (2006)) – are all cited as the 'sins of omission and commission' (Goodhand and Sedra 2007: 57). A de jure state may have been re-formed with the trappings of democracy, but the period post 2001 has seen the rise of an informal and shadow state.[4] Informal power relations dominate, are diffused through complex patronage networks and secured through access to an informal economy, of which the opium trade is but one, albeit significant, dimension. A variable pattern of localised and extended non-state regimes[5] has been created.

But in keeping with the focus of this book, and to explore a dimension of the Afghan economy that has received little attention precisely because there is so much effort to destroy it, the content and focus of this chapter is on the growth of the opium economy and its effects on rural change. Indeed, here we have an example of a commodity that has bucked the trend – the spread of technical change in a rural economy at an almost unprecedented rate that has absorbed labour and transformed the rural economy through its multiplier effects.[6] Here we have an example of dynamic growth in the agricultural economy based entirely on small-scale production of an agricultural commodity that has made a significant contribution to the growth of a country's GDP.

None of this is to downplay the complexity and multi-dimensional nature of the opium economy in Afghanistan – which includes both its intertwined role in supporting a war economy, a black economy and a peasant or coping economy (Goodhand 2005). But much of the attention has focused inevitably on the first two dimensions with rather less interest in the third. Moreover, although it is remarkable how the evidence can be shifted to suit the policy, there is a distinct tendency to view its role in relation to the logic of small-scale production in negative terms.[7] More recently a narrative about opium and small-farmer greed has emerged to handle the shift of production towards the south of the country and to legitimate aerial spraying efforts (Mansfield and Pain 2007).

The role of opium poppy in small-scale production and its effects on social relations is complex, and it is not easy to generalise about it. The purpose of this chapter is to explore the growth of the opium economy in one context in Afghanistan and to investigate the role of such a political commodity in rural change, and in so doing to respond directly to many of the themes that have featured in Judith Heyer's work and her interest in the empirical. Indeed, this chapter is an exercise in evidence building in a context where data are thin and elusive, in seeking to build understanding of causalities and linkages between the past and present, between geography, resources and identity and the scope for individual action, within a shifting environment of structural constraints and opportunities. Its methodologically plural approach responds to many of the strands of da Corta's argument (Chapter 2 in this volume) for the need for diverse and multilevel quantitative and qualitative analysis to understand rural change.

The essay is structured as follows. First, there is a general analysis of the dynamic growth of the opium economy, an understanding of which is necessary to locate the case study material. Second, summary case study material will be discussed, drawn from fieldwork from 2004 to 2008 in Balkh province in northern Afghanistan. Finally, there will be a more extended discussion of what can be learnt from the growth of the opium economy for a better theory of rural transformation in Afghanistan.

The growth of Afghanistan's opium economy

Table 10.1 summarises some of the estimates of key features of the growth of the opium economy since 1995.

Table 10.1 Summary statistics on Afghanistan's opium economy

	1995	2000	2001	2002	2003	2004	2005	2006	2007
Production (tons)	2,300	3,300	185	3,400	3,600	4,200	4,100	6,100	8,200
World market share (%)	~52	70	11	74	76	87	87	92	93
Number of provinces producing opium	8	22	11	24	28	34	26	28	21
Area under opium poppy (thousand ha)	54	82	8	74	80	131	104	165	193
As % of total agricultural land	n/a	n/a	n/a	n/a	1.6	2.9	2.3	3.65	4.27
Area under poppy/ area under cereals (%)	2.0	3.2	n/a	3.2	2.8	5.9	n/a	n/a	n/a
Gross farm income from opium per ha (US$)	1,000	1,100	7,400	16,200	12,700	4,600	5,400	4,600	5,200
Gross potential value of opiate exports (US$ million)	n/a	850	n/a	2,500	2,300	2,800	2,700	3,100	?
Gross farm income from opium (US$ million)	50	90	60	1,200	1,000	600	560	760	1000
Downstream income in Afghanistan (US$ million)	n/a	760	n/a	1,300	1,300	2,200	2,140	2,340	?

Source: UNODC 2003; UNODC/Government of Afghanistan (2004, 2006, 2007).

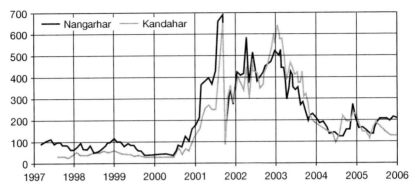

Figure 10.1 Dry opium prices in Kandahar and Nangarhar, 1997–2006 (US$/kg)

Source: Byrd and Jonglez 2006: 120.

Key features of the dynamics of the opium economy include the following. First, production of opium has quadrupled over a decade and Afghanistan's world market share has risen spectacularly, although the scale of more recent production against a long-assumed world demand (UNODC 2003) of 4,500 to 5,000 tons per year has yet to be reconciled. For Afghanistan this rise has meant that since 2001 the value of opium production has been in the range of 30–40 per cent of Afghanistan's GDP. Second – and underlying this increase in production – has been an expansion of area, which has included dimensions of both an intensification of production in core opium producing areas prior to 2001 as well as an expansion of cultivation into new provinces. However, despite this overall expansion, opium poppy cultivation has occupied a relatively small percentage of total agricultural land. Third, what has undoubtedly driven the expansion after 2001 has been the effect of the Taliban ban (see below) on opium poppy cultivation in the 2000/2001 season and its knock-on effects on opium prices (see Figure 10.1) which rose dramatically from the early months of 2001.

However, against this generalised story of expansion attention has to be given to the more subtle dynamics and shifting of cultivation (see Mansfield and Pain 2007 for a detailed discussion) between and within provinces (Table 10.2). Up until 2001 and coincident with the Taliban regime, opium production was largely concentrated in three provinces – Nangarhar, Helmand and Uruzgan (see Map 10.1) – located in the south and the east in the borderlands of Afghanistan, and the heartland of Pashtun tribes and the core of Taliban support.

In 2000, the Taliban issued an edict banning[8] the cultivation of opium poppy and the 2000/2001 cultivation season saw a dramatic drop (by 90 per cent) in national area. The one province in which it rose, Badakhshan, from 2,458 to 6,342 ha, remained in the hands of the Northern Alliance. After 2001, the area of opium poppy in the non-core provinces (to which it had been slowly spreading during Taliban rule) expanded, driven in part by the explosive effect of the rise in price (see Figure 10.1 above) and the ending of the widespread drought that had gripped Afghanistan since 1997.

Table 10.2 The percentage contribution of the core opium poppy–producing provinces and non-core provinces ('Others') to national area of opium poppy cultivation

Province	1994	1996	1998	2000	2001	2002	2003	2004	2005	2006	2007
Nangarhar	40.9	27.4	27.8	24.1	2.7	26.7	23.6	21.5	1.0	2.9	9.7
Badakhshan	2.4	5.7	4.4	3.0	79.3	11.1	15.9	11.9	7.1	7.9	1.9
Balkh	0	1.9	1.6	3.2	0	0.3	1.4	1.9	10.4	4.4	0
Helmand	41.7	43.7	47.9	52.2	0	40.5	19.2	22.4	25.5	42.2	53.2
Kandahar	5.1	5.4	8.2	3.7	0	5.4	3.8	3.8	12.5	7.6	8.6
Uruzgan	8.8	13.8	7.3	5.8	0	6.9	8.9	8.4	1.9	5.9	4.7
Farah	0	1.1	0.3	1.7	0	0.7	2.1	1.7	9.8	4.7	7.7
Others	1.0	1.0	2.5	9.4	17.9	8.4	24.9	28.2	31.7	24.5	14.1
Total '000 ha	71	57	64	82	8	74	80	131	104	165	193

Source: UNODC/Government of Afghanistan 2004, 2006, 2007.

Several points should be noted with respect to the post-2001 change in areas. First, there has been roughly a doubling of area from an average of 68,000 ha for the seven-year period between 1994 and 2000 to 125,000 ha for the six-year period from 2002. The fluctuations in area between years owe much to the fact that opium poppy is a crop that is highly responsive to climatic and management conditions, and that it performs poorly under continuous cropping and a poor crop one year has often encouraged farmers to exit from its production the next. Note should be made for example of the 21 per cent decline in area between 2004 and 2005 (from 131,000 ha to 104,000 ha – see Table 10.2) but a decline in estimated production of only 2.5 per cent (4,200 to 4,100 mt; see Table 10.1 on p. 200).[9]

Key provinces that saw a rise in area include both Badakhshan and Balkh, but from 2003/2004 the effects of provincial eradication efforts began to bite. Most notable is the case of Nangarhar which saw a decline in area from 2004 to 2005 of nearly 95 per cent (which was predictably called a success at the time) but it has since then begun to recover. The most recent example of a sharp decline in area is Balkh. Nevertheless, since 2005 there appears to have been a 'reconcentration' of opium poppy cultivation in the historical core provinces. What has driven this is a matter of debate: the UNODC/Government of Afghanistan (2007) has recently claimed that it has in effect been driven by the insurgency and greed, but there is stronger evidence to suggest that falling prices and relative returns in comparison with other crops, transaction costs in the market and counter-narcotics activities have played a critical role (Mansfield and Pain 2007). On this latter point, the origins of Afghanistan's opium economy can probably be traced to the closure of opium production in Turkey and Pakistan during the 1970s, combined with the emergence of political conflict in Afghanistan (Fazey 2007). Counter-narcotic activities have had a history of tending to displace production – the well-known effect of 'ballooning' of production – to elsewhere rather than to remove it, and such effects have undoubtedly been at play in response to counter-narcotic practice in Afghanistan.

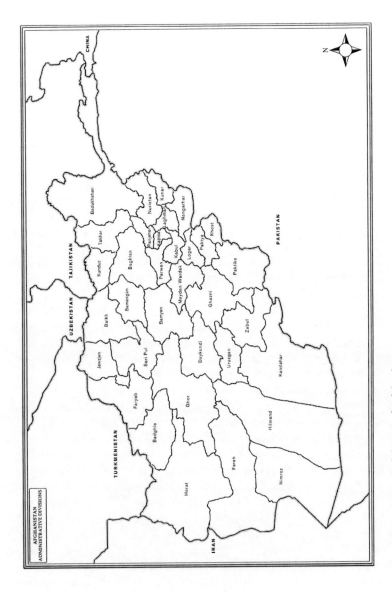

Map 10.1 A provincial map of Afghanistan

Source: www.aims.org.af/maps/national/political_divisions/political_divisions_34.pdf.

One must be careful, however, with the numbers, although it is the area estimates which have led the policy debate. Not only has there been a substantial shift in estimation methods since the UNODC-directed surveys were implemented, shifting from direct sample surveys to a combination of remote sensing and direct survey.[10] As a result, while the extent to which these are time series data may be questioned at least until 2006, UNODC and the United States government assessments (the latter done entirely by remote sensing) were telling rather different stories, an issue that has never been really discussed.

More significantly, the focus on aggregate statistics at the provincial level with problematic and incomplete district time series data has meant that very little attention has been paid to (or indeed interest has been shown in) patterns of cultivation between and within districts, or analytical enquiry into the drivers behind the diffusion and spread of cultivation. From an epidemiological perspective, this is precisely what one would be interested in. As David Mansfield has complained (2007a: 213):

> Why is it that, when it comes to a debate on opium poppy cultivation, the usual diversity that is at the forefront of discussions on Afghanistan is lost? Policymakers and development practitioners alike talk of 'opium poppy farmers' as if they are a homogenous group and refer to an 'aggregate' level of cultivation and 'average' crop returns.

It was precisely the need to gain a better understanding of the conditions and circumstances under which districts and farmers move in and out of the cultivation of opium poppy that led to the empirical fieldwork that is described in the next section.

The spread of opium poppy cultivation in Balkh[11]

The material that is presented here is drawn from a set of provincial studies that have sought to build longitudinal understanding of the dynamics of opium poppy cultivation. These studies[12] have been carried out working in locations contrasted by deep but shifting histories of opium poppy cultivation (Nangarhar), those with recent histories of significant expansion of cultivation (Balkh and Ghor) and those with little or no history of cultivation (Kunduz). They sought to develop a deeper understanding of changes in opium poppy cultivation, and the household and contextual factors that have influenced these trajectories.

A comment about research methods is needed. It will be appreciated that this is not a subject (or a location) that lends itself to quantitative methods or visible research teams. Field research has required a patient and diffuse process of relationship building, generalised discussions, cautious investigation and the seeking of triangulation and corroboration from multiple sources. This has been supplemented with remote sensing data on cropping intensity, although at present the methods used are not crop specific.[13] The evidence building is not systematic and there are inevitable gaps and areas of ignorance at several levels. Building the level of understanding reported here has taken time. Field research was carried out over effectively a twelve-month period working with one key research associate. Joint field visits were undertaken to build understanding of water distribution practices, settlement history and changing political contexts. The research associate working to a general checklist undertook informal discussions at village and household level, and wrote detailed transcripts that provided a basis for comment and debriefing. It goes without saying that all identities and locations are kept anonymous to protect informants.

Opium poppy cultivation in Balkh

Balkh has a ten-year recorded history (Table 10.3) of opium poppy production, although cultivation of the crop clearly predates this. According to these statistics, the major expansion of cultivation took place during 2005, although key informants from the districts place it earlier than this. The data indicate that the cultivation of opium poppy has been largely confined to just three districts, Balkh, Charbolaq and Chimtal which lie at the heart of the Balkh irrigation system, and all the field evidence supports this. The study focuses on Charbolaq and Chimtal districts. Table 10.3 shows the indicative[14] opium poppy area in Balkh for the three major opium-growing districts by district and year. What the UNODC data do not tell us, nor are they intended to do this, is the spatial distribution of cultivation within districts nor do they account for changing district distribution of cultivation. They provide an assessment of the incidence of cultivation but have nothing to say about causes or drivers of change.

The context

The irrigation system

The agricultural landscape of Balkh located on the northern Turkistan plains is dominated by a major irrigation scheme with a command area perhaps of 425,000 ha (ADB 2004) sourced from the Balkh River, a system that dates back more than a thousand years. Providing intensive irrigation facilities to at least four districts in Balkh through a network of eighteen canals, water is also diverted

Table 10.3 Indicative opium poppy area (ha) in Balkh for the three major opium-growing districts by district and year*

District	'94	'95	'96	'97	'98	'99	'00	'01	'02	'03	'04	'05	'06
Balkh				13	29	29	82	1	22	332		2,786	
Charbolaq				165	530	2,600	53			68		2,701	
Chimtal		1,065	532		485	1,428	2,451		153	617		1,878	
Other**							83	3	41	93		3,472	
Total	0	0	1,065	710	1,044	4,057	2,669	4	216	1,108	2,495	10,837	7,100

Source: UNODC/Government of Afghanistan 2005: 32; 2006.

Notes: *Opium poppy is mainly planted in the autumn and harvested in the following May, although there may be some rain-fed spring planting as well. The year therefore refers to the time of harvest. **'Other' comprised of eleven districts.

westwards to neighbouring Jawzjan province. The Balkh water management system is well described in a number of sources.[15] The picture that emerges is one of a historically complex system that is essentially on, if not beyond, the point of breakdown with respect to the implementation of rules of water allocation. During the long period of political instability, the upstream Sholgara district unilaterally expanded its water uptake through a further five canals (in addition to its legitimate seven canals) to support its rice cultivation area, effectively reducing water flow downstream. The same pattern is repeated as one moves downstream so that downstream districts and downstream locations within districts have been successively starved of water.

Chimtal district draws its water from two canals – the Chimtal and the Imam Sahib canal – and on the basis of Asian Development Bank estimates made in 2003 (ADB 2004) it is drawing over twice its allowable water. Balkh district was drawing nearly five times its allowable amount while Charbolaq was drawing just under its allowable amount. Opium poppy production appears to have been taken up in some of the better irrigated districts within Balkh province

The reasons for the breakdown of the Balkh water management system are complex (Lee 2003); decreased flows, increased demands, crop intensification processes balancing decreased individual farm areas, and expanding non-agricultural uses have all been combined with abuse of power and corrupt government to contribute to the collapse of former water distribution agreements.

Settlement history

Central to an understanding of Balkh is history and complex patterns of settlement and the associated development of the irrigation structures since the end of the nineteenth century. Drawing from N. Tapper (1973, 1991) and key informants, a summarised and simplified picture can be drawn.

In the late nineteenth century, the northern Turkistan plains, the most fertile areas of Afghanistan, had become severely depopulated, with the collapse of the northern khanates and the assertion of authority by Abdur Rahman. As a key part of a political strategy to gain political control of the north, a systematic process of settlement of the north by people from the south was implemented. During the first part of the twentieth century, settlers were primarily Durrani Pashtuns from the west and south (Kandahar), most of nomadic origins. From the mid 1930s, however, under the influence of Minister Muhammad Gul Khan Mohmand Durrani, dominance was balanced by the systematic settlement (in particular between Aqcha and Balkh) of Pashtuns of Ghilzai origin from eastern Afghanistan. Populations of Hazara and others were also forcibly resettled. As Tapper notes, and the field evidence amply confirms, settlement took place in the most favoured spots, primarily (although not always) upstream from existing settlements of Uzbeks, Aymaks, Arabs and Turkmen (N. Tapper 1991: 28).

Processes of settlement have continued to this day. In a context of population scarcity and land abundance up to the 1950s, competition for land and resources, particularly water, was not a basis for conflict. Tapper makes it clear that the settlers from the south were quick to establish political and economic domination over existing populations while 'local authorities turned a blind eye to Pashtun oppression, in conformity with what was essentially a tacit central government policy of political and cultural discrimination against non-Pashtuns' (N. Tapper 1991: 34). While ethnic identities could serve as boundaries in relation to resources and marriage, they often did not do so in relation to trade and exchange.

For the two study districts, Charbolaq and Chimtal, the settlement patterns are summarised in Table 10.4.[16] What is evident is that settlement history is different for each irrigation canal. In the case of the two canals in Charbolaq district, the top ends are settled almost exclusively by people of Pashtun origin, although each village traces its origins to different parts of the south; the further downstream and north one goes in this district, the greater the populations of non-Pashtuns, particularly at the bottom ends of the irrigation systems. In Chimtal district, in contrast, the upper reaches of the irrigation systems contain non-Pashtun villages with the majority of Pashtun villages being located downstream.

This account summarises a rather complex pattern of settlement and serves to point out that such patterns exist, and they have a historical basis, even if the exact chronology is not clear. However, the finer the scale of examination, the more complex these patterns become, not least because of problems about what and who defines a village. Examples were found, for example, of a village of non-Pashtuns being surrounded by *nawared* (new) (Pashtun) settlements. Officially these may be treated as one village, although often the local perspective is different.

The settlement of new people in major irrigation systems has implications for the design and management of the distribution of water both among villages and between upstream and downstream. At a time of water and land surplus in the 1930s and before, with an incremental process of settlement over a long period of time, it is doubtful that the consequences of new settlement were structured into irrigation management at a system level. The primary concern of the government at that time appears to have been to develop a system of taxation of water distribution.

Systematic information on irrigation design and the extent to which water flows and allocation times reflected concerns for equity in distribution is not available. What anecdotal information there is, and this is primarily based on what has been reported by individuals with a long history of engagement in water distribution at the district level (the *mirabashi*s, or water masters), indicates

Table 10.4 Patterns of ethnic identity by location in Chimtal and Charbolaq districts

	Chimtal district		Charbolaq district	
Canal position	*Imam Sahib*	*Chimtal*	*Charbolaq*	*Shasharak*
Top	Tajik/ Hazara	Mixed	Pashtun	Pashtun
Middle	Hazara	Mixed	Mixed	Mixed
Bottom	Pashtun/ Mixed	Pashtun	Mixed	Mixed

Source: Pain.

that there are structural inequalities built both into the irrigation system and into water distribution within the canals. There appears to have been no attempt or intention to allocate downstream villages longer irrigation times, for example, to compensate for reduced water flow. The existence of such inequalities is not in doubt. There were persistent reports of contrasts between potential yields for crops upstream in contrast with those downstream.

Informants commented that villages at the top end of the irrigation system in Charbolaq could easily produce double the yields of wheat of those at the bottom. A wealthy landowner at the top end of the irrigation system would have 40–50 jeribs (approximately 8–10 ha) of land, while a wealthy landowner at the bottom of the system would have at least 100 jeribs (20 ha), if not more. These inequalities were officially recognised and they provide the basis for taxation classes introduced during King Amanullah's time in the 1920s. Thus, land at the top end of the canals, which is termed 1 or 2 bawra,[17] is taxed at the rate of 5 Afs per jerib and land that is 3 or 4 bawra at the rate of 2 Afs per jerib.

Under conditions of water and land sufficiency, water distribution inequalities did not provide a point of friction between upstream and downstream villages. Villages at the bottom end of canals reported, as in the case of the Imam Sahib canal, that there was in the past sufficient water for them to be able to double-crop, with wheat during the winter period to meet household requirements, and a cash crop of either cotton or sesame to meet cash requirements. For the Turkmen villages at the bottom of the Charbolaq canals, large livestock holdings combined with a secure winter wheat crop provided for a robust and sufficient livelihood during the 1950s.

However, two things have happened since the 1950s. The first is the steady growth of population and increasing intensification of agriculture as households have sought to intensify production to meet the reduced land areas per household. The second change is the increased demand for water, since the drought of 1998, coupled with a decline in the water supply. The result has been increasingly acute water scarcity, emergence of conflict and the surfacing of underlying inequalities in water distribution and access. In Charbolaq district, upstream villages have exerted control over water distribution and severely reduced downstream water supplies. This has also happened in Chimtal district, but not to the same extent.

The effects of increasing population and decreasing water supply are most clearly evidenced by the intensity of double cropping in the areas served by the district canals as shown in remote satellite imagery (Pain 2007: 18). Upstream areas have double-cropped in all seven years since 2000 while downstream areas have only double-cropped in one to two years out of seven. The evidence from the field confirms this.

The diffusion and spread of opium in Chimtal and Charbolak

To understand the argument about diffusion and spread, it is first necessary to outline the key infrastructural features (Map 10.2) of these two adjoining districts.

The main road from Mazar-i-Sharif to Sheberghan runs east–west and is located in the southern end of Charbolaq district; a small but significant part of this district is located south of the road. The two irrigation canals, the Imam Sahib and the Chimtal canals run east–west through Chimtal district, which is located south of the main road. The Charbolaq and the Shasharak canals run diagonally east–north-west across Charbolaq district. Both sets of canals are divided into top, middle and bottom ends, which in the case of Chimtal run east–west, and, in the case of the Charbolaq canals, run roughly south–north. For the sake of discussion, these dimensions are overlaid with a matrix of three by six, with the squares sequentially numbered for ease of reference.

Three distinct phases of cultivation (prior to 1992; 1992 to 2001; 2001 to 2006) with specific spatial and temporal dimensions can be identified in these

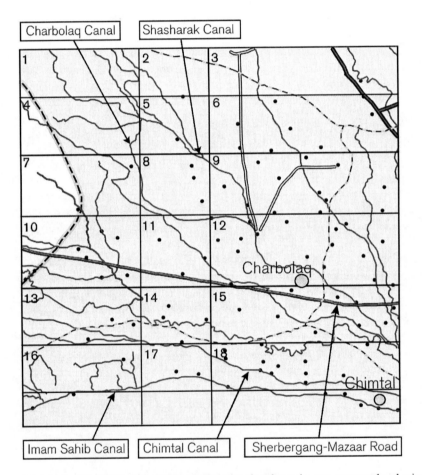

Map 10.2 Chimtal and Charbolaq districts showing the main east–west road and primary irrigation canals, and overlaid with a reference grid.

Source: Pain (2007).

two districts prior to 2006, with the possible start of a fourth phase in 2006/2007. These are linked to specific political periods, which can be simplified as follows. The pre-communist era (before 1978) was followed by the Soviet period to the fall of President Najibullah in 1992. From this time (1992–96), internecine conflict developed between the various Mujahideen groups, many of which were ethnically based and had emerged in response to the Soviet invasion. After the Soviet departure they fought for power and resources to fund themselves and then from 1994 they fought against the rise of the Taliban. The Taliban captured Mazar-i-Sharif and the north in 1996, ultimately confining the opposition to Badakhshan province in the north before the Taliban fell from power in late 2001.

Phase I – prior to 1992

During this period opium poppy cultivation was highly localised and limited in scope. There were consistent reports (Pain 2007: 10) that production at this time was limited to the upper and lower reaches (respectively squares 18 and 16) of the Imam Sahib canal, in Chimtal. Historically, cultivation, which certainly predates 1978, was small-scale, primarily for consumption by Turkmen people from the bottom end of Charbolaq (there are no exclusively Turkmen villages in Chimtal), and the crop was relatively low-value. Interestingly, there were no reports of prior production from the Turkmen villages. It is clear that there was a small and contained market for opium driven by local demand. It is also clear that the basic knowledge of opium production has long existed in Balkh, although the skills were not sufficient to handle the technological changes of the 1990s.

Phase II – from 1992 to 2001

This phase was characterised by intensive cultivation that was concentrated in specific locations. From 1992, around the time of the fall of the Najibullah government, there seems to have been the beginning of an expansion in the area of opium poppy cultivation in Chimtal and its emergence in Charbolaq and this increased significantly under the Taliban from 1996. All accounts point to cultivation being highly localised, and concentrated on the Chimtal canal (in contrast to the prior cultivation on the Imam Sahib canal), particularly in the middle and downstream ends and confined to these villages. Some reports (Pain 2007: 13) also indicated that cultivation may have started in the eastern end of the Charbolaq canal (square 12) toward the mid 1990s consistent with the UNODC data (see Table 10.3 above).

Phase III – from 2001 to 2006

This third phase may be described as generalised cultivation but with clear spatial patterning. From 2001 to 2002, all reports (Pain 2007: 13) are clear that opium poppy cultivation expanded dramatically and became much more widespread across the two districts. This is also consistent with the UNODC area statistics. Comments from informants, however, claim a much greater rate of expansion in the first few post-Taliban years than the UNODC figures indicate. There was a general expansion of cultivation, but within this expansion there were some distinct patterns. This phase was brought to an abrupt halt with the effective ban on opium poppy cultivation in the autumn of 2006.

Phase IV?

From the 2006/2007 cultivation season, both field observations and UNODC reports indicate that there has been a sharp decline in the area of cultivation. During fieldwork in March 2007 all informants reported that cultivation had stopped. Field observations were consistent with this. Fields where opium poppy was growing in March 2006, many of them within half a kilometre of the main road, had no opium poppy growing in March 2007, reflecting a shift in the local political climate and support for opium production.

Why these phases?

The phases of opium cultivation that can be identified prior to the 2006/2007 season are based on location (where it has been cultivated), intensity (the scale or area of cultivation), and extent (the overall area that it occupies), as summarised in Table 10.5.

Phase I saw localised, low-level, contained production. During Phase II, cultivation increased in intensity but remained contained, implying control over its cultivation. Finally, Phase III saw cultivation expand and become more dispersed, with variable intensity, but also with forms of regulation apparent in relation to access to the market as discussed below. Two important questions arise from this conceptualisation. First, what are the factors that explain the characteristics of each phase, and to what extent have these changed or shifted from phase to phase? Second, what are the factors that have caused a shift in phase or a transition from one phase to another?

Understanding the diffusion and spread of opium poppy in Balkh

With respect to Phase I, it appears that the major reason for its limited area and dispersed cultivation was that there was only a small local demand for opium

Table 10.5 Characteristics of the three phases

	Location	Intensity	Extent
Phase I	Contained	Low	Small
Phase II	Restricted	High	Medium
Phase III	Dispersed	Variable	Large

Source: Pain.

consumption which justified its production. It is not clear why the Turkmen populations who are reported to have been the major consumers did not meet their opium demand through their own production since water scarcities were not reported for that time. One possible explanation is that, after the official banning of opium poppy cultivation in Afghanistan after 1948, it was safer or easier for Pashtun populations to grow the crop than it was for the Turkmen, although historically it had been cultivated by the Turkmen people.

That there was an increase in opium cultivation leading to Phase II is corroborated by all sources, but what brought this about? Moreover, why did it assume its particular characteristics of being located only in specific areas but reportedly intensively cultivated in these, rather than spreading more generally within these districts?

There are a number of possible explanations. Some associate the expansion of poppy cultivation in the north with the coming to power of the Taliban and the capture of Mazar-i-Sharif in 1996. Informants indicated however that cultivation started to expand during Jumbesh rule (from 1992 to 1996) and that there were traders from the north engaged in the market, possibly exporting into Uzbekistan to the north. Whether this meant that cultivation of opium poppy was taken up more widely in the districts is not known but it is evident that by 1996 it had become firmly restricted to certain villages in Chimtal.[18] The UNODC data support this (see Table 10.3 above).

The expansion of opium poppy cultivation from its previously low level is likely to have been a result of an external demand penetrating the market, which shifted the profitability of the crop. Although price data do not appear to exist for this period, it is clear that it was not just a change in market conditions. There seem to be three dimensions to the change. First, external traders from Kandahar appeared and rapidly turned one village (in square 14) into a trade centre for the two districts. One informant commented that there had long been a history of trade in hawks between the cluster of village in squares 13 and 14 and Kandahar, dating back at least thirty years. Thus trade links were strong, cemented by common tribal identities.

Second, there appears to have been a transformation of technology. New opium poppy seed was brought from the south and, with the appropriate skills and lancing equipment, these new varieties had the potential to yield up to six times more opium than the traditional varieties. Third, beginning in 1992, major problems with water distribution began to develop. From the 1980s, underlying tensions between the multiple ethnic communities within the districts began to surface. This started with conflicts and tension between the Mujahidin groups. In 1989/1990 there was a severe shortage of water during internal conflict between Jamiat Islami (under Rabbani) and Hezb-e-Islami (under Hekmatyar). The Hekmatyar commander at the time, Juma Khan Hamadard, blocked the streams towards Charbolaq and Shasharak canals to prevent water flows to middle and bottom end villages that were connected to Jamiat.

Why did cultivation not spread more widely given these conditions? The cultivation of opium appears to have been regulated and restricted. As one informant put it, referring to 1996–2001: 'We lost the opportunity at that time – if we had cultivated we would be rich but we were scared of the authorities – they appeared in black turbans and we were scared they would find some reason to punish us.'

During 1992–96, under the rule of the Uzbek Jumbesh party, the communities of Pashtun origin suffered considerably. As the Taliban came to power in 1996, there was certainly retribution in these two districts for the power that the Jumbesh had wielded from 1992, contributing to the concentration of opium poppy cultivation in Pashtun areas from 1996. For example, in Chimtal district a significant group of leading Hazara from the cluster of villages in square 17 were executed. There is no wonder that a crop that was closely linked with trading networks of people from the Durrani Pashtuns from southern Afghanistan, and so intimately tied in with sustaining the means of power (Rubin 2000), should be so closely and effectively regulated.

Factors influencing the diffusion of cultivation after 2001

The documentary record shows clearly that there was a dramatic rise in market price of opium from the second half of 2000 and the first half of 2001. The price rose from around $50 per kg of dry opium in Kandahar and Nangarhar to over $500 by mid 2001 (Byrd and Jonglez 2006).

The opportunity to generate substantial income after years of hardship due to conflict and drought should not be underestimated as a driver of the spread of cultivation. However, cultivation required labour for crop management, skill for harvesting and water for irrigation. Closely related to this was the need for credit, although the effects of the rise in prices on the ability to raise credit and hire labour should be appreciated. Access to all three of these mattered. On the question of skill, some sources from the northern end, or downstream, in Charbolaq indicated that initially they did not have the skill for cultivation. It was only after labouring in the southern belt of the district that they acquired sufficient skill and knowledge to be able to cultivate the crop themselves. As one of them put it:

> We used to seek opium-poppy related jobs in other villages. I remember my hard work with good enough income on opium poppy farms in [squares 11 and 15]. My aim was to learn the lancing skills because we were not so skilled at that time [2001 and 2002]. Gradually over a couple of years we learned this skill very well and have been able to cultivate on our own lands since then. We cultivated and harvested opium in small pieces of our lands independently and gradually expanded within our village. Many of our farmers owning a lot of land were admitted to the opium poppy lands of other villages even though we had problems with them in the past.

This interesting comment, particularly the last sentence, from a Hazara informant, points to a history of social boundaries to the diffusion of cultivation skills.

It also points to the effects of the market expansion on lowering some of these boundaries.

It is also clear that initially while there was a pool of unskilled labour in Balkh in 2001 this was rapidly absorbed. There was also a particular shortage of skilled labour for harvesting in both districts. Although villages from the south started systematically to recruit labour from northern parts of the district to work on the opium crop, it is also evident that migrant skilled labour from Nangarhar became a significant part of the labour force for the crop for the first few years after 2001. The significance of the higher skill levels of Nangarhar labour should be noted. According to one source, the use of labour from Nangarhar could contribute a 20–30-per-cent difference in yield due to their ability to extract more opium resin through multiple lancing in contrast with less skilled labour.[19] Indeed, there were reports from numerous informants that Nangarharis had been coming to the north to work,[20] sometimes as sharecroppers even before Taliban times.

During 2005, some 5,000 Nangarharis were thought to be in Charbolaq district, in all probability driven by the effective prohibition on opium poppy cultivation in Nangarhar during 2005/2006 (Mansfield 2006). But as local labour gained skills, there came a point when the demand for Nangarhar labour declined. One informant recalled how one morning during the 2006 harvest, the village woke up to find that about a hundred Nangarhari workers had arrived overnight. The villagers reportedly asked the provincial administration to get them sent back and to stop any more coming, a request that was apparently met.

On the question of access to credit, much depended on who you were and where you lived. For those villages in the core of the opium area and well linked into the trading system, credit was reportedly easily available, either within the village or from traders. From those who were not part of these groups, credit could either be raised from within known networks or provided by traders with whom they had dealings for cotton or sesame. Credit, given largely in cash, appears to have been easier upstream rather than downstream, reflecting effects of the relative prosperity of these areas with income generated from opium and better connections into trader networks.

The third factor governing the spread of opium poppy was the availability of water. Here, contrasts have to be made between the bottom end of the Imam Sahib canal in Chimtal and the bottom end of the Shasharak canal in Charbolaq (Pain 2006:16). The villagers at the bottom end of the Imam Sahib canal are primarily of Pashtun origin. During the time of the Taliban when the management of the water distribution within the canal was under the control of a Pashtun *mirabashi*, they were reportedly able to deepen and widen their irrigation canal to pull through more water. The current *mirabashi* (a non-Pashtun) is apparently both well connected to the government and effective, and water distribution along the length of the Imam Sahib canal has not been subject to the degree of absolute control at the upper end as has been the case elsewhere. The result is that sufficient water gets through to the bottom end to support an opium crop. There is not enough water to cultivate wheat, and certainly not enough to double crop.

In contrast, in Charbolaq district, the water that gets through to the bottom of the Sharsharak canal is not even sufficient for drinking purposes. There has been very limited crop production in these areas. This varies according to location and canal, but generally there is much greater water scarcity at the bottom of the irrigation canals in Charbolaq than in Chimtal.

Factors affecting the returns to cultivation of opium poppy after 2001

Three major factors have determined the returns to opium poppy cultivation. The first is resources, such as water and other inputs (including access to credit for those inputs) that determine potential yield. The second is the social relations around cultivation: whether the cultivator owns the land, uses it as a tenant or sharecropper, landlord or labourer. The third is the price for which the opium can be sold.

Many informants in both districts made reference to major differences in opium yield according to location on the canal and the inputs that were applied, upstream well-irrigated areas with applied fertiliser yielding at least 50 per cent more opium than downstream. While yields are evidently highly variable according to both skills and available inputs, downstream villages are clearly at a disadvantage. Although there are no quantitative data to support the observation, field observation supported a picture of a higher percentage of the land under opium poppy cultivation that was more intensively cultivated at the top end of irrigation systems than at the bottom. In short, more land was allocated to opium cultivation in the more favourable areas and these also achieved higher yields than in the less favourable areas downstream.

Cultivation of opium poppy takes place through four main types of socio-economic relations. These can be characterised as follows:

1   a landowner cultivating on small areas using family labour and some hired labour for weeding and harvest;
2   a landowner using exclusively hired labour;
3   a landowner sharecropping out land;
4   contract growing.

Cutting across these four categories is the demand and availability of skilled labour, influenced by farm-gate prices for opium and wage rates. Mansfield (2002) estimating the relative returns on opium poppy cultivation according to social position shows how the US$3,000–3,870 gross value of output is divided up. The landlord/sharecropper ratio can vary from 90:10 to 50:50 depending on the specific terms of the agreement and the legacy of opium-denominated debt that exists between landlord and sharecropper. Data were not collected here to describe this in detail, but the effects from 2005 of declining prices and poor yields on employment opportunities in Balkh should be noted.[21] Note must also be made of the available data on land distribution, which indicate the relative proportion of those with and without land. These data are drawn from two sources. First, estimates that can be derived from a WFP Vulnerability Assessment Mapping undertaken during 2002/2003 (WFP 2002) and, second, estimates of the distribution of land ownership provided by informants during the fieldwork. The WFP data indicate that 20–35 per cent of households are landless, with higher values upstream. Field evidence indicated that it is more variable than this and that there were differences by location. For example, in one village, 90 per cent of households (square 2) were reported to be without land, comparable to the 80 per cent reported in a second village (square 16). In a third village (square 5), the proportion of landless households was relatively small, although about 60 per cent could only meet two to three months' requirement of grain from their land in a good year. Both sources thus point to major inequalities in land ownership, with a minority of large landowners and a significant number of landless or near landless households that are not grain secure from own production.

No systematic information is available on the distribution of small-scale production with local employment of labour, although it is likely that this was more common in the middle and downstream portions of the Charbolaq canals and the bottom end of the Chimtal canal. In part, this may have been determined by social identities. While it might be acceptable for a Hazara, for example, to work as labour on lands upstream, it would be less likely for non-Hazara to work as labour on Hazara land downstream. Villagers in mid- and downstream villages, for example, often commented that labour for the crop came only from within the village.

It is clear that hired labour was systematically drawn from downstream and midstream villages to work on the opium crop upstream. Landowners at the top end of the irrigation systems appeared to prefer to cultivate with hired labour and pay in cash. Those further downstream were more likely to sharecrop land (or hire land out to sharecroppers) and thereby share the risks of cultivation and pay labour through shares of the crop rather than cash. In the upstream areas, there were several examples of labour contractors who organised opium production either for landlords or for traders. These examples indicate the degree to which the production of opium poppy had become commercialised.

The third factor influencing returns is the price that can be obtained. The price depends on whether or not the producer has access to the main traders. For many, access is extremely limited, as for example the first quotation from a village in the heart of the opium belt in Charbolaq, suggests: 'It is very hard to see the main trader. It is difficult to understand the main buyer, the network is very strong and a lot of people are involved at other levels. We sell through commission agents.' Respondents from Chimtal confirmed this:

> The first harvest we sold. In each village of this belt there is a big guest room which receives two to five people from Helmand as guests who ask the middlemen to buy. We mostly sold to them [i.e. the middlemen] and were not allowed to meet the main dealers because of reasons of trust.

As many observed, selling through the middlemen or commission agents meant that they got a reduced price, although it was difficult to get precise figures on how much the differential in prices was.

These descriptions of market access provide an illustration of how the market is regulated by key actors, and how groups of solidarity often defined by ethnic identities have played a critical and important role in the evolution of the opium market within these two districts.

Outcomes

What have been the effects of the development and growth of the opium economy from 2001 to 2006 and why does this question matter? The effective cessation of opium poppy cultivation in Balkh (at least for the 2006/2007 season) is likely to have immediate effects on household incomes.

There can be no doubt that the growth of the opium poppy economy in these two districts has been significant and has injected an unquantifiable amount of cash into the districts, even if much of the overall value has been transferred out of the districts to trade and processing centres elsewhere. While caution and reservation should be attached to figures and numbers, taking the UNODC area figures from 2001 to 2006 (a cumulative total of 21,750 ha over these five years) and assuming average yields of 40 kg per hectare and an average price of US$75 per kg of opium, an order-of-magnitude figure of US$65 million gross has been injected over this five-year period into the two districts' economies at the farm-gate level. This does not take account of the undoubtedly higher margins on the trading of opium. If one considers that probably no more than one-third of all the villages in the two districts (40 of about 120) have been intensively cultivating opium poppy over this period, this sum could amount to an average of US$1.5 million per cultivating village over this six to seven-year period.

Two questions arise. First, what have been the effects of this cash infusion and how are these benefits likely to have been distributed within the districts according to social position? Second, what have been the effects of the growth of this market on underlying social structures within the district and the capacity of individuals to negotiate these? Has the growth of the opium economy simply consolidated pre-existing structures of identity and inequality, continuing a 'path dependent' trajectory? Or has the opium economy had a transforming effect shifting and reconfiguring social alliances and structures? First, the likely effects on household economies need to be considered.

Effects of opium cultivation on household economies

In looking for effects of opium cultivation, a number of factors need to be taken into consideration. First, potential returns to opium poppy cultivation are set by production levels as influenced by the management and inputs provided, for which location is an effective proxy, and area of cultivation. Second, the distribution of shares of production is determined very much by who you are and the conditions under which you cultivate, as owner cultivator, as sharecropper, or as labour. Third, what is realised from the share of production is set by the price that can be obtained and the settlement of any credit taken for production. Finally, account has to be taken of the period over which cultivation has been taking place as it is clear that some villages started cultivating opium poppy earlier than others.

None of these issues can easily be addressed with quantitative data. On the question of potential returns, there is likely to be a gradient of yield, reflecting availability of water and resources to provide inputs, combined with the period over which cultivation has been taking place moving from (relatively) high production upstream to relatively low production downstream over the five-year period. Second, with better market access and therefore less risk associated with production, landowners upstream have tended to use hired labour rather than sharecroppers. The returns to cultivation are therefore likely to have been higher to landowners at the top end rather than at the bottom although there are no systematic data to show this. Sharecroppers are likely to have had lower returns than landlords (see Mansfield 2007b). As noted above, the proportion of opium poppy that was sharecropped is likely to have been higher downstream, although there are no data on this. Then there are the returns to labour, which would have been variable depending on how much labour the individual contributes and how payment was distributed between payment in cash and payment in kind.

What do the reports from the field have to say on all this?

An upstream landowner (square 15), a trader in cotton and possibly a middle-level trader in opium reported that in 1994 there had been an earthquake as well as factional fighting in the village. His house had been destroyed and he gave his land on mortgage to get the money to rebuild his house. He was US$2,000 in debt as a result and reportedly there were some hundred households in a similar position to him. In the past, he had cultivated cotton and hashish, but he has a large household to feed with three brothers, uncles and two cousins living together.

> In reality, the only crop that provides enough income is poppy. Even women members of our family were doing the cultivation and harvesting in the yard. Except for me the rest of these boys (indicating his brothers and cousins) have not married yet. I was planning last year to earn huge money and was prepared to cultivate opium in all 5 jeribs to pay for one of my brothers' wedding this winter. Well-organised poppy cultivation is possible when all elements work together. You have to ensure marketing though its evidence (traders from Nangarhar, Helmand and Kandahar) should appear in the area during sowing, growing and processing; you must agree on cash and kind payment to labourers that we organise for them (outside traders) and feel safe and secure of your environment.

For a household without land the opium poppy crop also had significant benefits for the labouring opportunities and improved access to credit that it provided:

> 2001–2003 were the best years of income and prosperity and of saving for assets and livestock. Within those years I have been able to buy four goats and one cow and just last summer I sold them to repay my debts and resolve my economic difficulties. I used to work on farms in many villages. The terms of my work was getting one-quarter of the harvest. In the top-end village it was daily payment and even in villages like here and the neighbourhood I used to get advance cash to cover my family needs. (Square 8)

However, as the above quotation shows, while the opportunities to find work clearly improved, the benefits were much diminished compared to landowners. The comments from a small landowner (square 15) who has only 0.5 jeribs of land himself but supervised the production of opium on 3 jeribs for a landlord, illustrates this:

> I used to work as a senior farmer to supervise the land with poppy cultivation on a credit basis. The landowner gave me authority for supervising other labourers and my family members who are working on the land during processing. Last spring I was supervising 3 jeribs of land with poppy with one-quarter share at harvest time. Despite all these realities that I am talking about to you and I acknowledge my involvement in the opium poppy cultivation, still I am in the same economical situation that I was before; it is just like an increase of 15–20 per cent to my annual earnings out of all this hard work day and night.

What does not appear to have emerged here, in contrast say to Helmand or Nangarhar, is deep opium-denominated debt. The effect of the opium economy in Balkh on credit relations is a separate issue (Pain 2008), but suffice it to say that the development of opium poppy cultivation in Balkh largely took place after the boom-and-bust cycle of prices and the structure of credit relations in the districts appear to be rather different from those reported for Nangarhar and Helmand. Mansfield (2007b) found, for example, that 75 per cent of his sample (in Badakhshan province) who moved back into opium poppy cultivation in 2006/2007 had an average level of debt of US$1,721, nearly three times the level of those who had moved out of cultivation in the season. But the evidence from Balkh is that access to trader-sourced credit for opium poppy cultivation has been restricted to those who are well connected (and thus with land and in the most favourable areas). There were not widespread reports of legacies of debt from opium cultivation.

The multiplier effect of opium cultivation on the rural economy was significant. One informant noted how seven years previously there had only been two motorcycles in the district, and no motorcycle shops. By 2006, there were more than 500 motorbikes and 11 motorbike shops in the district centre.

For a carpenter, the house rebuilding programme fuelled by opium income had significant benefits:

> The opium poppy cultivation years [2001–2006] were good years for the shop with a lot of orders for making windows. Orders were coming everyday to my shop from this and neighbouring villages and I opened up another shop in my home village and sometimes was going there for marketing and receiving new orders. (square 4)

In sum, benefits from the opium economy were significant and trickled down through the social hierarchy. But as is clear from above, the returns to landowners and to labour were of different orders of magnitude. The differentials between returns to farmers and returns to district officials, and returns to farmers and returns to traders, were even greater.

The growth of the opium economy and its effect on underlying structures

Much of the argument of this chapter has concerned the determinants of opium poppy cultivation, arguing that opium poppy cultivation has to be understood in terms of underlying structures of inequality of power and access to resources. Given the extent to which it has increased in scale from Phase II to Phase III, it is also important to raise the reverse question: how has the growth of the opium poppy economy affected and perhaps changed underlying structures? There is no clear answer to this question, but there are some fairly ambiguous outcomes which hint at potential 'transformatory' consequences of the growth of this market.

During Phase II, when cultivation and the markets appear to have been closely regulated, reserving the benefits strictly to those who had control of the market, the more persuasive argument would be that the cultivation of opium served to consolidate existing inequalities and structure them more deeply.

The scaling-up of opium poppy cultivation since 2001 has possibly done the reverse. The immediate benefits of cultivation have certainly been more widely distributed, although it is clear that their distribution has not been equitable. The effects of cultivation have possibly been neutral in relation to practices of water distribution within the irrigation system. Cultivation upstream is not likely to have led to more restrictions on water release for downstream, given that opium poppy is not as water-demanding a crop as wheat and therefore there may have been water distribution benefits. The expanded market, through bringing about more interchange between different social groups, may also have subdued conflict, which may or may not have longer-term consequences. These are little more than speculations but they serve at least to question the implicit and widespread assumptions about the negative effects of the opium economy.

Concluding remarks

On 12 April 2007, an Afghan organisation in Kabul called the Institute for War and Peace Reporting posted the following report by IWPR trainees:

On April 8, about 60 landowners staged a protest in front of the governor's compound in Lashkar Gah, the capital of Helmand. They were demanding that the local authorities step in to resolve a dispute that was threatening to disrupt the all-important gathering of the opium crop. The hired labourers, who work as sharecroppers, had united to force landowners to give them half of the yield, when the owners insisted that one-fifth was a more reasonable share. The farm owners wanted the provincial government to mediate 'We spent all of our money growing the poppy,' complained one landowner. 'If the government doesn't help us with the harvesters, we'll lose everything.' But the workers in the fields are in a strong position. This year's harvest may well be the biggest ever. Hired labour comes at a premium since the work is dangerous in Taliban infested areas.

'Last year we had to beg from the landowners,' said Abdul Jamil, who gathers poppy every year. 'We wanted one-sixteenth of the harvest and we apologised even for that. But this season they need us more than we need them. They are offering a quarter, maybe a third. We are lucky to be united. If they want us to go into districts where the Taliban are, they'll have to pay us a lot of money.'

By April 9, the harvesters were back at work. According to unconfirmed reports, the Helmand government imposed a limit of one-quarter of the opium yield as a fair deal for the labourers.

The emergence of class interests is a rarity and possibly at present likely to emerge only in a relatively ethnically homogeneous area such as Helmand. Richard Tapper, writing of the north during the 1970s (R. Tapper 1988), detected a gradual emergence of class identities that were beginning to traverse ethnic divides. With the hardened conflicts over resources and the political deployment of ethnic identities in such an ethnically diverse context (in contrast to Helmand) class interests may well have become subsumed to ascribed ones in the north.

By contrast, in the mountain economy of Badakhshan in the north-east of Afghanistan, which is predominantly a Tajik area, for which descent is not so ideologically important, current fieldwork does hint at potential social changes driven by opium (Pain 2008). This is an area that has had a long history of opium cultivation, primarily in the more remote mountain valleys. The rise in prices from 2001 led to an unprecedented period of prosperity – colloquially called the 'opium festival years' or the opium revolution. For many households these are seen as years when for the first time they have been freed from debt relations and have accumulated surplus. Various informants talked about how this new experience meant that they would not go back to the old ways and dependent relations of the past and, as the opium economy is suppressed, they are migrating to find work, if necessary in the police or army. In part this also points to the historic role that opium poppy has played, providing a stay of history on the viability for farm-based livelihoods for those on marginal landholdings.

A wider question is the extent to which the growth of the opium economy and the surplus that it has generated has enabled a consolidation of power structures within the province given the extent to which the informal has blended with and consolidated formal institutions. There is evidence to suggest that the relative consolidation of power within Balkh and the relative security it has achieved is more likely to have been built on the opium economy than to have emerged despite it. The role of predation and illegal networks in the accumulation of capital and state-formation processes has a historical root in the early modern era (Tilly 1985). As Gallant (1999) has argued, 'military entrepreneurs' resourced and established through illegal activities can modernise and shift to more legal positions in state-building processes. What is happening in Balkh at the moment could possibly be interpreted in this light, but this is not the place to pursue this further as it moves the discussion well beyond the focus of this chapter.

However, as this chapter has argued, opium poppy cultivation and its expansion since 2001 has shifted the ground, softening some of the previous hierarchical and concentrated power relations and possibly reducing conflict and inequalities. How durable these changes will be remains unclear. Balkh as with the rest of Afghanistan remains an informal security regime (Wood and Gough 2006), but it may have become a little more secure than other parts of the country.

Notes

1 Source: Mr Rayne, Opium Agent, East India Company, 'The Siege of Krishnapur' at the time of the Indian Mutiny. J.G. Farrell (1973: 47).
2 One of the greater ironies is the fact that one of the core producing provinces in Afghanistan, Helmand, was the subject of intensive modernisation efforts by the Americans in the 1950s–1970s to build a centralised irrigation and settlement scheme around cotton (Cullather 2002); it largely failed at that time but success has at last been achieved, unfortunately with the wrong crop, as far as the Americans are concerned.
3 Available online: www.dailymail.co.uk/pages/live/articles/news/news.html?in_article_id= 468430&in_page_id=1770 (accessed 9 August 2007).
4 Conceptualised here for the context of civil war where the state is wholly informal (Wood and Gough 2006), it has also been applied to more formal states (Harriss-White 2003: 89) where it 'comes into being because of the formal state and it coexists with it'.
5 Regimes, either formal or informal in the sense that Wood and Gough (2006: 1698) apply the term, are 'rules, institutions and structured interests that constrain individuals'.
6 It is estimated that opium poppy requires 350 person days per hectare in contrast to about 36 for wheat and each hectare generates about 5.6 jobs in the rural non-farm sector.
7 The claims made in the US Counternarcotics strategy (Schweich 2007: 39) that '[a]dditionally many rural households are mired in debt. Estimates as to the total debt of poppy growers in Afghanistan are in the hundreds of millions of dollars. Many of the indebted have little choice but to grow a crop which yields the necessary income to meet obligations' are misleading and misrepresent the probable sources (which are unreferenced) of the data. The implication that households are 'mired in debt' due to opium is most likely drawn from the work of Mansfield in Nangarhar (Mansfield 2006) where opium is grown and from the work of Klijn and Pain (2007).
8 The reasons for this remain in debate. The mainstream view tends to see it as cynical inventory management while others would argue that it could also be interpreted as an effort in seeking wider legitimacy.

9 The decline in area was heralded as a success by the UNODC but with respect to the production it was moved to comment, 'unfortunately the production conditions have not been kind to us' (UNODC/Government of Afghanistan 2005).

10 'In a changing and challenging environment UNODC constantly strives and improves the survey methodology' (UNODC 2004: 80).

11 This section draws heavily from Pain 2006 and 2007 and summarises the key conclusions drawn from interviews and observations.

12 Under the auspices of the Afghanistan Research and Evaluation Unit, Kabul, and funded by the EC.

13 This information has been very kindly prepared and provided by Richard Brittan, working with the UK Drugs Team in Kabul.

14 Table 10.3 only contains data with a value greater than zero. Although since 2002 UNODC has entered zero values for pre-2002 district data implying no cultivation, earlier UNODC reports indicate no data rather than no cultivation for these districts. In 2004, no district-level data were collected.

15 See, for example, Lee 2003; ADB 2004.

16 Villages were mapped according to position on the irrigation canals. Several key informants assisted in identifying the ethnic identities of each village. Although ethnic identities are used to characterise communities, these are descriptive and simplistic labels. Ethnic or ascribed identities do not explain all, or predetermine how people behave or how they see themselves, and nor are they absolutely unambiguous categories. They have greater meaning for Pashtun and Turkmen communities where identity is clearly defined by descent, than, for example, for Tajik communities.

17 A bawra is the inverse of the proportion of land that can be irrigated each year: in the case of 1 bawra all land can be irrigated; in the case of 2 bawra half of the land can be irrigated; and in 3 and 4 bawra a third and a quarter of the land can be irrigated.

18 In Nangarhar, there are many reports (David Mansfield, personal communication) of land-scarce families going to Balkh during the Taliban years and leasing or sharecropping lands in Chimtal and cultivating poppy, consistent with comments from informants from Charbolaq.

19 In Nangarhar, skilled labour can be paid 350–500 Pakistan rupees per day in contrast to the 250–400 rupees per day of less skilled labour (Mansfield 2006).

20 Corroborated by Mansfield (2006) and (2007b).

21 IWPR (2007) notes farmer comments on the effect of declining prices reducing profitability ('Northern Province says "no" to opium' – available online: www.sim.ethz.ch/news/sw/details_print.cfm?id=17718 (accessed 16 June 2007). Mansfield (2007c) also notes the effect of the high cost of hired labour making returns to opium less than that of wheat, opium and potato in Badakhshan.

Bibliography

ADB [Asian Development Bank] (2004) *Emergency Infrastructure and Rehabilitation Loan Afghanistan Irrigation Component*, Technical Assistance Mission Draft Report, Balkh and Jawzjan Province Irrigation.

Byrd, W. and Jonglez, O. (2006) 'Prices and market interactions in the opium economy', in D. Buddenberg and W. Byrd (eds), *Afghanistan's Drug Industry: Structure, Functioning, Dynamics and Implications for Counter-narcotics Policy*, UNODC and World Bank.

Cullather, N. (2002) 'Damning Afghanistan: modernisation in a buffer state', *The Journal of American History*, 89(2): 512–37.

Farrell, J.G. (1973) *The Siege of Krishnapur*, London: Weidenfeld & Nicolson.

Fazey, C. (2007) 'Responding to the opium dilemma', in R.I. Rotberg (ed.) *Building a New Afghanistan*, Cambridge & Washington: The World Peace Foundation & Brookings Institution Press.

Gallant, T.W. (1999) 'Brigandage, piracy, capitalism, and state-formation: transnational crime from a historical world-systems perspective', in J. McConnell Heyman (ed.) *States and Illegal Practices*, Oxford and New York: Berg.

Goodhand, J. (2005) 'Frontiers and wars: the opium economy in Afghanistan', *Journal of Agrarian Change*, 5(2): 191–216.

Goodhand. J. and Sedra, M. (2007) 'Bribes or bargains? Peace conditionalities and 'post-conflict' reconstruction in Afghanistan', *International Peacekeeping*, 14(1): 41–61.

Harriss-White, B. (2003) *India Working: Essays on Society and Economy*, Cambridge: Cambridge University Press.

Institute for War and Peace Reporting (2007) 'Northern Province says "no" to opium', www.sim.lthz.ch/news/sw/details_print.cfm?id=17718 (accessed 16 June 2007).

Klijn, F. and Pain, A. (2007) *Finding the Money: Informal Credit Practices in Rural Afghanistan*, Afghanistan Research & Evaluation Unit Synthesis Paper, Kabul.

Lee, J.L. (2003) *Water Resource Management on the Balkh Ab River and Hazhda Nahr Canal Network: From Crisis to Collapse*, Report for UNAMA Northern Region, Central Asian Free Exchange.

Mansfield, D. (2002) 'The economic superiority of illicit drug production: Myth and reality, opium poppy cultivation in Afghanistan', paper prepared for the International Conference on the Role of Alternative Development in Drug Control and Cooperation, Munich, 7–12 January 2002.

—— (2006) *Water Management, Livestock and the Opium Economy: Opium Poppy Cultivation in Nangarhar and Ghor*, Kabul: Afghanistan Research and Evaluation Unit.

—— (2007a) 'Economical with the truth: the limits of price and profitability in both explaining opium poppy cultivation in Afghanistan and in designing effective responses', in A. Pain and J. Sutton (eds) *Reconstructing Agriculture in Afghanistan*, Rome & Rugby: FAO and Practical Action.

—— (2007b) 'Governance, security and economic growth: the determinants of opium poppy cultivation in the districts of Jurm and Baharak' in *Badakhshan, A Report to GTZ/AKDN, Kabul*. Available online: www.gtz.de/de/dokumente/en-eod-report-Badakhshan.pdf (accessed 31 March 2009).

—— (2007c) *Beyond the Metrics: Understanding the Nature of Change in the Rural Livelihoods of Opium Poppy Growing Households in the 2006/07 Growing Season*, Report for the Afghan Drugs Inter Departmental Unit of the UK Government.

Mansfield, D. and Pain, A. (2007) *Evidence from the Field: Understanding Changing Levels of Opium Poppy Cultivation*, Afghanistan Briefing Paper, Afghanistan Research and Evaluation Unit.

Pain, A. (2006) *Water Management, Livestock and the Opium Economy: Opium Poppy Cultivation in Kunduz and Balkh*, Case Study Series, Kabul: Afghanistan Research and Evaluation Unit.

—— (2007) *Water Management, Livestock and the Opium Economy: The Spread of Opium Poppy Cultivation in Balkh*, Case Study Series, Kabul: Afghanistan Research and Evaluation Unit.

—— (2008) *Opium Poppy Cultivation and Informal Credit*, Issues Paper, Kabul: Afghanistan Research and Evaluation Unit.

Rubin, R. (2000) 'The political economy of war and peace in Afghanistan', *World Development*, 28(10): 1789–803.

Schweich, T.A. (2007) *US Counternarcotics Strategy for Afghanistan*, Washington: US Department of State.

Suhrke, A. (2006) *When More Is Less: Aiding State-building in Afghanistan*, Working Paper 26, Madrid: FRIDE.

Tapper, N. (1973) 'The advent of Pashtun "Maldars" in north-western Afghanistan', *Bulletin of the School of Oriental and African Studies*, University of London.

—— (1991) *Bartered Brides: Politics, Gender and Marriage in an Afghan Tribal Society*, Cambridge: Cambridge University Press.

Tapper, R. (1988) 'Ethnicity and class: dimensions of intergroup conflict in north-central Afghanistan', in M.N. Shahrani and R.L. Canfield (eds) *Revolutions and Rebellions in Afghanistan*, Berkeley: University of California Press.

Tilly, C. (1985) 'War making and state making as organized crime', in P. Evans, D. Rueschemeyer and T. Skocpol (eds) *Bringing the State Back In*, Cambridge: Cambridge University Press.

UNODC [United Nations Office on Drugs and Crime] (2003) *The Opium Economy in Afghanistan: An International Problem*, Vienna: UNODC.

—— (2004) *Afghanistan: Opium Survey*, Vienna and Kabul: UNODC.

UNODC/Government of Afghanistan Ministry of Counter Narcotics (2005) *Afghanistan: Opium Survey*, Vienna and Kabul: UNODC.

—— (2006) *Afghanistan: Opium Survey*, Vienna and Kabul: UNODC.

—— (2007) *Afghanistan: Opium Winter Rapid Assessment Survey*, Vienna and Kabul: UNODC.

Wood, G. and Gough, I. (2006) 'A comparative welfare regime approach to global social policy', *World Development*, 34(10): 1696–1712.

WFP [World Food Programme] (2002) *Afghanistan Countrywide Food Needs Assessment of Rural Settled Populations: 2002–2003*, Vulnerability Analysis Mapping Unit and Partners, Kabul: WFP.

11 The marginalisation of Dalits in a modernising economy

Judith Heyer

This chapter focuses on Dalit[1] subordination in the liberalising and globalising economy of the late twentieth and early twenty-first century in India. Markets are deeply embedded in social, political and cultural structures which are as necessary for their functioning in liberalising and globalising economies as in any other economies. The role of 'traditional' institutions may increase as competition becomes more aggressive and states withdraw. This chapter looks at the role of caste in the context of liberalisation and globalisation. Based on intermittent fieldwork from the early 1980s to the early 2000s, the chapter looks at the way in which caste institutions have operated to subordinate Dalits. Their mode of operation has changed, but the outcome has remained very much as before.

Capitalists are using caste institutions to control labour in India. This has serious implications not just for Dalits but for the working class as a whole. Caste provides capital with an important instrument to divide and rule. It also makes it more acceptable for capitalists to ride roughshod over the rights of members of the working class as a whole. It helps the capitalist project that caste ideology is continually reinforced in the everyday practice of large numbers of people in all walks of life in India.

In this chapter I look at some of the economic aspects of the use of caste institutions in villages in South India over the period from 1980 to 2004. Over this period, the villages that form the basis of the study have seen the effects first of agricultural modernisation, at its height in the late 1970s and early 1980s, and then of industrialisation, which came to the fore in the 1990s and early 2000s. Caste was an impressive weapon in the hands of farmers in the era of agricultural modernisation up to the early 1980s in these villages. The state supported the use of caste too. Scheduled Castes (SCs) were extremely submissive, deferential and subordinated at this time, up against a sophisticated group of farmers who resorted to brutal caste practices that served their purposes well.

Industrialisation had a much more visible impact on these villages in the mid 1990s than in the early 1980s. One might have expected this to have benefited SCs. However, the vast majority of SCs were either completely excluded or included only at the margins of the industrial economy. Most of the new opportunities opened up by industrialisation went to people higher up in the caste hierarchy, not SCs.

There is a substantial literature showing that despite the growing modernisation of the economy, and positive discrimination policies and programmes in their favour, SCs are still overwhelmingly represented in the lowest ranks of the socio-economic hierarchy in India.[2] There have been political successes, notably in Uttar Pradesh, but these have not been accompanied by significant socio-economic gains.[3] There have been continuing problems for SCs in the recent period in India in a climate that is increasingly hostile to labour, and hostile to state intervention favouring the poor and the weak.

Coimbatore, the focus of this chapter, is in Tamil Nadu, a state that is at the forefront of industrialisation and urbanisation in India, and one of the better-placed states with respect to many human development indicators. It is also a state with high degrees of inequality, and high incidences of poverty, notwithstanding the generally better human development indicators relative to those of other states in India. It is a state where caste plays a particularly strong role as well.[4]

Coimbatore has long been at the forefront in Tamil Nadu both in respect to the modernisation of agriculture and in respect to industrialisation and urbanisation. It is also notable for its casteism, which is closely bound up with the success of the local economy. It is a sign of the degree of control that Caste Hindus have over SCs that atrocities against SCs have only recently begun to be reported from Coimbatore, unlike in other parts of Tamil Nadu where such reports have been significant since the early 1990s and before.[5]

Coimbatore was in the vanguard of agricultural modernisation in Tamil Nadu from the late 1950s, well ahead of the Green Revolution in the rest of India. In the 1980s and the 1990s, it was the high degree of urbanisation and industrialisation for which Coimbatore was known instead.

Coimbatore agriculture was based on (*thottam*) land irrigated by large open wells, dryland farming, and livestock. Its large open wells were the main source of irrigation.[6] The kavalai system, powered by bullocks, was used to lift water until the 1960s when electrified pump sets took over. The water table, which had been falling since the early decades of the twentieth century,[7] fell much more rapidly after electrification. The level of purchased inputs was very high in the 1960s and the 1970s. Agriculture remained relatively labour-intensive, however, as the degree of mechanisation of field operations remained low. Large landholdings gave way to small- and medium-sized as intensification proceeded.[8] In the 1980s, water shortages became acute and there was competition for labour from the industrial economy. This led to a fall in agricultural employment[9] and a fall in the cultivated area.[10]

Industrialisation has been based on medium- to small-scale enterprises rather than large in Coimbatore. In the 1980s and the 1990s, many of the medium-scale enterprises closed down, making way for smaller-scale enterprises. Small-scale industry has been the basis of high rates of growth since the 1980s.

SCs were strongly subordinated in the modernised agriculture of the 1960s and the 1970s. They remained very much at the bottom of the hierarchy in the industrialising economy that was characteristic of the 1980s and the 1990s as well.

The chapter starts with some background on the study villages. It goes on to provide evidence of SC subordination in 1981/1982. This is followed by a consideration of the position in 1996 when large numbers of people in the villages – but few SCs – had moved into non-agricultural occupations. There were changes in the social and political position of SCs in the villages, including reductions in the severity of practices associated with untouchability. However, the subordination of SCs remained acute. The chapter concludes with a discussion of the issues raised in the main body of the chapter.

The study villages

The study villages are 20–30 km from Tiruppur, and 40–60 km from Coimbatore. Tiruppur was the most dynamic centre of growth in the Coimbatore region from the mid 1980s until the early 2000s. It acted as a magnet for people from the villages from the mid 1980s onward.

During the first period of fieldwork in the early 1980s, agriculture was dominated by sophisticated small-scale agriculturalists running highly commercialised agricultural operations that were extremely profitable. Labourers came from all caste groups, but the majority were SCs.

Industrialisation was already significant in the region in the early 1980s, when the study villages were still overwhelmingly agricultural.[11] There were no industrial units in the villages. There was no commuting either. By the mid 1990s there were power-loom units, elastic factories and 'jetty'[12] factories; significant commuter populations, and migrants in the towns maintaining close contact with relatives in the villages too.[13] Agriculturalists were no longer as dominant, or as prosperous, as before. The irrigated area had fallen, and much of what was still irrigated was irrigated less intensively. Dry land had been taken out of cultivation. The numbers working in agriculture had fallen dramatically too.

The majority of members of the 'thottam farmer'[14] households that dominated the villages in the early 1980s were still pursuing agriculture and agriculture-related activities in 1996, though much less successfully than in 1981/1982. Large numbers of Caste Hindu members of other occupational groups had moved into non-agricultural activities. The majority of members of SC agricultural labourer households continued to work as agricultural labourers.

1981/1982: the caste and economic structure of the study villages

The 'study villages'[15] were relatively isolated from the urban and industrial economy in 1981/1982. They were still predominantly agricultural at a time when other villages in the vicinity were more involved in the urban and industrial economy.

The majority of agriculturalists in the study villages were Gounders, Naidus and Chettiars by caste. The majority of agricultural labourers were SCs. Other caste groups were represented in very small numbers only (see Table 11.1).

Thottam farmers, all of whom were Gounders, Naidus and Chettiars, dominated the study villages in 1981/1982. They made up 13 per cent of the households, and owned 61 per cent of the irrigated land (Table 11.2a). They were relatively small

Table 11.1 1981/1982 and 1996 caste and agricultural land (%)

	1981/1982		1996	
	HHs	*Land*	*HHs*	*Land*
Brahmin	0	1		
Naidu	6	13	4	12
Gounder	35	58	33	60
Chettiar	15	21	16	22
Thevar	1	1	1	1
Muslim	0	1		
Mudaliar	1	0	2	1
Valayar	0	0	0	0
Muthuraja	1	0	4	0
Vaniyar	0	1	0	1
Pandaram	0	0	1	0
Achari	3	1	2	0
Barber	3	1	3	1
Dhobi	2	0	2	0
Pannadi	11	1	16	1
Paraiyar	0	0		
Chakkiliyar	19	0	16	0
All	100	100	100	100

Source: Village Surveys 1981/1982, 1996.

landowners (Table 11.2b). The largest holding was 30 acres (much smaller than the hundred-odd acres of the previous generation). Agriculture was their main occupation. A small minority were cotton and/or groundnut oil traders as well.

The 1981/1982 generation of thottam farmers had bought land, dug wells, deepened wells and invested in equipment and machinery as well as houses and other farm buildings in the 1960s and the 1970s. They relied on large inputs of labour for cultivation. There were very few tractors. They operated in a wide range of input and output markets. They were involved in complex systems of finance, underlying which was the fear of bankruptcy, all too real a possibility with recent as well as more distant examples nearby. The most important irrigated crops were cotton, turmeric and sugarcane in 1981/1982. There was a wide range of minor crops, including fruits and vegetables. Very little paddy was grown in this area. Thottam farmers grew groundnuts and cholam (sorghum) on dry land, interplanted with a variety of other pulses and seeds. They kept small numbers of livestock, for milk for domestic consumption, and for draught power.

Farmers were getting very substantial support from the state in 1981/1982 in the form of subsidised input and product prices, investment in research, and so on. They had particularly good technical support from the Tamil Nadu Agricultural University in Coimbatore. Farmers associations were strong in the area, lobbying for the continuation and expansion of support from the state.

Table 11.2a Share of landholdings by occupational group and caste (agricultural labourers) in 1981/1982 (percentages)

Occupational group	House-holds	Thottam land	Dry land	Total land
Thottam farmers	13	61	31	44
Small farmers	23	33	45	40
*Trade and services	23	4	17	12
Agricultural labourers	43	2**	7	5
Caste Hindu agricultural labourers	13	2**	5	4
Pannadi agricultural labourers	11	0	1	1
Chakkililyar agricultural labourers	18	0	1	0
All	100	100	100	100

Table 11.2b Average acres of land by occupational group and caste (agricultural labourers) in 1981/1982

Occupational group	House-holds	Thottam land	Dry land	Total land
Thottam farmers	29	7.2	5.1	12.3
Small farmers	53	2.1	4.0	6.1
*Trade and services	52	0.2	1.6	1.8
Agricultural labourers	96	0.1**	0.3	0.4
Caste Hindu agricultural labourers	30	0.3**	0.8	1.1
Pannadi agricultural labourers	25	0.0	0.2	0.2
Chakkililyar agricultural labourers	41	0.0	0.1	0.1
All	230	1.5	2.0	3.5

Source: Village Surveys, 1981/1982.

Notes: *Also includes small number of SC households **Disputed thottam land.

Thottam farmers maintained tight control over labour, partly through their tradition of working in the fields alongside their labourers. They boasted a frugal everyday lifestyle but this was belied by substantial expenditures on marriages, festivals and life-cycle ceremonies, for which they purchased gold, consumer durables and clothing. This was an important part of their strategy of maintaining strong social relations among their own kin and caste groups to which they devoted large amounts of time and money. Kin and caste relations were crucial for getting access to finance, for spreading risks and for diversification of the entrepreneurial pool. Nearly all thottam farmers aspired to a future for their sons in agriculture in 1981/1982. They educated their sons up to at most Standard X.[16] This did not prepare them well for a future in urban and industrial activities. They did not foresee the necessity for this in 1981/1982.

'Small farmers'[17] operating alongside thottam farmers made up 23 per cent of households in the study villages in 1981/1982. They owned 33 per cent of the irrigated land (Table 11.2a). They were independent owner operators, much less heavily involved in markets than thottam farmers. Nearly all were members of the same caste groups as thottam farmers. Forty-two per cent of the households in the study villages were headed by agricultural labourers. Thirty per cent of these were Caste Hindu. The rest were from the two main SC groups: 27 per cent Pannadi,[18] a minority of whom had very small holdings of land; 43 per cent Chakkiliyar,[19] virtually none with any land at all.[20]

The remaining households in the village were headed by traders, government employees and providers of services, from a variety of castes. 'Traditional' trades, services and manufacturing activities had given way, partially at least, to government-related employment, including employment connected with electricity, as well as employment in hotels, teashops, retail shops, cycle shops and so on.

Labour relations in the study villages in 1981/1982

The wide range of crops, extensive irrigation and relatively low seasonality meant that there was year-round employment for relatively large numbers of agricultural labourers in the study villages in 1981/1982. Migrant sugar-cane crushing work, undertaken by 13 per cent of the male agricultural labourers, supplemented this.

Thottam farmers employed pannayals (permanent labourers), as well as large numbers of casual labourers in 1981/1982.[21] Pannayals were all male, and almost all Chakkiliyars.[22] Pannayals played a central role in the agricultural labour force: they worked both longer hours and more days in the year than casual labourers. They performed some of the more responsible tasks including the supervision of other hired labour. They and their families had closer ties with employers than labourers from other groups.

Chakkiliyar work with cattle and leather was crucial to the kavalai system of irrigation prior to the advent of electricity in the 1950s and the 1960s.[23] With the demise of the kavalai system, Chakkiliyars became field labourers for which the demand increased with the intensification of agriculture.

Pannayals were beck-and-call labourers working long hours on most days of the year and their annual earnings were considerably higher than those of casual labourers.[24] Discretionary benefits included time off, loans and 'help' with expenditure on health care, life-cycle ceremonies and so on. These were key instruments of control, which Chakkiliyars resisted by changing employers, buying produce in the local markets instead of from their employers, and getting loans from elsewhere. Thottam farmers complained bitterly about these moves in 1981/1982.

Chakkiliyar, Pannadi and Caste Hindu men and women worked as casual labourers. Casual labour was not as intensive or as dependable a source of income as pannayal labour. But casual labourers could choose to work less than six days a week. Older men and women usually did so. Younger women took very little time off for childbirth[25] or child rearing. Once children started going out to work, their mothers went less regularly. This was an important consideration for women worn out by the time their children started work, at the age of ten or twelve. Very few Chakkiliyar children went to school in 1981/1982.

Most Chakkiliyar parents thought school irrelevant at that time. Many thought that it spoilt children for labour as well.

Chakkiliyars were subjected to discriminatory treatment outside the workplace as well as within in 1981/1982. They played the drums at village festivals. They carried messages outside the villages. They handled dead animals, human excrement and waste. These roles carried small benefits in kind and were also regarded as a basis for considering Chakkiliyars polluting or 'unclean'.[26] Being forced to play these roles reinforced the subordination of Chakkiliyars here.[27]

Thottam farmers and others in the villages engaged in a whole range of untouchability practices, similar to those in other parts of India.[28] Practices still operating in the study villages in 1981/1982 included restrictions on where SCs lived; restrictions on how they got water;[29] restrictions on where they were served tea, and in what vessels they were served tea, at the teashop; and restrictions on where their children sat, and from what vessels their children drank water, at school. These, together with language conventions, and conventions about physical interactions, served as daily reminders of their subordinate status, many of them degrading and humiliating. It is difficult to exaggerate the psychological effect this had, including on aspirations and self-esteem.[30]

Chakkiliyars were largely excluded from state programmes targeted at the poor in 1981/1982. However, they did benefit from the SC housing programme. Chakkiliyars from two of the three colonies in the villages were in the process of acquiring new colonies in 1981/1982, through the auspices of thottam farmers.

The highly selective state support that Chakkiliyars got in 1981/1982 played into thottam farmers' hands. Not getting government loans, not getting support from the police, and so on, increased Chakkiliyar dependence on thottam farmers. The fact that the state was seen not to be concerned with Chakkiliyars in practice, despite official rhetoric to the contrary, conveyed an ideological message that was important too. Moreover, the hold of thottam farmers over Chakkiliyars was reinforced by the almost total absence of churches and NGOs.

Cederlof (1997) has documented the mission-backed struggle of Madaris (Chakkiliyars) trying to obtain some independence from Gounder control in Palladam in the 1930s and the 1940s. This was at its height in the early 1930s when there were major labour uprisings across Tamil Nadu and, according to Washbrook, perhaps for the first and only time in the twentieth century capital experienced a general threat from labour (Washbrook 1989). There has been nothing like it since. Washbrook (1989) suggests that some of the factors responsible have been the lack of critical mass and the obscuring of class relations in Tamil Nadu.[31] More obvious explanations in the Coimbatore case are poverty and vulnerability combined with the absence of alternatives (such as emigration), in the face of a well-organised and well-connected dominant caste that was able to maintain control over Chakkiliyars particularly well.

Pannadis, the other group of SC agricultural labourers in the study villages, were less numerous than Chakkiliyars. Many young Pannadi men were migrant sugar-cane crushers working all over Coimbatore district. They earned more than pannayals by doing this, but they lived and worked in very poor conditions for months at a time, and spent a lot of what they earned on the job. Pannadis also worked as casual labourers within the villages. A large minority had tiny holdings of land. Many also had small holdings of livestock. Pannadis had a much less intense and dependent relationship with thottam farmers than did Chakkiliyars. They could not ask for 'help' from thottam farmers with expenditures on things such as housing, ceremonies and festivals, and health care. They could not get thottam farmers to help them get access to state benefits either. This was part of the price they paid for greater autonomy within the village community. They suffered from many of the problems of migrant labourers,[32] but geographical mobility was also something that gave them an edge over Chakkiliyars, particularly as agriculture came under pressure later too.

Caste Hindu agricultural labourers, also less numerous than Chakkiliyars, were in a much stronger position than either Pannadis or Chakkiliyars, though some individual Caste Hindu labourer households were very poor. Half of the Caste Hindu labourer households had land. Many had livestock. Most of their income came from agricultural labour however. Caste Hindu labourers lived in the main villages and had access to more facilities and space than SCs. Whereas all Chakkiliyars and Pannadis were agricultural labourers, only a minority of Caste Hindus were. Many Caste Hindu labourers had the possibility of moving out of agricultural labour and prospects if they went to school. This was reflected in the fact that the majority of young Caste Hindus from agricultural labourer households were in school, in contrast to very small numbers of Chakkiliyars or Pannadis, in 1981/1982.

Caste oppression and agricultural modernisation

The study makes it very clear that one cannot assume that modern capitalist farming will be associated with less oppressive labour relations. Indeed, the opposite may be the case. There was a striking disjuncture between the sophistication of thottam farmers on the one hand and their oppressive and caste-based labour relations on the other, in the study villages in 1981/1982.

Thottam farmers clearly found it relatively easy to maintain an oppressive labour regime in 1981/1982. A number of factors contributed to this: (1) they were well entrenched, and the caste practices involved were well established; (2) they were able to offer an attractive enough deal to stave off resistance; (3) they were supported by state ideology and practice; and (4) they were exposed to very little pressure from below.

Chakkiliyars accepted the oppressive regime, with only minor resistance, because of (1) lack of support from state ideology and practice; (2) the security of livelihoods which employers were able to provide; and (3) the absence of better alternatives. The fact that Chakkiliyars put a high value on the security associated with their relationships with thottam farmers was not surprising given that their capacity to earn was their only resource, and that this was vulnerable to illness, accident, disability and their generally adverse household dependency ratios. They did not want to jeopardise what they had. Chakkiliyars also knew the lengths to which thottam farmers would go (from examples elsewhere in Tamil Nadu and the rest of India), making their lives intolerable in the villages, as well as withdrawing their livelihoods there. They would only risk this if they had alternatives that were better than those available in 1981/1982.

Their situation improved somewhat in the 1990s, as will be seen below. However, this was still far away in 1981/1982.

1996: Industrialisation combined with difficulties in agriculture

By 1996, the situation in the villages had changed dramatically. Agriculture had been in serious trouble since a drought in 1983/1984 when the decline in the water table came to a head. This more or less coincided with increased opportunities in the urban and industrial sectors. The availability of these increased opportunities was partly due to improvements in transport and communications. People in the study villages could commute in 1996, something they had not been able to do in 1981/1982. As significant though was the general expansion of small-scale industrialisation in the region, and the fact that this was reaching areas nearer to the villages. Some new industrial employment became available in the villages themselves too.

Industrialisation expanded dramatically in the area around the study villages between 1981/1982 and 1996. There was a decline of larger-scale manufacturing in the larger centres, and an increase in smaller-scale manufacturing in Coimbatore, Tiruppur, and smaller centres, as well as in the surrounding countryside. There was an explosion of knitwear and other light industry in Tiruppur in the 1980s and early 1990s, which has been well documented.[33] Tiruppur was an important centre as far as the study villages were concerned.

The growth of industrial opportunities coincided with the crisis in agriculture.[34] The response of thottam farmers was to sink deeper boreholes and to invest in compressor and submersible pumps.[35] The new technology was expensive, and it produced less water than before. The increased cost of labour was an additional problem for farmers. They had difficulty retaining enough labour, despite the fact that they were employing less labour than before (see Table 11.3 below, discussed in more detail). All of this appeared to have been completely unforeseen by farmers and others in the villages in 1981/1982.

Changes in employment and occupations

Moving out of agriculture

In 1981/1982 nearly three-quarters (73 per cent) of the male workforce worked in agriculture, roughly 40 per cent as cultivators, and 60 per cent as labourers (Table 11.3). The percentage of total village employment in agriculture in 1981/1982 was considerably higher than this as most women and girls worked in agriculture too.[36]

In 1996, just over 50 per cent of the male members of the workforce were employed in agriculture (Tables 11.3a and 11.3b). The percentage in rural non-agricultural employment had risen substantially, particularly in services and trade. The percentage in urban non-agricultural employment had risen even more. Most of this was in mills, factories and workshops to which people commuted from the villages. It is notable that very few women and girls from these villages were employed in the non-agricultural sector in places like Tiruppur where the overall proportion of women and girls in the workforce had been growing rapidly.[37]

People in different caste and occupational groups were participating very unequally in the changes (Table 11.3a and 11.3b). The majority of members of 1981/1982 thottam farmer households in the sample had stayed in the villages, some combining agriculture with trade and processing. Relatively small numbers from 1981/1982 thottam farmer households in the sample still represented in the villages had moved into urban non-agricultural occupations. The few that had were working in some of the few remaining large mills in Coimbatore and/or had set up businesses of different kinds elsewhere. There were a number who had returned to the villages after their businesses had failed too.

Very few thottam farmer sons, and only one quite exceptional daughter, in the 1981/1982 generation had gone into higher education. More of the next generation had embarked on the sorts of educational trajectories from which they could expect to go further later on. What was striking in 1996 (and 2003/2004) was how relatively little people from 1981/1982 thottam farmer households had been able to take advantage of the new opportunities that had been opening up.

The 1981/1982 small farmers and 1981/1982 Caste Hindu agricultural labourers had moved out of agriculture in large numbers, however. It was not that they had more education, or education that fitted them better for the move, than members of 1981/1982 thottam farmer households: but they were willing to take up positions that members of thottam farmer households were not willing to take up. These positions were attractive relative to small farming and agricultural labour in the short term. They were also seen as ways of getting into more attractive positions in the future. There were some who had taken this route who by 1996 were beginning to do quite well.[38]

Members of Chakkiliyar and Pannadi agricultural labourer households had been strikingly less successful in moving into either urban or rural non-agricultural occupations than members of Caste Hindu labourer households (see Tables 11.3a and 11.3b below). The majority of Chakkiliyars who had moved into rural non-agricultural occupations had moved into marginal occupations such as firewood cutting, coconut- leaf plaiting, and chappal repairing.[40] Pannadis moving into rural non-agricultural occupations had moved into services and trade.

In 1981/1982, large-scale enterprises in Coimbatore were the major outlet for people from the study villages wanting to move out of agriculture, and high-level connections were necessary to get into these. In 1996, small-scale enterprises nearer home were the target and the barriers included limited education, lack of relevant contacts, and lack of resources to finance the early stages of getting established there. Despite rapid growth leading to shortages of labour in the

Table 11.3a 1981/1982 occupations of male members of the workforce* (percentages in parentheses)

1981/1982 occupational group	Cultivators	Agric. labourers	Rural non-agric.	Urban non-agric.	All
Thottam farmers	50	0	2	1	53
	(94)	(0)	(4)	(2)	(100)
Small farmers	85	9	6	16	116
	(73)	(8)	(5)	(14)	(100)
Trade and services	2	15	68	15	100
	(2)	(15)	(68)	(15)	(100)
Agricultural labourers (AL)	0	180	9	9	198
	(0)	(91)	(5)	(5)	(100)
Caste Hindu AL	0	36	6	9	51
	(0)	(71)	(12)	(18)	(100)
Pannadi AL	0	62	1	0	63
	(0)	(98)	(2)	(0)	(100)
Chakkiliyar AL	0	86	2	0	88
	(0)	(98)	(2)	(0)	(100)
All	137	204	85	41	467
	(29)	(44)	(18)	(9)	(100)

Table 11.3b 1996 occupations of male members of the workforce* (percentages in parentheses)

1981/1982 occupational group	Cultivators	Agric. labourers	Rural non-agric.	Urban non-agric.	All
Thottam farmers	42	1	11	2	56
	(75)	(2)	(20)	(4)	(100)
Small farmers	40	17	15	36	108
	(37)	(16)	(14)	(33)	(100)
Trade and services	3	6	52	33	94
	(3)	(6)	(55)	(35)	(100)
Agricultural labourers (AL)	5	119	44	34	202
	(2)	(59)	(22)	(17)	(100)
Caste Hindu AL	5	10	18	14	47
	(11)	(21)	(38)	(30)	(100)
Pannadi AL	0	41	12	14	67
	(0)	(61)	(18)	(21)	(100)
Chakkiliyar AL	0	68	14	6	88
	(0)	(77)	(16)	(7)	(100)
All	90	143	122	105	460
	(20)	(31)	(27)	(23)	(100)

Source: Village Surveys 1981/1982, 1996.

Note: *Workforce defined as those in work, excluding unemployed, and very small numbers where data are missing too.

industrialising economy of the 1990s and early 2000s, getting opportunities with some prospects in the industrialising economy was not easy for people from the villages. Accounts of people who had been successful make clear the levels of human capital, material resources and networks required. People trying to get into industrial employment had to be reliable, robust and able to ride out periods of unemployment. Some non-SC landless agricultural labourers in the villages had some of what was required here. Most SCs did not. Chakkiliyars and others at the bottom of the hierarchy still had very limited resources in spite of the state support that they had been receiving in the 1980s and the first half of the 1990s (see below). Low aspirations and low self-esteem played a role here, too. SCs had the additional disadvantage of being willing to fall back on agricultural labour and being under pressure from their families to do so. This often meant that they were not able to hold out for long enough to get established in non-agricultural employment instead.

The difficulties faced by SCs from the villages in participating successfully in the industrial economy were the direct result of the legacy of their position in the agrarian economy. Their relative isolation, low levels of education, poor health, lack of financial resources, and lack of experience of anything other than agricultural labour, all played a part. There was an improvement in their position in the 1980s and the early 1990s, but it was too little, too late and too slow.

There was no direct correlation between education and the sorts of blue-collar occupations which people from the study villages had entered. However, for Chakkiliyars and Pannadis education may have been more important, both in helping to negotiate the urban environment and in obtaining reasonable employment there.[41] The educational achievements of the different occupational and caste groups are shown in Table 11.4.

To summarise: a large majority of members of 1981/1982 thottam farmer households on the one hand, and of SC agricultural labourer households on the other, remained in agriculture or agriculture-related employment in the villages in 1996. Members of 1981/1982 households in other groups had moved in larger

Table 11.4 1996 education of male members of the workforce by 1981/1982 occupational group (row percentages)

	0	I–V	VI–X	>X	DK	All
Thottam farmers	4	25	48	21	2	100
Small farmers	19	24	46	6	5	100
Trade and services	30	29	35	4	2	100
Agricultural labourers (AL)	64	18	15	0	1	100
Caste Hindu AL	9	51	36	2	2	100
Pannadi AL	67	13	19	0	0	100
Chakkiliyar AL	92	5	1	0	2	100
All	40	23	31	5	2	100

Source: Village Surveys 1981/1982, 1996.

Note: DK = no information.

numbers into the urban non-agricultural economy, the overwhelming majority into mills, factories and workshops. Pannadis had moved into such employment in greater numbers than Chakkiliyars, but in smaller numbers than members of Caste Hindu labourer households.

Remaining in agriculture

Agriculture still occupied just over 50 per cent of the male, and a very much higher proportion of the female workforce in the villages in 1996 (see Tables 11.3a and b on p. 235). Agriculture continued to be the main occupation of members of 1981/1982 thottam farmer households. Many had invested in new irrigation technology, and a number had bought land (1981/1982 thottam farmers held a slightly increased share of land in the villages in 1996). Having sunk much of their capital in an agriculture that was no longer producing high returns, they were now looking elsewhere. They were not finding it at all easy to move out of agriculture, however. The majority were waiting for the next generation, with more education, to do so. Meanwhile, 1981/1982 thottam farmers remained in the villages, less powerful in relation to labour, and less powerful in village social and political life than before.

The numbers of small farmers had declined significantly, although 1981/1982 small farmers as a group held an only slightly reduced share of the land. Some small farmers remaining in agriculture were doing better than before.

The proportion of agricultural labourers in the male workforce fell from 44 per cent in 1981/1982 to 31 per cent in 1996. Pay had increased[42] and hours were more regular and more strictly adhered to than before. The numbers of males had fallen more sharply than the numbers of females. There was also less child labour in 1996 than in 1981/1982. A much higher proportion of children were now in school.

Chakkiliyars had become increasingly dominant in the agricultural labour force as Caste Hindus, and Pannadis, had moved into other occupations. Many Chakkiliyars would have liked to have done so, too. They had found this difficult though. There was a reduction in extreme forms of untouchability as the power of Caste Hindus waned in the villages and as many of the up-and-coming Caste Hindus turned their attention elsewhere.[43] Chakkiliyars remained in villages in which their position had improved (better wages and conditions, less social and political exclusion, and more support from the state), but they still did not have access to land or other crucial resources.[44] They were still confined to relatively low-paid labour in an agriculture that was doing less well. Many members of the younger generation with some education no longer wanted to settle for a future as agricultural labourers. Many were having to do so, though.

Virtually no young men or boys were pannayals in 1996. Many who would previously have been pannayals were now in school. Terms and conditions of pannayal employment had improved greatly by 1996, but there were very few pannayals left by 2003/2004.[45] Sugar-cane crushing was still an important source of employment in 1996. It had almost completely died out by 2003/2004.

The expansion of state programmes and policies that were now reaching SCs had contributed to the general improvement in the position of SCs since the early 1980s. These included free school meals, access to subsidised food and essential commodities, and large numbers of housing grants and loans which were accompanied by improved services in SC colonies.[46] There had been a change in rhetoric too. It was no longer considered acceptable to treat SCs as badly as before. Chakkiliyars were becoming more assertive, challenging Caste Hindus. They were beginning to be able to get away with more in relation to their employers too. One should not exaggerate the changes though. There was still a lot that was very oppressive, demeaning and humiliating for Chakkiliyars in 1996 and the early 2000s.

There was a striking absence, not only in the villages but in the Coimbatore region as a whole, of Dalit political parties and Dalit movements such as those that were achieving prominence elsewhere in Tamil Nadu in the early 1990s.[47] It was also notable how few NGOs were operating in the villages. The only visible forms of political organisation were branches of the CPI and its agricultural workers union, which had been set up in the Pannadi hamlet in the mid 1980s. Their focus seemed to be on getting Pannadis to support meetings and demonstrations around larger issues in the region as a whole. Chakkiliyars were not involved in any of this. They acted quite separately from Pannadis where politics was concerned. There were two significant sets of localised political developments in the 1990s: (1) the setting up by Chakkiliyars of a branch of the APM (Ambedkar People's Movement) which operated from 1994 to 1999, and was replaced by the DYFI (Democratic Youth Federation of India) thereafter; and (2) the establishment of new panchayats which came into existence in 1996.

The APM

An APM branch was set up in one of the main Chakkiliyar colonies in the study villages in 1994,[48] with considerable resistance from thottam farmers.[49] The first issue it took up, the construction of a new Chakkiliyar temple, provoked a violent reaction from Caste Hindus 'who came with axes, knives and spades to destroy the work'. The police and the tahsildar intervened, settling the issue in favour of the Chakkiliyars.

The APM's next move was to petition the Collector for improved access to water and electricity. This resulted in separate water taps, and the right for Chakkiliyars to fill their pots themselves from the taps in the centre of the village if their own taps ran dry. The APM then took up the question of separate seating and separate drinking vessels for children in school, both of which were abolished in 1998.

The APM ceased to function in 1999, when one of the leaders left for a spell of construction work in Tiruppur and got involved with the CPI(M) DYFI. He set up a branch of the DYFI in the village when he came back. This did not appear to be nearly as active as the APM had been though, at least in the period up to 2004.

It was possible for Chakkiliyars to engage in more organised resistance in the study villages in the 1990s for several reasons: (i) they could afford to give up some of the patronage ties because wages had risen and state support had increased (food and housing particularly); (ii) thottam farmers no longer had such a stake in what happened in the villages; (iii) thottam farmers were no longer the only sources of livelihood; (iv) the state had helped to make SC oppression generally less acceptable, both through its rhetoric and through its actions, and (v) Chakkiliyars had more exposure through TV and other media to ideas, norms and so on, in the wider economy and society. Similar factors were behind a general increase in SC mobilisation in the Coimbatore region.[50] Chakkiliyar engagement in organised resistance in these villages was a part of this general increase.

The new panchayats

The first panchayat elections since the 1970s took place in 1996, with new rules, including specific reservations for women and SCs.[51] Two local Panchayat Union councillorships were reserved for SCs, one for a woman SC. One of the village panchayat presidencies was also reserved for an SC woman. In the 1996 election, Pannadis got the two positions reserved for SC women. In the 2001 panchayat elections, Chakkililyars got these two positions instead.

The panchayat reforms were more successful in these villages than in some other parts of Tamil Nadu.[52] This had a lot to do with the social and economic conditions that had emerged in this area by the mid 1990s.

Both the Panchayat President and the Union Councillor were key figures in relation to infrastructure projects benefiting people from all caste groups in the villages. This meant that Caste Hindus had to deal with them and show them some respect. Administrative officials treated them better, too. There was a definite sense of increased status, and an increase in 'voice' and visibility, both among Pannadis and among Chakkiliyars, by 2003 and 2004.

The state government has been criticised for simply making the new panchayats the implementing arm of the administration in Tamil Nadu.[53] Whether or not this criticism is justified, the fact that Pannadis and Chakkiliyars were involved in implementation, working with the administration, was a significant step.

In sum: (1) Caste Hindus had been taking advantage of many of the new opportunities in the non-agricultural economy, thottam farmers less so than others though, and (2) the majority of Chakkiliyars and Pannadis remained as agricultural labourers in the villages. Both Chakkiliyars and Pannadis had better standards of living and terms and conditions of employment than before. Their social and political position in the villages had improved as well. However, they remained very much at the bottom of the social, political and economic hierarchy. There was no sense in which they had experienced any improvement in their relative position here.

Urbanisation, industrialisation and caste subordination

It is significant that the relative position of SCs showed little sign of improvement as a result of the expansion of industrialisation and urbanisation between 1981/1982 and 1996 (and 2003/2004) in a region as dynamic as Coimbatore.[54]

The instruments of subordination in urban and industrial settings are different from those in rural and agricultural settings. The outcome may be very similar though. It is generally the case that there are less stifling untouchability practices in urban than in rural areas.[55] There may be less overt discrimination in low-level employment too.[56] There is enough militating against SCs even without the more extreme untouchability practices and overt discrimination however. Some of the particular barriers are their lack of relevant connections, their lack of relevant skills and experience, their physical and financial vulnerability, and their limited and perhaps even counterproductive (cf. Jeffrey, Jeffery and Jeffery 2005) education. These all make it difficult for SCs to get any but the most fragile footholds in the urban and industrial economy.

It is the relative position that is crucial here.[57] There have been improvements in SC education, but the education of others has been improving more. Lack of connections may become less important over time but only if enough SCs get into better positions in the urban and industrial sector. One might expect the position to improve for SCs as labour shortages develop further. There are many different ways in which employers can react to labour shortages, though. These may not necessarily be favourable to SCs.

Concluding remarks

We now return to the continued relevance of caste in the modern economy. The paradox behind the material presented in this chapter is that Coimbatore is *both* the region of Tamil Nadu in which the economy is furthest ahead, *and* the region in which caste plays the strongest role, and the position of SCs is weakest of all.[58]

It is often claimed that it is the particular caste combination that is responsible for the above. Much has been made of the reputation of Gounders as hard-working, puritanical, violent and relatively uneducated.[59] Gounders are also known for their close-knit local organisation[60] and what appear to be disproportionate amounts of time and resources invested in participation in life-cycle ceremonies. This is as much a characteristic of urban as of rural Gounders.

It may also be significant that only in Coimbatore and neighbouring regions in western Tamil Nadu do Chakkiliyars predominate among SCs. In other parts of Tamil Nadu, they are widespread but less numerous. Chakkiliyars own less land, and have lower levels of education, than other SC groups in Tamil Nadu. They are also by far the most seriously under-represented in government positions. Furthermore, they are known for their particularly low levels of geographical mobility.

Coimbatore has long been a harsh environment in which to make a success of agriculture: agriculture has relied on relatively high inputs of capital; it has been high risk; it has also been relatively highly commercialised. It is said to be to Gounders' credit that they have been able to make a success of such a harsh environment. This could be a reflection of the character of Gounders. It could also be a reflection of the environmental influences on the character and organisation of Gounders. Strong social networks could have been of particular importance for Gounders in the face of high levels of risk. Tight control over labour could have been important to safeguard high levels of investment of capital. The fact that Gounders worked in the fields alongside their labourers may have been driven by the difficulties of their agriculture, and have strengthened their control over labour as well. Chari (2004) quotes Nicholson writing in the late nineteenth century describing Gounders as small livestock keepers cultivating a few cereals with a 'want of energy and thrift'. Gounders earned their current reputation in the 1920s and the 1930s.[61]

Gounders in the study villages were clearly investing a great deal in maintaining Chakkiliyar dependence in the early 1980s. They strongly resisted Chakkiliyar acquisition of land, participation in education, resort to the market for food items, and for credit, and so on. Chakkiliyar subservience, and the lengths to which Chakkiliyars went to maintain good relations with thottam farmers, underlined the importance that Chakkiliyars attached to this dependence, too. The strength of Gounder resistance to Chakkiliyar moves to reduce their dependence makes clear the stake that Gounders had in all this.

Capitalists will build on strong caste institutions where there is a legacy of such. Where they are able to use caste institutions to increase their control over labour, it clearly benefits them to do so. What is perhaps surprising is that a modernised agriculture does not make it more difficult for them to do so.

Industrial employers were short of labour in the 1990s and early 2000s. Despite this, they employed very few SCs, except in the jobs (e.g. dyeing) that others were unwilling to do.[62] One might have thought that employers would favour SC employees for their pliability, and exploitability, as they did in agriculture. Employing SCs might also have given employers a means of control over non-SC labour – they could point to people willing to do the job for less. The factors that determine which labourers employers choose to employ in the urban/industrial economy are clearly different from those that apply in the agrarian economy, however. In the industrial setting, they seem to be resorting to long-distance recruitment to get the sort of pliability they want instead.

Neither the modernisation of agriculture, nor urbanisation and industrialisation, has led to significant changes in the relative position of SCs. SCs still face considerably greater barriers to progress than others among the working poor.

SCs will have to fight to rise in the economic and social hierarchy. It is all too easy to see a future in which their relative position continues to deteriorate, unless they can mobilise effectively to force changes that are more favourable from their point of view.

Acknowledgements

The research on which this chapter is based has been funded by the UK Department of International Development (DFID, formerly ODA), the Oxford University Webb Medley Fund, the Leverhulme Trust and the Queen Elizabeth House Oppenheimer Fund, at different stages. It has benefited greatly from the participation of Dr V. Mohanasundaram, my interpreter and co-researcher for most of the fieldwork since 1981/1982, and from the contributions of M.V. Srinivasan, Paul Pandian and Selva Murugan who did some of the fieldwork interviews. It has also benefited from discussions at seminars in Oxford and elsewhere, and with a large number of individuals, particularly S. Anandhi, Barbara Harriss-White, C. Lakshmanan, Karin Kapadia, K. Nagaraj, Aseem Prakash and Frances Stewart.

Notes

1 The term Dalit is used interchangeably here with the term Scheduled Caste (SC) to denote the lowest group in the caste hierarchy in India. The term SC refers both to the Scheduled Castes and to members of the Scheduled Castes. It is used in preference to Dalit in much of the chapter as this is a term used by people in the villages to identify themselves.
2 See, for example, Thorat, Aryama and Negi (2007) and references therein.
3 See, for example, Mehrotra (2006).
4 See, for example, Human Rights Watch (1999); Viswanathan (2005); Gorringe (2005).
5 See Pandian (2000).
6 There was some surface irrigation. This accounted for 30 per cent of the net irrigated area in Coimbatore in 1981/1982. Most of the rest was well irrigated. Less than 5 per cent was irrigated directly by tanks.
7 Sivanappan and Aiyasamy (1978).
8 Sivanappan and Aiyasamy (1978); Kurien (1981); and Harriss-White (1996) are the main sources here.
9 The proportion of 'main workers' in agriculture in Coimbatore district as a whole fell from 47 per cent in 1981 to 28 per cent in 2001, according to the Population Census.
10 Government of Tamil Nadu, Season and Crop Reports, annual; Population Census 1971, 1981 and 1991.
11 Population Census figures show that in 1981 the villages were even more strongly agricultural than in 1971, when 'traditional' non-agricultural activities had still been quite strong.
12 Men's underpants.
13 In the study villages, the proportion of the male working population working in agriculture fell from 75 per cent in 1981 to 50 per cent in 1996 (see below). Figures from the Population Censuses show that there were even greater decreases in other villages in the vicinity.
14 'Thottam farmers' are defined as farmers with well-irrigated land who employed permanent labourers in 1981/1982.
15 The 'study villages' comprise six hamlets in two revenue villages originally selected for the strength of their agriculture and their high levels of uptake of SFDA (Small Farmer Development Agency) and MFDA (Marginal Farmer Development Agency) loans in 1981/1982. A random sample of 20 per cent of households in these villages was interviewed between August 1981 and March 1982, a sample of 230 households

in all. The 1996 data came from a May–June resurvey of 85 per cent of the 1981/1982 sample households that still had descendants living in the villages. Some information about those who had left was also obtained. Both 1981/1982 and 1996 sample interviews were supplemented by interviews with people outside the sample. More selective interviews were conducted in May 2003 and August 2004, focusing particularly on SC housing, the Ambedkar People's Movement (APM), panchayats, and urban and industrial employment.

16 Standard X was the last year of secondary school at the end of which students sat for examinations leading to the Secondary School Leaving Certificate (SSLC).

17 'Small farmers' are defined here as farmers the bulk of whose income came from working their own land but who did not employ permanent labour.

18 Pannadis are Paraiyars.

19 Alternatively, Arunthathiyar, Madari, Sakkili *et al.* 'Chakkiliyar' is one of the names people in the study villages used to identify themselves.

20 There was one exception in the sample – a Chakkiliyar who had worked as a plantation labourer in Ooty (Oothacamund, now Udhagamandalam) where he had acquired a small landholding. There were also one to two Chakkiliyars outside the sample with 1–2 acres of dry land in the villages that they had bought with employer loans that had been worked off over long periods of time.

21 Eighteen per cent of male labourers were pannayals, and 67 per cent casual labourers. The rest were sugar-cane crushers who worked as casual labourers outside the sugar-cane crushing season.

22 The exceptions were an impoverished Pannadi and a mentally retarded Gounder.

23 Cederlof (1997) in her study of Madaris (Chakkiliyars) in a neighbouring taluk (Palladam) in the first half of the twentieth century elaborates on this in some detail.

24 The annual rate of pay for pannayals in 1981/1982 was Rs.2400/- for an adult doing the full range of tasks, with or without one or more meals per day. This was equivalent to the highest daily casual labour wage of Rs.7/- for 343 days of the year without taking account of any of the additional perks available to pannayals. Male wages for casual labour in 1981/1982 were Rs.5, 6 and 7/-; female Rs.2, 2/50 and 3/-.

25 Chakkiliyar fertility rates were still relatively high: households starting families in the 1960s and the 1970s had between one and six surviving children, an average of 3.5. Both the average and the dispersion were greater than in the case of thottam farmers who were controlling their numbers of offspring much more strictly.

26 When I first started fieldwork, I had to negotiate the terms on which I could interview both Chakkiliyars and others in these villages. The agreement eventually worked out was that I would visit the Chakkiliyar colony at the end of the day, and then leave without re-entering the main village, returning only the following day, by which time it would be assumed that I had had a bath. It would have been impossible to continue interviewing non-Chakkiliyars in the villages without this agreement.

27 See Arun (2007) for a good discussion of the way in which this operates in villages in north-eastern Tamil Nadu.

28 See Shah *et al.* (2006) for the sorts of practices that continue in much of India to the present day.

29 They got water from the main village borehole where Caste Hindus filled their pot first and then filled the pots of Chakkiliyars.

30 This is a recurring theme in literature on Dalits, particularly strong in writing by Dalits themselves.

31 Alexander (1989) makes a similar point too.

32 See Breman (1996); De Haan and Rogaly (2002).

33 See, for example, Chari (2004); Vijaya Baskar (2001); Singh and Sapra (2007).

34 Production figures available in the VAO's offices confirm the depth of this crisis. The reliability of these figures is questionable though.

35 In 1981/1982, the deepest wells in the villages were 120 ft with bores extending up to 220 ft. In 1996, bores were reaching 550 ft or more. In 2003/2004, the depth from which water was being obtained had reached 1200 ft.

36 Fieldwork data on female employment in the villages are not available for 1981/1982. However, data available from the Population Census confirm the fact that most women and girls in the workforce worked in agriculture in 1981.

37 Population Census 1981, 1991, 2001.

38 One such example was that of a young man who had rejected a relatively well-paid clerical job in favour of work as an errand boy in a banian factory in 1984 and who by 1996 was a production manager and in 2003 had started a small company of his own that was doing well. It had taken him twenty years to get to this point, though. Moreover, he was still having to work very hard as the owner of his own company in 2004.

39 One of these was quite exceptional in having become a peon in the Forestry Department. He was the most prominent Pannadi in other respects in 1996 too (see below).

40 There was one outstanding case again here, the 'Secretary' in charge of the VCACS, who was exceptional among Chakkiliyars in having passed SSLC as early as 1985. It was not until 1996 that another Chakkiliyar from these villages passed SSLC.

41 Jeffrey, Jeffery and Jeffery (2005) point out that education can be very damaging to the self-esteem of SCs though, given the content of current syllabi and the way SCs are treated in school. Harriss (1989) points to the low returns to education for Dalits too.

42 Daily agricultural wages for men were Rs.5/-, Rs.6/- and Rs.7/- in 1981/1982. In 1996 they were Rs.40/-, Rs.45/-, Rs.50/-. This represents an up to 200-per-cent increase using the Coimbatore rural rice price, and up to 175 per cent using the CPIAL. (The *India Labour Journal* is the source both for the rice price and for the CPIAL.) This overstates the real rise, though. There are a number of items of increased expenditure that are not included in the CPIAL, including things such as health care. Patterns of expenditure have changed much more dramatically in Tamil Nadu than in other parts of India, many new items being regarded as necessities which they certainly were not before.

43 There were other factors that had contributed to the reduction in extreme forms of untouchability too.

44 A new scheme was introduced in 2004 whereby TAHDCO (Tamil Nadu Adi Dravidar Housing and Development Corporation Ltd) gave loans which enabled SC women to buy land and convert it to thottam land with technical support and advice from the state. A prominent Chakkiliyar leader had applied for a loan under this scheme, nominally in the name of his wife, for a project that looked very risky given the high price and low productivity of the land and the heavy loan commitment involved.

45 There had been prosecutions for bonding labour in the early 2000s. One such prosecution in which a substantial loan was associated with the bonding of a pannayal had gone against the employer concerned. His reaction was to re-employ the pannayal, but no longer to lend more than very small amounts to him and other pannayals in his employment.

46 SC 'colonies' are separate, and often adjacent to, the main villages. The majority own their own houses and house plots in these colonies. The colonies were overcrowded and had no electricity or water supplies in 1981/1982. They had been improved and substantially expanded by 1996.

47 See Gorringe (2005) on one of these. Adiyamaan's Adi Thamizhar Peravai is the one long-standing Arunthathiyar (Chakkiliyar) social movement in Coimbatore.

48 The CSED (Centre for Social and Economic Development), a small NGO based in Avinashi, played a role in this. The CSED was one of only two NGOs playing any role in the study villages in the 1990s and early 2000s. The other was World Vision India.

49 When the establishment of the APM was announced, thottam farmers and others in the village threatened 'to stop Chakkiliyars from riding bicycles in the village', 'not to give employment to initiators in the village', and 'to file police cases against them'. They also approached MLAs (Members of the Legislative Assembly) in a bid to prevent the APM branch from going ahead.

50 Such an increase in mobilisation could easily spill over into violence. The CSED was keeping a record of community level confrontations that involved violence. The first community level violence that occurred, according to him, was a riot in Muriandampalayam over a Chakkiliyar brushing against the leg of a Gounder in a bus. Further incidents of community-level violence have been reported since then, too.

51 These were set out in the 73rd and 74th amendment to the Constitution of the early 1990s.

52 See Viswanathan (2005) for an example of the complete failure even to conduct elections in some cases where key positions were formally reserved for SCs; on violence including murder in others; and on simple de facto takeovers, non-SCs effectively running the show, in others.

53 Goyal (2006).

54 Breman (2007) makes a similar point in relation to south Gujarat where he finds that the relative poverty of those at the bottom of the hierarchy has barely changed over the more than fifty years for which he has been studying conditions in the area.

55 It is not easy for SCs to 'pass' as anything but SC in urban areas. Apart from the fact that it is difficult for them to do this, there are a lot of incentives for SCs to identify themselves as SCs in urban as well as rural areas in India today.

56 There are more in supervisory positions, and other positions for which education certificates are required, though. See also Jodhka and Newman (2007) on caste discrimination being implicit as well as explicit, those practising it not always realising they are doing so.

57 See Breman (2007) who has argued this powerfully in the south Gujarat case, too.

58 Pandian (2000) makes the point that less violent caste conflict has been reported from western Tamil Nadu (which includes Coimbatore) than from other parts of Tamil Nadu where SC advances have been more threatening to dominant castes, and that this may reflect the weakness of the SC position rather than its strength.

59 See Chari (2004), particularly, and De Neve (2003).

60 Beck (1972). The strong localised caste organisation of Gounders is a marked contrast to the caste organisation of Kaikkolars portrayed by Mines (1984), e.g. Chakkiliyar caste organisation mirrors that of Gounders, too.

61 According to Chari (2004), it was in the 1920s and the 1930s that they took advantage of opportunities arising from the introduction of new varieties of cotton to develop the entrepreneurial characteristics for which they are known today.

62 See Chari (2004); Vijaya Baskar (2001); De Neve (2003). Chari has written about Gounders reproducing agrarian relations in the textile industry in Tiruppur. Gounders may have been reproducing agrarian relations to some extent, but this did not extend to the employment of SCs.

Bibliography

Alexander, K.C. (1989) 'Caste mobilisation and class consciousness: the emergence of agrarian movements in Kerala and Tamil Nadu', in F. Frankel and M.S.A. Rao (eds), *Dominance and State Power in India: Decline of a Social Order*, New Delhi: Oxford University Press.

Arun, C.J. (2007) *Constructing Dalit Identity, Jaipur, New Delhi, Bangalore, Mumbai, Hyderabad*, Guwahati: Rawat Publications.

246   *Judith Heyer*

Beck, B. (1972) *Peasant Society in Konku: A Study of Right and Left Sub-castes in South India*, Vancouver: University of British Columbia Press.

Breman, J. (1996) *Footloose Labour: Working in India's Informal Economy*, Cambridge: Cambridge University Press.

—— (2007) *The Poverty Regime: Half a Century of Work and Life and the Bottom of the Rural Economy in South Gujarat*, New Delhi: Oxford University Press.

Cederlof, G. (1997) *Bonds Lost: Subordination, Conflict and Mobilisation in Rural South India, c. 1900–70*, Delhi: Manohar.

Chari, S. (2004) *Fraternal Capital, Peasant Workers, Self-made Men and Globalization in Provincial India*, Delhi: Permanent Black.

De Haan, A. and Rogaly, B. (eds) (2002) *Labour Mobility and Rural Society*, London: Frank Cass.

De Neve, G. (2003) 'Expectations and rewards of modernity: commitment and mobility among migrants in Tiruppur, Tamil Nadu', *Contributions to Indian Sociology*, 37(1/2): 275–304.

Gorringe, H. (2005) *Untouchable Citizens: Dalit Movements and Democratisation in Tamil Nadu*, London: Sage.

Government of India, Population Census, 1981, 1991, 2001.

Government of Tamil Nadu (various) *Season and Crop Reports*, Chennai.

Goyal, S. (2006) 'Human development in Tamil Nadu and Karnataka: a Comparison', in Vikram Chand (ed.) *Reinventing Public Service Delivery in India: Selected Case Studies*, New Delhi: World Bank and Sage.

Harriss, J. (1989) 'Vulnerable workers in the Indian urban labour market', in G. Rodgers (ed.) *Urban Poverty and the Labour Market: Access to Jobs and Incomes in Asian and Latin American Cities*, Geneva: ILO.

Harriss-White, B. (1996) *A Political Economy of Agricultural Markets in South India: Masters of the Countryside*, New Delhi: Sage Publications.

Human Rights Watch (1999) *Broken People*, New York: Human Rights Watch.

Jeffrey, C., Jeffery, P. and Jeffery, R. (2005) 'Reproducing difference? Schooling, jobs and empowerment in Uttar Pradesh, India', *World Development*, 33(12): 2085–101.

Kurien, C.T. (1981) *Dynamics of Rural Transformation: A Study of Tamil Nadu, 1950–75*, New Delhi: Orient Longman Ltd.

Mehrotra, S. (2006) 'Well-being and caste in Uttar Pradesh: why UP is not like Tamil Nadu', *Economic and Political Weekly*, XLI(40): 4261–71.

Mines, M. (1984) *The Warrior Merchants: Textiles, Trade and Territory in South India*, Cambridge: Cambridge University Press.

Pandian, M.S.S. (2000) 'Dalit assertion in Tamil Nadu: an exploratory note', *Journal of the Indian School of Political Economy*, XII (3/4): 501–18.

Shah, G., Mander, H., Thorat, S., Deshpande, S. and Baviskar, A. (2006) *Untouchability in Rural India*, New Delhi and London: Sage Publications.

Singh, N. and Sapra, M.K. (2007) 'Liberalization in trade and finance, India's garment sector', in B. Harriss-White and A. Sinha (eds) *Trade Liberalization and India's Informal Economy*, New Delhi: Oxford University Press.

Sivanappan, R.K. and Aiyasamy, P.K. (1978) *Land and Water Resources of Coimbatore District, Coimbatore*, Tamil: Nadu Agricultural University.

Thorat, S., Aryama, and Negi, P. (eds) (2007) *Reservation and the Private Sector, Quest for Equal Opportunity and Growth*, Jaipur: Rawat Publications.

Thorat, S. and Newman, K. (2007) 'Caste and economic discrimination: causes, consequences and remedies', *Economic and Political Weekly*, XLII(41): 4121–4.

Vijaya Baskar, M. (2001) 'Industrial formation under conditions of flexible accumulation: the case of a global knitwear node in southern India', unpublished Ph.D. thesis, Centre for Development Studies, Nehru University.

Viswanathan, S. (2005) *Dalits in Dravidian Land*, Pondicherry: Navayana Publications.

Washbrook, D. (1989) 'Caste, class and dominance in modern Tamil Nadu, non-Brahmanism, Dravidianism and Tamil nationalism', in F. Frankel and M.S.A. Rao (eds) *Dominance and State Power in Modern India: Decline of a Social Order*, New Delhi: Oxford University Press.

12 Shifting the 'grindstone of caste'?

Decreasing dependency among Dalit labourers in Tamil Nadu

Hugo Gorringe

If you ask whether there is a limit to untouchability, then there is not. You said that in the village where you stayed there was only one glass [not separate glasses for Untouchables]. If you think that means there is no untouchability that is not so. Even if there is one glass at the teashop things are not equal: in the administration of the village; in the Panchayat elections; in the allocation of common assets; the Panchayat meetings to resolve village problems, common resources, the pond, the temple. Who is given the lease to catch fish in the pond? How is water distributed? The downtrodden do not have rights to administer these common resources . . . From the President's residence to the teashop, untouchability persists. Untouchability is not only things like two tumblers, cycle [prohibition to ride through Caste Hindu areas], sandals [prohibition to wear] and so on, nor even like in Allallaberi where they had to bear the death news, prepare the body and dig the grave. These alone do not exhaust untouchability – they are the oppressive aspects of untouchability . . . But this untouchability is everywhere . . . In the name of caste, many economic opportunities are denied to them, their economic rights are denied . . . Now we also wish to breathe the wind of Independence which blew through the rest of India.

(Chandra Bose, Interview)

Caste in context

Kodankipatti is a small village some 20 miles outside Madurai in central Tamil Nadu. Alighting at the bus stop, by the main village square, one has to head away from the shops, the panchayat office and school and turn off down a sun-baked mud track to reach the cheri (Untouchable settlement). My visit was prompted by two Liberation Panther (Viduthalai Ciruthaigal Katchi (VCK), the largest Dalit movement in the state) activists who wanted me to encounter caste discrimination first-hand and to speak to people whose lives are most enmeshed within the entanglements of caste, class, power and resources. Few houses in the cheri had electricity; none had running water, bathrooms or toilets. They were, however, pucca houses – made of concrete or brick, with tiled roofs – and several of the inhabitants had consumer goods (televisions, radios, bicycles). At first sight, the residents, while not wealthy, were reasonably placed.

Interviewing cheri residents, however, revealed a pervasive sense of fear, vulnerability and inequality. 'We have only the land on which we live and ourselves,' said Arulmozhi, 'otherwise nothing in the village is ours or available to us. That we were born here has been rendered meaningless.' The interviews are littered with references to 'Them' – meaning Caste Hindus – and the fear that 'They' would 'do something'. Caste relations collapsed in the early 1990s when Dalit[1] villagers refused to 'continue doing the menial tasks they demanded of us'. Following this act of insubordination, Dalits were hounded from the village by an angry, stone-throwing mob that set light to the cheri. Government intervention enabled Dalits to build pucca houses and return to the village, but had resolved none of the underlying issues.

Balasubramaniam, a clerk in an insurance firm in Madurai, related how Dalits were still subject to social boycott:

> Now all the farming, all the land is in their hands and there is no work for us. We have to go to them for work but it's not there. Now we have to go elsewhere – to Madurai [a city 25 km away] and so on – for construction work, plumbing contracts and this sort of work . . . We used to go to them for coolie work, but then the conflicts arose and then they laid down rules and called the oor [main village] together and decreed that 'no one should call them to work'. If anyone employs us, that family is punished.
>
> (Interview)

The lack of resources extended beyond employment and income and was refracted by gender as well as caste. The cheri women mostly stayed at home, calculating that the social and economic costs of travelling into the city outweighed the benefits that might accrue, and their accounts reflected the routine aspects of caste tension: 'If we go to the pond to bathe they say we don't have the right to use it. They have even blocked off the pond. Then if we try to use poromboke [common wasteland] to go to the toilet we don't even have that right . . . they taunt us and threaten us (Maligai, Interview).

Contrary to Moffatt (1979), however, Dalits no longer accept their fate (if they ever did). The uneasy truce between the Caste Hindus and Dalits required the latter to accept daily indignities and threats which they were no longer prepared to tolerate. Shortly before my interviews, Dalit villagers staked a claim to the village square by trying to screen a film there. When this was prohibited, they disrupted the weekly market to emphasise inequalities in access to 'common resources'. The police response was to counsel caution and host peace committees. 'Even incidents that the Sub-Inspector witnessed firsthand', Arulmozhi bemoaned in the interview, 'he is able to present in a different light and say "cleanse your hearts, be patient".'

Three months after the interview tensions boiled over and, as Dalits fled the village again, twenty-four homes were ransacked and their contents strewn across the cheri (cf. Dinakaran 1999). Police swarmed to the scene to prevent further clashes, but the Dalits sheltered in a neighbouring village. If they anticipated a sympathetic welcome there, they were mistaken. As the villagers narrated the course of events to me, some VCK men interjected with disgust: 'You mean you abandoned the village without a fight?' It is indicative of current Dalit assertion that the immediate (rhetorical) prescription was retaliatory. Successive atrocities have fostered a disinclination to trust state intervention or negotiated settlements and cultivated a naive and often counterproductive belief in redemptive violence: 'Only if we return a hit for a hit', said Arulmozhi, 'will the grindstone shift.'

Introduction

The contradictions that characterise rural Dalit lives are epitomised in the quote and the case study above and admirably captured in Heyer's longitudinal studies of agricultural labourers in Coimbatore. She notes that even the least organised and most marginal of Tamil Dalit castes, the Chakkiliyars, were 'wrenching themselves from their moorings' for the first time. The 'moorings' themselves were beginning to change too' (2000: 3). Despite this, Heyer found that their achievements were not consonant with their opportunities and expressed surprise that Chakkiliyars 'could not improve their position more vis-à-vis their employers given the weakness of their employers' and 'that it was only in 1994 that something like the APM (Ambedkar People's Movement) was started and that Chakkiliyans were so worried about it jeopardising their relationships with employers when it did' (Heyer 2000: 28).

This chapter draws on my fieldwork in rural and urban Tamil Nadu to further explore these issues, and engage both with the above questions and with Heyer's long-term concern to analyse and address the situations of the chronically poor.[2] My data suggest that declining dependency has fostered challenges to the status quo, but a concomitant amelioration of the vicissitudes of caste or a diminution of vulnerability has not automatically ensued. Indeed, escaping the shackles of dependency has frequently been the precursor for renewed domination.

Contemporary caste 'moorings' are in flux and no longer tessellate with material structures. The chapter begins, therefore, by charting the extent to which caste structures are being contested, but it is important not to get too carried away and to ground such debates in the ongoing dynamics of social change. Caste inequalities will not be eradicated overnight and challenges to the status quo have presaged processes of retrenchment and retaliation as well as renegotiation. The chapter therefore offers an analysis of the various tributaries to Dalit activism and considers potential paths out of caste-accentuated poverty, focusing on migration, employment, education and group formation. In concluding, I consider the implications of these findings.

Declining dependency

Any discussion of caste in rural Tamil Nadu today, though, must begin by acknowledging the shifting contours of dependency and the increasing frequency with which caste norms are confronted. Numerous studies demonstrate the determination of Tamil Dalits to escape the most degrading forms of tied labour and dependency by any means available to them (Heyer 1989, 2000, this volume; Mosse 1994; Gorringe 2005). Dalit respondents thus asserted that when they play drums at village festivals and funerals now, they insist on cash payment. Others commute into urban centres to find work, set up home industries, borrow money from moneylenders rather than employers, join social movements, utilise government initiatives and, at the least, seek to educate their children: 'Educating our children is our desire as well,' as Chellamma put it, 'we wonder if God will help us to live in comfort.'

Their efforts generally amount to little more than the 'everyday resistance' of the weak (Scott 1985), but we should not downplay the significance of even minor acts of insurrection. Their importance is amplified by two considerations: first, as Mosse argues, 'Harijan identity is itself principally defined by dependence and service' (1994: 73). It is only in this context that we can comprehend the degree to which Dalits have progressed, and the extent to which even minimal resistance erodes the bases of caste hierarchy. These implications are certainly not lost on Caste Hindu landlords or farmers. Heyer (2000: 11) notes how thottam farmers felt threatened by any insubordination (seeking credit from moneylenders rather than thottam farmers for instance) that characterises the first tottering steps on the road to independence.

Madhiarasan, a BC farmer near Kodankipatti, likewise insisted that taxes for the village festival should not be collected from Dalits. After much prevarication his rationale was telling: 'they will turn around and say: "so, you came to collect taxes but you don't give us respect." They will ask for the deity to go to their houses' (Interview). Where assertive attitudes have taken hold, as in Kodankipatti, the dominant caste response is often repressive. As Chellamma explained: 'We still don't have anything to do with the people here, even after ten years we won't perform death duties or customary duties. We don't talk to them and they, if they see us, smoulder with anger' (Interview).

Secondly, these intimations of declining dependency are particularly salient because they indicate how the 'structures of mind' that kept the downtrodden in thrall are crumbling. This transformation and the attendant alteration in Dalit priorities, however, are neither universal nor always acknowledged. S. Martine, a social activist and advocate in Villupuram, thus, spoke of inferiority complexes:

> You must understand, their [Dalits'] instincts and creativity have been killed, he thinks that he is a no one. He has lost his identity. A challenge is to make this lion active, but it will be a slow process . . . and there are bound to be failures. It is hard to see when he drinks and fights and gambles, but they are like a sick people, they are living in a sick society.
>
> (Interview)

This paternalist attitude towards the 'indolent and ignorant' poor finds echoes in government reports and initiatives. The SC/ST Commissioner thus argued that Dalits have inculcated a 'psychological state of accepting deprivation and destitution as justified and proper' (Scharma 1990: iv). The Panchayat President of Kodankipatti, likewise, dismissed the fears and allegations of Dalit villagers. 'They have some sort of inferiority complex,' he insisted, 'they think of themselves as depressed' (Interview). The consensus between Dalit advocates and a dominant caste leader responsible for attacks on cheri residents should give the former pause for thought.

Too often the perceptions, attitudes and priorities of the rural poor are neglected (Chambers 1995). Dalits do lack access to, let alone control over, land, water, labour power or security, but the easy assumption that educated outsiders know what is best for deprived Dalits must be challenged. In Kodankipatti, for instance, Dalits' actions appear to be counterproductive and inimical to their interests. Indeed, strategies aimed at diminishing dependence regularly invoke a disproportionate repressive reaction (Mendelsohn and Vicziany 1999: 54), but travelling round Tamil Nadu it is clear that a sea-change in attitudes is extending (in varying degrees) to Tamil Nadu's most marginal communities. This is not to say that all Dalits are up in arms or refusing to perform the menial tasks required of them; almost every village had some households who conformed to caste stipulates, and some Dalits appear to remain in ignorance of the discourses of discontent articulated with increasing fervour by movements over the past three decades.[3]

Heyer (in Chapter 11 of this volume) observes that her respondents were still subordinate. None termed themselves 'Dalits' and they were characterised by low aspirations and self-esteem. Heyer has worked among the most vulnerable and least mobilised Dalits in the state, yet even here there has been a diminution in the extent to which thottam farmers can control Chakkiliyars. Racine and Racine (1998: 7) elsewhere argue that some Dalits share 'the consensus that places the Dalits at the bottom of the caste hierarchy and accept the rationale of a system based on "purity"'. Viramma, the elderly Dalit whose life story they narrate, supposedly 'accepts the concepts of karma and dharma', but a residual attachment to caste ideology no longer determines her actions to the extent of denying her children an education (Viramma, Racine and Racine 1997: 104). There are very few indeed who are completely ignorant of processes of caste change even if they yet lack the vocabulary of liberation.

Among the more politically conscious Dalits of my research, many not only reject caste prescriptions but are prepared to make sacrifices to enhance their sense of self-worth:

> In this village due to our awareness none of us are prepared to do this slave work [*adimai thozhil*]. Because we are not prepared to do this they have enforced a caste control [*kattamaipu*] on the village, a caste/village domination. This involves blocking any opportunities that should reach us, forcing us to do certain things under threat of punishment, denying us our rights. Now we have studied, and because we are a little educated and aware we refuse to do the most menial jobs our ancestors did. They [the dominant castes] cannot stomach our resistance!
>
> (Balasubramaniam, Interview)

What this suggests is a fundamental transformation of aspirations. Even among marginalised Chakkiliyar labourers, Heyer's work demonstrates the rapidity with which priorities altered. Within a generation, those whose primary focus was on the need for an immediate income – as seen in the preponderance of child labour – have begun to reorient themselves towards the acquisition of transferable assets such as education. Heyer (2000: 9) records how the expectation that Chakkiliyars would work as pannayals (tied labourers) in 1981/1982 had evaporated by 1996 and Dalits who had never held such posts recounted this with pride. This repudiation of conspicuous markers of subordination is ubiquitous where movements are active. Dalit assertion, however, has social and geographical limits and attitudinal transformations cannot be attributed solely to the campaigning work of Dalit activists. It is to a consideration of the factors underpinning caste change that we now turn.

Land and labour: agricultural assets

'The most important asset as far as landless agricultural labourers are concerned', Heyer (1989: 33) observes, 'is labour power'. Nearly 80 per cent of working Scheduled Castes (SC) in Tamil Nadu are employed in the agrarian sector, and 64 per cent work as agricultural labourers so this is undeniable (Gorringe 2005: 154). 'Coolie work', however, was primarily a survival strategy. The recurrent refrain was 'we have nothing'. Of late, therefore, several factors including Dalits' increasing rejection of degrading labour, a decline in the agricultural sector, and a diversification of urban and industrial opportunities have shifted the horizons of Dalit interviewees beyond agricultural work.

Recent decades have witnessed a gradual decline in agriculture in terms of productivity (soil health and crop yields) and capacity (availability of land and rural work) (Government of Tamil Nadu 2003; Shah 2007). While labour power remains an asset, therefore, agriculture provides a tenuous path to security at best. The fragility of this economic platform is compounded by the seasonal nature of agricultural work and, more perniciously, by the legal wage differential between male and female labourers. While Dalit women field workers offer a source of income, the 'feminisation of agrarian labour' has been fuelled by the decline in male agricultural work due to mechanisation and the 'the very low wages that are paid to women' (Kapadia 1995: 209–10).

Recently, the imbalance between labour and reward in combination with group-based status acquisition has led some Dalits to withdraw women from work (Kapadia 1993; Heyer, Chapter 11 in this volume). The rejection of poorly paid drudgery is welcome but the outcomes are politically ambiguous. Withdrawal from work certainly reduces household earnings and – especially when part of a Sanskritising process – can decrease the autonomy of women and reinforce patriarchal tendencies (Deshpande 2002). Since female income benefits the household more than male earnings, wage differentials and/or the withdrawal of female labour have wider significance (Mencher 1988). As Mathivanan of the Working Peasants' Movement (WPM) argues:

Now I work for eight hours and receive Rs.60. My wife works those same eight hours but she only gets Rs.30. Of the Rs.60 I get for my eight hours only 30 gets home, but the 30 rupees a woman gets – exactly Rs.30 salary is expended on the home and the children and for other necessary items. Then if women got the salary that men do the family could develop and grow better.

(Interview)

Equal wages are the central plank of a WPM campaign that emphasises the gendered experience of caste and reveals the imbrication of landlessness and gender inequalities. Land reform is advocated to enable Dalit women to reap the full benefit of their labour.[4]

This tendency to focus on Dalit landlessness is widespread: 'The most important thing is to get land. Without land we cannot get near any demands' (Mathivanan, Interview). From his perspective, land connotes more than an economic asset since those lacking land 'are seen as worthless'. It is bound up with a desire for self-determination and independence: 'Now we go to work for a daily coolie of Rs.20–30. If we had our own land to work on, we who are hungry ten days a month would at least have *kanji* [old rice steeped in water] to eat. One acre per person would be sufficient for this' (Interview).

Consequently, land tops Dalit movement demands and has occasionally informed the programmes of governments seeking the Dalit vote. Addressing the VCK's Munnurimai Maanadu (Land Rights Conference) in June 2007, thus, Chief Minister (CM) Karunanidhi endeared himself by stressing that 'his government was distributing agricultural lands to the poor' (Hindu 2007a). The importance of land is apparent then, but land acquisition was neither a major route out poverty nor a preferred strategy for Dalit respondents.

The automatic championing of land redistribution must be tempered in the light of local contingencies and relationships. Since Dalits lack control of water sources and labour and are vulnerable to caste conflicts, land may not be a profitable investment: '[Land] is quite costly to operate. Land may also limit agricultural labourers' ability to participate in the most lucrative wage labouring at peak seasons; and it may limit agricultural labourers' mobility' (Heyer 1989: 37). Much of the land distributed in populist government programmes, furthermore, is of poor quality or not irrigated. Pai argues that the 'traditional structures of rural dominance based on land and social status are undergoing change, and that ownership of land is not as important a source of power and prestige as in the past' (2000: 192). Her findings, however, have been contested (Jeffery, Jeffrey and Jeffery 2001) and fly in the face of my data (Gorringe 2005).

Since the majority of Dalits in the state are landless,[5] this is clearly not the basis of contemporary Dalit assertion, and it would take an unprecedented programme of land reform that addressed inequalities in social relations to 'realise this dream' (as Karunanidhi referred to it). More immediately, therefore, there is a pressing need to improve the conditions of agricultural labour, which will dominate Dalit employment for the foreseeable future. The Government of India's 2005 National Rural Employment Guarantee Act (NREGA) has potential here.

The act provides 'a minimum guaranteed wage employment of 100 days in every financial year to rural households with unemployed adult members prepared to do unskilled manual work' (Chakraborty 2007: 548). This recognition of the right to work and the insistence on state (rather than contractor) provision is incredibly significant in the context of caste based social boycotts. State intervention here could reconstitute and stabilise labour relations. Shah, thus, envisages labour-intensive 'asset-creating works that . . . could tackle problems of unemployment, environmental regeneration and agricultural growth' (2007: 46). Not everyone, however, is as optimistic.

Chakraborty notes the limited uptake of the scheme and cautions against 'elite capture' (2007: 551; cf. Mosse 2007); the NREGA is said to suffer from familiar failings of unaccountability and understaffing (Ambasta, Shankar and Shah 2008); and even Narayanan's (2008) more positive review points to a lack of childcare facilities as a serious impediment. The longevity, commitment to, and objective of state schemes is also uncertain. In 2002, for instance, the reigning CM, Jayalalitha, proposed to regenerate the rural economy with a Comprehensive Wasteland Programme. As activists noted, this plan to cede agricultural land to corporate giants would privatise common lands required for toilet purposes and grazing. Furthermore, some of the earmarked land was inhabited by Dalits awaiting title deeds (Thamukku 2002: 2; Viswanathan 2003). The NREGS is better placed to benefit rural labourers (Narayanan 2008). Indeed, it was 'making a real difference and being taken up quite widely in villages in Tiruppur district in 2008–9' (Heyer, personal communication). Heyer notes that the programme has improved since its inception, but scepticism of state programmes was rife among my respondents and reflected in news reports (*The Hindu* 2009). Consequently I stress the role of community groups in monitoring and publicising state initiatives.

Migration and the non-farm economy

Lacking land or sustainable employment, commuting and migration have enabled Dalits to escape dependency by undertaking caste-neutral jobs or by working beyond the dominant caste's sphere of influence. Improvements in infrastructure and the expansion of urban centres with employment opportunities are significant here. The existence of a bus route, thus, enabled Kodankipatti Dalits to seek alternate sources of income. Partly as a consequence of improved transport links and the social networks attending them, Dalits in suburban villages are more autonomous than their less connected neighbours (Gorringe 2005: chapter 3).

Declining dependency need not entail material advancement though: many interviewees travelled to urban centres from satellite villages, often enduring trips of two hours on potholed roads with unpredictable and infrequent bus services. The working conditions faced by labourers in towns and cities are often atrocious, and lead Mendelsohn and Vicziany (1998) to describe a 'new Indian proletariat' engaged in unskilled, manual labour in demeaning conditions. Most respondents found it hard to gain anything other than casual work: 'The barrier to entry into the secure labour force', as Harriss-White states, 'is not geographical but social' (1996: 249).

Sundari (2005) captures the variable effects of migration as a livelihood strategy. Migrating for work may increase income, she argues, but often at the expense of diminished networks and assets. Migration, for instance, correlates with child labour and can mean a loss of amenities and entitlements (for example, ration cards) (Sundari 2005: 2303). Given environmental degradation in urban areas – and the appalling state of slums and run-down estates where respondents often lived in cramped conditions – her call for schemes to minimise rural to urban migration is important.

Pay and physical conditions thus cannot explain increasing Dalit migrant labour. The explanation rather is twofold: the push factor of declining rural opportunities and the pull factor of employment untainted by caste status. Indeed, while some respondents had secure employment in urban areas, migrants dreamed not of urban squalor but the prospect of a government or 'foreign job'. The number of Dalits who achieve these goals is infinitesimal, but the mere possibility has generated a discourse that reinforces aspirations towards higher-status employment. High-profile caste attacks on Dalit villagers who prospered from remittances (Kodiyankulam, for instance; Gorringe 2005: 162) have generated awareness of these opportunities.

The cumulative impact is an increasing diversification of employment, but even caste-free opportunities are mediated through caste relations in the form of heightened tensions on the ground for instance. While out-migration is promising for frustrated young villagers and can boost the rural economy through sustained remittances and family ties, incidents like Kodiyankulam have led some Dalits to sever rural linkages. This can mean that the most vulnerable and least-networked rural Dalits face boycotts or are compelled to accept demeaning work. The alternate opportunities increasingly offered by the non-agricultural sector are significant therefore.

'The non-agricultural rural economy is no longer marginal; it is of central importance in the reproduction of rural society' (Harriss-White and Janakarajan 1997: 1475). Development optimists, such as the World Bank (1997), suggest that the non-farm sector is raising real wages and providing employment and a new wave of capitalist development has seemingly revitalised the rural economy in Tamil Nadu.

Dalit respondents, particularly in Karur district, had profited from expanding opportunities and invested in weaving and textile home industries. Dalit Liberation Movement activists, however, noted that the benefits were attenuated by an increase in child labour, especially where children were withdrawn from school to this end. Semi-autonomous, subcontracted householders utilise family members as cheap or unremunerated labourers in weaving, fireworks, beedi and other industries (Group Discussion). Nihila's study, of tanning industries in western Tamil Nadu, similarly suggests that the prospects for employment may be rising, but 'the quality of the employment has deteriorated' (1999: WS-26).

The expansion of the non-agricultural sector has largely been in unskilled, small-scale commodity production (Harriss-White and Janakarajan 1997: 1475), and may, therefore, perpetuate the casualisation of labour, poverty and landlessness.[6] Furthermore, there is no reservation in the private sector. Harriss-White and Janakarajan thus do not view the non-agricultural sector as offsetting the poverty of the most disadvantaged, since it is 'biased against women, against the lowest castes and the poorest classes' (1997: 1476). Heyer (2000) found that Dalits were repeatedly frustrated by the mirage of a thriving non-agricultural sector and notes that some respondents had reverted to agricultural labour.

Dalits in Kodankipatti and elsewhere echoed this and called for government enterprises to provide jobs. 'In the higher-caste milk societies and dairies', they insisted, 'there is no work for Dalits' (Group Discussion). Dalits continue to depend on wage labour since they lack the connections or capital to set up their own businesses.[7] Politically driven rights-based initiatives such as the NREGA (above) could be significant here, but steps are required to free Dalits from forms of tied labour and to guard against the privatisation and exploitation of natural resources. For all the gains offered by the growing non-farm economy and rural infrastructure, to credit Dalit uplift to material developments alone would be misplaced. Pai's (2000) assertion that education rather than land or legislation may offer the quickest route for upward mobility resonates in this context.

Empowering education?

'If you want your children to advance', Subramani – a bricklayer and VCK activist – insisted, 'put them to school. Put them to school and make men [sic] of them; escape the slavish instinct' (Interview). 'We are educated now' was a common utterance intended to convey a break from the past. Such accounts equate education with empowerment, which enables Dalits to gain skills, confidence and autonomy from caste structures (see Pai 2000). Dalits across Tamil Nadu increasingly see education as an escape route.

Contemporary Dalit movements recognise education's value and encourage affiliates to continue with education. 'Once we are educated,' as Kamaraj, an VCK activist, put it, 'we cannot go for slave work, we will seek employment elsewhere' (Interview). While observations and interviews supported Pai's (2000) findings, further probing offered a less sanguine assessment. Citing widespread poverty among Dalits, thus, Kamaraj continued: 'If there is a struggle to eat, how can one think about education?' (Interview). As several studies note, the costs of education are high (both in income forfeited and expended), and the rewards uncertain (Heyer 1989; Jeffrey, Jeffery and Jeffery 2004).

Empowerment optimists treat education as a black box, but more nuanced analyses note the variable quality of, and access to, education. Across rural Tamil Nadu schools were located in the main oor, rendering it intimidating or impossible for Dalit children to attend during caste conflicts. Absenteeism was rife and schooling often reinforced social divisions. Teachers rarely discriminated openly against Dalits, but subtle forms of differentiation included calling scholarship recipients forward (identifying them as Scheduled Castes) (Edwin, Interview). F. Matthew, a Christian Paraiyar teacher at a Catholic school, called for more Dalit teachers to act as role models, but he hid his caste background to facilitate interaction with all students (Interview).

There are efforts to improve the quality and accessibility of education, and Epstein, Suryanarayana and Thimmegowda (1998) point to decentralised ventures like the Indira Gandhi National Open University (IGNOU – a distance-learning enterprise) as exemplars. Recent reports note IGNOU's village-based capacity-building programmes and emphasise that their programmes are tailored to local skills shortages (Padmanabhan 2004; Krishnakumar 2007). The Vice-Chancellor Professor Pillai, however, noted that there was still a stigma associated with distance learning and a premium placed on certificates (Mahadevan 2006). Consequently, the Dalit Student Federation's (DSF) Kadirvelu emphasised: 'the value of a degree is being lost as many do degrees simply for the qualification rather than with a view to future prospects' (Interview).

In the villages around Vellore the consequences were evident in the number of educated and unemployed young men. As Rajasekhar noted: 'You come here any day around ten or eleven o'clock,' he insisted, 'I can show you a group of thirty to thirty-five Dalit youth just sitting around wasting their time' (Interview). Assessing the value of education, in other words, must consider the availability of employment: 'Many of the girls have studied well,' Arulmozhi from Kodankipatti observed, 'but look around: have any of us gone anywhere? We all remain here because there is no work for us' (Interview).

Jeffrey, Jeffery and Jeffery (2004) and Thorat and Newman (2007) offer analogous findings, and note that social barriers impede Dalits' search for jobs. Epstein Suryanarayana and Thimmegowda sum up the ambiguity surrounding formal education: 'Education has undoubtedly been one of the most important keys to rural development in South India. However, the evidence . . . also indicates some negative effects: for instance, massive rural outmigration and large numbers of frustrated educated/semi-educated unemployed young villagers' (1998: 220).

In an attempt to address skills shortages and the frustration of the educated unemployed, IGNOU aims to develop a knowledge-led rural economy. The focus on literacy and ICT (Information and Communication Technology) skills emphasises capacity-building and knowledge transfer. Crucially, the programme avoids reliance on private enterprise and existing power holders and aims to increase rural–urban links and share information about a range of issues from policy to disease prevention (Padmanabhan 2004).

This broader conception is important as formal education can be individualistic. Indeed, activists frequently berated high-fliers who neglected their social origins. Organisations, such as the DSF in Vellore, thus sought to retain links between educated Dalits and their roots. A lack of networking and support within Dalit groups was commonly cited as explaining why other castes secured better employment than Dalits (cf. Jeffrey, Jeffery and Jeffery 2004; Thorat and Newman 2007). To address this, the DSF offered material support to impoverished students, but also required each graduate to mentor two students from their village to emulate them. The emphasis here is on the group significance of individual achievement. Movements can mediate and amplify the effects of education by establishing tuition centres and after-school sessions to foster a culture of learning for instance. While shifting patterns of land ownership, employment, state intervention and education have facilitated Dalit resistance, therefore, socio-political mobilisation inspires and reinforces social mobility.

Organising for change

'Groups formed among poor people', as Heyer, Stewart and Thorp (2002: 322) argue, 'are likely to improve societal equity, not only by improving incomes but also by increasing political and bargaining power':

> 'Because the VCKs have raised their head and are a radical movement under Thirumavalavan, we can be somewhat comfortable . . . This has given us a buttress'
>
> (Balasubramaniam, Interview)

Movements like the Liberation Panthers lack resources and infrastructure but their actions are profound; they hold the state to account, press for the implementation of 'Dalit-friendly' legislation and publicise caste abuses. The presence of movements in villages across the state helps raise awareness of social entitlements and ideals, fight court cases, counter the fear of change and caste conflict, and provide an example for others to follow. While Dalit movement organisations are tenuous in rural areas – they are largely absent in Heyer's area and often exist in name alone in mine – their impact is widespread. Dalits in Kodankipatti and nearby villages insisted that the VCKs had done nothing for them but still acknowledged the confidence they derived from their one-sided affiliation.

Crucially, perhaps, movements have inverted the stigma attached to being 'untouchable' and enhanced confidence and self-esteem. Ananda Paraiyar, an educated VCK affiliate, found that friendships repeatedly dissolved when he revealed his caste so he added 'Paraiyar' to his name to emphasise that there was nothing to be ashamed of. Such decisions are possible only in the advent of Dalit mobilisation: 'There are places today (today!) where one can't wear shoes through the *oor* [Tamil word for 'village'], where a well-dressed Dalit had the clothes torn off his back for his presumption. So for me to be well dressed – wearing trousers and shirt – and to speak my name is a big thing!' (Interview).

Dalit movements have made Dalithood a positive (or at least not stigmatised) identity and tackled inferiority complexes inculcated by caste ideologies. Untouchability is bound up with socio-cultural norms that escape standard measures of poverty. The pursuit of employment that is de-linked from caste, thus, may be materially counterproductive but it offers respondents self-respect and dignity. 'A decrease in drudgery' here is 'an important aspect of poverty alleviation' (Heyer 2000: 19). In these terms, Dalits are immeasurably better off, yet material poverty and social vulnerability persist.

Caste pride before a fall?

That Dalits must choose between status and well-being is especially puzzling given 'the weakness of their employers' (Heyer 2000: 28). Indeed, the Tamil Nadu Human Development Report (THDR) notes that employers have not been able to suppress wages which increased, even in real terms and especially in the agricultural sector, over the 1990s (Government of Tamil Nadu 2003: 27).[8] Partly as a consequence, the THDR celebrates a 'dramatic decrease' in poverty levels. The percentage of people living below the poverty line has fallen from 45.8 per cent in 1987/1988 to 21.1 per cent in 1999/2000 (Government of Tamil Nadu 2003: 34). Vera-Sanso's (2007) observation of increased expenditure on non-essential items among Chakkiliyars complements these findings. She and others, though, point to continuing poverty and vulnerability.

The TDHR data on nutrition also conflict with the poverty statistics, but the report fails to coordinate its findings (cf. Vijayabaskar *et al.* 2004). THDR thus notes that 46.6 per cent of children under five are underweight. Furthermore, 'when data are analysed by caste, results show that children from SC households tend to be the worst-off among all communities ... It is clear that the socio-economic status of the household has a direct effect on nutritional status' (Government of Tamil Nadu 2003: 49–51). Heyer (2000: 19) refers to such conundrums as a 'standard of living paradox'.

The disparity between poverty rates and well-being partly reflects the continuing impact of caste structures, and the THDR notes that Scheduled Caste women labourers face more harassment and are poorer than other social groups (Government of Tamil Nadu 2003: 96–8). The contradiction, however, is partially explained by changing Dalit priorities and practices ranging from altered consumption patterns (rice rather than grains) to the rejection of caste work.

Dalits operate within a field of power, and resistance at one level may rebound in another. Emphasising status and dignity, thus, can mean Dalits eschew more reliable (but demeaning) employment opportunities and incur debts at higher interest rather than rely on the goodwill of a patron. The rhetoric of 'dying with dignity' can also undermine the achievements of mobilisation. Concerted activism, for instance, helped secure government housing, land and amenities in some areas, but deteriorating caste relations and a decline in agricultural jobs can bind Dalits to rural housing with no work or compel them to abandon their assets and migrate in search of income. As Laksmanan from Kodankipatti averred: 'The Caste Hindus retain control because they know we have no resources and that, ultimately, we will have to go to them for help. The government should take full responsibility for us and teach skills and set up small industries, otherwise we will have to return to them [higher castes]' (Interview).

This quote encapsulates contemporary Dalit politics. While campaigns to redistribute land, reservations and education have had some success, political mobilisation increasingly emphasises the emotive issues of caste pride and status acquisition (Gorringe 2006). Identity- and status-based tactics, however, can be counterproductive in the immediate rural context since caste pride facilitates group cohesion on the basis of exclusion. Heyer, Stewart and Thorp (2002: 321) note some of the problems of exclusive groups, and to these we may add the threat posed by counter-mobilisation – both internal and external.

The flipside of caste pride is group enmity and the generation of conflicts which adversely affect the most vulnerable people in society. The weakness of elites here is double-edged. While they no longer have exclusive control over resources – thus facilitating Dalit mobility – a prevailing sense of insecurity and wounded pride has fuelled a Backward Caste backlash in which perceived Dalit 'misdemeanours' are met with 'extravagant revenge' (Mendelsohn and Vicziany 1998: 54; Gorringe 2005: chapter 3). Socially isolated Dalits, therefore, repeatedly emphasised their vulnerability and pleaded for VCK activists to intervene on their behalf.

Activists insisted that present suffering would reap dividends in future, but caste-based mobilisation erodes the efficacy of Dalit claims-making groups, too. An identity-oriented approach paves the way for ever-narrower terms of engagement. Pallars, Paraiyars and Chakkiliyars thus demand their own leaders and are further subdivided by tactical preference, political allegiance and sub-caste concerns. Consequently, the solidarity on which an effective challenge to caste hierarchy depends has been diluted (cf. Gorringe 2006).

The move to political contestation has further weakened Dalit activism. While Dalit parties gain more coverage and support than movements ever did, these benefits are superficial. Support in the form of voting requires little expenditure of time or energy, so numbers count for little (cf. Pai 2000), especially as activists are seen as acquiring a 'party-mentality' and 'selling out' for the rewards of institutionalisation. An increase in material incentives may entail a reduction in voluntarism (Heyer, Stewart and Thorp 2002), and the grassroots of Dalit movements are evaporating.

Group action aids development where it is focused, sustained and mapped on to active local networks. Dalit mobilisation reflects gender norms, however, and these characteristics are most evident among the secondary, women's wings: caste pride and militancy typify the hegemonic masculinity of the 'main' move-ments while local networking and organisation are the female preserve. This disjunction occasionally undermines the rhetorical commitment to women's rights, and the defence of group identity can adversely affect the autonomy of Dalit women: status-seeking behaviour has entailed the adoption of dowry, male activism has placed a heavier burden on supporting households, and caste conflicts impede Dalit women's access to public space.

It is the women's wings, however, that offer examples of the sustained commitment and organisation required to safeguard Dalit mobility. In a neigh-bouring village to Kodankipatti, for instance, Amulakka was one of a group of fifteen women in a credit union: 'We saw that all loans available here were for a huge amount of interest, and we questioned why we were forced to use such loan sharks. So, we have started up this union for ourselves' (Interview). Though modelled on an NGO pilot project, the scheme was more sustainable because it relied on mutual support and targeted issues that affected the women directly (access to credit, but also caste abuse, discrimination in ration shops, and access to drinking water). Their initiative and foresight are commendable but are born of necessity. As Amulakka observed in elucidating the rationale for the union: 'The women have more responsibilities and household expenditure and so they need the help more than men' (Interview).

Given the extent and success of Dalit mobilisation to date, both male and female networks offer a resource for equitable development. Best results, however, demand less top-down, power and control modes of organisation and a recapturing of the grassroots links that made them such a dynamic force against discrimination in the 1980s and 1990s. Localised, small-scale and targeted projects and networks do not lend themselves to rhetorical flourishes like 'a hit for a hit', but where movements have organised on this basis their gains have been impressive (cf. Thorp, Stewart and Heyer 2005: 917; Pattenden 2005).

Conclusions and implications

Running through this research is the interplay between social and material factors and the assertion that poverty cannot simply be measured in economic terms. Consideration must be given to the intangible goods of self-esteem, pride and dignity, which cannot be read as individual attributes but must be viewed in their group context. The experience of poverty is entangled with social status and is mediated by gender and caste. This finding is not novel but needs reemphasising in light of the THDR's blindness in this regard.

The THDR notes the pivotal importance of the primary sector. It rightly views declining productivity with alarm given the high proportion of people living in rural areas and dependent upon agricultural labour (Government of Tamil Nadu 2003: 132). The report thus considers how to increase economic growth and productivity. In addressing enrolment and retention levels and the quality of education, similarly, the recommendations refer to teacher recruitment and infrastructural improvements (ibid.: 134). Finally, the report seeks to ensure 'full-equality for women' by raising wages and employment opportunities (ibid.: 135–6). There is no reflection on the social conditions of labour, or its own findings that SC women are especially vulnerable to poverty and abuse.

Poverty in rural Tamil Nadu is inextricably bound up with caste as Chandra Bose illustrates at the beginning of the chapter. 'Isolation, political marginalisation and social exclusion', as Thorp, Stewart and Heyer argue, 'are . . . central to poverty and need to be addressed before long-term economic initiatives can be successful' (2005: 917). 'Without affecting the well-being of the dominant castes', Chandra Bose states, 'how will the lower castes get a solution?' Increasing non-agricultural opportunities could reinforce Dalits' independence from dominant landlords, but could equally marginalise Dalits further as others benefit from caste connections and attitudes (cf. Jeffrey, Jeffery and Jeffery 2004; Thorat and Newman 2007).

Contrary to the belief of Tamil Nadu Adi-Dravidar Welfare Minister, A. Thamizharasi, education and vocational training alone cannot address the inequities of caste (Hindu 2007b). First, education, skills training and assistance to entrepreneurs need to ensure that vulnerable social groups benefit. For instance, when recruiting teachers, Dalit role models could be selected and mechanisms developed to tackle endemic absenteeism and routine discrimination. Relying on the black box of 'education' and the invisible hands of the market in rural South India will allow discriminatory barriers to persist. Micro-organisation by the poor and marginalised is hugely significant here in addressing power imbalances and auditing the delivery of government projects (cf. Pattenden 2005; Ambasta, Shankar and Shah 2008).

Dalit movements in my research were pivotal to wrenching caste from its 'moorings', inculcating a sense of independence and monitoring government action. Rural Dalits face multiple barriers: physical and psychological insecurity, lack of resources and poor education. These disadvantages are 'cumulative' (Oommen 1990: 255), and political mobilisation, especially if it is sustained and rooted in local community participation, may be necessary to challenge the status quo. Where asymmetries in power are mapped on to resource allocations, Chambers rightly notes, 'the struggle against poverty is, has to be, a struggle for political and physical power' (Chambers 1983: 166). Equitable development in Tamil Nadu requires us to 'shift the grindstone of caste'.

Acknowledgement

This chapter was written as a paper for 'Rural development retrospect and prospect: a workshop for Judith Heyer'. I am grateful for Jens Lerche's insightful discussion of the original paper and to other participants for their observations and engagement. I am thoroughly indebted to Barbara Harriss-White and Judith Heyer for their detailed and constructive editorial reading of the chapter.

Notes

1 'Untouchables' are the lowest strata of the caste hierarchy. In 1950, the practice of untouchability was prohibited and Untouchables officially became 'Scheduled Castes' (SCs) by reference to a list of castes entitled to positive discrimination (reservations). Politically active SCs in Tamil Nadu, however, call themselves Dalit ('downtrodden'). While not all SCs use the term, I do so here because activists see other terms (Untouchable, SC, harijan) as demeaning. Backward Caste (BC) is the category of low-caste groups allotted reservations due to their social status. Many BCs, however, are politically powerful.
2 Empirical data were collected between 1998 and 1999. The multi-sited ethnography focussed on Dalit movement activists, motivations, modes of operation and ideological aspirations. The data consists of 30 group discussions, 32 formal and 30 informal interviews with activists, leaders, academics and non-participating Dalits. Interviews were complemented by participant observation.
3 Mosse (2007: 27) testifies to the power of such discourses when he notes that everyday social conflicts in his field-site are packaged in the language of caste because it is effective and carries weight.
4 Were land reform to be achieved on this basis, however, women would be left to mind the home, the family and the land. Inherent in such analysis is the conceptualisation of women's time as flexible and elastic.

264 *Hugo Gorringe*

5 Those Dalits who do own land fall into the category of marginal landowners, and their land is seldom irrigated (Gorringe 2005: 154).
6 Indeed, the Tamil Nadu Human Development Report (2003) notes a huge increase in marginal labour.
7 See Kapadia (1995); Harriss-White (1996); Harriss-White and Janakarajan (1997); and Prakash (Chapter 14 in this volume).
8 It is significant that this wage rise accompanied an increase in marginal labour. It is unlikely that higher wages could offset the casualisation of labour (see Vijayabaskar *et al.* 2004).

Bibliography

Ambasta, P., Shankar, V. and Shah, M. (2008) 'Two years of NREGA: the road ahead', *Economic and Political Weekly*, 43(8): 41–50.
Chakraborty, P. (2007) 'Implementation of employment guarantee: a preliminary appraisal', *Economic and Political Weekly*, 42(7): 548–51.
Chambers, R. (1983) *Rural Development: Putting the Last First*, Harlow: Longman.
—— (1995) 'Poverty and livelihoods: whose reality counts?', *Environment and Urbanization*, 7(1): 173–204.
Deshpande, A. (2002) 'Assets versus autonomy? The changing face of the gender–caste overlap in India', *Feminist Economics*, 8(2): 19–35.
Dinakaran (1999) 'More clashes between groups', *Tamil Paper*, Special Correspondent, 21 June 1999.
Epstein, S., Suryanarayana, A. and Thimmegowda, T. (1998) *Village Voices: Forty Years of Rural Transformation in South India*, New Delhi: Sage.
Gorringe, H. (2005) *Untouchable Citizens*, New Delhi: Sage.
—— (2006) 'Banal violence? The everyday underpinnings of collective violence', *Identities*, 13(2): 237–60.
Government of Tamil Nadu (2003) *Human Development Report*, New Delhi: Social Science Press.
Harriss-White, B. (1996) *A Political Economy of Agricultural Markets in South India*, New Delhi: Sage.
Harriss-White, B. and Janakarajan, S. (1997) 'From Green Revolution to rural industrial revolution in South India', *Economic and Political Weekly*, 32(25): 1469–77.
Heyer, J. (1989) 'Landless agricultural labourers' asset strategies', *IDS Bulletin*, 20(2): 33–40.
Heyer, J. (2000) *The Changing Position of Agricultural labourers in Villages in Rural Coimbatore, Tamil Nadu, between 1981/2 and 1996*, QEH Working Paper Series 57, Oxford: University of Oxford.
Heyer, J., Stewart, F. and Thorp, R. (2002) 'Conclusions' in J. Heyer, F. Stewart and R. Thorp (eds) *Group Behaviour and Development: Is the Market Destroying Cooperation?*, Oxford: Oxford University Press.
Hindu (2007a) 'Support leaders who work for welfare of Dalits', *The Hindu*, 18 June 2007. Available online: www.hindu.com/2007/06/18/stories/2007061854990800.htm (accessed 18 June 2007).
Hindu (2007b) 'Education alone can empower Dalits, says Minister', *The Hindu*, 5 October 2007. Available online: www.hindu.com/2007/10/05/stories/2007100560590800.htm (accessed 27 February 2008).
Hindu (2009) 'Women seek assured wages under NREGS', *The Hindu*, www.hindu.com/2009/09/24/stories/2009092452540300.htm (accessed 25 September 2009).

Jeffery, R., Jeffrey, C. and Jeffery, P. (2001) 'Social and political dominance in western UP: a Response to Sudha Pai', *Contributions to Indian Sociology*, 5(3): 213–35.

Jeffrey, C., Jeffery, R. and Jeffery, P. (2004) 'Degrees without freedom: assessing the social and economic impact of formal education on Dalit young men in North India', *Development and Change*, 35(5): 963–86.

Kapadia, K. (1993) 'Marrying money: changing preference and practice in Tamil marriage', *Contributions to Indian Sociology*, 27(1): 25–51.

——(1995) *Siva and Her Sisters*, Boulder: Westview.

Krishnakumar, G. (2007) 'Opening up rural knowledge connectivity', *The Hindu*, 6 February. Available online: www.hindu.com/edu/2007/02/06/stories/2007020600080100.htm (accessed 22 February 2008).

Mahadevan, G. (2006) 'Inclusive growth is IGNOU's priority', *The Hindu*, 11 December 2006. Available online: www.hindu.com/edu/2006/12/11/stories/2006121100590800.htm (accessed 22 February2008).

Mencher, J. (1988) 'Women's work and poverty', in D. Dwyer and J. Bruce (eds) *A Home Divided*, Stanford: Stanford University Press.

Mendelsohn, O. and Vicziany, M. (1998) *The Untouchables*, Cambridge: Cambridge University Press.

Moffatt, M. (1979) *An Untouchable Community in South India*, Princeton: Princeton University Press.

Mosse, D. (1994) 'Idioms of subordination and styles of protest among Christian and Hindu harijan castes in Tamil Nadu', *Contributions to Indian Sociology*, 27(1): 67–104.

——(2007) *Power and the Durability of Poverty: A Critical Exploration of the Links Between Culture, Marginality and Chronic Poverty*, Chronic Poverty Research Centre Working Paper 107.

Narayanan, S. (2008) 'Employment guarantee, women's work and childcare', *Economic and Political Weekly*, 43(9): 10–13.

Nihila, M. (1999) 'Marginalisation of women workers', *Economic and Political Weekly*, 34(16/17): WS21–7.

Oommen, T. (1990) *Protest and Change*, New Delhi: Sage.

Padmanabhan, B. (2004) 'A vision for rural India', *Frontline*, 21(19). Available online: http://frontline.in/fl2119/stories/20040924003711200.htm (accessed 26 February 2008).

Pai, S. (2000) 'New social and political movements of Dalits', *Contributions to Indian Sociology*, 34(2): 189–220.

Pattenden, J. (2007) 'Trickle-down solidarity, globalisation and dynamics of social transformation in a South Indian village', *Economic and Political Weekly*, 40(19): 1975–85.

Racine, J. and Racine, J. (1998) 'Dalit identities and the dialectics of oppression and emancipation', *Comparative Studies of South Asia, Africa and the Middle East*, XVIII(1): 5–20.

Scharma, B. (1990) *The Report of the Commissioner for SCs and STs: 29th Report: 1987–1989*, Faridabad: Government of India Press.

Scott, J. (1985) *Weapons of the Weak*, Berkeley: University of California Press.

Shah, M. (2007) 'Employment guarantee, civil society and Indian democracy', *Economic and Political Weekly*, 42(45/6): 43–51.

Sundari, S. (2005) 'Migration as a livelihood strategy: a gender perspective', *Economic and Political Weekly*, 40(22/23): 2295–303.

Thamukku (2002) 'Comprehensive wasteland programme', Thamukku, *Newsletter of the Dalit Resource Centre*, 3(12): 2.

Thorat, S. and Newman, K. (2007) 'Caste and economic discrimination: causes, consequences and remedies', *Economic and Political Weekly*, 42(41): 4121–4.

Thorp, R., Stewart, F. and Heyer, A. (2005) 'When and how far is group formation a route out of chronic poverty?', *World Development*, 33(6): 907–20.

Vera-Sanso, P. (2007) 'Increasing consumption, decreasing support: a multi-generational study of family relations among South Indian Chakkiliyars', *Contributions to Indian Sociology*, 41(2): 225–48.

Vijayabaskar, M., Swaminathan, P., Anandhi, S. and Balagopal, G. (2004) 'Human development in Tamil Nadu: examining linkages', *Economic and Political Weekly*, 39(8): 797–802.

Viramma, Racine, J. and Racine, J. (1997) *Viramma: Life of an Untouchable*, trans. W. Hobson, London: Verso.

Viswanathan, S. (2003) *Land Reforms in Reverse?*, Frontline, 20(5). Available online: www.frontline.in/fl2005/stories/20030314001205300.htm (accessed 27 February 2008).

World Bank (1997) *India: Achievements and Challenges in Reducing Poverty*, Washington, DC: World Bank.

13 Liberalisation and transformations in India's informal economy

Female breadwinners in working-class households in Chennai

Karin Kapadia

Introduction

In this chapter, the findings of a small pilot research project that I carried out in February 2008 in Chennai are used to explore key issues in the literature on contemporary urban India. Crucially, my micro level evidence appears to confirm what economists are finding at the macro level about the detrimental effects of liberalisation policies on the poorest sections of the population (Bhalla 2007; Chandrasekhar and Ghosh 2008, 2007a; Ghosh 2008a; Sen and Himanshu 2007; Srivastava 2007). My field data also raise important questions about trends in the employment of women workers and about the significance of women's work in India's low-wage urban informal economy.

India's poorest are often the lowest castes, that is, the Scheduled Castes or Dalits, the ex-'untouchables', who, in rural India, still constitute the largest percentage of landless agricultural labourers (Jha 2007; Heyer and Gopal Jayal 2009). Recognition of this double burden of class and caste that the poorest in India have to bear helps us to understand the processes by which the poor stay poor. This needs emphasis because the poorest are not only oppressed by economic class-based poverty, but also by the specifically caste-based form of dispossession that is termed caste discrimination (Ghosh 2008a, 2006a; Gorringe 2005; Lerche 1999). Further, India's culture and economy are pervaded by 'male bias' (see Elson 1991 on this concept) – a systemic bias in favour of men, extending from the household to the highest reaches of the economy, and resulting in pervasive discrimination against women in multiple ways. Muslims, many of whom are very poor, in addition face particular kinds of discrimination (Kalam 2007; Robinson 2007; Shah 2007; Wilkinson 2007), but its severity varies significantly by region, being much milder in Tamil Nadu than in the north (Fakhri 1999). My field investigations highlighted the complex ways in which class, caste, gender and religion contribute to widening the gap between the rich and the poor. My focus here is on the poorest urban working classes – the 'urban poor' – in the processes of socio-economic transformation. In particular, I discuss the possibility that in contexts where it is increasingly difficult for men to find employment, the burden on female primary breadwinners might be increasing so significantly that this might be leading to a feminisation of the low-wage informal economy. I link this possibility to longer-term socio-cultural and socio-economic changes that have transformed kinship and mutuality in Tamil Nadu over the last four decades.

The selection of women respondents

In the space of a ten-day field visit I met about fifty people in Chennai's slums, some of them very briefly. I had in-depth conversations with some thirty women in a range of informal-sector occupations. I was able to visit about half of these thirty women more than once and this improved the quality of the information they offered. Households were selected using the criterion that they should contain women doing paid work. My first contacts with the women respondents were made through NGOs and political organisations that were engaged in assisting them – in particular, a large Christian educational institution that ran a crèche for working mothers from the slums nearby and the Marxist Communist Party (the CPM) which had organised several workers' trade unions in Chennai's informal sector. Perhaps because of their trust in these organisations, the women I met were willing to talk to me, even though they were unceasingly busy with domestic work, childcare and, in some cases, home-based beedi-making work, when I met them. I met a wide range of women workers – Muslims, Hindus, Christians, Dalits and non-Dalits – but all of them were very poor and struggling to eke out a living in very difficult conditions in the slums of Chennai. Despite the small number of households visited, this brief field visit raises several interesting questions regarding the nature of transformations in the urban informal economy in the context of globalisation and liberalisation processes. Women workers in several different low-wage informal-sector occupations were interviewed in different locations. However, here I focus on only three occupations: (1) construction work, (2) beedi making, and (3) domestic service. The other informal-sector occupations I investigated briefly included embroidery and garments production in an export unit, flower- garland making, home-based tailoring for private customers, the making and vending of snack food (*idli*) on the street, and home-based outwork tailoring for a garments workshop.

This essay is in five parts: (1) transformations in Tamil kinship and mutuality, (2) macro, meso and micro levels of analysis, (3) the significance of low-wage women's work and women's breadwinning for the economy, (4) working conditions, labour relations and labour unions, and (5) tentative conclusions.

Transformations in Tamil kinship and mutuality

Female breadwinners in contexts of increasingly patriarchal kinship systems

A major finding from my field visit was the surprisingly large number of female primary breadwinners that appeared to be emerging in the low-wage informal economy. I had sought out poor women working in the informal sector in a fairly random way and had expected that I would find largely male breadwinner households in which women's paid work was secondary. This, certainly, is the local assumption about breadwinning in Chennai. The fact that around half of the thirty or so women whom I interviewed in some detail were the primary breadwinners of their households suggests that this assumption about male breadwinning may be quite wrong. If this finding is confirmed by further research it will prove to be one of great significance.

In rural Tamil Nadu, in the lowest castes and poorest classes, the vast majority of women traditionally worked outside the home in agriculture, together with the men of their families and communities (Dyson and Moore 1983; Kapadia 1995a). Such work was regarded as entirely acceptable, even in small landholding households. Members of the poorest rural caste/class sections – both Dalits and 'caste-Hindus' – did not perceive women as losing status if they did outside paid work: this was solely an upper- caste/class view. However, these rural gender norms have undergone a remarkable transformation in urban, 'modern' Tamil Nadu, where the poorest, lowest castes are eager to imitate the norms of the wealthy upper classes. This is not an imitation of Brahmin caste values, the so-called 'Sanskritisation' process put forward by Srinivas (1962). 'Sanskritisation', or the imitation of Brahminical behaviour, has had very little purchase in Tamil Nadu, due to the pervasive influence of the Dravidian Movement and Periyar's ideology of 'Self-Respect' (Geetha and Rajadurai 1998). Periyar's anti-Brahminism had a huge influence on the consciousness of even the poorest Dalit castes (Kapadia 1995a). What the urban lower castes copy is upper-class behaviour, signalling the supremacy of class status over caste status in contemporary Tamil Nadu – and in contemporary India (Kapadia 2002a, 2002b). However they don't look to the city's westernised elite for role models. Instead, it is the wealthy, conservative Tamil castes that are their moral exemplars.

These conservative rich castes continue to value the norms of female seclusion and, particularly, female subordination. This may be partly why poor urban women workers are subjected to strict new social controls by their male kin (especially their husbands and their brothers), who, today, seek to control their mobility, their earnings and their sexuality. Peri-urban Dalit women in modern non-farm employment are subjected to – and resist – similar controls. Documenting these processes, S. Anandhi, an insightful observer, notes that today one finds a 'context of [a] strengthening of patriarchal values, even while women try to affirm their new-found autonomy. The new patriarchal social norms ultimately limit the 'choice' and 'free-will' of women' (Anandhi 2007: 1058). Many factors contribute to this new and increasing patriarchalisation of Tamil society (also discussed in Kapadia 2002b). Dramatic indicators of this important socio-economic transformation of society are the recent increase in female foeticide and the falling sex ratio in Tamil Nadu (Agnihotri 2003; Athreya and Chunkath 2000) – signalling a tragic devaluation of women in a region previously celebrated for the relatively high status of women compared to most of North India (Dyson and Moore 1983). In all these processes, however, there are signs that women – perhaps particularly Dalit women – are strategically negotiating with and resisting the new patriarchal controls.

Over the last fifty years there has been increasing class differentiation within the Tamil castes. This class differentiation within castes has meant that older forms of Tamil 'preferential marriage' with close relatives, especially cross-kin, have been increasingly abandoned by better-off families in favour of marriage with upwardly mobile 'strangers' – non-kin within the same sub-castes (Kapadia 1995a: 46–67). The introduction of so-called 'dowry' – a device enabling a capital transfer to the bridegroom's family from the bride's family among the better-off classes (see Heyer 1992 on Gounder 'dowry') – was still in a nascent stage in rural Tamil Nadu in the late 1980s, when I did my first field research (Kapadia 1995a). 'Dowry' was beginning to replace 'brideprice', the traditional marriage system, which had highlighted women's valued place in rural Tamil society (ibid.). Crucially, marriage with cross-kin gave a very central place to a woman's natal family: they controlled the lives and marriages of her children. The almost proprietary rights that a woman's brother had over her children gave Tamil kinship a matrilateral emphasis, suggesting that it once was closely related to the kinship systems found in the contiguous cultural domains of Kerala and Sri Lanka (Kapadia 1995a: 14–15). Most importantly, Tamil women in all castes, including the Tamil Brahmin castes, could call on the continued support and close physical proximity of their natal kin after marriage, in sharp contrast to marriage in Gangetic North India. This continued support had several reasons – one was that a woman's agricultural labour was greatly valued and was regularly called on by her natal family even after her marriage. Another reason, noted above, was her brothers' almost proprietary rights over her children.

Among the poorest castes, especially the landless Dalit castes, a woman's fertility was of far greater social concern than her sexuality (Kapadia 1995a). This was for several reasons. Dalits had been historically dispossessed and forbidden the ownership of land (Habib 1983). Questions of inheritance therefore did not arise. Traditional kinship structures devalued the status of husbands and empowered brothers, and every child was viewed as a valuable source of labour power.

The profound changes that have occurred in Tamil kinship and mutuality are thrown into relief when we remember that, until very recent times, rural Dalit women controlled their own sexuality. This crucial element in Dalit social history has been ignored by most scholars, resulting in the fallacious assertion that Dalit and other landless very low-caste women have 'always' suffered from the 'threefold' discriminations of class, caste and patriarchy. Rural Dalit women did suffer from extreme disadvantages imposed by their class and caste locations, but in terms of gender norms within their own communities they were significantly better off than women in the wealthier, higher castes. This fact was regularly commented on, in my presence, by upper-caste women interviewed in earlier work who greatly envied the Dalit women their untrammelled mobility and relative autonomy (Kapadia 1995a). Among the Dalit castes it was easy for a woman to leave a violent or alcoholic husband. Both women and men had extramarital affairs which were common knowledge but caused little concern. Today the breakdown of traditional kinship structures is well under way and the natal family support that women called on, which so greatly strengthened their position within marriage, is fast disappearing, leaving lower-caste Tamil women far more vulnerable than they were before.

The increasing socio-economic differentiation between women and men in terms of employment and education has further worsened lower-caste women's status and increased their economic dependence on men. Thus, to understand the decline in the socio-cultural and economic status of lower-caste Tamil women today, we have to view their present predicaments in the context of the withdrawal of their kinship-based economic and social support. Within this context, the two processes of differentiation that I have discussed have been key – first, the still ongoing class differentiation within caste, replacing traditional isogamous (same-status) close-kin marriage with hypogamous (marrying up) 'stranger' marriage. Second, the increasing socio-economic gender differentiation between women and men within the same households. Their joint participation in agricultural labour has now given way to a situation where women with very little education have to depend on men with more education and better employment opportunities.

Anandhi is one of the few researchers to comment on the remarkable changes in Tamil kinship support structures. She reports an elderly Dalit woman as saying, 'In those days . . . [t]here was *no taboo attached to those who gave birth to a child before marriage*. There was community support even for those who made this mistake' (2007: 1058; emphasis added). This observation should alert us to the enormous cultural differences that have existed between the Dalits and the upper castes in Tamil Nadu until very recently. This should also warn us that, even today, when Dalit norms may appear very 'urbanised' in Chennai, these behaviours may not mean the same thing as the conservative norms of the city's wealthier classes. On the basis of the social history of rural Tamil Dalits I would expect this to be the case: namely that in Chennai today, apparently 'urbanised' behaviours may in fact encode very different cultural values for low-income Dalit women from those of better-off 'caste-Hindu' women, even though they seem to be similar. But this hypothesis would need detailed, longer-term ethnographic investigation to be substantiated – or rejected.

Women's work contexts in Chennai

In 2008, in Chennai, we found that households in which women were primary breadwinners were important across all the occupations that we studied. Significantly they also appeared to be prominent across religious and caste identities. It was class identity – belonging to the poorest sections of society – as well as, paradoxically, the new gender norms, particularly the specific forms of patriarchalisation under way in much of urban Tamil Nadu, that were among the complex factors behind the increasing incidence of primary female breadwinning. Our Chennai field data suggest that when impoverished families are on the breadline, it is the women, who are often already secondary breadwinners, who have to take on the main responsibility, as primary breadwinners, even if this goes against the new norms of their 'urbanised' caste identity. Their paid work creates many problems for low-waged urban women and, due to the new patriarchal norms, does not appear to give them autonomy or to automatically 'empower' them, contrary to the expectations of social scientists.

Padmini Swaminathan has put this paradox well: 'Approached from any discipline . . . women's participation in paid employment and particularly participation outside the household domain has uniformly been given a positive connotation' (2005a: 1).[1] Based on her own research, Swaminathan argues that the reality of women's work in Tamil Nadu today is precisely the opposite of these expectations: [C]ombining the tasks of production and reproduction . . . has a serious impact on well-being. For . . . poor working women . . . the wages received are no compensation for the high work intensity and the *pervasive practice of sexual harassment that they have to put up with on a day-to-day basis* (Swaminathan 2005a: 2; emphasis added).

Anandhi states that though working women 'have greater autonomy, this has also led to greater surveillance by men' (2007: 1058). While women workers lack control 'over the oppressive work conditions and social norms' (2007: 1059) their male kin always seek 'to exercise control over the physical mobility, earnings and sexuality of employed women' (2007: 1058).

These important feminist analyses of urban women's work argue that many of the claims made about the 'empowering' effects of women's paid work may not apply in Tamil Nadu's changing socio-cultural contexts. The paradoxes they highlight are of central importance to one of my contentions, namely that the very specific gendering of low-income women workers appears to construct them as docile, cheap labour, ready for urban employers to exploit. The possibilities for meaningful autonomy appear to be out of their reach at the present time.

Macro, meso and micro levels of analysis

My central argument is developed here by considering three levels of the economy: the macro (national) level, the meso (state and city) level and the micro (household) level. First, at the macro level I briefly review important recent analyses of statistical data. These analyses lay bare the class-structuring of the Indian economy and the destructive impact of neo-liberal policies on the poor. Second, at the state (and city) level I consider evidence of the caste segmentation of the economy. Finally, from a feminist perspective, I analyse gender relations within the working-class home and their implications for the wider economy. Nota bene: at all these levels of analysis, gender, caste/ethnic and class identities are also of great importance. It is purely for heuristic reasons that my argument is structured in this way. My central focus is on the household level, because this is where my field data are strongest. My main arguments will concern impoverished urban women workers.

The macro level

The current globalisation of India's economy consists of several elements, including, pre-eminently, the liberalisation and deregulation of the economy, the deliberate casualisation/informalisation of jobs, with a steady increase in low-grade, low-paid informal-sector work and an increasing inflow of foreign direct investment (FDI) across the spectrum of Indian services and manufacturing (Bhalla 2007; Chandrasekhar and Ghosh 2006, 2007b, 2008; Harriss-White and Sinha 2007; NCEUS 2007). Fundamental to India's present attractiveness to foreign investors are the lower labour costs across occupations when compared with the costs of labour in the developed economies and even in some other developing economies. But how are these lower labour costs, e.g. in the computer software industry or in BPO (business process outsourcing) sustained? They are sustained in a variety of ways, all including, crucially, the squeezing of labour costs at the bottom of the economy. In other words, the vulnerability of female and male workers and the deplorable, dangerous and highly exploitative conditions of women's and men's work in, for example, the construction industry, allow the middle classes 'to work for less', thus sustaining the relatively lower wage rates that make the computer software and BPO sectors so attractive to foreign investors. The different sectors of the economy are quite highly integrated, so that the very low wages and appalling conditions of work at the bottom of the economy *subsidise the salaries of the upwardly mobile Indian middle classes* (Ghosh 2008b; Srivastava 2007). As Ghosh has rightly put it: '*It is seldom recognised that the recent economic expansion has come about because of the contribution of the mass of Indian workers* rather than a few high-profile corporate magnates. Yet this huge contribution remains not only unsung, but unrewarded even in monetary terms' (2008b; emphasis added).

Chandrasekhar and Ghosh (2007a) describe the wages and working conditions at the lowest levels of the economy as an indictment of the neo-liberal policies that have enabled economic growth without social equity. They and others point out that India's spectacular economic growth has not been accompanied by commensurate growth in employment, observing, 'This makes growth non-inclusive in a country like India where there are no unemployment benefits and other social security schemes. This also ... accentuates inequality' (National Conference 2007).

The meso level

Here I consider the caste structuring of the labour market and of labour relations in the informal economy, arguing that caste discrimination is a sophisticated economic and political weapon. Our field study suggests that caste identity is crucial in segmenting even low-wage jobs in Chennai's informal labour markets. We found that those jobs that offered higher wages, and therefore higher status, were entirely monopolised by 'Caste Hindu' workers – these were, especially, jobs in the construction industry and also those in an embroidery export unit.

Construction work is extremely arduous, and dangerous, but it is comparatively well paid – at least in comparison with the abysmal wages that others at the bottom of the economy earn. So it was significant that all the construction workers we met were, without exception, of Vanniyar caste. Vanniyars are a powerful upwardly mobile omnibus caste category – including many sub-castes – with several million members. They constitute the single largest caste category in Tamil Nadu. Though extremely poor in some areas, the 'Caste Hindu' Vanniyars are well organised politically and have succeeded in gaining Most Backward Caste reservations for themselves. Their growing political power has been marked by sharp – and often very violent – clashes with Dalits in those areas where impoverished Vanniyars are just above Dalits in local hierarchies.

Similarly, there were no Dalits at all among the relatively well-paid workers in the embroidery export unit we visited – all the workers were ''Caste Hindus' with some education. On the other hand, domestic service, which is very low paid and is universally regarded as very low-status work, appeared to be largely the preserve of Dalit women. All the flower-garland wage workers we met were Dalit as well. Though paid more than domestic servants, their work was very arduous and their working conditions poor. This remarkable caste-based segmentation of occupations, even at the very bottom of the economy, is a significant indicator of the obstacles that Dalits in Tamil Nadu face. Our findings are confirmed by much other research (including de Neve 2005; Harriss 1980, 1982; Heyer in this volume; Kapadia 1995b).

In sum, there is considerable evidence that 'Caste Hindus' deliberately keep the Dalit castes out of all those occupations that offer higher wages and even the smallest degree of upward social mobility. In an alarming economic context of growing rates of unemployment and a paucity of jobs (Chandrasekhar and Ghosh 2007b), it appears that the more powerful castes corner the better jobs, leaving almost none for impoverished Dalits. Thus, neo-liberal arguments that the liberalisation of the Indian economy benefits everyone are utterly misleading. On the contrary, liberalisation is widening the already huge gap between the rich and the poor in India. Those who are better off use the well-established strategic instrument of caste discrimination to safeguard their own political and economic interests and to keep others, especially Dalits, 'down'. Newspaper reports make it crystal clear that this is indeed how many Tamil 'Caste Hindu' communities think: their concern is to ensure that they keep Dalits 'in their place' – by which they mean deferent, servile and completely subordinate (Gorringe 2005).

An extensive literature shows that caste discrimination is not an anachronistic remnant of ritual hierarchy, nor has it ever been a religious response: on the contrary, caste discrimination has been and continues to be a sophisticated economic and political instrument of class subjugation (for recent contributions see Madheswaran and Attewell 2007; Thorat and Newman 2007). So-called 'caste' is a socio-cultural construction: it is an 'ideology' in the Marxist sense, a deliberate mystification of social reality by the politically and economically dominant classes in order to protect their vested interests. It is no surprise, therefore, that caste identities continue to thrive and that caste discrimination is used very actively to deliberately segment labour markets in ways that benefit better-off 'Caste Hindus' and prevent the upward mobility of Dalits.

It is thus no accident that a large majority of the IT professionals in Chennai are either Brahmins or upper castes. Not only do the upper castes – who are identical with the upper middle classes – monopolise the new IT jobs, they also strongly defend the globalisation and liberalisation policies of the government, precisely because they are doing so well out of these policies, as shown by Fuller and Narasimhan (2007: 143–4) for Chennai and Upadhya (2004) for Bangalore.

The micro level

We now turn the analytical gaze to gender relations within the household. Gender relations vary sharply in the highly differentiated caste, class and religious groups that constitute the different sections of Chennai society. I argue here that gender relations are crucially important to what is happening in the urban informal economy. Our case studies suggest that impoverished women workers very often have to subsidise and support male workers – their husbands, if they are married (as in our field data) and their brothers, if the women are unmarried (as in Anandhi, Jeyaranjan and Krishnan 2002). This subsidising and support happens in several ways: first, through women's unpaid labour within the household in the form of their unending care work and domestic work (cf. Folbre 1994 on the importance of women's unpaid work to the economy). Second, it happens through the cultural norms that give men extensive authority over women. The paradox is that the hegemonic gender norms, recently appropriated by Dalit and lower-caste 'Caste Hindu' men, valorise male breadwinning. But, partly due to major changes in employment structures, low-waged working-class men are finding it increasingly difficult to find suitable employment (Chandrasekhar and Ghosh 2007a; Ghosh 2006a). They therefore often contribute either very little or even nothing at all to family income – while demanding that they be fed, cared for and housed by their working wives. Why are they allowed to get away with this? Partly it is because it is generally recognised that they are not able to access productive employment. But it is often also because of the power of the patriarchal norms that they invoke. Sometimes it is also because of the violence that men use against women who defy them. Several accounts (Anandhi, Jeyaranjan and Krishnan 2002; Swaminathan 2005a) suggest this, as do our own case studies. Thus a central paradox remains: for Chennai's impoverished working-class women, 'nagarikam' ('urban sophistication') connotes the continuing attempt by working-class husbands to subordinate them, while at the same time requiring them to go out to work to support their husbands.

The conditions of work at the lowest levels of the informal economy in Tamil Nadu are appalling. They are not only very detrimental to health but also confront female workers with the frightening dangers of endemic sexual exploitation (Swaminathan 2005b). Poor working women, across caste and religion, therefore usually see it as a very unwelcome imposition when they are forced by their male kin to take on arduous, unpleasant and sexually dangerous wage-work outside the household. Thus, indigent men try to have it both ways – on the one hand they demand the female subordination that is part of the recently adopted hegemonic family model, but, on the other hand, they are unable to offer the male breadwinning – with its implicit protection of female sexual 'honour' – that is at the heart of the upper-class model. Thus, they try to enforce patriarchal values, but lack the material resources needed to legitimise these values (Anandhi, Jeyaranjan and Krishnan 2002). Women are left to deal with the resulting contradictions, forced by family survival needs to be breadwinners in a lower-caste context that now decries and devalues female autonomy and independence (also see Vera-Sanso 2001).

Swaminathan has observed, 'The search for cheap prices has more often than not been translated to mean a search for cheap labour, with women's labour bearing the brunt of the changing nature of the capitalist onslaught' (2005a: 3). The macro-level analyses discussed above, the recent research of Anandhi , Jeyaranjan and Krishnan (2002), Anandhi (2007) and Swaminathan (2005a, 2005b) and my own anecdotal evidence of significant numbers of primary female breadwinners together suggest that Swaminathan's insight is of general relevance. Perhaps the brunt of the current liberalisation and globalisation processes is indeed being borne, in all its weight, by impoverished, 'cheapened' women workers. If this is the case, it raises the important question of whether a feminisation of the very low-wage urban workforce is under way, not only in Chennai, but also elsewhere in metropolitan India (see Roy 2008 for Kolkata). I use the term 'feminisation' deliberately, in order to draw analytic and policy attention to these important recent changes in the roles of women workers in the informal economy. My data raise the question of what the wider implications of such a feminisation of the low-wage informal economy might be.

The significance of women's low-wage work and women's breadwinning for the economy

Apart from the important reasons already discussed, it also appears that demand from employers is a key factor in the possible feminisation of jobs: Chennai employers see women workers as easier to discipline, and categorise them as secondary, not primary, wage earners. Employers therefore pay women significantly less than men. Chennai's women workers are seen as much cheaper and far more docile than male workers, and, consequently, as less likely to go on strike. If we are witnessing a feminisation of the urban low-wage economy, then this process is resulting in a transition from a low-wage male workforce to an even lower-wage female workforce.

I found anecdotal evidence suggesting that such a process might be under way. We came across a young Muslim man in north Chennai, who was employed as a cleaner in one of the new corporate offices associated with the burgeoning software industry and the BPO call centres. Because the new corporates pay much higher wages for cleaning jobs than do ordinary households, these better-paid jobs have been monopolised immediately by young men. The new jobs are dignified by an English term that is retained in Tamil – they are called '*housekeeping velai*' ('housekeeping work'). There is no mention here of the specificities of these jobs, which include cleaning toilets and sweeping – 'inferior' and 'polluting' tasks that have traditionally been associated with the Dalit castes and with women. The young man told us that he and his friends, who were all employed in this new 'housekeeping work', had discovered that acquaintances elsewhere in the city were getting higher wages for the same kind of work. They had therefore consulted their contractor, who had advised them to demand more from their management, and to threaten to go on strike, because the corporate was reneging on its promise to the contractor.[2] When, with this encouragement, they made this threat, they were immediately told that their wages would be raised. When we spoke, this raise had just been promised.

This narrative should be read together with another story, from another male informant, who also happened to be Muslim. He claimed that there was a strong trend, on the part of all urban employers, to prefer women workers to men. Pointing out that local cultural norms had a lot to do with the behaviour of men after work hours, he said that, after work, women workers hurried home to look after their children, but men did no such thing. Instead, they congregated in various places to relax with their friends. During their chats, men asked each other about work and pay – and found out very quickly if cleaners in other offices were earning higher wages than themselves. Women, on the contrary, had no such opportunity to meet and therefore had much less information about the labour market. He insisted that, even if women knew that higher wages were being paid elsewhere for the same work, they were extremely unlikely to go on strike because they felt that they carried the primary responsibility for feeding their families and therefore could not risk losing their jobs. These interesting observations suggest that the dynamic that is at work in female breadwinner households is, as I have already noted, at odds with the assumptions made in much of the Euro-American literature on women earners, to the effect that paid work 'automatically' gives women power and status. On the contrary, our data suggest that the cultural dynamic at work here is deeply harmful to women's interests, while being extremely profitable for employers.

This is because among the poorest and lowest castes/classes there is increasing acceptance of a norm that places the responsibility for family breadwinning on the shoulders of women, while denying them the rights and privileges that normally attend wage earning. Moreover, this is happening within a patriarchal-ising social context, where men are the arbiters of power. Such a culturally legitimated notion of responsibility without rights for women within the household domain plays directly into the hands of employers, who, within the factory or work site, are able to extract the maximum work from women for the minimum of wages. In other words, the 'docile' female worker is constructed primarily within the household, not in the workplace, but she is kept firmly in her sub-ordinated place in the workplace too.

The paradoxical dynamic that I describe here is widespread in India – it is not limited to Tamil Nadu by any means. This dynamic consists of the social perception that, in extremis, when impoverished men are unable – or, as often happens, unwilling – to take on the burden of breadwinning, this responsibility is automatically devolved to women. This is despite the fact that women are generally perceived as 'weaker' than men and almost universally regarded (except in rural Dalit communities and impoverished tribal communities) as requiring to be firmly subordinated by men at all times. In other words, the paradox is that men see themselves as the unquestioned heads of their households and as the patriarchal arbiters of power and rule, despite the fact that they are not fulfilling their pre-eminent male role of being the main breadwinners. The fact that they thus lack legitimacy for their claim to absolute authority creates conundrums and dilemmas that they, in the final event, resolve with violence, in order to subordinate women (cf. Anandhi, Jeyaranjan and Krishnan, 2002).

Gooptu's research among unemployed male jute-mill workers in Kolkata has uncovered a situation that seems startlingly similar to that described by Anandhi, Jeyaranjan and Krishnan (2002) and Anandhi (2007) in Tamil Nadu. Gooptu observes:

> In the social and political milieu of the mills, a 'male public sphere' had been forged, and this was accompanied by an ideological emphasis on the domestic role of women . . . Against this background, women's recent re-entry into the workforce has had significant implications for social identities and gendered subjectivities. Not only are women now taking up employment, usually part-time self-employment and working as domestic servants, they have adopted other coping strategies as well . . . Men have responded in contradictory ways to this situation of women's workforce participation and their assertiveness. While they are eager for women to generate income, they fear the erosion of their own authority or they fear that this could lead to sexual laxity . . . Many emphasised that home-based low paid work is not likely to be accepted by men, for men are used to a different work regime and culture, and it would be demeaning or beneath their dignity and status to do these seemingly menial, 'feminine' jobs, of low status and poor pay.
>
> (Gooptu 2007: 1928)

Breman (2004) has documented a very similar de-industrialised context where unemployed male textile mill workers in Ahmedabad refused 'demeaning' work and sent their wives out to support their families. Chitra Joshi (2003) has reported a similar survival strategy from de-industrialised Kanpur.

Gooptu's observations above recall some of the key themes discussed by Anandhi and Swaminathan regarding men's perceptions of women's work. It is important to note her male informants' comments on the appropriateness – or not – of certain kinds of 'feminine' jobs for men. As we have just seen, when cleaning jobs were suddenly paid much more because they were in the new corporate offices, what was otherwise indubitably a 'feminine' job was immediately transformed into a (largely) male monopoly, because of the relatively high wage on offer.

The phenomenon of men refusing, or seeking to abandon, work they consider 'demeaning or beneath their dignity' has had very significant consequences in the context of bonded/tied labour, both in agriculture (da Corta and Venkateshwarlu 1999) and in rural small-scale industry (Kapadia 1999a, 1999b). Here, men's refusal to continue doing demeaning work has had important implications because they have exited from the humiliating conditions of tied work by transferring their debts and their bonded status to their wives, who have thus been converted from free wage labour into bonded labour. Further, it is very clear that the huge exodus of male labour from agriculture and the resultant feminisation of the agricultural workforce (a new trend that was noted quite early in Kapadia and Lerche 1999) is part of a dynamic where men leave work that is poorly paid to seek better-paid, higher-status work elsewhere. But they leave it to their wives and female kin to look after their children and to provide for the survival of their households.

While the National Commission for Enterprises in the Unorganised Sector (NCEUS) does indeed note the feminisation of agricultural labour in its important and comprehensive Report (NCEUS 2007), it unfortunately does not consider the possibility that this feminisation may mean a huge increase in the percentage of rural female primary breadwinners – nor do its policy discussions sufficiently consider the wider implications of the feminisation of agriculture for the rural poor.

There is significant recent evidence that the burden of breadwinning on poor rural women may indeed have become extreme. This evidence exists in the fact that the recent National Rural Employment Guarantee Act (NREGA) studies that have provided a breakdown of numbers of workers by sex suggest that NREGA work is being taken up primarily by women in many parts of rural India. Women hugely outnumber men, providing 80 per cent to 90 per cent of the NREGA workforce: in Tamil Nadu 'women constitute an overwhelming proportion (more than 80 per cent) of NREGA workers' (Narayanan 2008: 10). And in Rajasthan, 'According to the collector of Dungarpur . . . about 90 per cent of the NREGA workers are women . . . The reason for the greater participation of women is that the men have migrated out' (Bhatty 2006: 1966).

All this evidence suggests that the significance of women's work – especially impoverished women's work – may be huge and growing in the Indian economy. It is undoubtedly so in agriculture and this may possibly be the case in the urban informal economy as well. Yet women's work, even in 2008, is still almost completely ignored by India's policymakers. One of the central aims of this chapter is, therefore, to call for very urgent policy attention to low-wage women's work and breadwinning – and to the important issues that they raise for the wellbeing and survival of the poorer 75 per cent of the population.

Working conditions, labour relations and labour unions

The women we met worked in uncertain, very low-paid jobs, which had no legislative protection of any kind – even the beedi-workers in our case studies were all casual workers, entirely vulnerable to the whims of their employers. Because of time constraints we were not able to delve into women's working conditions in detail. However, we were able to get a rough impression of certain aspects of labour relations.

Construction labour

We witnessed very poor working conditions for construction workers – for example, we found a wailing baby hung in a cloth cradle inside an extremely dangerous, busy building site. Crèches are supposed to be provided at work sites – but they do not exist. The NCEUS notes the deplorable fact that statutory provisions and protection for construction workers have been completely ignored by state governments (2007), while a recent editorial in the *Economic and Political Weekly* declares that it is outrageous that state governments have so totally ignored their statutory duties to construction workers that most of them have not even bothered to set up the statutorily required welfare boards (Editorial 2008: 5).

None of the construction workers we saw wore protective gear of any kind. Women construction workers spoke of workplace accidents as if they were commonplace, everyday events – one middle-aged woman had fallen off the ladder just the previous day. She showed us her bandaged shoulder. She had received no help from the employer or her contractor. These women workers also told us of workplace deaths – two of them had lost their husbands, who had been crushed to death in workplace accidents. The central government has passed legislation requiring compensation to be paid to the families of construction workers killed in workplace accidents. But these benefits are administered by welfare boards, and, to avail of benefits, construction workers have to register themselves with these boards. Most workers are totally unaware of this requirement. A recent newspaper report states that of 'an estimated 40 lakh construction labourers in the State [Tamil Nadu] . . . [only] 11 lakh had registered themselves with the welfare boards. Many construction workers were still unaware of the welfare boards' (The Hindu 2008). A woman worker who had lost her husband in such an accident was told, in our presence, by the CPM union leader that she could not hope to get any compensation because she had not been registered at the time of the accident. This is shockingly unfair, given the extreme poverty of most construction workers. But this situation also highlights the fact that, while workers need the support of an active union to access even their statutory rights, even this is not enough when the state remains recalcitrant. Within the ten days of our field visit, the CPM-organised construction workers were called out on strike to demonstrate in front of the Tamil Nadu State Social Welfare Board office against the government for its indifference to their plight. Their grievance was that the various promised benefits had not been disbursed, including the compensation for work-related injury and death. The comments of the women after their demonstration were eloquent testimony to their indignation against the state government.

It is significant that, though the great majority of construction workers we met were female, their union leader was male. This phenomenon, of the leader being male despite the vast majority of union members being female, was found in both the CPM construction workers' union and the CPM beedi workers' union. The male union leader told us that he was very upset that the ruling DMK party continued to treat CPM labour demands with disdain, even though both these political parties were partners in the national coalition government. His ruminations did not interest the women workers: what engaged them were the injustices they faced.

Beedi work

The beedi workers' union seemed even worse than the construction workers' union. Here again, it was the CPM that had organised beedi workers in an impoverished Muslim residential area in north Chennai. But the relationship between the male Muslim union leader and the Muslim women workers was highly problematic. Despite his seeming sympathy for the women workers, he appeared to have been bought over by the management. When we were sitting in his office he gave us an account of the industry that was extremely sympathetic to the employers. The fact that his rendition of 'the beedi story' came just minutes after an extremely lacklustre strike that he had organised made his allegiance seem even more dubious.

I had made a point to be present at the beedi workers' strike as I was interested to see how Muslim women would behave on strike – would they march bravely through the streets? Would they shout and wave flags? I was disappointed: the so-called 'strike' was so quiet that it was almost a secret! When we arrived we found a dozen women standing in absolute silence in a little huddle by the locked gate of the beedi factory. They were being harangued by the union leader, but even he was speaking rather softly, not trying to draw the attention of the general public. The general air was one of depressed embarrassment, rather than defiance.

Later 'H', one of the few younger beedi women workers, told us that the union leader had called the strike to protest the unfairly low price that was being paid to beedi workers. In this area, virtually all the beedi workers were women – only a handful of elderly men still did this work. According to long-standing labour laws, beedi workers have rights and protections (NCEUS 2007), but none of these rights or protections existed for the women workers we met because they were now informalised and categorised as casual labour even though they had been doing this work for decades.

Beedi work is home-based – these Muslim women did their beedi work in-between their domestic and childcare tasks, working steadily all day. H and others told us that they should have been getting Rs.55 per thousand beedis, the number of beedis a worker is expected to make in a day, but they were being paid only Rs.35 per thousand. The women had learnt that other beedi factory owners in Chennai were paying their workers Rs.55 so they felt very aggrieved.

They said, 'If we argue with them, asking for a better wage, they just say, "If you don't want to do this work, don't do it! Leave!"'[3]

The account of the CPM union leader centred on the difficulties faced, not by the women workers, but, on the contrary, by the Muslim factory owners. He told us that beedi was a 'dying industry' because beedi smokers had become 'modern' and now preferred cigarettes. In his view, the women workers were therefore being unreasonable in making demands, because the factory owners were having to curtail production and faced 'many difficulties'. Most of them had moved their factories out of north Chennai into rural Tamil Nadu, he said, because rural female labour was 'not so difficult' and made fewer demands. The women whom he claimed to represent were, in his view, lacking in skill and were slow, inferior workers who did not understand that their product had a declining market and who therefore made 'unreasonable demands for better wages'. This union leader seemed, by his own account, to have been completely co-opted by the employers.

During our discussions, the women expressed their frustration and utter helplessness regarding their work conditions. They said that Muslim women today preferred other, slightly better-paid employment. Those who did not have very young children and who were able to leave their homes for a few hours every day went to the 'plastics' workshops and factories to collect home-based 'outwork'. They sat at home, paring the rough edges off small plastic bottles, which they carried home from the workshops in huge sacks. This 'plastics' home-based work paid only a little better than beedi work, but, our informants emphasised, it was better work because it was 'not so humiliating'. They found beedi work humiliating because it involved them in interminable quarrels with the middlemen over wages, as the problem of defective leaves came up almost daily. Fed up with this and their miserable wages, they no longer regarded beedi work as a proper job, but saw it as merely a secondary occupation with which to fill in leisure time.

The most impoverished Muslim women, they said, actually worked on the shop floor in the plastics factories. But 'decent' Muslim women avoided such work, because the mixed-sex shop floor carried the constant threat of sexual abuse from the supervisors and male workers. Impoverished women – across religion and caste – avoided mixed-sex work because of routine sexual harassment. This explains why most poor women preferred home-based work: it kept them safe from men.

Our field visits to the beedi workers made it starkly obvious to us that the living conditions of our Muslim respondents were even worse, in some cases, than those of our Dalit respondents. It is only very recently that the central government has acknowledged that very many Muslims are deeply impoverished and almost as much in need of special assistance as Dalits and Scheduled Tribes (Basant 2007). The NCEUS has recently provided important evidence on this, too, showing that Muslims are in fact much worse off than the Other Backward Classes, and only just above the Dalits and Scheduled Tribes with regard to the incidence of poverty and lack of education (Sengupta, Kannan and Raveendran 2008: 59).

Domestic service

In February 2007, Chandrasekhar and Ghosh published an important paper investigating the actual numbers of women employed in various activities in urban India. They stated:

> The results are quite startling, especially in the context of the much-trumpeted high output growth rates which are widely felt to have predominantly affected urban India in positive ways ... The biggest single increase after apparel – and the category of work that is now *the single largest employer for urban Indian women* – has been among those employed in private households. In other words, *women working as domestic servants now number more than 3 million, and account for more than 12 per cent of all women workers in urban India.*
>
> (Chandrasekhar and Ghosh 2007a; emphasis added)

They observed in another paper:

> It is indeed disturbing to see that the greatest labour market dynamism has been evident in the realm of domestic service. This is well known to be poorly paid and often under harsh conditions – and certainly, it cannot be seen as a positive sign of a vibrant dynamic economy undergoing positive structural transformation.
>
> (Chandrasekhar and Ghosh 2007b)

My case studies entirely support this analysis. Domestic service was both the most widespread occupation we came across, as well as the most despised. It had the lowest status of all the jobs we encountered, precisely because wages were so dismally low. The caste status of women in domestic service also tended to be low – almost all the women domestics we met were 'Adi Dravidar' (Paraiyar Dalits).

As in the rest of India, domestic servants in Chennai today are very largely female (Neetha 2004). Thirty years ago the domestic servant in Chennai was a full-time worker, working from early morning to evening in one household, in a work relationship that usually lasted many years. This relationship, with its feudal overtones, has become much rarer today, when a domestic servant seldom works all day for the same family. Instead, she works for one or two hours at most for three to four families every day – and her relationship with her employers has very little of the old patron–client overtones about it. Recently, agencies have started to provide migrant, young, largely non-Dalit women as trained, live-in maids, a phenomenon noted elsewhere in metropolitan India (see Neetha 2004 on Delhi). These young women constitute a better-paid, superior category of domestic servant. Our Dalit respondents, on the contrary, were just impoverished women who desperately needed paid work. They found their employment in low-paid domestic service through their neighbours, acquaintances or kin, not through any agency.

When we spoke with 'M', who worked as a domestic servant, we had to sit down in the middle of the road, on a very tattered reed mat. I was acutely embarrassed by the total lack of privacy for our interview, because we quickly gathered an interested audience. But we had no choice; M's rented home was a tiny concrete cubicle, so small that even three people could not sit on the floor. Sitting in the dust in that slum road, M told us that, unlike those in government jobs, their monthly wages did not go up to meet inflation – and that therefore it was very obvious that those who depended on this type of waged work (i.e. waged work that was not unionised or index-linked to inflation) suffered the most from inflation. I asked M whether she could not put this to her employer, to press her for a pay rise. M looked at me quizzically for a moment, then said, with a touch of scorn, 'She reads the newspapers every day – do you think she doesn't know?' I was silenced.

Our case studies suggested that by 2008 impoverished Dalit women were very much a part of the market for domestic servants. This marked a sea-change in caste mores in the city. Forty years earlier it had been very rare for an upper-caste household to employ a Dalit servant because of the upper-caste belief that a Dalit would 'contaminate' their home. Today even Brahmin families employ Dalit servants. The NCEUS notes that caste-wise, across India, the largest percentage of domestic workers today are Dalits (NCEUS 2007). This is clearly because of the low pay and the very low status held by domestic service. Significantly, the NCEUS also notes that there has recently been a very significant increase in the demand for domestic servants in India's large cities and urban areas (ibid.). This increasing demand from the growing middle classes probably explains the tightening labour market for domestic servants in Chennai though from a low level.

The NCEUS also notes that one of the biggest obstacles faced by domestic servants today is that they lack trade unions, largely because domestic servants were historically not considered to be full-fledged workers and so – like most workers in the informal economy – were totally ignored by the trade unions (NCEUS 2007). However, fledgling attempts at unionisation are being pursued in some of the largest cities, including Chennai, some of them under the auspices of the New Trade Union Initiative (NTUI). One of the difficulties this initiative faces is, ironically, a lack of support from the established trade unions who continue to be extremely patriarchal. Sujata Mody, a Chennai union leader of women working in domestic service has stated that the trade union movement continues to have scant respect for working women (Pallavi 2006). None of the women domestic servants whom we met was a member of any union.

Despite gaining access to domestic service, all the Dalit women we interviewed faced a hidden barrier – none of them was ever asked to cook. This is significant because, in conservative upper-caste understandings, the kitchen has to be carefully guarded from 'pollution' (cf. Dickey 2000: 479). The fact that busy middle-class housewives – several of whom were in full-time employment – took on the burden of cooking every day, instead of giving their maidservants this chore, tells us something rather worrying about caste sensibilities in Chennai. It is no accident at all that the subtle intricacies of the caste prejudices of the modernised middle classes begin to be revealed within the home, for social identities start at home.

Tentative conclusions

In this chapter I have focused on a section of the low-wage informal economy and have argued: (1) that the participation of women workers is surprisingly large, and (2) –even more surprising and more important – that a large number, maybe half, of these women workers are the main breadwinners of their families. If this latter finding is indeed more widely the case, this tells us at least two things.

First, that government policymakers and planners need to give women workers much more policy importance than they have so far. If it is indeed impoverished women who carry the burden of family survival when all else fails (and the NREGA data so far appear to suggest this), then the enormous importance of women's labour has to be given its due importance and structures of support and protection put in place – as indeed protection and labour rights need to be put in place for male workers, too. A simple way to start here might be to ensure that: (1) women are given exactly the same wages as men for the same work; (2) to ensure, too, that minimum wages are set at a decent level, and (3) that these minimum wages are actually paid. Decent minimum wages which ensure a living wage – a wage which supports a family – will need to be paid to women as well as men, if our findings here are found to represent the wider picture.

Second, if large numbers of low-waged women are becoming the primary earners of their families, then something deeply paradoxical is happening in contemporary South India. There are, unfortunately, many signs that indicate that women's status in South Indian society is steadily worsening: (1) the transformation of South Indian kinship and the breakdown of cross-kin marriage systems have meant a dramatic erosion of natal family support for women; (2) the spread of so-called 'dowry' demands has meant that the birth of daughters is now often seen as an unwanted financial liability (this has been accompanied by the spread from North India to South India of 'dowry murders' ('bride-burning') and 'dowry harassment' (the harassment of brides by their in-laws)); (3) falling sex-ratios are spreading in South India, and (4) television – which is very biased towards deeply male-biased North Indian values – is greatly aiding both an epidemic of consumerist values and a commodification and denigration of women. Violence against women is already widespread and society is becoming less, not more, safe for women. This is despite the rising rates of education and well-paid employment for upper-class and elite women. In this male-biased socio-economic context, it seems clear that when impoverished women are forced, by family poverty and male unemployment (or male recalcitrance), to go out to earn a living, this is not a positive sign of female empowerment. Far from it, this is yet another sign of the many ways in which women are being instrumentally used by men – both their husbands and their employers – to further male interests. Given that male-biased norms permeate society – and all levels of government

– it is not surprising that no notice is taken and very little policy attention is given to working-class women's huge participation in the economy and to their crucially important role as family providers, whether primary or secondary.

Whether or not there is actually a feminisation of the low-wage informal economy going on, women's participation in this low-wage economy is clearly immense and growing. It demands policy attention and it demands government support, as indeed do the women themselves. They deserve welfare and government assistance for their families, statutory regulation of their working conditions, protection for their unions, and, at the very least, decent wages for their hard labour. Labour rights are not only their right – they are their due. Because it is on their backs that the current 'economic miracle' of 10-per-cent growth is being built. The desperately low wages and appalling conditions of work at the bottom of the economy that women workers face are destroying them and their families. This exploitation is indefensible. The authors of the important NCEUS Report have shown that a shocking 75 per cent of India's population continues to be poor: 'An overwhelming majority of the Indian population, around three quarters, is poor and vulnerable and it is a staggering 836 million as of 2004–2005' (Sengupta, Kannan and Raveendran 2008: 58). They also point out that 444 million or 40.8 per cent of the population are extremely poor and very vulnerable (ibid.). In the context of the current spectacular economic growth, the worsening standards of living of Indian labour, both female and male, are utterly inexcusable. All the specious arguments made by the government and the corporates, to defend the 'flexibilisation of labour' and their meretricious neo-liberal policies, are shown up as completely unjustifiable and deeply damaging to the vast majority of the Indian people, who continue, even in 2008, to constitute India's labouring poor.

Acknowledgement

I am deeply grateful to S. Anandhi, whose advice and support were invaluable in making this research possible. I also thank Padma Balaji, who very ably assisted my research for ten days in Chennai in February 2008. Judith Heyer and Barbara Harriss-White have provided unfailing encouragement: Judith Heyer's input has been huge. I am particularly indebted to Jayati Ghosh for her quick response to my queries and her helpful advice on further readings. I hope to discuss her helpful response in a forthcoming paper. Any mistakes in this chapter are mine.

Notes

1 Page numbers here refer to the printout of the text emailed to me by the author as I was unable to access the book.
2 This incident is an atypical example of subcontracting in India – usually the subcontracted workers are paid by their own contractor and have to demand their wage rise from him, not, as in this case, from the corporate management. But the subcontracted workers in this instance are entirely typical in another way – they are

part of the huge and growing informal workforce that is employed in formal enterprises – one of the central strategies by which formal-sector firms evade labour laws and also evade responsibility for disciplining workers, while simultaneously gaining access to vulnerable workers who can be exploited far more easily and paid much lower wage rates. Ghosh (2008b) discusses the massive and growing use of a female informal workforce in subcontracted labour; Parry (1999, forthcoming) and NCEUS (2007) provide ethnographic and statistical evidence, respectively, on the use of informal labour in very large formal-sector enterprises.

3 They had an additional complaint, which was that they were being paid even less through a sustained deception. To wrap a thousand beedis, they were given a certain number of dried leaves by their contractor. These dried leaves had to be cut down to the right size, filled with tobacco powder, rolled up into little cheroots and tied. But the dried leaves were always of poor quality: many had to be thrown away. The women were forced to buy extra leaves from their contractors at their own cost to make up the required thousand beedis. Thus a woman often had to make an extra outlay of Rs.5–10 per day, reducing her actual earnings to a paltry Rs.25 for an entire day's labour.

Bibliography

Agnihotri, S. (2003) 'Survival of the girl child', *Economic and Political Weekly*, 38(4): 4351–60.

Anandhi, S. (2007) 'Women, work and abortion: a case study from Tamil Nadu', *Economic and Political Weekly*, 42(12): 1054–9.

Anandhi, S., Jeyaranjan, J. and Krishnan, R. (2002) 'Work, caste and competing masculinities: notes from a Tamil village', *Economic and Political Weekly*, 37(43): 4397–406.

Athreya, V. and Chunkath, S.R. (2000) 'Tackling female infanticide: social mobilisation in Dharmapuri, 1997–99', *Economic and Political Weekly*, 35(49): 4345–8.

Basant, R. (2007) 'Social, economic and educational conditions of Indian Muslims', *Economic and Political Weekly*, 42(10): 828–32.

Bhalla, S. (2007) 'Inclusive growth', National Conference on Making Growth Inclusive with Reference to Employment Generation, 28–29 June 2007, Jawaharlal, New Delhi: Nehru University. Available online: www.macroscan.com/spfea/jun07/PDF/Sheila_Bhalla.pdf (accessed 15 May 2008).

Bhatty, K. (2006) 'Employment guarantee and child rights', *Economic and Political Weekly*, 41(20): 1965–6.

Breman, J. (2004) *The Making and Unmaking of an Industrial Working Class*, New Delhi: Oxford University Press.

Chandrasekhar, C.P. and Ghosh, J. (2006) 'Working More for Less'. Available online: www.macroscan.org/the/employment/nov06/emp281106Working_More.htm (accessed 15 May 2008).

Chandrasekhar, C.P. and Ghosh, J. (2007a) 'Women workers in urban India'. Available online: www.macroscan.org/fet/feb07/fet060207Women_Workers.htm (accessed 15 May 2008).

—— (2007b) 'Recent employment trends in India and China: an unfortunate convergence?', April 5. Available online: www.macroscan.org/anl/apr07/anl050407India_China.htm (accessed 15 May 2008).

—— (2008) 'Global inflation and India', 8 April 2008. Available online: www.thehindu businessline.com/2008/04/08/stories/2008040850360900.htm (accessed 15 May 2008).

da Corta, L. and Venkateshwarlu, D. (1999) 'Unfree relations and the feminisation of agricultural labour in Andhra Pradesh, 1970–95', in T.J. Byres, K. Kapadia and J. Lerche (eds) *Rural Labour Relations in India*, Frank Cass: London.

de Neve, G. (2005) *The Everyday Politics of Labour: Working Lives in India's Informal Economy*, Delhi: Social Science Press.

Dickey, S. (2000) 'Permeable homes: domestic service, household space and the vulnerability of class boundaries in urban India', American *Ethnologist*, 27(2): 462–89.

Dyson T. and Moore, M. (1983) 'On kinship structure, female autonomy and demographic behavior in India', *Population & Development Review*, 9(1): 35–60.

Editorial (2008) 'State apathy towards construction workers', *Economic and Political Weekly*, 43(21): 5.

Elson, D. (1991) 'Male bias: an overview', in D. Elson (ed.) *Male Bias in the Development Process*, Manchester: Manchester University Press.

Fakhri, S.M. Abdul K. (1999) 'Caste, ethnicity and nation in the politics of the Muslims of Tamil Nadu, 1930–1967', unpublished Ph.D. thesis, University of Cambridge.

Folbre, N. (1994) *Who Pays for the Kids?: Gender and the Structures of Constraint*, Routledge: New York.

Fuller, C.J. and Narasimhan, H. (2007) 'Information technology professionals and the new-rich middle class in Chennai (Madras)', *Modern Asian Studies*, 41(1): 121–50.

Geetha, V. and Rajadurai, S.V. (1998) *Towards a Non-Brahmin Millennium: From Iyothee Thass to Periyar*, Calcutta: Samya.

Ghosh, J. (2006a) 'Case for caste-based quotas in higher education', *Economic and Political Weekly*, 41(24): 2428–32.

—— (2006b) 'The jobless young', December 8. Available online: www.macroscan.org/cur/dec06/cur081206Jobless_Young.htm (accessed 16 May 2008).

—— (2008a) 'Caste and discrimination in higher education: evidence from the National Sample Surveys', April 8. Available online: www.macroscan.org/fet/apr08/PSDE.pdf (accessed 15 May 2008).

—— (2008b) 'The crisis of home-based work', May 5. Available online: www.macroscan.com/cur/may08/cur170508Home_Based%20_Work.htm (accessed 15 May 2008).

Gooptu, N. (2007) 'Economic liberalisation, work and democracy: industrial decline and urban politics in Kolkata', *Economic and Political Weekly*, 42(21): 1922–33.

Gorringe, H. (2005) *Untouchable Citizens*, New Delhi: Sage Publications.

Habib, I. (1983) 'The Peasant in Indian History', *Social Scientist*, 11: 21–64.

Harriss, J. (1980) *Urban Labour, Urban Poverty and the So-called 'Informal Sector'*, Bulletin October, Madras Institute of Development Studies.

—— (1982) 'Character of an urban economy: 'small-scale' production and labour markets in Coimbatore', *Economic and Political Weekly*, 17(23/24): 945–54/993–1002.

—— (1989) 'Vulnerable workers in the Indian labour market' in G.B. Rodgers (ed.) *Trends in Urban Poverty and Labour Market Access*, Geneva: ILO.

Harriss-White, B. and Sinha, A. (eds) (2007) *Trade Liberalisation and India's Informal Economy*, New Delhi: Oxford University Press.

Heyer, J. (1992) 'The role of dowries and daughters' marriages in the accumulation and distribution of capital in a South Indian community', *Journal of International Development*, 4(4): 419–36.

—— 'The marginalisation of Dalits in a modernising economy', in this volume.

Heyer, J. and Jayal, N.G. (2009) 'The challenge of positive discrimination in India', CRISE Working Paper no. 55, Oxford: University of Oxford.

Hindu, The (2008) 'Construction workers plan statewide demonstration', *The Hindu*, 23 June. Available online: www.hindu.com/2008/06/23/stories/2008062354640600.htm (accessed 17 May 2008).

Jha, P. (2007) 'Some aspects of the well-being of India's agricultural labour in the context of contemporary agrarian crisis'. Available online: www.macroscan.org/anl/feb07/anl220207Agrarian_Crisis.htm (accessed 15 May 2008).

Joshi, C. (2003) *Lost Worlds: Indian Labour and Its Forgotten Histories*, Delhi: Permanent Black.

Kalam, M.A. (2007) 'Conditioned lives?' *Economic and Political Weekly*, 42(10): 843–5.

Kapadia, K. (1995a, 1996) *Siva and Her Sisters: Gender, Caste and Class in Rural South India*. Boulder: Westview Press and New Delhi: Oxford University Press.

—— (1995b) 'The profitability of bonded labour: the gem-cutting industry in rural South India', *Journal of Peasant Studies*, 22(3): 466–83.

—— (1999a) 'Responsibility without rights: women workers in bonded labour in rural industry', in D. Bryceson, C. Kay and J. Mooij (eds) *Disappearing Peasantries?: Rural Land and Labour in Latin America, Asia and Africa*, London: IT Publications.

—— (1999b) 'Gender ideologies and the formation of rural industrial labour in South India today', in J. Parry, J. Breman and K. Kapadia (eds) *The Worlds of Indian Industrial Labour*, New Delhi: Sage Publications.

—— (2002a) 'Introduction: the politics of identity, social inequalities and economic growth', in K. Kapadia (ed.) *The Violence of Development: The Politics of Indentity. Gender and Social Inequalities in India*, London: Zed Books.

—— (2002b) 'Translocal modernities and transformations of gender and caste', in K. Kapadia (ed.) *The Violence of Development: The Politics of Indentity. Gender and Social Inequalities in India*, London: Zed Books.

Kapadia, K. and Lerche, J. (1999) 'Introduction', in T.J. Byres, K. Kapadia and J. Lerche (eds) *Rural Labour Relations in India,* London: Frank Cass.

Lerche, J. (1999) 'Politics of the poor: agricultural labourers and political transformations in Uttar Pradesh', in T.J. Byres, K. Kapadia and J. Lerche (eds) *Rural Labour Relations in India*, London: Frank Cass.

Madheswaran, S. and Attewell, P. (2007) 'Caste discrimination in the Indian urban labour market: evidence from the National Sample Survey', *Economic and Political Weekly*, 42(41): 4146–53.

Narayanan, S. (2008) 'Employment guarantee, women's work and childcare', Economic *and Political Weekly*, 43(9): 10–13.

National Conference (2007) 'Program statement', National Conference on Making Growth Inclusive with Reference to Employment Generation, 28–29 June 2007, New Delhi: Jawaharlal Nehru University. Available online: www.macroscan.org/spfea/jun07/spfea 020707_JUN_IIAS.htm (accessed 18 May 2008).

NCEUS (2007) *Report on Conditions of Work and Promotion of Livelihoods in the Unorganised Sector National Commission for Enterprises in the Unorganised Sector*, New Delhi: Government of India. Online. Available online: www.nceus.gov.in/Condition_ of_workers_sep_2007.pdf (accessed 19 May 2008).

Neetha, N. (2004) 'Making of female breadwinners: migration and social networking of women domestics in Delhi', *Economic and Political Weekly*, 39(17): 1681–8.

Pallavi, A. (2006) 'Unfair to women', *Business Line*, May 12. Available online: www. blonnet.com/life/2006/05/12/stories/2006051200090200.htm (accessed 16 May 2008).

Parry, J. (1999) 'Lords of labour: working and shirking in Bhilai', in J.P. Parry, J. Breman and K. Kapadia (eds) *The Worlds of Indian Industrial Labour*, New Delhi: Sage Publications.

—— (forthcoming) 'Sociological Marxism in Central India: Polanyi, Gramsci and the case of the unions', in C. Hann and K. Hart (eds) *Market and Society: The Great Transformation Today*, Cambridge: Cambridge University Press.

Robinson, R. (2007) 'India Muslims: the varied dimensions of marginality', *Economic and Political Weekly*, 42(10): 839–43.

Roy, A. [2003] (2008) *Calcutta Requiem: Gender and the Politics of Poverty*, New Delhi: Pearson Education.

Sen, A. and Himanshu (2007) 'Employment trends in India: a fresh look at past trends and recent evidence', National Conference on Making Growth Inclusive with Reference to Employment Generation, 28–29 June 2007, New Delhi: Jawaharlal Nehru University. Available online: www.macroscan.org/spfea/jun07/spfea020707_JUN_IIAS.htm (accessed 18 May 2008).

Sengupta, A., Kannan, K.P. and Raveendran, G. (2008) 'India's common people: who are they, how many are they and how do they live?', *Economic and Political Weekly*, 43(11): 49–63.

Shah, G. (2007) 'The condition of Muslims', *Economic and Political Weekly*, 42(10): 836–9.

Srinivas, M.N. (1962) 'A note on Sankritisation and westernisation', in M.N. Srinivas *Caste in Modern India: And Other Essays*, London: Asia Publishing House.

Srivastava, R. (2007) 'Widening exclusion: informalisation in the Indian economy'. National Conference on Making Growth Inclusive with Reference to Employment Generation, 28–29 June 2007, New Delhi: Jawaharlal Nehru University. Available online: www.macroscan.org/spfea/jun07/spfea020707_JUN_IIAS.htm (accessed 15 May 2008).

Swaminathan, P. (2005a) 'The trauma of "wage employment" and the "burden of work" for Women in India', in K. Kannabiran (ed.) *The Violence of Normal Times: Women's Lived Realities*, New Delhi: Women Unlimited.

—— (2005b) *Trapped into Living: Women's Work Environment and their Perceptions of Health*, Mumbai: CEHAT.

Thorat, S. and Newman, K.S. (2007) 'Caste and economic discrimination: causes, consequences and remedies', *Economic and Political Weekly*, 42(41): 4121–4.

Upadhya, C. (2004) 'A new transnational capitalist class? Capital flows, business networks and entrepreneurs in the Indian software industry', *Economic and Political Weekly*, 39(48): 5141–51.

Vera-Sanso, P. (2001) 'Masculinity, male domestic authority and female labour participation in South India', in C. Jackson (ed.) *Men at Work: Men, Masculinities, Development*, London: Frank Cass.

Wilkinson, S. (2007) 'A comment on the analysis in Sachar Report', *Economic and Political Weekly*, 42(10): 832–6.

14 Dalit entrepreneurs in middle India

Aseem Prakash

Introduction

It has long been argued that any socio-economic relationship configured under the organised political power of the upper castes reinforces the 'traditional marginality' of Dalits. In this essay, the question whether this process persists to this day and applies to owners of capital (not simply to the labour force) will be explored. In the late nineteenth century, Jotirao Phule (1881) argued that the predominant control of the day-to-day running of all types of government institutions by 'Bhat-Brahmans' resulted in the pauperisation of peasants and farmers as well as rampant social discrimination and the economic exclusion of Dalits. Further, reacting to the Swadeshi movement, Phule (ibid.) noted that economic nationalism had become a smoke screen to conceal and preserve the socio-economic and religious superiority of the upper castes. Accordingly, the discourse of Dalits draws our attention to two kinds of colonialism: British colonialism and 'Brahminical colonialism', the latter preceding the former. The latter has its roots in Hindu scriptures which provide divine justification for caste-based discrimination and domination – both economic and social. British colonialism, in spite of its negative features, made available certain normative and cognitive tools to fight Brahminical colonialism. The ideas of the enlightenment provided a reason to believe that inter- and intra-social group relationships can be configured on an egalitarian basis. These very ideas also led to the demise of the colonial empire and the development of political democracy. Political democracy, henceforth, became the basis of political equality (one person one vote irrespective of social location) and also galvanised hopes for economic prosperity.

However, it is increasingly perceived that Indian democracy has provided political empowerment to Dalits but has failed to empower them economically. Omvedt (n.d.) advances the view that the Nehruvian model and state protectionism retained the caste base of society and restricted social mobility. The Indian state did not take, or enforce, measures sufficient to alter the unequal socio-economic relationship between upper castes and Dalits because state power was itself structured under the domination of upper castes. Panini (1996) argues that even the private ancillary industries and accompanying economic opportunities which emerged under state protectionism were cornered by the upper castes. Omvedt (n.d.) also argues that the ongoing globalisation has the potential to open a sea of opportunities for the weaker sections and hence she advocates free markets.[1] Similarly, Prasad (2008) puts forward the view that the principle of the caste system – blood and occupational purity – is dissolving under the impact of the wealth creation of markets.

So, on the one hand, the disjunction between political equality and the vast economic inequality between upper castes and Dalits is seen by many scholars potentially to be bridged by free-market policies. The logic is that the market has the potential to eliminate discrimination and bias because it represents the interaction of free individuals maximising their utilities. On the other hand, Dalit intellectuals and activists insist that the Indian state should support the creation of a Dalit bourgeoisie.[2]

It is against this backdrop that we analyse the outcome of the political and economic desire on the part of Dalits to enter the market as owners of capital and to trade in various goods and services. Our aim is to understand the attempts of Dalits in middle India[3] to earn a living, as well as generate surplus, through trade and commerce. We show that the interaction of economic agents in the market is mediated and influenced by the social structure and the social contexts in which the economic agents live. But before we analyse the evidence, we need to take stock of existing theories pertaining to markets and discrimination.

What the existing theories tell us

Theories of discrimination in the labour market explain how workers having the same endowments – skills, education, experience and so on – but not belonging to the 'dominant' race, caste, gender, or religion command less income. Most of these theories were explicitly developed for understanding discriminatory practices in labour markets. Although they do not directly relate to our own inquiry, since we are trying to understand market outcomes for the owners of capital, they nevertheless provide crucial insights because our research has confirmed that economic discrimination in the labour market is a result of the same social processes which are used to marginalise Dalits when they enter the market as owners of capital.

Several economists of the neo-classical school have attempted to capture the discrimination inherent in market operations. Thus, Gary Becker explains discrimination in terms of a 'taste for discrimination'. An individual is a discriminator because he has a taste for it and he 'must act as if he were willing to pay something, either directly or in the form of a reduced income, to be associated with some person instead of others' (Becker 1971: 14). Becker's work does not deal with caste discrimination but it has influenced authors working on discrimination in general and caste discrimination in particular. Akerlof analyses the possibility that the economic agent who transacts with lower castes may 'suffer the stigma of the outcastes [and hence economic loss]. If the punishment of becoming an outcaste is predicted to be sufficiently severe, the system of caste is held in equilibrium irrespective of individual tastes, by economic incentives; the predictions of the caste system become a self-fulfilling prophecy' (Akerlof 2005: 49). He also shows that the sanction of caste renders the market less competitive such that the 'successful arbitrageur', if any, will not be a winner but a loser, as a social 'outcaste'. Building on insights of Akerlof, Scoville's model (1996) explains the segmentation of the labour market through caste identities which to him essentially mean the 'suppression of competition' and the absence of 'institutional change'. These analyses share the following assumptions: the caste system is hereditary and endogenous; it segments the labour market; the values inherent in the caste system shape collective consciousness but it is the individual who refuses to go against dominant beliefs because of the fear of possible adverse outcomes; discrimination in the long run translates into suppression of competition resulting in imperfect/inefficient market outcomes (the inefficient allocation of labour, low profit, low wages). Since, according to the neo-classical school, the discrimination practised by individuals in the market has a non-economic origin, it breeds inefficiency and it will wane over time.

The emphasis on the individual means that these models fail to explain the mechanism through which the 'taste for discrimination' is exercised (Banerjee and Knight 1985). Further, they also do not reveal the economic basis of discrimination (the question of the production of surplus and of which castes appropriate it) (Deshpande 2000: 388).

Drawing on neo-classical theory, new institutional economics (NIE) privileges the role of institutions[4] in determining market outcomes. Baldly stated, NIE is normatively concerned with increasing market efficiency by lowering transaction costs with the help of institutions which are perceived to be legitimate.[5] The NIE school revisits history and finds that the gains from trade were best achieved in societies which successfully evolved towards impersonal institutions (secure property rights, legal institutions to arbitrate the violation of contracts, and corresponding political and bureaucratic institutions) because practices such as personal ties, voluntaristic constraints and ostracism are not allocatively efficient forms of exchange (North 1990: 107–31).

NIE, as with its predecessor (neo-classical economics), retains the central role of competition but highlights the role of impersonal institutions and the modern state[6] in reducing transactions costs and enhancing competitiveness. The historical evidence generated suggests that impersonal/formal institutions lower transaction costs and hence promote competition which in turn can lead to growth.[7] However, Williamson points out that NIE considers informal institutions as given (Williamson 2000: 596). The source of strength of NIE, factoring in institutions to understand market outcomes, also becomes a source of weakness because of its lack of emphasis on informal institutions.

In the Indian context, Harriss-White, who explores the economic roles of informal institutions, reminds us that there is no contradiction between the informal institution of caste and corporatist capitalist development (Harriss-White 2003:

176–99). This crucial insight becomes a springboard to probe several questions that remain unanswered in the NIE account. How do we understand the nature of competition in a market which, on the one hand, ensures a positive outcome for the leading players belonging to dominant social groups, while, on the other hand, it results in adverse terms of incorporation and marginalisation for many? How do we factor in the presence, and at times domination, of informal institutions (caste, religion, etc.) that significantly influence market outcomes in favour of dominant social groups? In order to answer these questions, we need to understand the relationships and practices which contribute to the blurring of boundaries between informal and formal institutions governing markets. The crucial answer is perhaps best provided by the authors belonging to the school of social embeddedness.

The most important contribution of the social embeddedness school is to flag the failure of 'mainstream' economists to incorporate social structure into their analysis. It was Polanyi who pointed out that the economy is an instituted process of interaction and is embedded in both economic and non-economic institutions (Polanyi 1957). In this school, there are three sets of scholars with similar ideological roots but crucial (internal) differences.

The first set of scholars that we discuss works primarily from the United States and help us understand the crucial role of social networks in the market. White (1981) suggests that economic actors take each other's behaviour into account through the medium of what he calls 'joint social construction – the schedule of terms of trade'. Granovetter suggests that economic actions are embedded in social networks, built on kinship or friendship and trust or goodwill, which sustain economic relations and institutions and also govern economic rewards and punishments (Granovetter 2005: 33). In substance, the analyses of these authors help us understand that economic activities require cooperative action in the market which finds its expression in social networks.

The second set of scholars originating from the CEPREMAP research centre in Paris argue that market forces, though very important, are only one of the contributing factors for capitalist development. Institutions, collective identities, shared visions, common rules, norms and conventions, networks, procedures, and modes of calculation are essential to the processes of accumulation. The French scholars not only highlight the social embeddedness of market relationships but also flag the important role of civil society in nurturing and sustaining the norms and conventions practised and observed in market transactions (Boyer 1990: 25–60).[8]

These arguments help us to understand the reasons why marginalised social groups like Dalits face adverse inclusion in the markets. Social networks in the market can be formed on the basis of caste location and can create adverse conditions for business people belonging to Dalit communities. However, we still don't have a convincing answer to the question why caste-like groups endure and shape economic transactions. Here we draw on the works of a third set of scholars belonging to the school of social embeddedness who work on India.

Thorat (2006) shows that Dalits find themselves excluded from the market or at best included in it on adverse terms. The privileges and rights of individuals are determined by virtue of being members of particular castes. A casteist ideological landscape shapes the operation of the market economy and limits the occupational mobility of Dalits by means of restrictions on capital, land, labour, credit, other input markets and in those services necessary for any economic activities.

The emphasis on caste as an ideology helps us to make the critical link between exclusion and discrimination. Individuals are excluded, or adversely included, because of deep-rooted social values. Thorat underlines the fact that discrimination has a material basis since exclusion or adverse inclusion always works in favour of the material interests of the dominant castes. Some of the writings on caste and modernity point to the dissolving of socio-economic relationships based on caste.[9] On the other hand, Harriss-White remarks that 'elements of the caste system are often rearranged leaving the principles intact' (2003: 177). She further explains that caste-like groups refuse to dissolve because caste in its corporatist[10] avatar provides institutional as well as ideological support for configuring distinctive production relations. First, this implies that the ideology of caste still forms the basis of various corporatist projects. In this sense the ideology of caste forms part of the social structure of accumulation.[11] Second, it provides the basis for building networks in the market, thwarts competition, mobilises resources, controls labour and so regulates the market (ibid.: 197). Third, caste helps to support the informal politics of the market. The politics of the market governs the operation of the market. Exchange regulated through caste blurs the boundaries between state, market and civil society. It forms the basis of contacts for informal or illegal dealings within both formal (both political and economic) and informal institutions (ibid.: 178). As a result, economic transactions in the market are mediated through social structures that in turn ensure that transactions are enforced through social conventions. The state either abstains from this or provides tacit consent.

Summing up

The three schools converge on several issues. First, all of them agree that caste is a material reality and a source of discrimination in markets. Second, all of them locate such discrimination in the realm of civil society. Third, the state is an important institution in all three theoretical frameworks, albeit the role of the state is understood differently. These schools also differ from each other in crucial ways. The neo-classical school maintains that while the source of discrimination lies in the realm of civil society the flag bearer of discrimination is the individual. The individual adheres to the dictates of dominant values of civil society for fear of penalties, at the cost of thwarting competition in the markets, which in turn results in imperfect market outcomes. The neo-classical school, therefore, predicts that discriminatory practices will wane in the long run. This school cannot explain the factors responsible for the persistence of discrimination in the economy. A plausible response to this is provided by NIE, which emphasises institutions – both formal and informal – that influence and determine market outcomes. The NIE economists consider informal institutions as 'given' and generate historical narratives to show that competition in the market leads to a reduction in their influence and also gives birth to institutions driven by impersonal codes. Both the neo-classical school and NIE stress the necessary institutional arrangements – political, legal and economic. In this sense, both schools argue that impersonal institutions can mitigate exclusion and discrimination practised in civil society. The school of social embeddedness exposes the fragility of these two positions. Here the theoretical understanding of competition and institutions is radically different. Scholars developing this approach have concluded that that the market functions with the help of networks, conventions and relationship created through social and personal ties. Social networks are used to thwart competition, procure and regulate credit, discipline labour, source information, and so on. Informal institutions in the markets reflect and express these hierarchised social relationships. In the Indian context, scholars point out that the social networks in markets are configured, inter alia, through caste, religion, gender, age, ethnicity and space (Harriss-White 2003). Caste as an ideology and as a social institution serves two crucial purposes. First, caste is used as an institution to meet the practical regulative demands of market competition. Second, more specifically, caste ideology helps to configure a regime of accumulation in the market which has been aptly described as a 'social structure of accumulation'.

With this backdrop, we analyse the attempts of Dalits in middle India to enter markets as owners of capital and earn their living, as well as create a surplus, through trade and commerce. In doing so, we cannot avoid concluding that the market is mediated and influenced by the social structure and the social contexts in which the economic agents live.

Dalit business: general profile of the sample

Our analysis draws on material from detailed interviews of 90 Dalit business persons in 6 states and 13 districts in middle India[12] carried out at the end of 2006 and beginning of 2007. The objective of this research was to examine the agency of Dalit capitalists. The business people we interviewed were perceived by fellow Dalits to be successful, though many of them consider themselves at the periphery of the class of peers among whom they work, earn and survive. The community's perception was the basis of our identification of 'successful' business people. Some were also identified through references given by other business people during the course of their interviews. Table 14.1 shows that 'small' and 'average'-sized businesses together represent nearly 65 per cent of the total in the sample. Twenty per cent of the sample operates 'very big', 'big' and 'middle'-sized business. The sample tapers sharply with increasing size.[13]

Table 14.1 also shows the type of business in which our respondents are involved. Nearly one-fifth of our respondents owned economic enterprises which

Table 14.1 Type and size of economic ventures (percentages in parentheses)

	Very big (more than 5 crores)	Big (1–4.99 crores)	Middle range (between 50–99 lakhs)	Average range (5–50 lakhs)	Small (4.9–2 lakhs)	Petty (less than 2 lakhs)	Total
Caste-related	2	1	2	12	6	3	26 (29)
Earlier restricted and considered taboo	0	0	2	2	4	4	12 (13)
General	1	2	6	13	10	4	36 (40)
Liberalised market	0	2	0	5	2	2	11 (12)
Specialised	0	1	0	3	1	0	5 (6)
Total	3 (4)	6 (7)	10 (11)	35 (39)	23 (26)	13 (14)	90 (100)

Source: 2006–7 survey.

related to their respective caste location (sanitary ware, clothes washing, cleaning services, leather work, hair cutting, etc.). The second type, in which nearly 11 per cent of our respondents were involved, comprises trade in goods and services earlier disallowed to Dalits by the Hindu social order (educational coaching, trade in food products, etc.). Nearly two-fifths of business people in our sample are found in the third category which we have called general economic ventures (trade in wood, handlooms, grocery shops, etc., as well big businesses such as mining, construction, manufacture and sale of ceramic ware, etc.). Thirteen percent of our respondents are found in our fourth category which covers the many newer avenues for business that have been created by the ongoing integration of the Indian economy with the global economy (trade in communication, electronics and computers). Lastly, our fifth category covers the remaining 6 per cent of our respondents who are involved in economic activity in which participation is contingent on higher education (economic activities related to medicine and hospital services, etc.).

In this analysis, developing questions generated from the earlier theoretical discussion, we first examine how and from where Dalits source their initial capital to enter markets and trade their goods and services. We then go on to look at the constraints they face in operating their ongoing businesses once they have acquired the initial capital to set them up. By exploring these questions we aim to understand markets from the perspective of the experience of Dalit entrepreneurs. Where appropriate we use quantitative information, but we focus on interpreting Dalit narrative. It may be pertinent to explain that, while interviewing these business people, our approach was primarily directed at understanding their success in the markets. However, in the process of their sharing with us their entrepreneurial experiences, we came to understand how their business practices were constrained because of their caste. During fieldwork, while tracing their business histories, we made every effort to ensure that we did not elicit exaggerated responses by asking leading questions.

Dalit entrepreneurs in the market

We start with a narrative which illustrates simultaneous processes of accommodation and rigidity. A building contractor from Ahmedabad who supplies workers, and construction and building material, explained to us:

> The money in construction of the flats is invested by Patels and Baniyas but people like me supply construction labour. I bring labour from my village and even from other states . . . There is no caste conflict in Gujarat. All conflict is over money . . . [Patels and Baniyas] never question my caste, but if I try and step in their shoes of managing my own small business, they will question my caste and ensure that I don't exist in business.

The labour contractor first explains his inclusion in market processes in which caste is not questioned by upper-caste economic 'masters'. This may be understood as illustrative of the accommodative character of the market-based system of accumulation, which is adapting to the requirements of the 'new' economy. The Dalit labour contractor from the low caste is included as a junior partner. At the same time, however, he is not given space to step into the shoes of his 'masters' in the market. The second characteristic of the market is its rigidity. The interviewee perceives that, if he attempts to emulate his 'masters', the social norms of caste will be invoked and go against his accumulation strategy. How do we understand the apparently contradictory nature of such processes?

To some extent existing market players attempt to maintain the status quo – that is, the nature of market processes is rigid. This is reflected in Dalit perceptions that institutionalised attempts are made by the upper castes to block them from staking accumulation claims in the market. At the same time, the market may also contain a certain amount of flexibility and accommodate the economic interests of Dalits. The dominant market players may permit their entry and operation under certain conditions. Market processes can shape new socio-economic alliances between erstwhile labour (Dalits) and capital (the upper castes).

A model of pure rigidity would imply that all economic actors in the market are positioned within a given structure in which they have specific economic roles, responsibilities and duties determined by the structural principles of capital and the logic of the division of labour. Any attempt by labour in general – and social groups who have historically performed the role of labourers in particular – to enter the market as owners of capital is resisted. This model of rigidity portrays the case where caste overlaps with class. On the other hand, a pure accommodative model of market-based accumulation permits people to acquire capital, invest and earn surplus, irrespective of their social location. In its not so pure form, it will reflect the possibility of Dalits as owners of capital being integrated into economic processes to varying degrees. Hence, caste may not necessarily overlap with class.

Our ethnographic evidence suggests that market-based accumulation operates along the continuum between pure rigidity on the one hand and complete accommodation on the other. However, in all cases, Dalit owners of capital experience adverse inclusion in market processes. A more rigid process implies extremely adverse inclusion while a more accommodative process implies moderate adverse inclusion. Further, the extent to which market processes tend towards either end of the continuum are not only decided by the market but are also shaped by the balance of forces in the wider socio-economic and political realms.

The strength of market operations of entrepreneurs hinges on their ability to mobilise initial credit. Later, when they start operating in the market, they have to negotiate other dynamics in the market whose outcomes are economic in nature but are shaped by social factors. In the following pages, we take up for discussion, first the experience of Dalit entrepreneurs in putting together capital for initial entry into the market, and second their experience of ongoing operations once they are established. These two aspects also delineate how markets are shaped by twin aspects of rigidity and accommodation while resulting in adverse outcomes for Dalit entrepreneurs.

Initial credit for market entry

Dalit entrepreneurs rely on a mixture of institutional credit, informal credit, social networks, own savings and the proceeds of the sale of assets to enter markets and trade in various goods and services. Dalit entrepreneurs experience both accommodation and rigidity in entering markets shaped by social institutions.

Institutional credit

Institutional (formal-sector) credit is used very widely in India. It is extended by banks (public as well as private), development schemes of the government of India and state governments, along with cooperative financial institutions. It is generally much cheaper than credit from informal credit sources. It is also usually considered to be devoid of extra-economic compulsions.

A majority of our interviewees reported that their attempts to approach government institutions and banks for credit involved them in numerous visits, constant harassment and rent-seeking by officials. Nearly 80 per cent of our interviewees applied for credit from nationalised banks, nearly 65 per cent of them unsuccessfully. Similarly, more than 85 per cent applied for credit from government agencies, more than 50 per cent unsuccessfully. Several of the government agencies were created exclusively for funding Dalit economic ventures. In some cases, in Madhya Pradesh for example, the state government launched explicit initiatives to encourage Dalit entrepreneurs by providing credit as well as an assured market for goods.

Caste prejudice in the provision of institutional credit

Caste prejudice is seen in the testimonies discussed below to be a powerful factor responsible for the denial of institutional credit to Dalits.

A laundry owner from Lucknow pointed out that the geographical segregation of his community translates into his exclusion from credit. He told us that his community, Dhobis, resides in Dhobi Katra (the ghetto of the community that has traditionally washed clothes) in the Mehmodabad area of Lucknow. He pointed out that the very mention of Dhobi Katra invoked condescension as well as contempt in the minds of credit officials. He explained:

> As soon the officer [person dealing with my loan request] learnt that I reside in Dhobi Katra, his behaviour changed. He explained to me that I would be unsuccessful in managing a modern laundry and would lose all my money in the market. He further told me to continue with my washing activities on the riverbank as well as ironing clothes. He went to the extent of suggesting that I should buy my son a new cart to iron clothes so as to augment my family income . . . You tell me, if my father and grandfather have washed clothes on the bank of Gomti, does it mean both I and my son also have to wash clothes similarly? I had decided that I would not wash clothes on the bank of the river any more and whoever wants to get their clothes washed and starched has to come to my shop. I will not go door to door collecting clothes for washing and then returning them back . . .

The interviewee explains his understanding that the loan is not denied because of an adverse credit rating but due to his identification with a particular caste whose members reside in a particular area of the city. The narrator is upset by the view of the official who thought that he was incapable of managing any business in modern markets. He was also appalled when the official advised him to buy another cart for ironing clothes in order to supplement the family income. The narrator agitatedly posed the question: why should he and his son continue to work at the riverbank like his forefathers? This particular case also speaks volumes about the increasing social assertion of Dalits and their refusal to accept the position ordained by the Hindu social order.

Another aspect of Dalit assertion is reflected in the aggressive political mobilisation of Dalits in many parts of the country, particularly in the state of Maharashtra. The growing assertiveness of Dalits is resisted by the upper castes. The testimony of a medical doctor illustrates this. The doctor approached the Maharashtra State Financial Corporation (MSFC) for a loan in order to start a nursing home. He informed us that his loan application was rejected and that the MSFC official said, 'The Mahars[14] in Maharashtra are cornering all the government's resources, all political parties support you because you are an important vote bank.' Here, the narrator's community is being accused of being pampered as a social group because of its political clout. There is an implicit assumption in the accusation that community members are not deserving and that the political compulsions of various political parties to get Dalit votes ensures diversion of precious resources to them. Another fact which is being revealed by the statement reported to have been made by the upper-caste official is a fierce contempt not against a particular individual but against the Dalit community as a whole. In refusing credit to this Dalit entrepreneur, the upper-caste official also seems to be questioning the political decisions of the country which has given the Dalits an institutionalised medium to claim equality with upper castes.

A similar experience was recounted by a very unusual Dalit woman entrepreneur who owns a large ceramic factory in Ahmedabad. When she was trying to use the surplus earned through trading in retail coal to start her ceramic factory, she approached a public-sector bank for a loan of Rs.5 lakhs with a proposal to hypothecate her land worth Rs.12 lakhs. She recalled her experience with the bank manager as follows: 'He was of the opinion that providing loans to Harijans[15] means wasting money since most of them don't know how to do business. He also told me that if he gives all the money to Harijans, the bank will shut down and he will also lose his job . . .'

Finally, a supplier of domestic help and cleaning staff to offices in Ahmedabad told us:

> I had a dream of having a registered office and supplying workers to offices and homes. For this, I required an office. I applied for a loan of 1.5 million rupees. I wanted the loan against the security of my house the present market value of which is nearly 5 million rupees. The bank officer rejected my application and told me that we people don't need money for this kind of business; everyone in my community is a labourer. He further told me to go away and also told me that I should not disturb him everyday. The officer also told me that I did not even have the resources to feed myself and was trying to raise a loan. He did not even have the patience to understand that I am proposing a new kind of venture . . . Now I operate from a small tea joint at Vastrapur . . .

These four narratives emphasize the continuing power of caste which sustains, mediates and influences outcomes even in engagements with formal institutions such as state-controlled banks. Dalit entrepreneurs feel that the denial of initial credit for entering the market is strongly connected to systematic discrimination practised against them by the upper castes.

Successful applications for institutional credit

Around 35 per cent of the applicants to banks among those we interviewed were granted credit. Similarly, a range of government institutions granted credit to nearly 50 per cent of the respondents who applied for it. The four factors (Table 14.2) which seem to be most prominent in enabling them to obtain access to formal credit are: (1) the presence in the lending institutions of family members who can influence the process of loan sanction; (2) bribery and rent-giving; (3) local political contacts, and (4) business partnerships with upper castes. In a minority of cases, NGOs working for the cause of Dalits facilitated access to credit, both from the government and from banks.

Table 14.2 Factors facilitating access to initial capital

Loan facilitated by:	Number of respondents	
	Bank	Government
Official procedural outcome	NA	2
NGO	2	3
Family person in lending institutions	7	11
Local political contacts	4	7
Upper-caste business partner's influence	NA	5
Bribery	12	8
Government servant – business controlled and managed through proxy	0	2
Total	25	38

Source: 2006–7 survey.

Informal credit

Almost all of our interviewees obtained credit from informal sources. This often meant a very high interest rate, ranging from 3 to 6 per cent per month, and also the mortgage of their assets. In a few cases, such as leather work, credit was made available by a big business person in the same sector. In such cases, the credit was tied to a commitment to supply goods at less than the market price as well as at non-negotiable interest rates that were high. Capital was also raised through social networks. Almost all respondents informed us that they borrowed some money from family members and caste friends to meet the shortfall in their initial investment in the markets. Such initial help was very crucial, especially for Dalit interviewees classified as small and petty entrepreneurs. The sums borrowed from relatives and friends ranged from Rs.3,000 to Rs.35,000. Surprisingly, none of the interviewees who sourced money from within their own caste (30 per cent) paid interest. Nearly 90 per cent of the interviewees also raised money through social networks outside their own castes. Just over 70 per cent of these borrowers were paying relatively low interest rates (between 1 and 2 per cent per month).

Summing up

This complex amalgamation of degrees of rigidity and accommodation invariably results in adverse inclusion in the markets. Rigidity is sought to be maintained by invoking stereotypes[16] in order to remind Dalits that they are unfit for modern business dealings. Upper-caste discourse rests on the recognition and approval of caste differences with an objective to construe Dalits as a population who are best at earning their livelihood as labourers, rather than as owners of capital. However, it is almost impossible to maintain complete rigidity because of the ever-increasing assertion of Dalits in the socio-political and economic realms and because of the general changes taking place in the economy and society. This results in a degree of accommodation but mostly on adverse terms. Initial credit from formal institutions is obtained by a few, not just because they are entitled to it, but because they can use particular connections (which may not come without a cost). Informal credit comes with various conditionalities such as adverse terms of trade,[17] high interest rates and so on.

Ongoing business operations

In spite of the barriers to credit imposed by formal credit institutions, the Dalit entrepreneurs we interviewed had managed to enter the market as owners of capital and pursue their desire for accumulation within the market. Their attempt to enter the market and operate as 'free' economic agents gives them a distinct experience of market processes. We now look at this.

Social networks

Social networks can be grounded in acquired qualities such as skill and reliability or an ascribed characteristic derived from religion, caste, family and kinship ties, and regional identity. These may be further strengthened by their class location. They are used to negotiate the constraints experienced in markets through interpersonal relationships operating outside the regulatory framework of the state.[18] Our field material shows that social networks based on ascription play an important role in relation to market information for newer businesses, getting orders and supplies, fulfilling credit needs, arranging labour supplies, influencing price, influencing regulatory institutions, and so forth.

The dominant social groups mostly operate a closed network, working to each other's advantage. It is almost impossible for Dalit entrepreneurs to be members of social networks configured by their upper-caste peers. A general merchant in Lucknow told us:

> In my business, there is no godfather . . . I don't get any goods for my shop on credit . . . only people who have their uncle and other relatives as wholesalers get goods on credit . . . one should have a social status to command prestige in society, establish friendly relationships and social networks especially for profitable business . . .

Here, social status is equated with upper caste and only people belonging to upper castes can do business profitably. In other words, the narrator perceives powerful social networks in the market as being necessary for business and that such social networks are grounded in upper-caste identity from which he is automatically excluded.

Many of our interviewees perceived that their lack of social networks prevented them from procuring bulk orders. It also restricted their access to credit on the terms (time, quantity and rate of interest) available to other entrepreneurs in their class of business operations. A large number of them reported facing problems in procuring initial orders – several respondents felt that their former employers were instrumental in ensuring a lack of business at the initial stage. Others felt that the lack of working capital (further reduced by market/credit impediments[19] forcing them to take high- interest loans and also pay rent-seekers to operationalise their business) made their business propositions less competitive. The following two testimonies from a courier company and a brick-kiln owner from Pune elaborate these points. The courier company owner explained:

> The really big orders for letter despatch are given by big private companies. This is where I lose in the market. My work is much appreciated by my existing customers. However, I am not able to get big business orders for two reasons. First, I don't have any contacts in the big companies. Even if I develop some contacts, I am not in a position to do business with them. They release payments monthly. I don't have enough capital to wait for one month for the payment. I don't get credit from the market. Other franchises of DTDC[20] are controlled by Marathas and Gujaratis.[21] They have enough contacts in the market to obtain credit and are able to do business with big companies . . .

The respondent differentiates the normative construct of the market from its operating principles. The former means that any individual can enter the market and pursue his accumulative endeavours (for instance, he perceives that his services keeps his customer happy and hence his business should grow), while the latter refers to the hindrances experienced by individuals not belonging to the 'right' social networks (he fails to get large orders or raise sufficient credit). The narrator explains that social networks inspired by caste location and regional identity are not only crucial in procuring orders but are also important for accessing resources for meeting the requirements of big orders.

Likewise, the brick-kiln owner felt that he was not able to earn large surpluses from his business operations, which in turn restricted his business expansion plans. He explained:

> I own one brick kiln. I don't have resources to invest in a second brick kiln. All owners of kilns help each other. I once got a very big order from a farmhouse at Khadakwasla. I was short by 50,000 bricks. None of the kiln owners helped me. I had to take credit from the open market at an interest rate of 6 per cent. Usually, brick-kiln owners give credit to each other at 2–3 per cent . . . Mostly, I have to take credit from the open market for any big order I get. This lowers my profit and hence I am not able to invest in the second kiln.

The brick kiln owner tells us that his accumulation attempts as well his ambition to invest in the expansion of his business are both constrained by the business practices of upper-caste 'peers'. Such practices include the refusal of his upper-caste 'peers' to share resources with him (he perceives that sharing of resources is a normal practice in his sector of trade), and an unfriendly credit market.

The regulation of credit by the upper-caste networks is not the only factor constraining the accumulation endeavours of Dalits. A handloom business and boutique owner in Vidisha explained:

> As per the market's principles all handloom workshops release their labour for the other, as and when required . . . Last March, I got a big order from Delhi. None of the workshops released their labour and I had to get my order prepared from Hoshangabad and Bhopal at a higher cost . . .

The handloom workshop owner is perturbed by the fact that his plans for accumulation in the market are hampered by the strict regulation and control over labour supply by the social networks of upper-caste 'peers'. Due to lack of cooperation from his 'peers', he had to rework his accumulation strategy and structure a different workforce supply chain. The latter, he points out, did not produce the best results, but was the only option available to him.

The above four narratives indicate ways in which Dalit entrepreneurs' endeavours in the market are constrained by their lack of social networks and the subordinating activity of the firm owners who are formally their peers. Such networks are not merely economic interest groups (market players having common economic interests emanating from pursuing the same trade or profession) but are configured on the basis of caste and family, or caste and regional social identity. Further, the use of social networks inspired by upper-caste social location are an institutionalised attempt to mitigate competition from relatively new entrants who also happen to be Dalits. In other words, not only are Dalits handicapped by their own social networks, but caste and regional identities are also deployed by upper castes to marginalise Dalits in the market.

Caste prejudice among former employers

The interviewees reported that their ambition to move to the position of trader in various goods and services from the status of workers was severely handicapped by the prejudices of upper castes. Employers were perceived by our Dalit entrepreneurs to be instrumental in creating multiple impediments to market entry. Out of the 90 business persons interviewed, 57 of them (nearly 64 per cent) were earlier working in the same sector as wage workers. In other words, they acquired the skills and basic capabilities to earn and manage the present business while working in economic units controlled by upper castes. The interviewees reported that their movement from 'worker' to 'manager/owner' was seen both by their upper-caste employers and by their caste peers as a step that does not suit the 'status' of workers.

As with officials controlling access to credit, former employers seem to be prejudiced about the kind of economic activity members of the Dalit community can possibly undertake. Thus, while trying to raise finance, the sanitary-ware shop owner in Pune was dissuaded by his former employer. As he said: 'My old employer told me that we are not capable of doing business, we should be doing hard labour and put in extra effort to earn more money instead of starting our own business . . .'

Sites

Another problem faced by Dalit entrepreneurs was their difficulty in getting tenancies. Nearly 50 per cent were refused as tenants at least once in their search for physical space to carry out their economic activities. This denial was perceived as discrimination because they were Dalits. In some cases it was perceived to be due to the obstructive influence of a former employer as well.

Labour force

An overwhelming majority (90 per cent) also had difficulty in recruiting workers. Even when the workers belonged to the same caste, they feared a backlash from upper-caste employers.

Supplies

Many Dalit entrepreneurs had resorted to a strategy of supplying goods and services at lower prices than those being charged by their upper-caste 'peers'. In her interview, a 'very big business' owner and manager of a ceramic manufacturing unit informed us that her business reached such a scale through the sustained supply of goods at a much lower prices than her upper-caste counterparts.

Now a renowned trader in ceramic products in Gujarat, she started as a small-time coal supplier. Her business strategy was to deliver coal at the door and charge substantially less money than the upper-caste suppliers who were also not ready to deliver coal at home. She informed us that during the 1970s this business strategy helped her upper-caste customers to forget her caste and trade with her (the same people refused to buy cooking coal from her because she was a Dalit – *bhangi* [a formerly untouchable caste restricted to cleaning latrines and handling corpses]). The lower profit was compensated for by higher sales.

There are certain economic activities in our sample from which Dalits were traditionally barred because it was believed that their touch would 'pollute' the goods – render them unfit for upper caste touch or consumption (notably food and related items and also education). Entrepreneurs trading in 'mid'-sized wholesale food and beverages businesses, we were told, supply their customers at a slightly lower profit margin than their upper-caste business rivals, which keeps the trade lines open to them. As explained by a wholesale supplier of beverages in Jaipur:

> It is with great difficulty that I am able to set up my own business. Earlier, I used to work for a local trader. My duty was to supply goods from his shops to homes of different customers. I thought of starting my own business . . . My wife and two daughters prepare different food items at home and I supply them to different shops in the city. It was really difficult to get

established in the market. None of the *baniya* traders used to buy my goods. Nobody told me explicitly but I perceived that they were not buying from me because of my low-caste origin. Money has great power. I started selling my goods at a price lower than the market price. Several shop owners started buying my goods. Still, if I sell my goods at the market price, nobody will buy them . . .

Similar to the experience of the Jaipur entrepreneur, the wholesaler in food items at Ahmedabad pointed out the following:

I get fewer days to pay and other entrepreneurs take more time than usual to make a payment for the goods supplied by me. The rule of the market is that the wholesaler gets his money within one week or ten days but I don't. I have to visit them, at least ten times to get my payment released . . . Why should I fight? It might jeopardise my business . . .

In both the narratives above, we notice that the Dalit entrepreneurs are aware of their adverse inclusion but choose not to protest. Not objecting to the discriminatory practices of their upper-caste business colleagues is an accumulation strategy for them. They realise that traditional social norms, according to which the mere touch of a Dalit will pollute food, can be invoked to expel them from the market.

When Dalits operate as owners of hotels and are in direct interaction with consumers, their size of operation seems to be constrained by their caste and the location of the business. Their hotels are generally found in localities inhabited by Dalits. In other areas, the successful food entrepreneurs are 'tolerated' as long as they are not a threat to their rivals. However, if their Dalit rivals threaten their profit, upper- caste food traders publicise their caste. Our case studies of Dalit food entrepreneurs in Pune and Jaipur exemplify this. A Dalit woman supplying lunch boxes to offices who experienced the wrath of upper castes told us: 'The food prepared by me was very popular. However, when the popularity of my food affected the business interest of Manjerekar[22] [an upper caste], he went and told everybody that I am Dalit. Thereafter, the demand for my food was reduced by more than half . . .'

In the case of a Dalit-controlled and -managed educational coaching institute, it was perceived by our interviewee that upper-caste children and their parents stayed away from his institute on the assumption that his educational qualifications were a result of the state's affirmative action and he did not have the intellectual ability to train others. He told us: '[E]verybody thinks that I cannot teach because I have acquired education due to reservation policies . . .' In response to this and also because of his ideological inclination, the respondent started coaching Dalit students at concessional rates.

The credit market is certainly most unfriendly to Dalit retail trade in food. The credit market's social and sectoral unfriendliness is also spatially constructed. For instance, the Dalit entrepreneur operating a small food outlet in a 'general locality' in the prime area of the town is mostly refused credit but the same entrepreneur when operating from a Dalit locality in the same city is extended credit. A small outlet owner serving tea and refreshments at Kanpur explained:

> I used to work at Arya Nagar as sweeper. My job was to clean the public drains. I was allotted a shop at Arya Nagar by the Municipal Corporation under the Dalit quota. The biggest constraint in my business operation was that I never got credit from the wholesaler while purchasing cooking oil, cooking butter and tea. The wholesalers used to think that my business will not be profitable because I am a sweeper by caste and the shop was in a predominantly upper-caste area. Now it seems they were right. Most of my customers were my sweeper friends who would come and buy tea and bread pakora [a kind of vegetable burger] after their work in the morning. There was not much profit. I rented out that shop and now I have opened the shop here [Khatik[23] colony]. Here my caste is not a baggage and I get more customers . . . I do get some credit from the wholesaler. However, others get credit for fourteen days and I am given credit for seven days. If I default, I have to pay interest of 6 per cent.

In this case, the advantage of the norms of the state, permitting the narrator to get a shop in an upper-caste area, is tempered by the discriminatory processes dominant there. The wholesaler rightly perceived that the tea outlet/shop in a predominantly upper- caste area would not attract customers because the owner was identified as Dalit, and hence he refused credit. The dominant discriminatory values in civil society forced the tea outlet/shop owner to shift his business to a predominantly Dalit area where his economic efforts would attract more consumers. The wholesaler is now ready to extend credit but at a rate higher than the prevailing market rate. The narrator experiences inequitable treatment even when his business is seen to be economically viable.

Upper-caste partnerships

There are certain sectors of trade and services in our sample where Dalits hold a relative advantage over others. The relative advantage arises for two specific reasons. The first is due to an initiative of one of the federal units of the Indian state – Madhya Pradesh – to provide an assured market to Dalit entrepreneurs through government procurement of goods supplied by them along with the facility of a loan. The second relates to their involvement in the economic activities traditionally associated with their respective sub-castes.

Here, their relative advantage has not meant that Dalit entrepreneurs are able to accumulate successfully in the market. The shortage of capital and inability to raise credit on the part of Dalit business people provides an opportunity for better-capitalised upper-caste traders with capital to enter into business alliances with them. So we find more than half a dozen case studies from Madhya Pradesh where an upper-caste alliance has enabled a Dalit business person to 'overcome' the lack of capital and other resources in the interests of accumulation. In a few cases, the upper-caste partner's capital and social contacts are able to influence the sanction of larger government contracts and the Dalit is de facto reduced to the status of a junior partner (although legally the government contract has to be in the name of the Dalit).

In other instances, Dalit business people have been reduced to the position of supervisor/manager of the economic activity legally carried out in their name. A few of the interviewees claimed that they have to abide by the 'logic' of the market – that is, returns must be allocated proportionate to capital rather than to capital and work efforts. For instance, a supplier of computers to state government offices working from Bhopal told us:

> Before starting this business, I tried my hands at several activities but was not successful. The state government gave us an opportunity and also an assured market, the government also provides loan to us. However, we need huge investments in the computer business. My father and forefather do not have any accumulated wealth. Therefore, I took Tandon[24] as my business partner. He invested a lot of money and therefore his share in the business amounts to 70 per cent . . . Tandon also has a transport business and hence I have to do all the work in the computer business . . .

A similar structural logic was documented in several caste-related activities, in the leather goods sector, sanitary ware, iron work and carpentry. As a result, the entry of big firms in the market has marginalised communities who have traditionally specialised in leather-related trade. Dalit traders are unable to compete with economies of scale because of the lack of availability of the credit that is needed.[25] This has meant that the majority are reduced to supervisors or workers in factories controlled by dominant castes while a minority now work as contract producers for the big upper-caste traders. A Dalit leather goods manufacturer in Agra told us:

> Agra has thousands of small leather workshops. In the last few years, these small workshops have been either taken over by Punjabis, Gujaratis and Baniyas. Several of these businessmen are located outside Agra. The original owners of the workshop have been relegated to the position of supervisors or workers in their own workshop. My workshop also supplies leather goods to a businessman from Dharavi, Mumbai. He gives raw material to us and we make the leather product. We are paid per piece for all the leather goods we supply to him.

In a similar vein, a Dalit woman owning a beauty parlour in 24 Parganas, West Bengal, explained:

> Nowadays, people are very conscious about hygiene, beauty and health. Beauty parlours are mushrooming all over. Most of the investment in the beauty parlours in our district is by petty Marwari traders of Kolkata. Instead of having their own shop, the traditional barber is an employee. I have somehow survived because of my goodwill and hard work but I don't have money to invest in a modern beauty parlour cum health club.[26]

The boom in the real-estate sector has increased the demand for sanitary ware, metal work and carpentry. Our interviewees reported that their inability to raise credit from the market in order to produce larger quantities and overcome large payment delays forced them to accept the help of an upper caste partner who could raise and invest money. In such cases, the profit was shared in proportion to the capital investment even though the business was managed by the Dalit. However, in one of our case studies of 'very big' business in sanitary ware, the same strategy was used to raise capital, but in the course of time the owner's savings were sufficient to enable him to move into an independent venture.

These testimonies also reflect a crucial trend which has been witnessed in the last decade in India at all levels of the economy, namely, the centralisation of capital and decentralisation of production processes. The saloon owner indicates that the surplus controlled by upper-caste owners is increasingly being invested in all sectors including vocations hitherto considered as 'polluting'. The entrepreneur from Agra explains the recent changes in economic policies that have resulted in massive investments in the leather sector by big capitalists. As a result, many of the manufacturers who could earlier be considered big in terms of their annual turnover have slid down to the status of average- or small-size business. Further, many small manufacturers even had to close shop and are working as wage labour in big production units which have come up after the deregulation of the leather sector.[27] It appears that in the face of tremendous social change, Dalits are finding it increasingly difficult to compete with upper-caste peers who control relatively scarce capital. The markets still retain Dalits but only at the lower end of the chain.

Conclusions

Our analysis shows how market outcomes are embedded in the existing social structure. Following our theoretical discussion in the second section where we argued that market outcomes in India are neither a) governed by the forces of demand and supply, nor b) structured by formal institutions, we turned to research showing how they are shaped by existing social institutions which form India's social structure of accumulation. Caste in India is one of the crucial components of the social structure of accumulation. What role does it play?

Our Dalit entrepreneurs choose to enter the market because of the normative emancipating promise that it offers. However, from our interviewees' accounts of their experience, we saw that caste as an ideology (a set of beliefs, norms, values and practices) nurtures – rather than dissolves – discriminatory attitudes and behaviour by members of the upper castes against Dalits. We also saw that the ideology of caste has a social as well as an economic basis. The social basis manifests itself through the stereotyping of Dalits in which they are expected to be true to dominant social constructs which mandate them to serve the society manually and consider them to be unfit for any 'higher' economic role. By higher role is meant a role involving education, technological sophistication and continued exposure to upper castes on the basis of either equality or acquired characteristics. The social role of the ideology of caste may not have any immediate economic motives (such as those of bank officials involved in denial of loans to Dalits even when (s)he is legally entitled, or refusal to eat food prepared by a Dalit restaurant owner, etc.). However, it always harms/damages the economic interests of Dalits. The explicit economic objectives of the ideology of caste can be invoked by upper castes to structure favourable economic returns to them at the expense of Dalits (e.g. non-Dalit caste identity is used to prevent competition in markets, suppress prices, reduce Dalit profits, earn higher interest rates, negotiate profitable partnerships with Dalits, etc.). So both the social and economic basis of caste ideology may lead to adverse economic outcomes for Dalits.

As discussed in several of our testimonies, caste ideology does not seem to function through its socio-religious principles: the practice of purity and pollution. Instead it works cleverly, at least in markets, to maintain an unequal power relationship between the upper castes and Dalits. Further, due to the ever-increasing socio-political assertion of Dalits, it is not possible for the upper-caste owners of capital to prohibit Dalits entirely from market entry and accumulation. As a result, Dalits are incorporated at least to some extent in market-based accumulation processes, but on unfavourable terms. The unfavourable accommodation of Dalits is structured and maintained by social networks.

In other words, caste ideology can create solidarity between individuals belonging to the same castes carrying out similar economic activities. Such solidarity propels the configuration of social networks in markets that protect and promote the economic interests of their members. Social networks are also carved out through the identities of religion and region. The dominant social networks in markets are mainly coterminous with upper castes and may or may not overlap with religion and with region of origin. The dominant social networks in markets were not created explicitly to resist Dalit entrepreneurs but they adhere to the social and economic basis of the ideology of caste which invariably works against the economic interests of Dalits. It also appears from the testimonies of Dalit entrepreneurs that the dominant social networks are tightly knit bodies (sometime organised as trade bodies) which mostly work in the economic interests of their members. Their network resources (credit, information, control over labour supply, etc.) are not available for non-members, especially Dalits. On the other hand, Dalits do appear to have weak social networks in markets. The accumulation endeavours of Dalits in the market are sustained by what Granovetter has called the 'strength of weak ties' (Granovetter 1973). The weak social networks of our Dalit entrepreneurs are expressed through ascriptive ties (configured through caste identity) and facilitate access to formal as well as informal credit, using local political leaders to influence the state and so forth. Business ties with upper castes (partnerships) and market relationships with dominant market players (accepting adverse inclusion as a matter of strategy) are also part of the repertoire of weak ties. The objectives of the weak networks facilitating Dalit accumulation are similar to those of the dominant social networks of the upper castes. However, the socio-economic relationships inspired by weak networks do not follow repeated exchanges. For example, while a local politician may help the Dalit entrepreneur once to access credit, there is no surety that he may again help the Dalit entrepreneurs to resolve his problem with the municipality, as happens through the social networks of the upper castes. In the latter case, as a matter of routine a promissory note of credit, for example, becomes almost formalised as informal legal tender. Further, even if there is repeated exchange involving a Dalit (for instance, when a Dalit operates with an upper-caste partner or when they tie transactions with the upper castes), the outcomes are experienced as asymmetrically beneficial to upper castes.

This discussion gives us convincing evidence to conclude that operations of the modern market will not automatically dissolve caste identities since they 'restrict' competition. In fact, our evidence reveals how caste can be used to meet demands to circumscribe competition. These markets seem to be efficient, though not necessarily from the perspective of Dalits, even when the capacity to enforce of formal regulatory institutions is conspicuous by its absence.

Acknowledgement

The origin of the chapter lies in the work of Barbara Harriss-White (2003). The author is extremely grateful for her comments. The chapter would also not have been in this shape without the critical scrutiny and comments of Judith Heyer and without the assistance in the field of Amrita Dutta (see note 26). All its limitations are solely mine. The chapter is part of a larger research project 'Outcastes, Tribes and Modern Indian Capitalism', funded by Oxford University's John Fell Fund and organised by Barbara Harriss-White. We are grateful to the fund for supporting this research project.

Notes

1 Omvedt (n.d.) argues that the skilful use of markets and people (in the manner it has developed in information and technology) has to be extended to the areas such as agriculture and simple consumer goods, which still employ the largest numbers of people. Along with this, education and modern technologies – including the controversial areas of biotechnology and irrigation – have to be truly universalised.

2 This demand was made at the conclave of intellectual and activists working for the cause of Dalits at Bhopal in what is popularly known as the Bhopal Declaration. The declaration called on the Indian state to provided credit and assured business to Dalits and Adivasis in proportion to their population. For the full text of the Bhopal Declaration, please visit http://ambedkar.org/. Also see (Nigam 2002).

3 We use the term middle India to describe the thirteen cities where we conducted our interviews. As a phrase it represents a spatial category. For more details, see note 12.

4 North (1991: 97) defines institutions as 'humanely devised constraints that structure political, economic and social interaction. They consist of both informal constraints (sanctions, taboos, customs, traditions and codes of conduct), and formal rules (constitutions, laws, property rights).'

5 North (1992: 3). Further pointing out the lacuna in the neo-classical school, North writes, 'Institutions are unnecessary in a world of instrumental rationality; ideas and ideologies don't matter; and efficient markets – both economic and political – characterise economies.' For a discussion on market (in)efficiency, see North (1995: 19–20).

6 See North (1981: 20).
7 Neo-classical economics and NIE seem to converge on the point that the market is a realm of impersonal exchange, characterised by economic transactions between equal and autonomous individuals motivated by profits. All kinds of markets and diverse institutions of economic exchange (ranging from the purchase and sale of goods and services in cyberspace; hi-tech operations on the Mumbai Stock Exchange; utilising political connections and rent giving for information; credit exchange notes worth millions scribbled on dirty pieces of paper; the patronage-based retail CG road market at Ahmedabad; sand markets in Patna surviving on muscle power and political clout, and so on) are subsumed under the universalistic framework of a singular market. Any perceptible patterns of economic exchange falling outside the framework distort demand and supply and set in motion externalities (transaction costs of various kinds) which reduce profits or raise the costs of goods and services. Hence, any distortions will naturally wane.
8 Also see Jessop (n.d.).
9 Reviewed in Harriss-White (2003: 176–8).
10 A '(m)ode of economic regulation that that limits class conflict inter alia by involving both capital and labour in managing markets' (Harriss-White 2003: 197).
11 The theory of the social structure of accumulation analyses the relationship between capital accumulation processes and the set of social institutions that affects those processes. The central idea is that capital accumulation over a long period of time is the product of the role played by supporting social institutions. For a detailed discussion of the Social Structure of Accumulation, see Kotz (1994a, 1994b).
12 The interviews were distributed across states as follows: 8 Gujarat, 15 Madhya Pradesh, 20 Maharashtra, 10 Rajasthan, 27 Uttar Pradesh and 10 West Bengal. The interviewees were overwhelmingly male. We tried our best to identify women entrepreneurs but were unable to locate more than three women entrepreneurs.
13 The classification of size as well as type of business does not correspond to the classification of the government of India but was developed specifically for our needs. The government of India divides small-scale enterprises into manufacturing and services. It further divides them as per their size – micro, small and medium – measured in terms of investment in plant and machinery/equipment, excluding land and building (Government of India 2007a: 9). Instead, we divide the types of business into manufacturing and services and developed a fivefold classification to bring home the discovery that a miniscule proportion of Dalit business people are present in the emerging modern sectors or in the sectors which require high levels of skill. Further, instead of taking investment as the defining feature for size, we have taken per annum turnover (gross output) as the criterion of understanding the size, since the actual worth of several of the enterprises (for instance, retail/wholesale trade in food, supply of lunch boxes, coaching institute, courier services, etc.) could not be captured in terms of investment. We have classified the size distribution into six categories – petty, small, average, middle, big, very big (whereas the government of India has three categories – micro, small and medium) in order to capture the great diversity encountered in the field research.
14 Mahars are classified as a Scheduled Caste community in Maharashtra. They are considered to be politically powerful and are reported to constitute 9 per cent of Maharashtra's population.
15 Harijan literally means 'children of God'. The term was coined by Mahatma Gandhi for the ex-untouchables. The term is used all over India but has quite a prominent usage in Gujarat – the birthplace of Gandhi.
16 Bhabha (1999: 370) describes stereotype as major discursive strategy. It is a form of knowledge and identification that vacillates between what is always in place, already known, and something that must be anxiously repeated.

17 The assured supply of goods to creditors at lower than the prevailing rates, business partnership with upper caste on unequal terms, etc.
18 See White (1981); Burt 1983; Granovetter (1973), 2005; Podolny (1993).
19 This will be developed in the following section.
20 DTDC (Desk to Desk Courier) claims to be 'India's Largest Domestic Delivery Network Company'. Its website says that it delivers letter to the remotest places in India with the help of 4,000 business partners (franchisees) spread across the length and breadth of India. See www.dtdc.in/.
21 Gujarati is a regional identity. However, it is Patels and Kunbis, classified as 'Other Backward Castes' (Intermediary Castes), which dominate this sub-sector.
22 The surname Manjerekar is generally used by people belonging to the dominant Maratha community.
23 Khatik or Sonkar are classified as Scheduled Caste. There are many stories about the origin of their caste. However, one of the widely accepted stories in the region of central Uttar Pradesh is that earlier they were used to rear and hunt pigs.
24 Tandons are Hindu upper-caste Khatris. The word Khatri is generally considered to be a Punjabi adaptation of the word Kshatriya.
25 The problem has been aggravated by the downscaling of Leather Boards by the respective state governments (our respondents belonged to the states of Gujarat and Uttar Pradesh), which supported Dalit producers and manufacturers of leather goods.
26 This interview was conducted in Bengali by Amrita Dutta, who assisted the author in conducting the interviews in West Bengal – Hooghly and 24 Parganas. Her crucial help is gratefully acknowledged.
27 The Dalit entrepreneur from Agra seems to be affected by the policy regime guiding economic liberalisation. The production of leather accessories is no longer reserved as small-scale industry (For official notification see Government of India 2007b.) It is presently a 'special focus' area for export. Both in Agra and Kanpur (the two cities in which we interviewed leather goods manufacturers), it was perceived that the current trade regime has become more exploitative. In other words, there is an additional tier of appropriation in the form of the big capitalist, while the exploitative relationships between the local trader (now the raw material supplier on behalf of big capitalist) and Dalit manufacturers continue to persist. Due to this economic restructuring, we were told, earnings have fallen substantially while dependence on the patronage of upper-caste traders has increased.

Bibliography

Akerlof, George A. (2005) 'The economics of caste and of the rat race and other woeful tales', in G.A. Akerlof (ed.) *Explorations in Pragmatic Economics: Selected Papers of George A. Akrelof and Co-authors*, Oxford: Oxford University Press.
Banerjee, B. and Knight, J.B. (1985) 'Caste discrimination in the Indian urban labour market', *Journal of Development Economics*, 17: 277–307.
Becker, G.S. (1971) *The Economics of Discrimination*, Chicago: The University of Chicago Press.
Bhabha, H. (1999) 'The other question: the stereotype and colonial discourse', in J. Evans and S. Hall (eds) *Visual Culture: The Reader*, London: Sage.
Boyer, R. (1990) *The Regulation School: A Critical Introduction*, New York: Columbia University Press.
Burt, R. (1983) *Corporate Profits and Cooptation*, New York: Academic Press.
Deshpande, A. (2000) 'Recasting economic inequality', *Review of Social Economy*, 58(3): 381–99.

Government of India (2007a) *Annual Report*, Ministry of Small Scale Industries: Government of India.

Government of India (2007b) *Exim Policy – 2002–2007*, Government of India Ministry of Finance.

Granovetter, M. (1973) 'The strength of weak ties', *The American Journal of Sociology*, 78(6): 1360–80.

—— (2005) 'The impact of social structure on economic outcomes', *Journal of Economic Perspectives*, 19(1): 33–50.

Harriss-White, B. (2003) *India Working: Essays on Society and Economy*, Cambridge: Cambridge University Press.

Jessop, B. (n.d.) 'The social embeddedness of the economy and its implications for economic governance'. Available online: http://eprints.cddc.vt.edu/digitalfordism/fordism_materials/jessop2.htm (accessed 21 June 2008).

Kotz, D.M. (1994a) 'The regulation theory and social structure of accumulation approach', in D.M Kotz, T. Mcdonough and M. Reich (eds) *The Social Structures of Accumulation: The Political Economy of Growth and Crisis*, Cambridge: Cambridge University Press.

—— (1994b) 'Interpreting social structure of accumulation theory', in D.M. Kotz, T. Mcdonough and M. Reich (eds) *The Social Structures of Accumulation: The Political Economy of Growth and Crisis*, Cambridge: Cambridge University Press.

Nigam, A. (2002) 'In search of a bourgeoisie', *Economic and Political Weekly*, 37(13): 1190–93.

North, D.C. (1981) *Structure and Change in Economic History*, New York: WW Norton & Company.

—— (1990) *Institutions, Institutional Change and Economic Performance*, Cambridge: Cambridge University Press.

—— (1991) 'Institutions', *The Journal of Economic Perspectives*, 5(1): 97–112.

—— (1992) 'Institutions and economic theory', *The American Economist* 36(1).

—— (1995) 'The new institutional economics and Third World development', in J. Harriss, J. Hunter and C.M. Lewis (eds) *The New Institutional Economics and Third World Development*, London: Routledge.17–26.

Omvedt, G. (n.d.) 'Globalisation and Indian tradition'. Available online: www.ambedkar.org (accessed 21 June 2008).

Panini, M.K (1996) 'The political economy of caste', in M.N. Srinivasan (ed.) *Caste: Its Twentieth-century Avatar*, New Delhi: Viking.

Phule, J. (1881) 'Shetkarya Asud (The Whipcord of the Cultivators)'. Online. Available http://ambedkar.org (accessed 21 June, 2008).

Podolny, J. (1993) 'A status based model of market competition', *The American Journal of Sociology*, 98(4): 829–72.

Polanyi, K. (1957) *The Great Transformation: The Political and Economic Origins of Our Times*, Boston: Beacon Press.

Prasad, C.B. (2008) *Markets and Manu: Economic Reforms and Its Impact on Caste in India*, Centre for the Advanced Study of India, University of Pennsylvania. Available online: http://casi.ssc.upenn.edu/research/papers/Chandrabhan_2008.pdf (accessed 21 June 2008).

Scoville, J.G. (1996) 'Labor market underpinnings of a caste economy: foiling the Coase theorem', *American Journal of Economics and Sociology*, 55(4): 385–94.

Thorat, S.K. (2006) 'Caste system and economic discrimination: lessons from theories', in S.K. Thorat, Aryama and P. Negi (eds) *Reservation and Private Sector: Quest for*

Equal Opportunity and Growth, New Delhi: Indian Institute of Dalit Studies and Rawat Publication.

White, H.C. (1981) 'Where do markets come from?', *The American Journal of Sociology*, 87(3): 517–47.

Williamson, O.E. (2000) 'The new institutional economics: taking stock, looking ahead', *Journal of Economic Literature*, 38(3): 593–613.

15 Stigma and regions of accumulation

Mapping Dalit and Adivasi capital in the 1990s

Barbara Harriss-White with Kaushal Vidyarthee

Introduction

Six decades after 1947, Scheduled Castes and Tribes, or Dalits and Adivasis – a quarter of the Indian population – still suffer severe discrimination, in spite of protective provision and the positive discrimination measures built into the constitution shortly after independence. A significant index of these effects is the extent to which Dalits and Adivasis have entered the market economy, not as wage labour, but by establishing themselves in business. Using data from the Economic Census (1990 and 1998),[1] we have constructed maps showing the differing indices of participation by Dalits (Scheduled Castes (SCs)) and Adivasis (Scheduled Tribes (STs)) in business during the 1990s, when the liberalisation of the Indian economy led many observers to expect significant changes in deeply rooted institutions such as caste. In this chapter, we show that the effects of discrimination vary markedly between regions and states, and between Dalits and Adivasis. Some prima facie surprising results in respect of change in the 1990s suggest a challenging new research agenda.

We first outline the history of discrimination against Dalits and Adivasis, and the potential significance for change which liberalisation is generally assumed to offer. We then present the findings of our research, and confront them with such explanations for Dalit discrimination as have hitherto been proposed – explanations from economics and from political sociology. While some of the hypotheses behind these explanations deserve further exploration, none of the explanations accounts for our findings. This is a situation which calls for the kind of fine-grained field research which has been practised by Judith Heyer and it is for this reason that this All-India analysis forms part of the book.

Untouchability, ethnic 'otherness' and the contemporary structure of accumulation

Discrimination against Dalits and tribal people is so deeply entrenched that positive discrimination in their favour was built into the Constitution and has subsequently formed the basis of a politics of aspiration, defence and claim.[2] Certainly the opportunities for mobility and security provided by the Indian state have been of tremendous importance to Dalits. Over and above Reservations, about which there is a large critical literature (reviewed in Thorat, Aryama and Negi 2005), the mere establishment of a labour force of sanitary workers paid by the local state at twice the market rate for unskilled labour, and endowed with work rights, has been an important achievement for sweepers. So has been access to municipal marketplace space, when space to conduct business is routinely denied to Dalits in the 'open market', physical entry to which is a matter of struggle for them. Yet the Indian state has been quite unable to prevent the stigmas of untouchability and of tribal 'otherness' from clinging to a substantial proportion of the population, severely limiting their economic, or 'market' freedoms.

Caste persists as a component of India's social structure of accumulation. Formal, state-regulated institutions are estimated to order only about 40 per cent of India's GDP. For the rest, the relationship between the economy and the state is at best indirect. A set of non-state social institutions and organisations bring order to the large and growing informal economy, and caste and ethnicity are central to it.[3]

'The caste system is an economic order,' observed the Chair of the Tamil Nadu Commission for SC/STs as recently as 1999 (Human Rights Watch). Would it were so simple. If it ever had been a system, now, when caste is recognised through combinations and subsets of attributes such as ritual purity, occupation and inherited property rights, diet, rules of endogamy (which may be routinely broken), religion, language and the political categories of states, it can no longer be defended as a 'system' and least of all in regard to outcastes or Dalits. The category of Dalit is not always restricted to the descendants of untouchables. While the Dalit Panthers' definition encompasses SCs and STs, it does much more, extending to landless labour, poor peasants and working women in its class approach to the mobilisation of oppressed people. Others see a social–cultural continuum between SCs and tribes resulting from their common origin.[4] This is rejected by those Dalit scholars who distinguish tribes from untouchables through their 'remote' sites, their material culture and their kinship and religious differentiation from the Hindu social order.[5] Meanwhile, untouchables comprise many castes or caste-like social groups, and there is no consensus on whether untouchables are – or ever have been – inside the caste 'hierarchy' at its very base, or outside it with a cultural distinctiveness shaped by social exclusion.

As for being an economic order, like other non-state elements in the social structure of accumulation, caste has a perplexing capacity to dissolve, as ascriptive characteristics give way to acquired ones (such as skills, compliance and trust, experience and creative competence), and as capital becomes mobile. But at the same time it persists and transforms itself as a regulative structure of the economy – sometimes in the same site.[6] There are macro-economic consequences to this paradox: capital cannot be assumed to move from uses affording low to those offering high rates of return; and voluntary unemployment (where high castes still refuse to 'work down' in stigmatised occupations) may coexist with occupational immobility and involuntary unemployment (among low castes which are excluded from access to work on non-economic grounds – though see Kapadia, Chapter 13 in this volume, for evidence of change).

Not only does social science have to explain non-state 'economic order' and non-economic order in the economy,[7] but the instance of caste also shows how a given component of the social structure may work in different relational ways in different positions in the economy. It is not only a matter of change in a socially constructed institution diffusing throughout society over time.[8] Institutional change in one part of society can also coexist with institutional defence, reinforcement and petrification elsewhere. Attempts to exert agency may be experienced as deviance and be punished. Lack of change may not be due to lack of agency within an institution but instead due to pressure against change from outside it.[9]

Over the last sixty years, whenever they have been studied comparatively, Dalits and Adivasis – a quarter of the Indian population[10] – have been shown to have had very little choice and least economic mobility. Most SC women are still confined to casual agricultural labour, and most men supplement this work with construction, sanitary work and carcass skills. In 2000, SCs and STs were roughly twice as likely to be poor, unemployed and illiterate as non-Dalits.[11] They face serious and pauperising discrimination in parts of the rural economy.[12] Yet towns, although usually seen as centres of creative institutional destruction and progress, are often no better. The organised sector has an appalling record of recruitment of SCs and STs.[13] They are even under-represented in business in the two-thirds of the economy that is unregistered and informal. Twelve per cent have businesses as against 41 per cent of the non Dalit–Adivasi working population and they are overwhelmingly confined to petty production and trade.[14] Despite the achievements of Reservations, Dalits and Adivasis who have entered the professions are a disproportionately small minority both of the Dalit and Adivasi populations and of people in the professions.

Thorat and his team use US theories of race and gender to recognise two kinds of process which enforce and police the deprivation and discrimination experienced by Dalits: unfavourable exclusion and unfavourable inclusion.[15]

With respect to unfavourable exclusion, although caste is not longer a system, it works most systematically against Dalits and Adivasis. They still often face exclusion from labour markets, credit, land markets, rental markets, services, agricultural inputs and consumer goods. Econometric analysis suggests that for SCs the poverty effects of this exclusion operate through social constraints on labour market diversification and economic mobility, while the relative poverty of STs works through locational remoteness and disadvantage as well.[16]

With respect to unfavourable inclusion, Thorat, Aryama and Negi record caste-specific variations in the terms and conditions of contracts, in prices (lower for commodities sold, higher for those bought), slow queue behaviour and 'living-mode exclusion' – that is, poor-quality services in education, housing, health, access to common property resources, to public space and to other infrastructure (e.g. decent roads, water, drainage and electricity).[17] When treatment is so pervasively different, the distinction between unfavourable inclusion and exclusion is open to doubt. From evidence of denial of access to temples, retarded access to political rights, blocked access to skilled labour opportunities in the corporate sector, the police and the judicial system, Thorat, Aryama and Negi conclude with Ambedkar, except that it is now six decades later than when he wrote, that Dalits are far from being full citizens.[18] And even the evidence summarised by Thorat *et al.* does not fully capture the specificities of all the 'unfavour' still due to the contaminating power of stigma and pollution. The mere revelation of caste identity of educated people in cooperative exercises under experimental conditions results in a significant lowering of performance all-round, in which both the confidence and the payback expectations of the lowest castes are disproportionately reduced.[19]

The significance of liberalisation

The research reported here is concerned with market freedoms and with changes in the economic position of Dalits and Adivasis over the first decade of 'liberalisation' from 1991. Economic research on SCs and STs is scarce but has generally focused on their roles in the wage labour force, in the case of SCs, and the transformations of common property, shifting cultivation and debt relations in the case of STs. But over half of India's workforce is self-employed or owns businesses. The extent to which such 'self-employment' (also known as petty commodity production, micro-enterprise and super-exploitation) is a manifestation of efficiency or rather of distress, or is a residual or seasonal part of complex labouring portfolios in and out of agriculture – whether and when self-employment is disguised wage labour or an independent crucible for accumulation – are all questions that are hotly debated, unresolved and unresolvable here.[20] Most of the businesses are small, with a family labour force, employing wage workers if and when they grow.[21] In the noteworthy absence of well-enforced protective labour laws and other promotional institutions and of enforceable protective social security rights, their entry into the business economy, their transition from reserve army and proletariat to petty producer and thence to capitalist (being cautious about teleology) has to provide the routes out of poverty and towards accumulation and wealth.[22] The research reported here is concerned with SCs and STs as owners of capital rather than as labourers.

The 1990s are generally accepted as a time when India's incorporation into the global capitalist system accelerated.[23] It is noteworthy that over the last 150 years, all of the major social-economic theorists, whatever their differences, have predicted that capitalist modernity would destroy archaic forms of exchange. Marx thought it would come about through the labour struggle; Weber through the rationalities of planning; Veblen through the effects of curiosity, industrial processes and engineering on the creation of a business class; Schumpeter through the practice of entrepreneurship, creative destruction and corporatism; Myrdal and many modern development economists such as Akerlof – who formally modelled caste – through the efficiency requirements of markets; institutional economists such as North through the effects of technology and technical change. The founding fathers of modern Indian sociology – Madan, Srinivas and later Panini – certainly see contract replacing custom. And anthropologists such as Parry, Searle-Chatterjee and Sharma have observed how the state-organised production of entirely new intermediate goods and final commodities has created a cosmopolitan labour force in the melting pot of urban sites and the urban-industrial economy.[24]

Yet, the persistent condition of Dalits and Adivasis is evidence that while archaic forms of exchange and economic regulation may dissolve, the process is by no means straightforward.[25] Aspects of identity such as caste are not just ignored or confined to the dustbin of history but are also cherished and reworked as regulators – not only in the economy but also inside the state apparatus. Furthermore, they transform corporatist institutions of collective action, business associations, which are necessary preconditions to, and accompaniments of, economic competition. A range of social and economic processes may develop in close physical proximity and even in the same social space.[26] Rather than accelerating the destruction of old forms of exchange, India's liberalisation may be better understood as increasing the tension between forces dissolving social forms of regulation and those intensifying them or creating new forms.[27] This process will be socially and spatially uneven.

The rest of this chapter examines economic outcomes for Dalits and Adivasis at the start and end of the last decade of the twentieth century. Our initial analysis puts the question in its simplest form – hypothesising that unevenness in their economic chances will be reduced by the modernising forces embodied in liberalisation – and we already have good reasons to investigate it sceptically. We explore All-India unevenness across economic sectors, through the political space of states and over time.

Evidence and method

Aggregated analyses of the condition of Dalits and Adivasis merge caste with ethnicity because those of lowest caste and ethnic status have many life conditions in common. Indeed, we saw earlier that they are understood by some as having a common origin. Even when examined separately, bland categories – 'Scheduled Castes' and 'Scheduled Tribes' – are classified on a par with Backward Castes (BCs) and other politicised caste groups. These categories are further stylised in formal economic models – models of the transaction and enforcement costs of nonconformity, of caste as a voluntary stable equilibrium, of a system expressed in third-party penalties for rule-breaking, and so on.[28] All these approaches ignore the special relations of untouchability and tribal 'otherness', and strip caste relations of their complexity, dynamism and violence. Quantitative analysis cannot escape these problems, and the evidence and methods we use in this exercise are no exception. Yet the results of the research we have done are so striking, have such clear potential significance for policy, and provoke such challenges for explanation and further research as to demand publication and debate.

The population censuses provide data for 'Scheduled Castes' (SC) and 'Scheduled Tribes' (ST) and total population (rural and urban) by state for the years 1991 and 2001. While SCs are disproportionately agricultural and industrial labourers and self- employed artisans, STs are disproportionately cultivators, forest hunters and gatherers and fishers.[29] The Economic Census supplies a data base comprising the number of private, overwhelmingly 'own account', enterprises (OAEs) by SC, ST and other castes, rural and urban, by state for the years 1990 and 1998 (see Appendix 1 at the end of this chapter). 'Enterprises' in this context are economic undertakings 'not for the sole purpose of own consumption'.[30] We have no All-India information about the size distribution of enterprises.[31] Nor do we know how they are gendered. We also do not know the reliability of the sampling and survey procedures involved. The data are for ten sectors of the economy in 1990 and for fourteen in 1998. Over and above the problems of matching business data for 1990 and 1998 with demographic data for 1991 and 2001, not to mention the further difficulties for aggregation of the changes in sectoral classifications over the 'short decade' of 1990–98, the arbitrary sectoral categories are awkward for both theory and interpretation.[32] It should also be noted that there are no disaggregated data for the participation of self-employed SCs in sanitary services, refuse collection, recycling and so forth: this category of work is invisible, a taboo in official systems of classification. In addition, the territories of states (which were also reclassified over this period) produce distortions to India's agro-ecological regions. The latter may still be culture regions as they were known to be in the 1930s.[33]

With due caution these data may be used to produce indices of participation (PI):

SC or ST enterprises (SCE) in sector *i*, state *x* / total enterprises in sector *i*, in state *x* / SC or ST Population (SCP) in state *x* / total population in state *x*

$$\frac{SCEix}{\Sigma Eix} \Big/ \frac{SCPx}{\Sigma Px}$$

A value of 1.0 represents absence of bias or a state of parity: i.e., the proportion of Dalit enterprises equals the proportion of Dalits in the state. A rank of <1 denotes disproportionately low participation or 'negative discrimination' in the market, and >1 disproportionately high participation or 'positive market discrimination'.

These indices have in turn been mapped,[34] using the Geographical Information System (GIS), to produce forty maps of discrimination in the participation of Dalits as owners of capital in the Indian economy in the 1990s.[35] In the discussion which follows, we draw illustratively on a subset of these maps.

General trends over the 1990s

During the 'short decade' of the 1990s the absolute total number of enterprises in India increased by a quarter (Table 15.1). While this increase took place, the proportion of all enterprises owned by Dalits remained stable at 13 per cent. In fact, the involvement of Dalits in this general increase took two opposite forms. While the proportion of enterprises owned by STs increased by two-thirds, that owned by SCs actually declined by 15 per cent.[36]

The Economic Census data suggest that between 1990 and 1998 the number of firms grew from 22 to 28 million. From Table 15.2 it is evident that by far the most important category of firm – some 38 per cent in both 1990 and 1998 – is in wholesale and retail trade (a comparison of the 1998 disaggregation with the 1990 data shows that hotels and restaurants are only 4 per cent of all firms). Community social and personal services – mainly health, education personal and community services, rather than IT and back office sectors – also declined relatively, from 19 to 16 per cent. Together, by the turn of the century, trade and services constituted 56 per cent of GDP but 67 per cent of enterprises. Manufacturing firms accounted for 23 to 20 per cent of the total number of firms (while being about 22 per cent of GDP – roughly commensurate with their share of total enterprises).[37] They declined over the period (or perhaps retreated further into the informal economy). It may not be sufficiently appreciated how important the livestock sector is to the structure of India's non-farm enterprises; it rose from 8 to 10 per cent of firms from 1990 to 1998.

But these opposite trends were uneven across the sectors of the economy.[38] STs saw strong increases in their roles in the primary and secondary sectors (by 66 per cent and 54 per cent respectively) but a very striking rise of 125 per cent in services.[39] SCs, by contrast, saw their participation as owners in the agricultural and livestock sectors decline by 16 per cent; they saw little growth in the manufacturing sector and a mere 24-per-cent increase in their participation in the service sector. It is clear that the process of entry into the market as owners of capital, however small the firms, takes different forms for STs and SCs. It is greatly differentiated across the sectors of the economy and easiest in the provision of services. This sectoral unevenness increased rather than declined during the 1990s. Our starting hypothesis – that unevenness in the economic incorporation of Dalits and Adivasis will be reduced by the modernising forces of liberalisation – is refuted.

Table 15.1 Dalit firms (1990 and 1998)

	Total no. firms (millions)	% ST pop.	% ST firms	% SC pop.	% SC firms
1990 (1991)	22.2	8.1	2.9	16.5	9.9
1998 (2001)	27.7	8.2	4.4	16.2	8.4

Source: Census and Economic Census data.

Table 15.2 The distribution across sectors of private enterprises in India

Sectors in 1990	Total private enterprises (SC+ST+general)	%
1 Livestock raising	1,693,944	7.65
2 Agricultural services, forestry, fishing & hunting	549,098	2.48
3 Mining & quarrying	47,143	0.21
4 Manufacturing	5,131,524	23.18
5 Electricity, gas & water supply	10,557	0.05
6 Construction	221,162	1.00
7 Trade, hotels & restaurants	9,373,327	42.34
8 Transport, storage & communication	628,054	2.84
9 Finance, real estate, business & others	351,806	1.59
10 Health, education, community services, etc.	4,125,573	18.63
11 Others (n.a.d)	8,645	0.04
12 Total	22,140,833	100.00

Sectors in 1998	Total private enterprises (SC+ST+general)	%
1 Raising livestock	2,842,792	10.26
2 Agricultural services	595,218	2.15
3 Mining & quarrying	34,072	0.12
4 Manufacturing	5,481,722	19.78
5 Electricity, gas & water supply	12,159	0.04
6 Construction	283,200	1.02
7 Wholesale trade	705,605	2.55
8 Retail trade	10,538,516	38.02
9 Restaurants & hotels	1,162,915	4.20
10 Transport	883,266	3.19
11 Storage & warehousing	69,197	0.25
12 Communication	167,850	0.61
13 Finance, business & allied activities	597,711	2.16
14 Community, social & personal services	4,334,534	15.64
15 Unspecified activities	5,648	0.02
16 Total	27,717,190	100.00

Source: Economic Census data (1990; 1998).

Strong regional patterns emerge from the maps (see Appendix 2 at the end of this chapter). First, SCs and STs are distributed differently across India's states. In terms of people, the proportion of SCs to total population is greatest in the north and south-east and least in the far west, the north-east and the state of Kerala in the south. Their growth rates are fastest where they are least densely distributed. By contrast STs are most relatively dense in the centre and the north-east and least dense in the north and south. Their growth rates are fastest in south central India.[40] Meanwhile, the proportion of Dalit enterprises takes a somewhat different spatial expression from enterprises in general. SC enterprises are proportionally most abundant in the NE where their absolute incidence in the generally sparse population is among the lowest.[41] For SCs, extreme PI values of over 10 are common in these north-eastern states. By contrast, ST enterprises match the distribution of population but to a far lower extent.[42]

Between 1991 and 2001, there was no change in the demographic regions.[43] But maps of the participation index (PI) for all private enterprises show that the apparent effects of 'negative discrimination' against SCs spread during the decade throughout the south and intensified in a belt from Rajasthan and Gujarat, through Uttar Pradesh to Bihar and Chhattisgarh.[44] The opposite happened for STs: the PI indices show increases in relative participation focused in the region of Orissa, Jharkhand and Chhattisgarh, but extending in a general region along the eastern littoral – spreading westwards from the east during the 1990s.[45]

Spatiality of Dalit and Adivasi discrimination

The simplest generalisation that may be made is that the maps reveal that, where SCs and STs are each relatively most densely distributed in the population, they are each relatively least densely distributed as owners of firms in the non-farm economy. Beyond this aggregate conclusion, however, relationships are nuanced.

The regions of discrimination observed at the All-India level and for all private enterprises are now examined by sector, first for SCs and then for STs for 1990 and 1998. Despite the limitations of the data, they strongly suggest that different sectors show different patterns of regional distribution, which intensify both positively and negatively during the 1990s.

Scheduled Castes

Agriculture – and livestock:[46] In 1990 SCs were disproportionately prominent in agriculture in the north-east and under-represented in the west of India. By 1998, however, negative PIs had spread throughout the country.

Non-agricultural business in general:[47] In 1990, SCs were strongly under-represented in business in the south and relatively over-represented in Himachal Pradesh, Madhya Pradesh and the north-eastern states; but by 1998 their dispro-portionately low participation had spread in the southern regions as far north as Karnataka, making a solid region of low participation throughout South India – together with a northern one in Uttar Pradesh and the north-west.[48]

Mining, quarrying and construction: SCs are disproportionately active in these sectors in large parts of India. By 1998, 'positive discrimination' had spread to a belt in the centre and north but the whole of South India had developed a negative bias.[49]

Manufacturing: In 1990, relative SC participation in business was positive in central India and low in the south-east and north-west. Over the eight years studied in the 1990s relative disadvantage spread to Karnataka in the south and to Gujarat and Rajasthan in the north-west; while positive advantage started emerging in a wider belt in central and north central India.[50]

Trade, hotels, etc.: The participation of SCs is strongly negative in 1990 except in Orissa and the north-eastern tribal states. There appear on the face of it to be powerful entry barriers at work. The pattern persists in 1998.[51]

Transport, storage, communications, finance, real estate: There is persistently low participation of SCs in these sectors throughout India, except in the north-eastern states.

Personal and community services (including health and education): These are sectors where the impact of reservations in education and public service might be thought to be most manifest. But the participation of SCs is generally disproportionately low, and increasingly so through the decade except in Orissa, the north-eastern states and parts of North India.

Scheduled Tribes

Agriculture and livestock: Controlling for the distribution of tribal people, in 1990 they were disproportionately concentrated in agriculture in a north–south spine in eastern India and under-represented where they are also the smallest proportion of the population – in western India. But, in 1998, while they were withdrawing from the livestock economy, their relative disadvantage was declining – and even turning to relative advantage in the north-west.[52]

Non-agricultural business in general: Whereas, in 1990, the participation of STs was disproportionately low everywhere except for Uttar Pradesh and Sikkim and Mizoram in the north-east, by 1998 there is a striking increase in participation 'spreading' from the eastern littoral.[53]

Mining, quarrying and construction: Relative to their population, STs are disproportionately concentrated in this sector in a patchy scatter of regions around the periphery/littoral of India.[54]

Manufacturing: In 1990, STs were relatively concentrated in a northern belt extending east to Orissa and disproportionately under-represented elsewhere; by 1998, their under-representation had been reduced somewhat in the south of India.[55]

Trade – wholesale, retail and hotels: STs were under-represented in trade throughout India in 1990, with the exception of Uttar Pradesh and Assam. By 1998, however, their participation had greatly improved in the south, though the central belt showed no improvement. The more highly disaggregated classifications for 1998 confirm this trend.[56]

Transport, storage and communications: The participation of STs is patchy and shows no pattern.

Finance and real estate: STs are relatively absent in a central belt, but by 1998 their participation had improved in Uttar Pradesh, Bihar, Andhra Pradesh, Tamil Nadal and the north-east.

Education, health, personal and community services: During the decade a significant positive change was witnessed in the south of India.

To sum up these findings: The regionalisation of the economic participation of Dalits and Adivasis – and their entry barriers – are highly differentiated in sector-specific ways, and differ substantially as between SCs and STs. Over time, while the relative disadvantage of SCs appears to spread, especially in the southern states, the relative advantage of STs spreads inland from the east, and throughout the south.

We can now turn to the explanation of these regional patterns and trends.

Explanations from economics

Given that both the sectoral and the regional distributions are characterised by significant diversity, it is likely to be difficult to use the normal principle of parsimony to explain the phenomenon of several types of uneven participation at the state and All-India level. However, an attempt to explain SC/ST participation as owners of firms was made in 2006 by Charlotte Murphy, guided by Stefan Dercon. It showed that certain factors that might be expected to be at the root of differentials in advantage may be eliminated as being irrelevant at the All-India level of analysis using state-level data.[57]

Murphy's attempt to explain Dalit participation in the business economy was driven by the paucity and availability of data. From the data deployed, some tentative hypotheses may be generated. There are five:

1   Urbanism will dissolve rooted discrimination; new goods and socially dis-embedded exchange will favour the upward mobility of Dalits and their entry into business.
2   Education has both a capacitating, capability-expanding role and is widely thought to lead to the dissolving of archaic social arrangements. It may be predicted to facilitate entry into the business economy.
3   The average landholdings of SCs, STs and Other Castes (OCs) may be considered a proxy for collateral for credit which is predicted to ease entry to business.
4   The proportion of Dalits in the population may be considered a proxy for the density of their social networks. Social networks are known to be essential to entry into the business economy.

5   By contrast, the extensiveness of brute poverty is predicted to be a barrier
to entry into the business economy because entry requires a modicum of
initial capital.

Not only may these variables be used to explain entry, but state-level variations
in their values may be predicted to drive regional variations in SC/ST participation
in the business economy. None of these hypotheses are particular to the era of
liberalisation. Nor do hypotheses about economic mobility address the problem
of differential sectoral barriers to entry.

Murphy simplified the ten sectors in 1990 and fourteen in 1998 to three for
both periods. (See Appendix 15.1 for these sectors, and for the sources of all
the data and methods used.) Here we relate her results to the five hypotheses:

1   Holding crude caste categories constant, the degree of urbanisation was found
to matter only to the class of total enterprises and not to any of the three
sectors. Even at the crudest level (Other Castes (a.k.a. the 'main population'), SCs and STs) it was significant only at the 10 per cent probability
level and would be rejected as significant by most economists. Even as a
trivial result it is odd, because it is indeed to be expected that non-
agricultural firms are located in towns. The role of rural sites in the
accumulation trajectories of SCs and STs clearly needs further research, as
do the roles of towns as economic barriers to entry to socially disadvantaged
people.

2   Education was also statistically significant in the aggregate. It mattered most
to the chances of STs, where a 1 per cent increase in literacy resulted in a
10 per cent increase in ownership of enterprises. For SCs, however, there was
a significant but very poor response. A 1 per cent increase in their literacy
was related to a mere 0.001 per cent increase in enterprises owned. SCs are
apparently not able to profit from education by using it to start businesses.[58]
Education had no effects in the primary sector (agriculture); it had significant
effects in the secondary sector (manufacturing and extractive industry) both
for the main population of other castes (an elasticity of 5 per cent) and for
STs (10 per cent). In the tertiary, service sector, it had a large and significant
effect only for STs. For the main population and SCs the effect was statistically
significant but negligible in practical terms.

3   Landholdings, as a proxy for collateral for credit, were not significant at
the level of all enterprises. The average size of Dalit landholdings was significantly related to the frequency of their incidence in the agricultural sector
itself. But the regressions in terms of changes over the period 1990–98
revealed severe barriers to Dalit land acquisition. In the secondary (manufacturing) sector the relationship was slight, negative and of low significance.
Land does not appear to drive entry to the industrial sectors. In the tertiary
(services) sector the proxy for creditworthiness was significantly but negatively related to enterprise ownership.

4   The hypothesis about social networks, taking as proxy the proportion of Dalits in the population, proved insignificant and has to be rejected. The proxy may be inappropriate. The most that can be squeezed from the result is the implication that, where Dalits are currently most confined to the casual wage labour market, this does not necessarily imply that they cannot own firms – but there is certainly no strong positive association. Clearly the issue needs further research at lower levels of aggregation.

5   So does the hypothesis about poverty as a barrier to entry. Head-count poverty had negligible effects and was not statistically significant. Other poverty measures might produce different results. And changes in poverty may be driven by changes in education, with the knock-on differential effects discussed earlier.

In sum: This first attempt to explain the economics of Dalit participation implies that, in regions (or states) where STs have been made literate, this education drives a large increase in their capacity to enter the secondary and service sectors. The service sector may also hold fewer barriers to entry than the secondary and primary sectors. But the service sector is highly differentiated and it is low-end services that will have low entry barriers. Then throughout India the accumulation trajectories of SCs and STs may favour rural areas because the relationship between their firms and urbanisation, though positive in the aggregate, is found to be weak. In regions (or states) where SCs and STs have larger landholdings than their All-India average, they are, however, less concentrated in the secondary and tertiary sectors. So we cannot assume that agricultural profits are an investment springboard. There is also no relationship between Dalits in the wage labour force and entry to business – either agricultural or non-agricultural.

If the data relevant to this level of analysis cannot be refined (which is one avenue for further econometric investigation), then these All-India results direct us towards forms of analysis which use other kinds of evidence and other, more fine-grained levels of aggregation. In particular, local-level research needs to examine Dalit and Adivasi incorporation into the rural non-farm economy, and to explore the history of processes and relationships which block and resist their economic agency.

Explanations from political sociology

In 1999, John Harriss published research devoted to explaining success in poverty alleviation in India in terms of differences between pro-poor political regimes. As with Murphy's work, this research is highly relevant to any attempt to account for differences in the success of the Dalit population in the business economy, because Dalits are disproportionally poor. Harriss borrows from Dieter Rueshmayer the proposition that the effectiveness of democracy lies in its being able to differentiate politics from other systems of inequality and other forms of domination, both market- and non-market-mediated. Because this political differentiation rarely happens, civil society must be the mechanism for monitoring

and enforcing the democratic quality of politics. As a result, the broader politics
of any regime needs distinguishing from party politics; and both will enter into
any explanation of growth that reduces poverty. The former, 'regime structure',
melds the politics of agrarian classes with the levels of development of agrarian
and industrial capitalism and of the working class. The latter, 'party politics',
requires an understanding of ideology, party organisation and the class and caste
alliances involved. Harriss also updates[59] a taxonomy of the relations of caste
to class in India in the early 1980s borrowed from Roderick Church,[60] because
Church perceived that political regimes in India's democracy were crucially
dependent on the extent and mode of participation of lower castes. Church found
'the only people systematically excluded from a share of political representation
and policy benefits were the castes below the middle castes and above the
scheduled castes' – a comment we find tellingly neglectful of the actual condition
of the bottom quarter of the population.

The typology that results from Harriss's analysis of state regimes according
to the modes of incorporation of 'lower castes and classes' is presented in summary
form in Table 15.3 and we have mapped it – Appendix 3. Four comments can
be made on the table and the map.

First, the category of 'lower castes and classes' conflates a very large fraction
of the Indian population with significantly different economic interests, locations,
prospects and caste relations. Church defines 'lower castes' as those supplying
'artisanal goods and services'. The occupations to which SCs are mainly confined
– agricultural labour, carcass, sanitary and construction work – and the distinctive
property rights regimes through which tribal people hang on to agricultural land,
waste land and forest resources, and their double marginality from party politics
and from that of civil society,[61] were not regarded as being critically distinct
aspects of the politics of poverty and of micro-level economic growth.

Table 15.3 Typology of state regimes according to modes of incorporation of 'lower
castes and classes'

Class	Characteristics	States
Ai	Persistent upper-caste/class Dominance. Congress strong.	Madhya Pradesh; Orissa; Rajasthan
Aii	Effective challenges by middles castes/classes. Congress collapsed – i.e. dominance and alliances broken.	Bihar; Uttar Pradesh
B	Middle-caste-dominated regimes. Congress effectively challenged but not collapsed. Stable two-party competition and accommodation with lower castes.	Andhra Pradesh; Gujarat; Karnataka; Maharashtra; Punjab
C	Low castes/classes more strongly represented. Congress lost dominance early on.	Kerala; Tamil Nadu; West Bengal

Source: Harriss (1999).

Second, the distinctively tribal north-eastern region (in which there are both a substantial tribal elite and relatively striking SC involvement in the non-agricultural economy) is absent from the classification – neither Assam nor Arunachal and the other north-eastern states are included.

Third, while West Bengal is classed with Kerala and Tamil Nadu as states where Congress lost dominance early on, and where low castes and classes are more strongly represented in party politics – that is, the most pro-poor political regimes – there is good empirical evidence to suggest that West Bengal has not incorporated SCs and STs systematically into the party structure. The CPI(M) is generally reluctant on principle to take caste openly into class politics, but it does not have a conspicuously good record in the alleviation of poverty, especially when its multidimensional nature is taken into account.[62] And our maps of Dalit discrimination show that neither Kerala nor Tamil Nadu, both noted for achievements with respect to poverty, empowerment and self-respect, are at all notable for their achievement with respect to Dalit and Adivasi entry into the market economy as owners of firms.

Lastly, while the two classes of regimes which have the poorest incorporation of lower castes and classes do have a certain territorial integrity and regional character, there is a significant information loss between the map of the 'pro-poorness' of political regimes and the maps of the economic incorporation of Dalits as owners of enterprises. Jos Mooij's comparative study of food politics and policy regimes in India (1999) revealed one state with developmental and pro-labour food politics surrounded by quite predatory states, making the point – relevant here – that in India starkly different politics and political regimes can be separated by the power of 'thin' political borders. While political regimes can differ in adjacent states, the relations between the 'pro-poorness' of political regimes and the economic participation of Dalits and Adivasis will itself differ – an issue that clearly needs further research.

In sum: pro-poor growth has been conceived in Harriss's project – generally as a set of policies sectoralising and targeting 'low castes and classes' – and not as a set of transformations happening while SCs and STs claw their way into business, while they overcome the exercise of their economic agency as being treated by others as a punishable form of deviance, or while they are confined to a deliberately limited state of clientelage.[63] The analysis of pro-poor political regimes does not produce regions which map easily on to those of Dalit and Adivasi economic incorporation and exclusion. New research is needed on the modes of political incorporation explicitly of Dalits, and on the relation between these modes and their economic achievements outside the spheres of wage labour, the professions and public service.

Conclusions

The Economic Census data we have used yield strong results, of considerable interest for policy and development politics. They also generate a research agenda because their explanation is far from obvious: our first attempts to explain them as reported here got but limited purchase.

At the state level, there appear to be inverse though different spatial relationships between the relative density of SCs and STs in the population and their relative participation in the non-farm economy as owners of firms.

The categories of SCs and STs are usually lumped together in All-India analysis of poverty and social exclusion. They are even aggregated into larger social entities such as 'lower castes and classes' (see the political sociological analysis of Harriss 1999) or 'oppressed people' (as by the Dalit Panthers; see Kumar 2008). Our maps of their entry into the economy as owners of businesses show this to mask the political-economic processes involved. Not only are SCs and STs incorporated in widely differing regional and sectoral patterns but their historical trends are different. In the aggregate, their involvement as owners of firms did not change in the 1990s. But, while the proportion of enterprises owned by STs increased by two-thirds between 1990 and 1998, the proportion owned by SCs actually declined by 15 per cent. 'Human development' – in the form of education – had radically different and contradictory effects on SCs and STs. If liberalisation is dissolving archaic forms of regulating exchange, it is doing so unevenly and slowly.

Our All-India analysis, disaggregated by state, shows that India has a series of regions of relative advantage and disadvantage for SCs and STs. While sectors may be distinctively spatially organised, they are coherent, and they also change in coherent ways: Table 15.4.

SCs have entered mining, quarrying and construction and are most consistently prevented from entering trade, transport, food, hospitality and service sectors, the last of which is driving Indian growth. STs have a relative disadvantage in all sectors of the non-agricultural economy but have been able, with the help of improvements in literacy, to move into services – though, it is likely, at the low end.

Over time, it is remarkable that SC disadvantage has intensified in South India, in exactly those states where the politics of self-respect (Tamil Nadu) and

Table 15.4 Summary of regions of incorporation of Dalits in India

SCs *East advantaged; west disadvantaged*	*North advantaged; south disadvantaged*	*Relative advantage everywhere*	*Relative disadvantage everywhere*
Agriculture	Non-agricultural in general; manufacturing	Mining; quarrying; construction	Trade; transport; storage; finance; real estate; services
STs *East advantaged; west disadvantaged*	*North advantaged; south disadvantaged*	*Patchy/ no pattern*	*North and south-east advantage*
Agriculture	Manufacturing; trade	Mining; quarrying; construction; trade; transport; storage; communications; services	Non-agriculture in general

of the Communist parties (Kerala) have been notably active. It is also remarkable that in the north-eastern tribal states, while there is a very low absolute distribution of SCs, there is high SC participation in sectors to which there are clear barriers elsewhere. The region is liberating to the few who migrate there and cross its severe political hurdles to entry.

By contrast, over the first decade of the 'era of liberalisation', the low participation of STs in the ownership of firms was strikingly reduced, in a process that appears to be diffusing westwards from the eastern littoral. This seems to be an untold story of 'pro-poor growth' from conditions of great disadvantage. At the All-India level this process of transformation is associated with lagged responses to improvements in literacy – though whether STs in business are still likely to be confined to petty production and trade needs to be researched.

In general, although India has a unique policy response to the centuries of discrimination meted out to the lowest quarter of its population, the policy of Reservations has not been found to have a strong impact on the participation of Dalits and Adivasis in those public services which we were able to map. 'Pro-poor growth' – in an informal capitalist economy where unions, decent minimum wages, protective labour laws and social security exist but are all very thin on the ground – must provide routes by which wage labour can accumulate wealth through ownership. It is of the first importance, practically and theoretically, to discover whether entry barriers to the different sectors of the business economy are economic, social, or both, why that is, and why they vary regionally.

As with the sex ratio, where regions may be broadly defined but where All-India explanations have proved harder to obtain,[64] so with the regionalisation of Dalit and Adivasi incorporation and discrimination, historical explanations for the complex patterns that exist are needed at a lower level of aggregation than that of states. The problem needs complementary and different kinds of research at aggregate and disaggregated levels and the question then arises of the basis for theorising the relevant regions.[65]

Five dimensions of enquiry commend themselves for comparative research. First, the processes and relationships generating or blocking firm-owning opportunities in the rural non-farm economy, and differential resistance to Dalit and Adivasi entry into the urban business economy, need investigating.[66] Many detailed questions can be suggested: the roles of migration and remittance compulsions; the regional character of Forward Caste hegemony and of OBC (Other Backward Caste/Class) and MBC (Most Backward Caste/Class)[67] resistance to Dalit and Adivasi assertion in different regions; the regional roles of religion, language and other moral communities on the stratification of economic trajectories and migration routes; the role of employment in the armed forces in liberating starting capital and entry; reasons for regional variations in access to wholesaling and thus to trade credit.[68]

Second, the key relations for poverty reduction between Dalit and Adivasi ownership and management of land, water, forests and livestock, wage labour, self-employment and the employment of others need comparative class analysis grounded in field research. Research on agrarian class formation, migration and economic mobility suggests that these relationships are likely to involve the rural and urban non-farm economy in complex combinations of (micro) property and labour which work in nuanced ways and which resist an easy teleology.[69] One question for example would concern the relationship between relative participation in the business economy and political organisation in agriculture – the degree of success of claims for minimum wages by SC and ST workers and of their claims to land under land and tenancy reforms. The starter hypothesis would then be that, where SCs and STs have consolidated gains either as labour or as owners or tenants, they are less likely to invest in the non-farm economy (as a response either to distress using loans or to opportunities to use their savings).[70]

Third, in view of the contradictory role of education in the form of basic literacy, more needs to be known about the needs of the differentiated capitalist economy for Dalit and Adivasi 'human development'. This would inform a more general understanding of the nature and dynamics of the non-market institutions without which labour cannot be reproduced for the capitalist production cycle. Fourth, research is needed that examines individual economic agency – agency that is locally understood as deviance – which would reveal the policing and punitive processes confronted, and thus improve our understanding of the violence of institutional change in market economies. Finally, more needs to be known about the regional modes of political incorporation or exclusion of Dalits and Adivasis as highly differentiated and gendered categories. This requires research into the relation between political regime structures and party politics as they pertain to SCs and STs and the economic achievements of this quarter of the population not only as labour but also as owners of businesses.[71]

Here, problems of data will be serious. Even in the Economic Census databases only the most voluminous and disaggregated form will reveal the structure of ownership of refuse collection, butchering, recycling and sanitation services. The data to which we had access were also not gendered. Factors deemed irrelevant for All-India policy may in fact prove highly relevant at other, local scales. The implications for politics and development policy – whether positive, critical or normative – will be local and differentiated.

The advent of 'globalisation' has dealt a body blow to our understanding of regional geography.[72] The regional relations between agro-ecology, culture, politics, local capitalism and their relation to the global system need revitalising, both for their intrinsic value and for the insights this will surely yield into social structures of exploitation and capitalist wealth creation. That a large and new research agenda on the contemporary history of regional and local processes of discrimination, economic incorporation and accumulation of Dalit and Adivasi men and women has taken this long to be added to the Dalit activist research agenda does not indicate its lack of urgency in – or of relevance for – contemporary India.

Acknowledgements

This project has emerged from Barbara Harriss-White's work on the social structure of accumulation in India's informal economy (2003, 2004, 2008) (and what Kate Meagher (2004) has called 'identity economics'). But the present focus on Dalits has also been nurtured by discussions on rural labour and caste over the last quarter-century with Judith Heyer and by the experience of writing the *Socialist Register 2001* paper on 'Mapping India's world of unorganised labour' jointly with Nandini Gooptu. Nor could it have happened without timely data compiled and provided to us by Pinaki Joddar and support from Prof Alakh Sharma, Aseem Prakash and staff at the Institute of Human Development (IHD); or without galvanising conversations about the position of Dalits in the non-farm economy with Professors Sukhdeo Thorat and Yoginder Alagh in December 2005. The research has benefited from discussion at the Contemporary South Asian Studies Seminar as well as the Workshop for this book in Oxford in 2007 and at the British Association of South Asian Studies Conference in 2008. We are grateful for all the constructive engagement. The results of the regression analyses are drawn from Charlotte Murphy's MSc thesis, 2006, Oxford University, which used the IHD's data. That research was supervised by Professor Stefan Dercon and we are also grateful to both of them.

Notes

1 Collected and published by Central Statistical Organisation (CSO), Government of India. Available online: www.mospi.nic.in/economic_census.htm.
2 Thorat, Aryami and Negi (2005) give a good introduction to the constitutional protections pioneered by Ambedkar against the violation of the rights of Dalits. These comprise equal access: civil, political and economic; penalties for denial of access; empowerment in education, public service and the legislature; safeguarding, monitoring and enforcement. As they observe, it is clear Ambedkar's project involved the creation of a comprehensive strategy for the economic development of Dalits (2005: 16–24).
3 The informal economy uses money regulated by the state but firms are not registered for all required purposes – or at all. They either operate below tax thresholds or evade and avoid tax; and they also avoid and evade protections to labour afforded under the many labour laws and Factories Acts; they ignore land-use planning and laws regulating the environment (see Harriss-White 2003; Jairaj and Harriss-White 2006; Harriss-White and Sinha 2007; Ruthven 2008).
4 De Golbery and Chappius (2000: 303), according to whom the 'first occupiers' of the Subcontinent were driven to the remote margins as tribal people, or integrated adversely into Hindu village society as outcastes. Tribals are thought on balance to have living standards inferior to SCs.
5 Clarified in Kumar (2008).
6 Parry (2007), contrasts the cosmopolitan labour force in the Bhilai Steel Plant with the caste stratification on the local industrial estate, and in the market town serving these two planned development projects. So here, planned development has had two quite different outcomes in terms of the social stratification of the economy; regulative planning has had less of a transformative effect than full-blown state participation and the formalisation of wage labour.
7 By which we mean order derived from forms of domination that also have sites outside the economy and do not depend on market value for their reproduction. The reproduction of the cycles of accumulation cannot take place, however, without these forms of instituted power. These may have physical sites – such as gender in the household, religion and the temple. Change in their regulation of the economy may

well emerge from change in the way these forms of power operate outside the sphere of economic provisioning.

8 See Basile and Harriss-White (2003) for a detailed analysis of the caste-corporatist regulation of the small town business economy that illustrates this point.

9 See Harriss-White (2007) for an attempt to make a general statement about institutional policing and punishment when agency is experienced as deviance.

10 SCs amount to 16.5 per cent and STs 8.5 per cent (Thorat, Aryami and Negi 2005: 1).

11 Deaton and Dreze: cited in Sen (2002); Gang, Sen and Yun (2008).

12 Research by ActionAid in 550 villages in 2000/2001 showed the denial of access to agricultural wage labour in 36 per cent of villages, discrimination in wages in 24 per cent, barriers to construction labour because of the contamination to the purity of domestic space in 33 per cent, denial of access to irrigation water in 33 per cent, denial of access to the purchase of land and to common property resources in 21 per cent, forbidding to trade in 35 per cent and prevention of access to milk cooperatives in 47 per cent (reported in Thorat, Aryami and Negi 2005: 25–6).

13 Relational recruitment prevails in the private organised sector and high castes, especially Brahmins, are over-represented. In Pune Brahmins and Marathas are 50 per cent of the organised labour force and in Coimbatore Brahmins alone are about half (Thorat, Aryami and Negi 2005: 25–9). See also the research into first-stage rejection of Dalits in corporate recruitment by Thorat and Attewell (2007) and Thorat and Newman (2007).

14 Thorat, Aryami and Negi (2005: 24–5).

15 Thorat (2002).

16 Gang, Sen and Yun (2008).

17 So those responsible for the public cleanliness on which market economies depend are denied the basic infrastructure they help to provide.

18 Thorat, Aryami and Negi (2005: 3–14); Thorat and Attewell (2007); Thorat and Newman (2007).

19 Hoff and Pandey (2004).

20 See Banaji (1977); Vaidyanathan (1986); Chandrasekhar (1993); Jayaraj (2004); Harriss-White (2009) and Lerche, Chapter 3 in this volume.

21 They have proved hard to theorise. Kalecki referred to such forms of capital as 'intermediate'. Such firms embody the contradictory class positions of capital and labour. Petty production has also been theorised as disguised wage labour, or really subsumed under capital, though formally independent.

22 This is not an argument against workplace activism for better conditions of wage work. It is merely a response to the oppressive and exploitative conditions under which most Dalits labour.

23 Of course, the Indian economy liberalised, but without accelerated growth, during the 1980s. Some scholars point to the 1960s as the origin of liberalisation in the failure of planned industrial development and the onset of industrial deceleration (McCartney 2006). Das Gupta (2008) tracks Indian FDI (foreign direct investment) and argues that, from the 1960s, the institutional preconditions for liberalisation were being laid, finding also that significant deceleration was confined to the Post-Emergency period of 1977–80. Yet others saw no planned development, so no liberalisation at all. This is particularly relevant to the comprehensive demobilisation of labour in the late 1940s. With respect to the labour force a minute fraction was ever entitled under planned development, so the labour force in general can hardly have been liberalised, for it was always formally unregulated (see Chibber 2003 for the urban labour force and Breman 2007 for rural labour).

24 See the review in Harriss-White (2007) for references.

25 To cast this as 'modernity versus tradition' misconceives modernity. To cast this as a binary is itself a misleading simplification, for these processes will actually generate a range of outcomes.

26 Mhaskar (forthcoming) examines the political economy of Mumbai households in which the older generation of unionised textile workers has been made redundant and absorbed into the caste-regulated informal economy, while some of the younger generation find new white-collar jobs in the cosmopolitan service economy.

27 Harriss-White (2003: chapter 9); World Bank (2006: 179).

28 Akerlof (1976); Banerjee and Knight (1985); Scoville (1996).

29 De Golbery and Chappuis (2000: 321–32). Their dominant occupation defies easy regionalisation. SC artisanal dominance is scattered; SC cultivation tends to be found in the north and agricultural labour conversely in the south, forestry in the south-west and services in the north-east. ST forestry is the dominant ST occupation in the west; artisans in the east and agricultural producers and labourers in the centre. While STs are territorially concentrated in the centre, north-west and north-east, they are least urbanised around the land and coastal peripheries of the country (Chapman and Pathak 1997).

30 They are further classified into private; cooperative; private non-profit (such as a temple), and state institutions controlled by households (of which there are extremely few).

31 Though in Arunachal Pradesh, for instance, a tribal state, we have independent sample survey verification that over 90 per cent of enterprises have fewer than ten employees (Dr V. Upadhyay, Pers. Comm., March 2007); and long-term research on the evolution of a South Indian market town over twenty-five years has revealed that SC firms are few and unstable in number and confined to general merchants, transport and fuel, a very few grocery shops and the low-end margins of the silk manufacturing industry (Basile and Harriss-White 2003; Basile, forthcoming: chapter 9, table 6).

32 In 1990, these are livestock; agriculture and forestry; mining; manufacturing; utilities (electricity, gas and water); construction; trade, hotels and restaurants; transport, storage and communications; finance and real estate; and health, education community and personal services. In 1998, they are livestock; agricultural services; mining; manufacturing; utilities; construction; wholesale trade; retail trade; restaurants and hotels; transport; storage; communication; finance and real estate; and community social and personal services.

33 Thorner (1995) and see endnote 63.

34 The choropleth categories guard against the distorting effects of extreme values of these simple ratios.

35 A disaggregation by rural and urban site is also work in progress.

36 While the proportion of the total population registered as tribal remained approximately constant between 1991 and 2001, the proportion of SCs fell from 16.5 to 16.2. This may be error or the product of relabelling and upward mobility. SCs and STs have a different identity politics but its impact on self-identification is unknown. Nor do we have the answer to the question whether the relabelling or any possible error has a differential impact on the sectors into which the economy has been classified. It is unlikely, however, to affect the strong results that emerge.

37 (2007). Available online: www.india_at_a_glance.

38 Murphy (2006).

39 See Appendix 1 for the sectoral composition of these gross – but conventional – aggregations.

40 See de Golbery and Chappuis (2000: 309–11) for growth rates.

41 In Arunachal, for instance, SCs migrate-in, obtain Inner Line Permits, rent licences from Arunachal STs, achieve far higher returns in historical (or new) occupations than in their regions of origin and remit resources home. This is a one-generational process and the next generation has no automatic rights.

42 Appendix 2, Maps 15.1 and 15.2.

43 Appendix 2, Maps 15.3 and 15.4.

44 Appendix 2, Maps 15.1 and 15.3.

45 Appendix 2, Maps 15.2 and 15.4.
46 Appendix 2, Maps 15.3 and 15.11.
47 Appendix 2, Maps 15.4 and 15.12.
48 Excepting Kerala.
49 Appendix 2, Map 15.14.
50 Appendix 2, Map 15.14.
51 Except for hotels and restaurants in the north-eastern states. Trade was disaggregated into wholesale and retail in 1998 and hotels and restaurants were distinguished. See Appendix 2, Map 15.15.
52 Appendix 2, Maps 15.7 and 15.18.
53 Appendix 2, Map 15.18.
54 Appendix 2, Map 15.21.
55 Appendix 2, Map 15.20.
56 Appendix 2, Map 15.22.
57 It certainly does not follow, however, that factors rejected as insignificant at the All-India level will not play a role in the detail of regions, a feature of the long-standing debates over explanations for the much simpler and bolder All-India regions for aspects of the sex ratio.
58 De Golbery and Chappuis's maps of district-level data on SC and ST literacy show regions in excess of 30 per cent SC and ST literacy confined to a thin strip along the west coast and a patch in central India (2000: 312–13) with an extension to the north-east for STs. The same regional pattern of advantage is much diluted for the rural population as a whole with an additional patch of high literacy in the north-west.
59 Harriss sees the principal ways in which the current era differs from that of the 1980s as being the criminalisation of politics (politics as venture capitalism) with implications for the selective inclusion and rationing of the poor; intensified competition for the spoils of office and therefore rampant factionalism – with no necessary implications for anti poverty policy as distinct from other kinds of policy; increasingly weak party organisation (except for cadre-based parties: the CPM, the BJP/Shiv Sena and the DMK/AIADMK) – but these strong parties have no determinate impact on poverty; and lastly the development of alliance politics and intensified political accommodations, though these kinds of politics generally fail growth and human development (1999). So it seems that the differences between current politics and those of Church's period, while being significant in themselves, do not yield strong hypotheses about their impacts on poverty or pro-poor growth. The recent rise of Dalit politics in the very large state of Uttar Pradesh (160 million population) and the protests by the OBC Gujjars demanding ST status in Rajasthan need relating to the roles they play in the economies of their respective states.
60 Church saw upper castes aligned with landlords, business owners and professionals, middle castes being on the land, and low castes supplying artisan goods and services. The particularities of the occupations to which SCs are increasingly confined and the distinctive property rights regimes through which tribal people relate to land, waste and forest resources are not mentioned.
61 Sarkar (forthcoming).
62 Ghosh (1998); Harriss-White (2008: chapter 1).
63 Prakash, in this volume.
64 Bardhan (1982); Dyson and Moore (1983); Agnihotri (2000).
65 Theories may emerge from analysis of district-level data, as in Chapman and Pathak's (1997) work on the economic and social variables characterising urban systems or Agnihotri's (2000) district-level analysis of the sex ratio. Land and water relations together with the labour demands of agriculture and modes of extraction of the marketable surplus have informed other regionalisations (Baker 1993; Rukmani 1994; Thorner 1995; Palmer-Jones and Sen 2003).

66 In this respect, the findings for Vietnam of Minot, Baulch and Epprecht (2006) of the significance of marketplace infrastructure and agro-ecology for spatial variations in poverty may help to generate testable hypotheses for India. See also the path-breaking research on Dalit business of Prakash (in this volume), though this has been confined to relatively big business in cities.

67 OBC, MBC: official designation Other Backward, Most Backward *Classes*. Often used to denote Other Backward. Most Backward *Castes* in practice too.

68 These owe much to discussion with Judith Heyer. On the last question of the multiplier effects of wholesaler credit (posed by Kunal Sen from an earlier draft of this essay), while our maps suggest no straightforward relationship, we can see that SCs are best represented in wholesaling in Orissa where they also have high participation rates. Absolutely thin on the ground in Uttar Pradesh, they are relatively well represented in wholesaling and, indeed, also manufacturing and construction even if finer-grained research maps show that it ought not to be extrapolated to the whole of India.

69 See Heyer, in this volume; see also the special issue on 'Rainfed Agriculture' of the *European Journal of Development Research* edited by Supriya Garikipati (2008) for detailed evidence of the complexity of distress-induced livelihood portfolios involving wage work, petty production and trade in and out of agriculture, in the locality and in migration flows.

70 Kunal Sen, Personal Communication.

71 The special politics of the smaller states: Goa, Pondicherry, Sikkim, Manipur Nagaland and Tripura for which the existing data are unsystematic call for dedicated research.

72 See Skinner (1985) on the Annales School; and Chapman (2007) on regional geography.

Bibliography

Agnihotri, S. (2000) *Sex Ratio Patterns in the Indian Population: A Fresh Exploration*, New Delhi: Sage.

Akerlof, G. (1976) 'The economics of caste and of race and other woeful tales', *Quarterly Journal of Economics*, XC: 4.

Baker, C. (1984) *An Indian Rural Economy, 1884–1955: The Tamilnad Countryside*, New Delhi: Oxford University Press.

Banaji, J. (1977) 'Capitalist domination and the small peasantry: Deccan districts in the later nineteenth century', *Economic and Political Weekly*, 12 (33/34): 1375–1404.

Banerjee, B. and Knight, J. (1985) 'Caste discrimination in the Indian urban labour market', *Journal of Development Economics*, 17: 277–307.

Bardhan, P. (1982) 'Little girls and death in India', *Economic and Political Weekly*, 17(36): 1448–50.

Basile, E. (forthcoming) 'A Marxist–Institutionalist analysis of rural capitalism in South India: the case of a Tamil market town after the Green Revolution', unpublished D.Phil. thesis, University of Oxford.

Basile, E. and Harriss-White, B. (2003) 'Corporatist capitalism: the politics of accumulation in South India' in R. Benewick, M. Blecher and S. Cook (eds) *Asian Politics in Development*, London: Cass.

Breman, J. (2007) *Labour Bondage in West India: From Past to Present*, Oxford: Oxford University Press.

Chandrasekhar, C.P. (1993) 'Agrarian change and occupational diversification: non-agricultural employment and rural development in West Bengal', *Journal of Peasant Studies*, 20(2): 205–270

Chapman, G. (2007) '-graphy: the remains of a British discipline', *Journal of Geography in Higher Education*, 31(3): 353–79.

Chapman, G. and Pathak, P. (1997) 'Indian urbanisation and the characteristics of large Indian cities revealed in the 1991 Census', *Espace, Populations et Societes* 53(2–3): 193–210.

Chibber, V. (2003) *Locked in Place*, Princeton: Princeton University Press.

Church, R. (1984) 'The pattern of state politics in Indira Gandhi's India', in J. Wood *et al.*, *State Politics in Contemporary India*, Boulder: Westview.

Das Gupta, C. (2008) 'State and capital in independent India: from dirigisme to neoliberalism', unpublished Ph.D. thesis, SOAS, University of London.

Dyson, T. and Moore, M. (1983) 'On kinship structure, female autonomy, and demographic behaviour in India', *Population and Development Review*, 9(1): 35–60.

Gang, I.N., Sen, K. and Yun, M.S. (2008) 'Poverty in rural India: caste and tribe', *Review of Income and Wealth*, 54(1): 50–69.

Garikipati, S. and Harriss-White, B. (2008) 'India's semi-arid rural economy: livelihoods, seasonal migration and gender', special issue, *European Journal of Development Research*, 20(4).

Ghosh, M. (1998) *Natural and Social Resource Use and the Poor in Rural West Bengal*, IDRC, Visva Bharati.

de Golbery, L. and Chappuis, A. (2000) 'Minorités defavorisées en Inde: intouchables et tribaux, approche cartographique', in C.Z. Guilmoto and A. Vagnet (eds) *Essays on Population and Space in India*, Institut Français de Pondichery.

Government of India (2007). Available online: India_at_a_glance.gov.in

Harriss, J. (1999) 'Comparing political regimes across Indian states', *Economic and Political Weekly*, 34(48): 3367–77.

Harriss-White, B. (2003) *India Working: Essays on Economy and Society*, Cambridge: Cambridge University Press.

—— (2004) 'Social stratification and rural households', in B. Harriss-White, S. Janakarajan, *et al.*, *Rural India Facing the 21st Century*, London: Anthem.

—— (2007) 'Informal capitalism: social order, agency and deviance', Plenary address to the International Conference of Heterodox Economics, Bristol Business School, July 2007.

—— (2008) *Rural Commercial Capital: Agricultural Markets in West Bengal*, New Delhi: Oxford University Press.

—— (2009) 'Globalisation, the financial crisis and petty commodity production in India's socially regulated informal economy', *Global Labour Journal*.

Harriss-White, B. and Gooptu, N. (2000) 'Mapping India's world of unorganised Labour', *Socialist Register 2001*, London: Merlin Press.

Harriss-White, B., Janakarajan, S. *et al.* (2004) *Rural India Facing the 21st Century*, London: Anthem.

Harriss-White, B. and Sinha, A. (eds) (2007) *Trade Liberalisation and India's Informal Economy*, New Delhi: Oxford University Press.

Heyer, J., in this volume.

Hoff, K. and Pandey, P. (2004) *Belief Systems and Durable Inequalities*, World Bank Policy Research Working Paper 3351, Washington, DC: World Bank.

Jairaj A. and Harriss-White, B. (2006) 'Social structure, tax culture and the state: Tamil Nadu, Indian', *Economic and Political Weekly*, XLI(51): 5247–57.

Jayaraj D. (2004) 'Social institutions and the structural transformation of the non-farm economy', in B. Harriss-White S. Janakarajan *et al.*, *Rural India Facing the 21st Century*, Anthem: London.

Kumar V. (2008) *Defining the Dalits*, Centre for the Study of Social Systems, Jawarhalal, New Delhi: Nehru University.

McCartney M. (2006) 'The long-term effects of short-term shocks: a hysteresis approach to Indian economic development', unpublished Ph.D. thesis, SOAS, University of London.

Meagher, K. (2004) 'Identity economics: informal manufacturing and social. Networks in south-eastern Nigeria', unpublished D.Phil. thesis, University of Oxford.

Mhaskar, S. (forthcoming) 'The emergence of post-industrial capitalism in India : urban spatial restructuring and changing class relations in Mumbai', unpublished D.Phil. thesis, University of Oxford.

Minot N., Baulch, B. and Epprecht, M. (2006) *Poverty and Inequality in Vietnam: Spatial Patterns and Geographic Determinants*, Research report 148, Washington, DC: IFPRI.

Mooij, J. (1999) *Food Politics and Policy in India*, New Delhi: Oxford University Press.

Murphy, C. (2006) 'The power of caste identity in private enterprise ownership', unpublished MSc thesis, University of Oxford.

Palmer-Jones, R. and Sen, K. (2003) 'What has luck got to do with it? A regional analysis of poverty and agricultural growth in rural India', *Journal of Development Studies*, 40(1): 1–31.

Parry, J. (2007) 'Hegemony and resistance: trade union politics in central India', Marett Lecture, Exeter College, University of Oxford.

Prakash, A. in this volume.

Ramachandran, V.K. and Swaminathan, M. (eds) (2002) *Agrarian Studies: Essays on Agrarian Relations in Less-developed Countries*, New Delhi: Tulika.

Rueshmayer D. *et al.* (1992) *Capitalist Development and Democracy,* London: Polity.

Rukmani R. (1994) 'Urbanisation and socio-economic change in Tamil Nadu, 1901–91', *Economic and Political Weekly*, 29(51/52): 3263–72.

Ruthven, O. (2008) 'Global value chains in local context: a social relations perspective from South Asia', unpublished D.Phil. thesis, University of Oxford.

Sarkar, S. (forthcoming) 'State and labour: a genealogy of the idea of "condition of labour" in colonial India', unpublished D.Phil. thesis, University of Oxford.

Scoville, J. (1996) 'Labour market underpinning of a caste economy: failing the caste theorem', *American Journal of Economics and Sociology*, 55(4).

Sen, A. (2002) 'Agriculture, employment and poverty: recent trends in rural India' in V.K. Ramachandran and M. Swaminathan (eds) *Agrarian Studies: Essays on Agrarian Relations in Less-developed Countries*, New Delhi: Tulika.

Skinner, Q. (1985) *The Return of Grand Theory in the Human Sciences*, Cambridge: Cambridge University Press.

Thorat, S. (2002) 'Oppression, denial and Dalit discrimination in the 1990s', *Economic and Political Weekly,* 37(6): 572–8.

Thorat, S. and Attewell, P. (2007) 'The legacy of social exclusion: a correspondence study of job discrimination in India', *Economic and Political Weekly*, 42(41): 4141–5.

Thorat, S. and Newman, K. (2007) 'Caste and economic discrimination: causes, consequences and remedies', *Economic and Political Weekly*, 42(42): 4121–4.

Thorat, S., Aryama and Negi, P. (2005) *Reservation and the Private Sector*, Indian Institute of Dalit Studies, Delhi.

Thorner, D. (ed.) (1995) *Ecological and Agrarian Regions of South Asia*, Karachi: Oxford University Press.

Vaidyanathan, A. (1986) 'Labour use in rural India: a study of spatial and temporal variations', *Economic and Political Weekly*, 21(52): A-130/A146.

World Bank (2006) *World Development Report*, Washington, DC: IBRD.

Appendix 1: Sources and treatment of data for the regression analyses

1   Data on enterprises

For the fifteen major states (which were not reclassified during the period), the ten economic sectors in 1990 and fourteen in 1998 in the Economic Census were aggregated into three:

1   primary (agriculture and livestock)
2   secondary (mining, manufacturing, utilities, construction)
3   tertiary (trade, hotels, transport storage and communication, finance and real estate, community and personal services).

2   Data on poverty

Data on inequality was obtained from the World Bank database. Data on rural and urban expenditure came from the Indian National Sample Survey (NSS) 46th Round for 1990 and the 54th Round for 1998; from these, proportions under the Poverty Line were calculated using deflators: the Ministry of Labour's Consumer Price Index for Agricultural Labour was used for rural data and the Consumer Price Index for Industrial Labour for urban.

3   Data on mobility

1981 and 1991 literacy data from the Indian Census were used as relevant to the 1990/1991 and 1998/2001data respectively. These were lagged to proxy the effect of an increase in literate people dispersing into the economy.

4   Proxy for collateral for credit-driving investment in the non-farm economy, also a poverty proxy to reduce the problems of endogeneity

Operational landholdings and the percentage of operational landholdings worked by SCs/STs were obtained from the Fertiliser Statistics for India, 1986 (for 1990/1991) and 1999/2000 (for 1998/2001) and the Agricultural Census, 1996 for the later period.

5   Evidence of urbanisation was obtained from rural/urban population data in the Indian Census for 1991

A series of fixed-effects, logarithmic regressions were run using levels and using changes; with states as cases, and dummy variables for SCs and STs, for rural and urban populations and for 1990 and 1998. These regressions were run for all enterprises and then in truncated forms for each of the primary, secondary and tertiary sectors (Murphy 2006).

Appendix 2

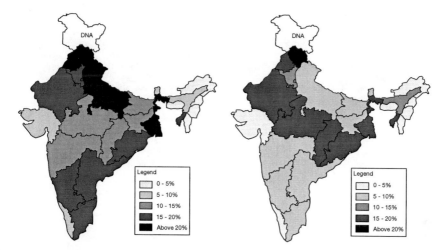

Map 15.1
Intensity of SC population (%),
1991 Census

Map 15.2
Intensity of SC enterprises, 1990–91

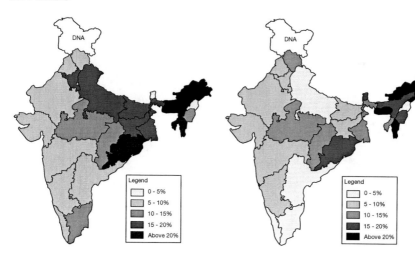

Map 15.3
PI-SC (1990–91) agricultural
enterprises

Map 15.4
PI-SC (1990–91) non-agriculture
enterprises

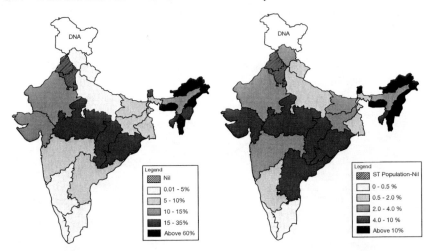

Map 15.5
Intensity of ST population (%),
1991 Census

Map 15.6
Intensity of ST population (%), 1991
 Census of ST enterprises (%), 1990–91

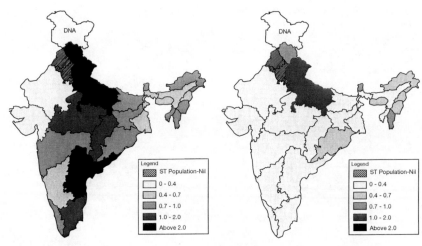

Map 15.7
PI-ST (1990–91) agricultural
enterprises

Map 15.8
PI-ST (1990–91) non-agricultural
enterprises

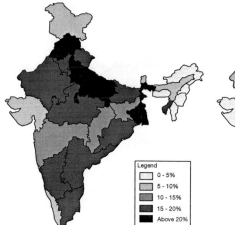

Map 15.9
Intensity of SC population (%),
2001 Census

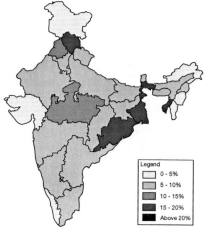

Map 15.10
Intensity of Map 9: Intensity of SC
population (%), 2001 Census SC
enterprises (%), 1998

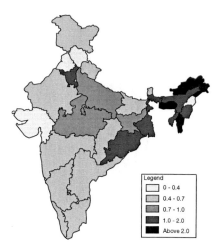

Map 15.11
PI-SC (1998) agricultural enterprises

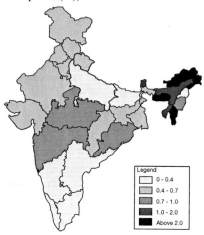

Map 15.12
PI-SC (1998) non-agricultural enterprises

346   *Barbara Harriss-White with Kaushal Vidyarthee*

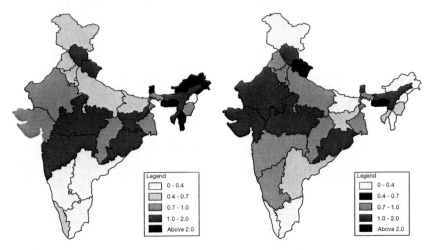

Map 15.13
PI-SC (1998) manufacturing

Map 15.14
PI-SC (1998) construction

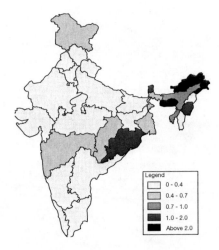

Map 15.15
PI-SC (1998) wholesale trade

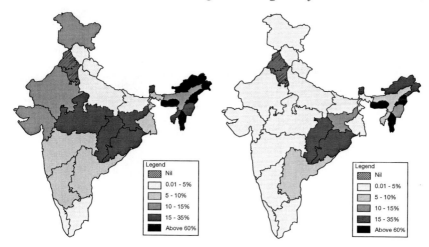

Map 15.16
Intensity of ST population (%),
2001 Census

Map 15.17
Intensity of ST enterprises (%), 1998

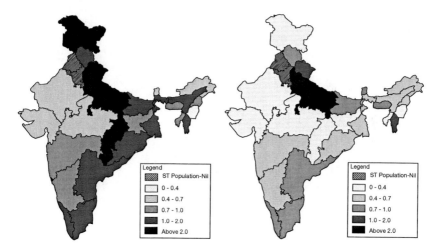

Map 15.18
PI-ST (1998) agricultural enterprises

Map 15.19
PI-ST (1998) non-agricultural enterprises

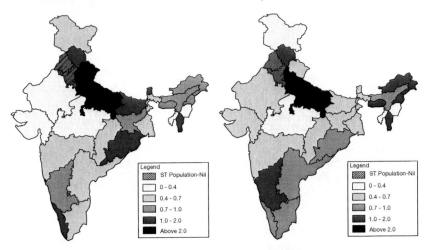

Map 15.20
PI-ST (1998) manufacturing

Map 15.21
PI-ST (1998) construction

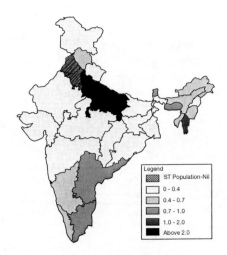

Map 15.22
PI-ST (1998) wholesale trade

Appendix 3

Map 15.23
Map of state regimes according to modes of incorporation of 'Lower castes and classes'

Glossary

Adivasi(s)   tribal people of India
Af/s   Afghani, the Afghan currency, roughly 50 to the US$
Baniya   trading community in northern India
bawra   inverse of the proportion of land that can be irrigated each year: in the case of 1 bawra all land can be irrigated; in the case of 2 bawra half of the land can be irrigated; and in 3 and 4 bawra a third and a quarter of the land can be irrigated
BC   Backward Caste
beedi (bidi)   an Indian cigarette
Bhangi   formerly untouchable caste associated with cleaning latrines and handling corpses
bridewealth   transfer of wealth which accompanies the movement of a bride to the groom's family
castes   hereditary groups in Hindu society distinguished by social status and ritual pollution
cess   tax
Chakkiliyars   leather-working Dalit caste
cheri   Dalit hamlet in rural India
Companía Chilena de Tobacco   Chilean Tobacco Company
Dalit   member of oppressed castes/a former untouchable
Dhobi   people whose traditional livelihood came from washing and ironing clothes
dop (or tot) system   daily provision of alcohol to farm workers by their employers
ganyu   casual agricultural labour in Malawi
Gujjar   multi-religious, 'martial' ethnic group in Afghanistan, Pakistan and India
Harijan   Gandhi's term for untouchables, ex-untouchables
Hazara   third largest ethnic group in Afghanistan
hypogamous   kinship alliance in which the group concerned marry down in status terms
idli   cake made of fermented rice and gram powder
isogamous   alliance which is equal in status

jerib   unit of land: 2 jeribs = 1 acre of land
jong   young man (South Africa) – formerly a 'coloured' person (derogatory)
Jumbesh   Afghan faction/political grouping
katapila   unlicensed money dealers (Southern Africa)
kavalai   bullock-operated lift irrigation device
Khatik   formerly untouchable caste said to have been associated with rearing
  and hunting pigs
Khatri   Punjabi adaptation of the word Kshatriya
Khoi   indigenous people of south-western Africa
Mahar   powerful Dalit community in Maharashtra
Manjerekar   surname generally used for people belonging to the Maratha
  community
mirabashi   water master (Afghanistan)
monopsony   exchange where there is only one buyer
nagarikam   cosmopolitan, modern, a move away from caste
Naxalite (insurgency)   set of armed Maoist organisations
oor   Tamil word for 'village'
outcaste   *see* Dalit
own account enterprises   small firms; self-employment
Pannadis/Pallars   Dalit labouring caste
pannayals   bonded agricultural labour
Paraiyar   Dalit labouring caste
parastatal   organisation legally independent of the state but run in the public
  interest
Pashtun   one of the major ethnic groups in Afghanistan
plaasvolk   workers on South African farms
platteland   countryside/rural areas in South Africa
Scheduled Castes   castes officially listed as former untouchables
Scheduled Tribes   officially listed tribes
soudure   annual hungry season in Africa, which can last from a few weeks to
  several months
sub-castes   endogamous sub-group of a caste
Swadeshi movement   economic nationalist movement
tendu   leaf: tobacco substitute
thottam   well-irrigated land in Tamil Nadu, South India
untouchables/untouchability   members of the lowest Hindu caste or people
  outside the caste system; the term was declared illegal in the Indian
  Constitution of 1947 but nonetheless has widespread currency
Vaniyar   large agricultural caste group in South India

Index